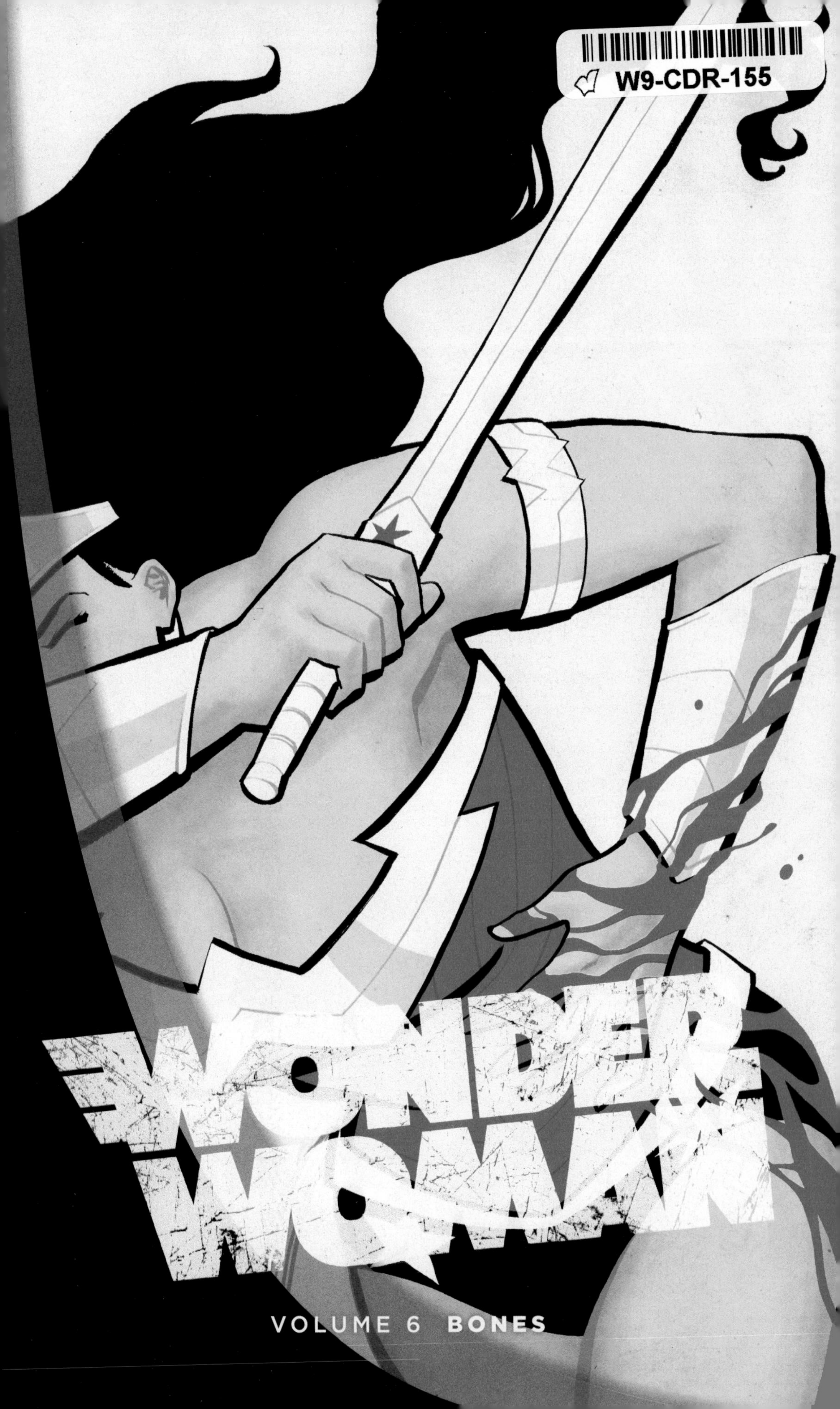

WONDER WOMAN

VOLUME 6 BONES

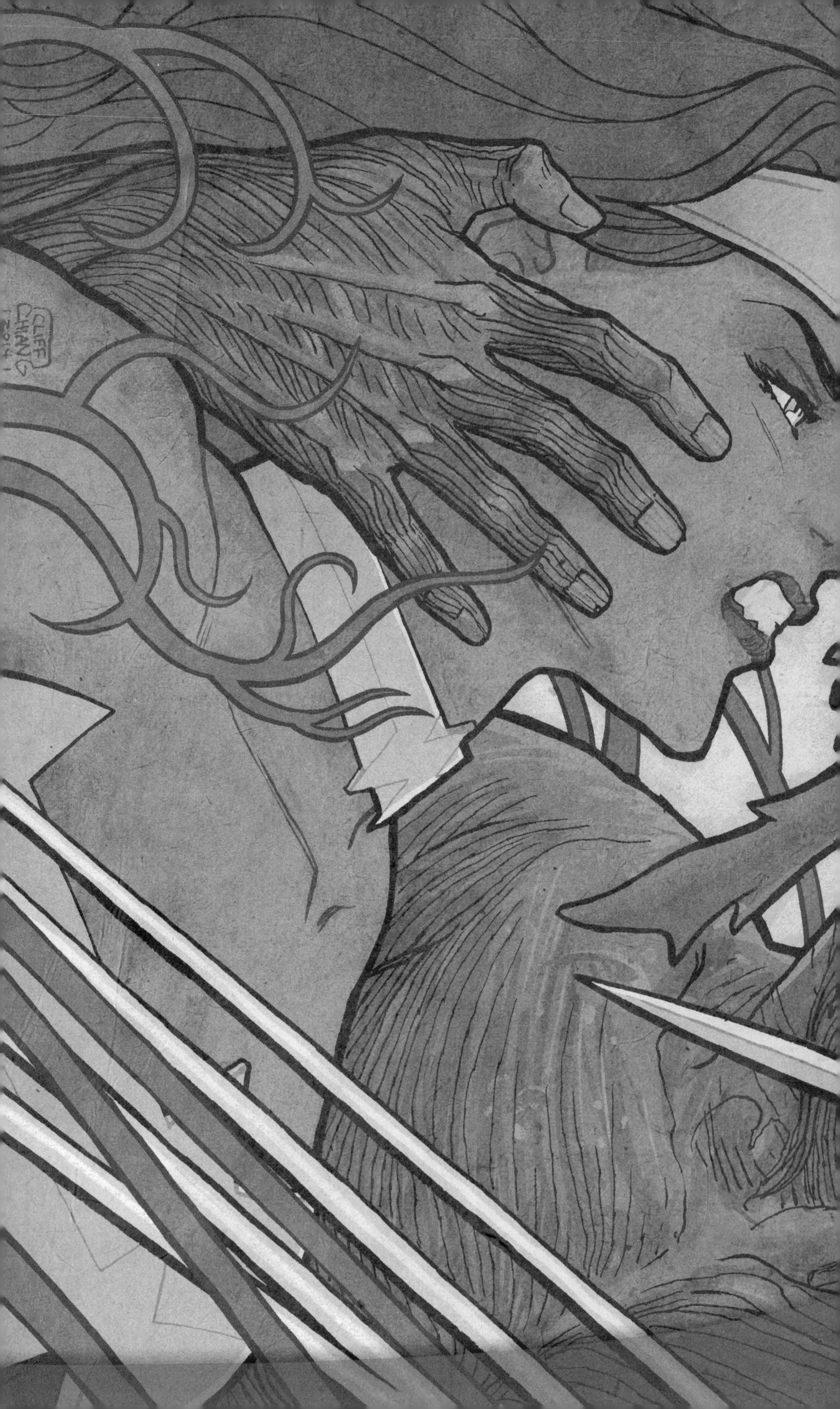
CLIFF CHIANG 2014

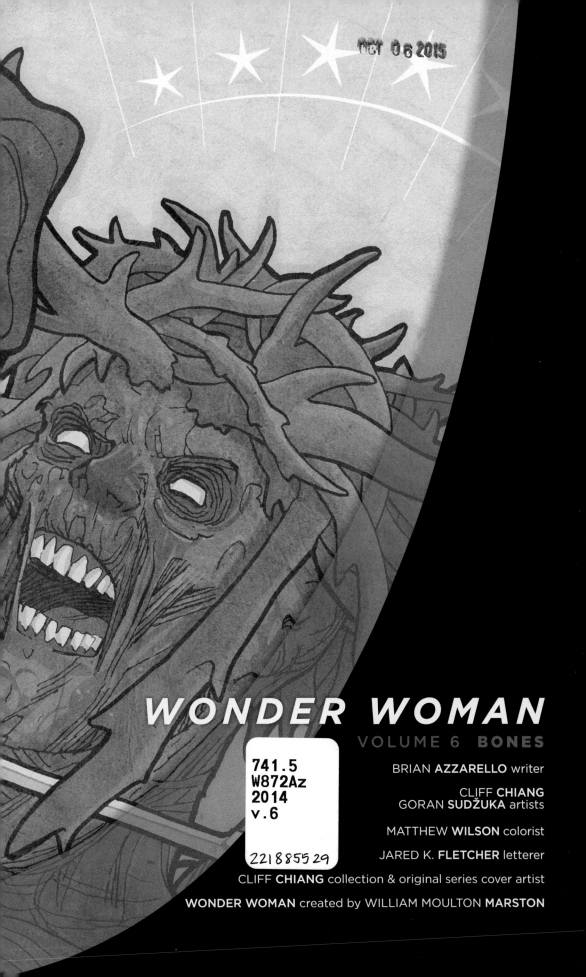

WONDER WOMAN

VOLUME 6 BONES

BRIAN **AZZARELLO** writer

CLIFF **CHIANG**
GORAN **SUDŽUKA** artists

MATTHEW **WILSON** colorist

JARED K. **FLETCHER** letterer

CLIFF **CHIANG** collection & original series cover artist

WONDER WOMAN created by WILLIAM MOULTON **MARSTON**

MATT IDELSON and CHRIS CONROY Editors – Original Series JEB WOODARD Group Editor – Collected Editions
RACHEL PINNELAS Editor ROBBIE BIEDERMAN Publication Design

BOB HARRAS Senior VP – Editor-in-Chief, DC Comics

DIANE NELSON President DAN DIDIO and JIM LEE Co-Publishers GEOFF JOHNS Chief Creative Officer
AMIT DESAI Senior VP – Marketing & Global Franchise Management NAIRI GARDINER Senior VP – Finance
SAM ADES VP – Digital Marketing BOBBIE CHASE VP – Talent Development
MARK CHIARELLO Senior VP – Art, Design & Collected Editions JOHN CUNNINGHAM VP – Content Strategy
ANNE DEPIES VP – Strategy Planning & Reporting DON FALLETTI VP – Manufacturing Operations
LAWRENCE GANEM VP – Editorial Administration & Talent Relations ALISON GILL Senior VP – Manufacturing & Operations
HANK KANALZ Senior VP – Editorial Strategy & Administration JAY KOGAN VP – Legal Affairs
DEREK MADDALENA Senior VP – Sales & Business Development DAN MIRON VP – Sales Planning & Trade Development
NICK NAPOLITANO VP – Manufacturing Administration CAROL ROEDER VP – Marketing
EDDIE SCANNELL VP – Mass Account & Digital Sales SUSAN SHEPPARD VP – Business Affairs
COURTNEY SIMMONS Senior VP – Publicity & Communications JIM (SKI) SOKOLOWSKI VP – Comic Book Specialty & Newsstand Sales

WONDER WOMAN VOLUME 6: BONES

DC Comics, 4000 Warner Blvd., Burbank, CA 91522
A Warner Bros. Entertainment Company.
Printed by RR Donnelley, Owensville, MO, USA. 7/31/15. First Printing.
ISBN: 978-1-4012-5775-0

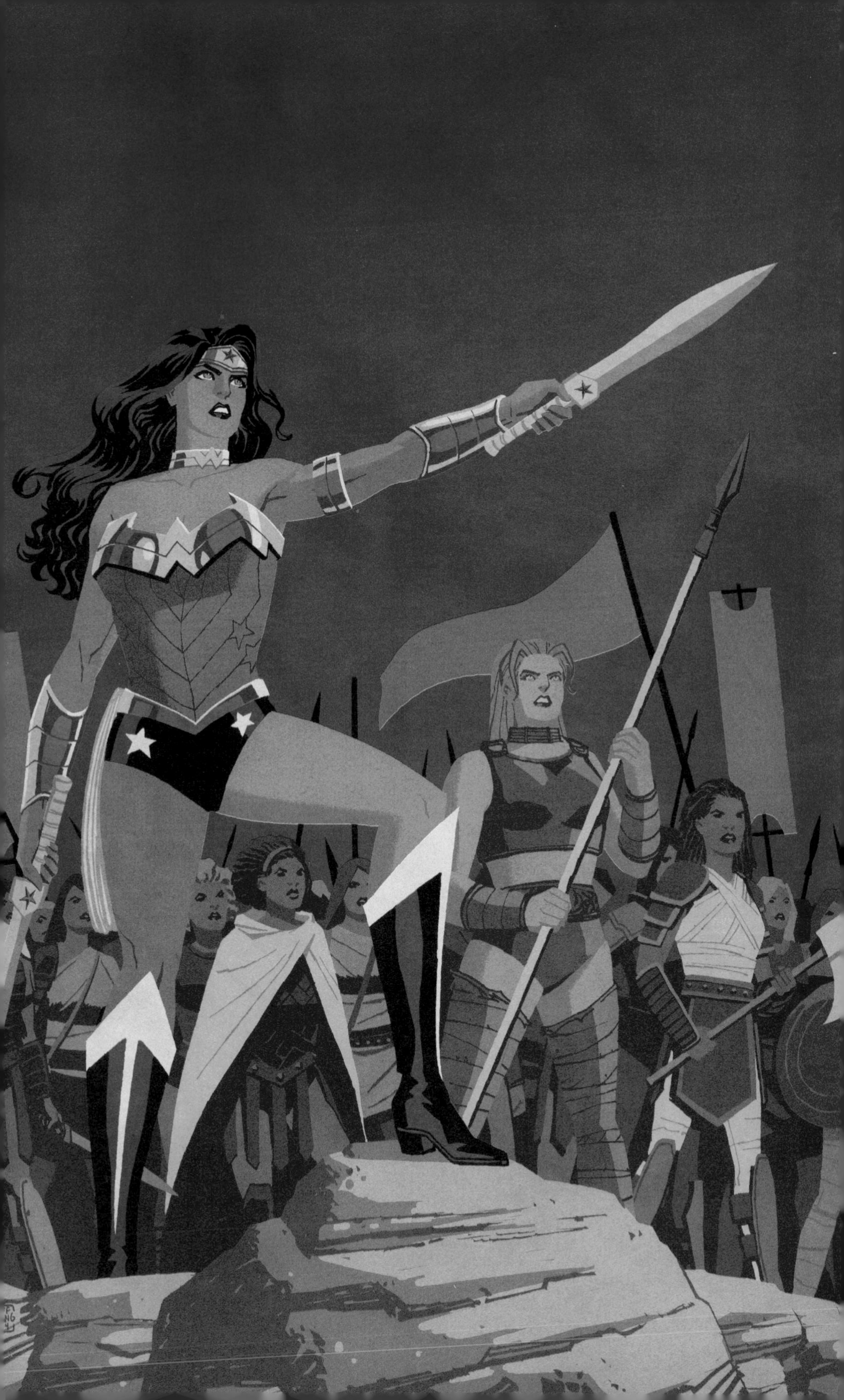

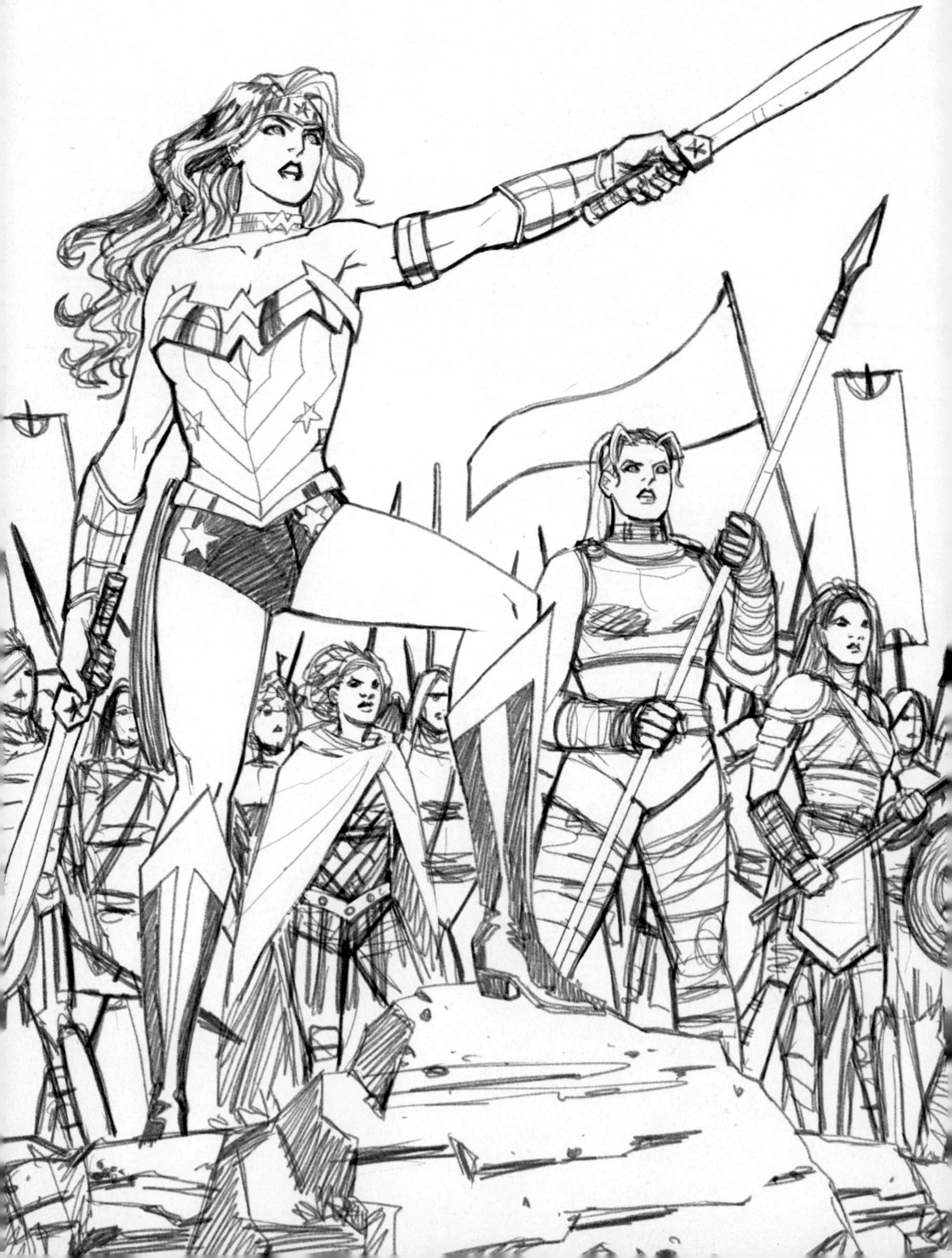

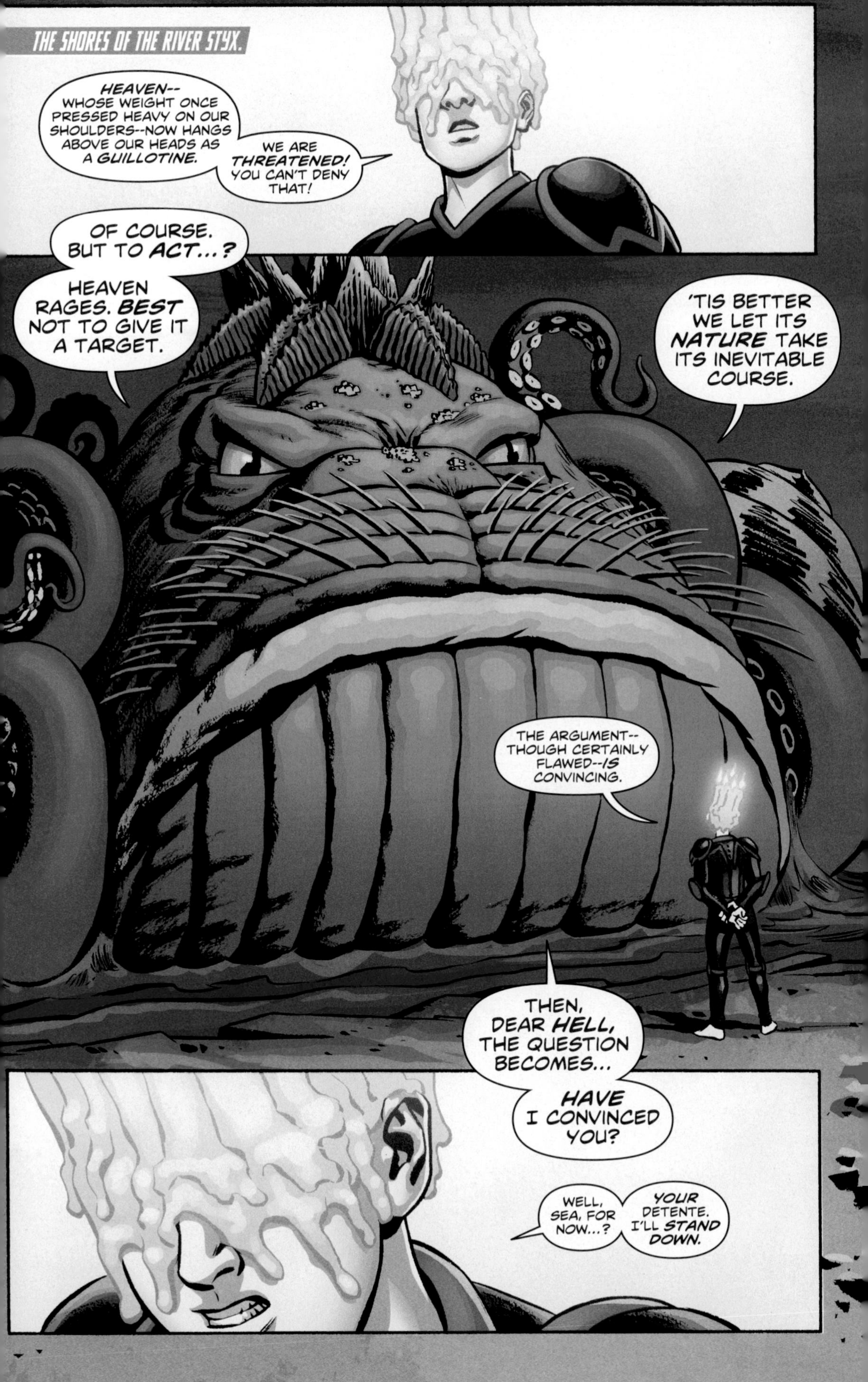
THE SHORES OF THE RIVER STYX.
HEAVEN--WHOSE WEIGHT ONCE PRESSED HEAVY ON OUR SHOULDERS--NOW HANGS ABOVE OUR HEADS AS A GUILLOTINE.
WE ARE THREATENED! YOU CAN'T DENY THAT!
OF COURSE. BUT TO ACT...?
HEAVEN RAGES. BEST NOT TO GIVE IT A TARGET.
'TIS BETTER WE LET ITS NATURE TAKE ITS INEVITABLE COURSE.
THE ARGUMENT--THOUGH CERTAINLY FLAWED--IS CONVINCING.
THEN, DEAR HELL, THE QUESTION BECOMES...
HAVE I CONVINCED YOU?
WELL, SEA, FOR NOW...?
YOUR DETENTE. I'LL STAND DOWN.

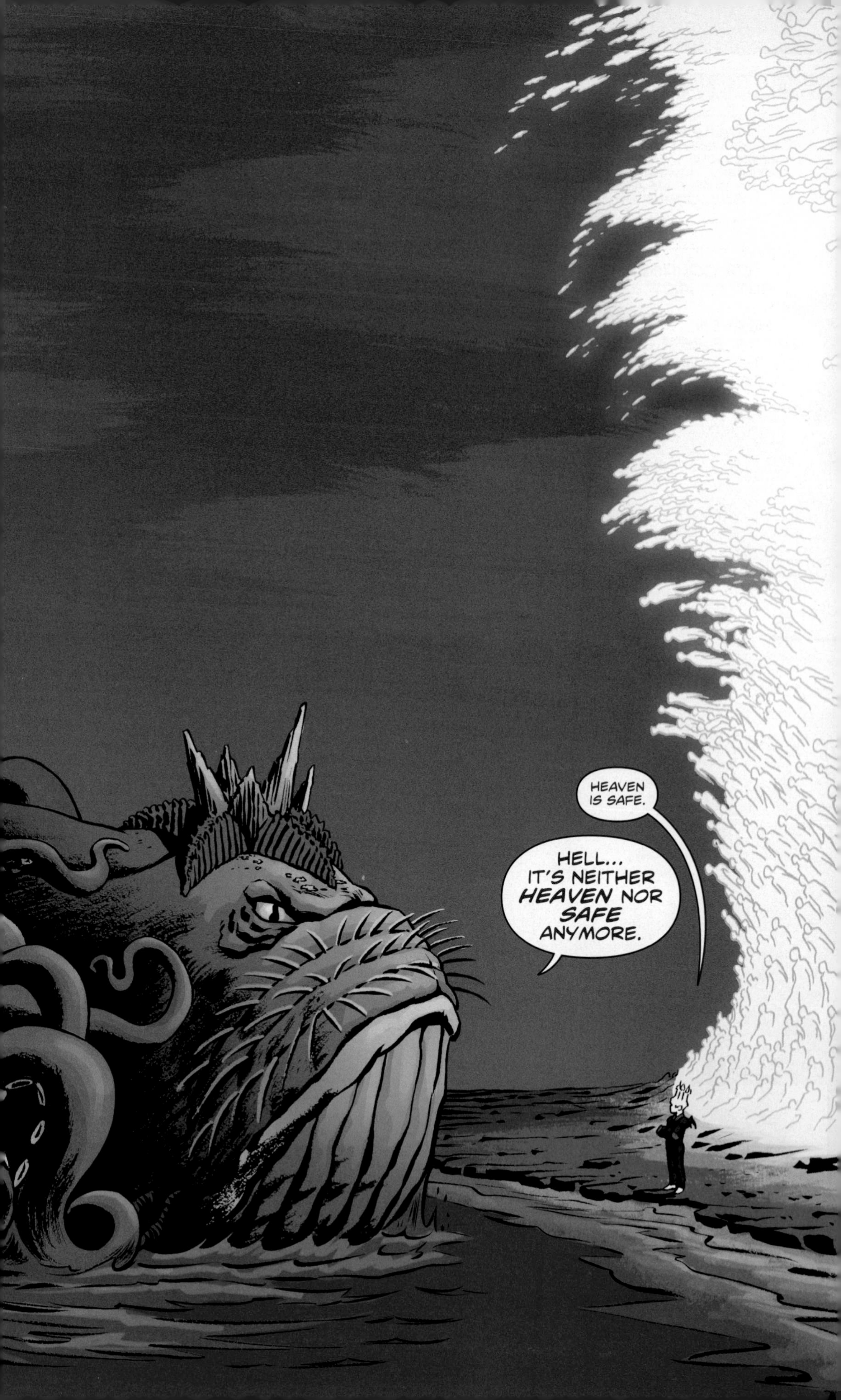
HEAVEN IS SAFE.
HELL... IT'S NEITHER HEAVEN NOR SAFE ANYMORE.

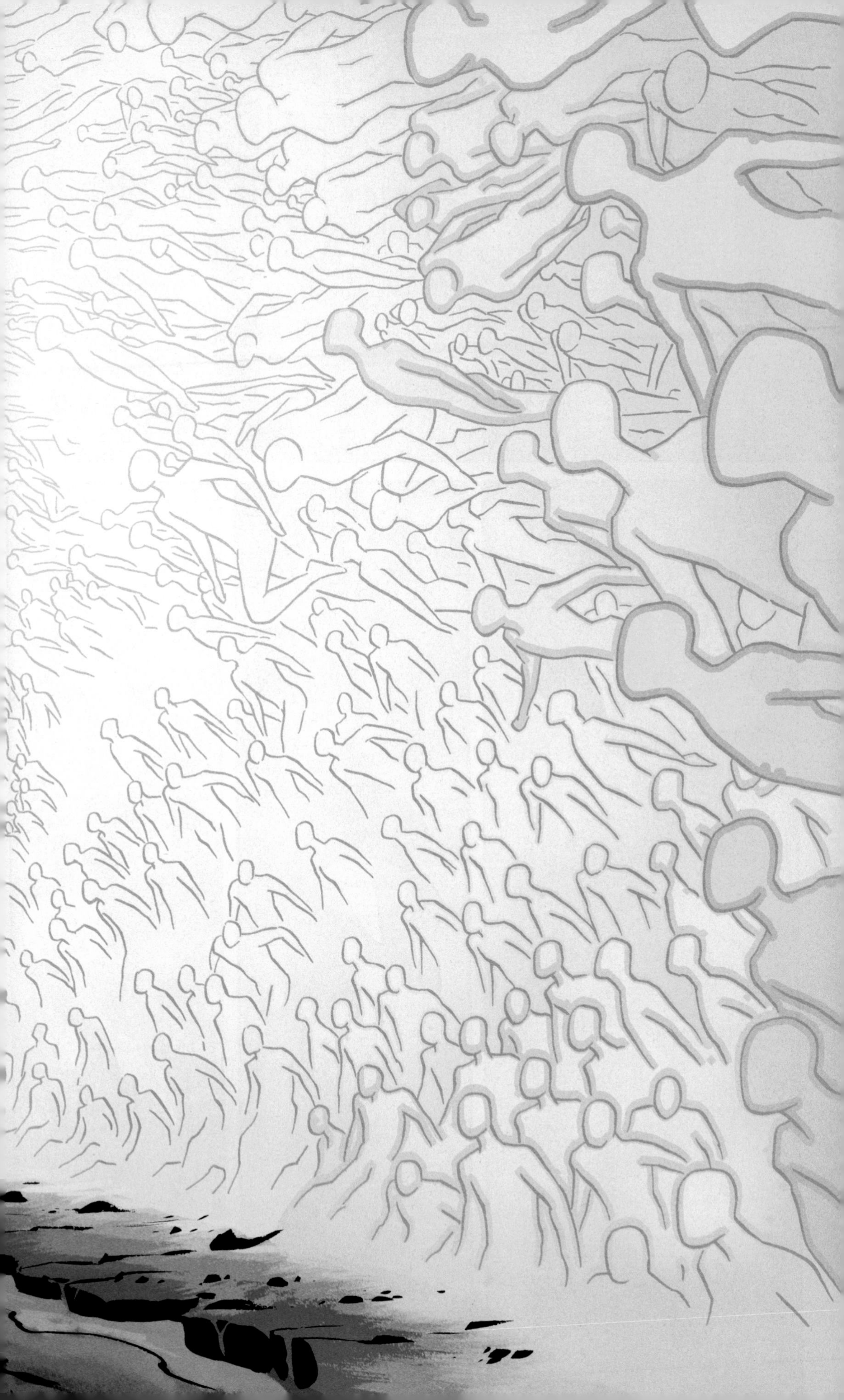

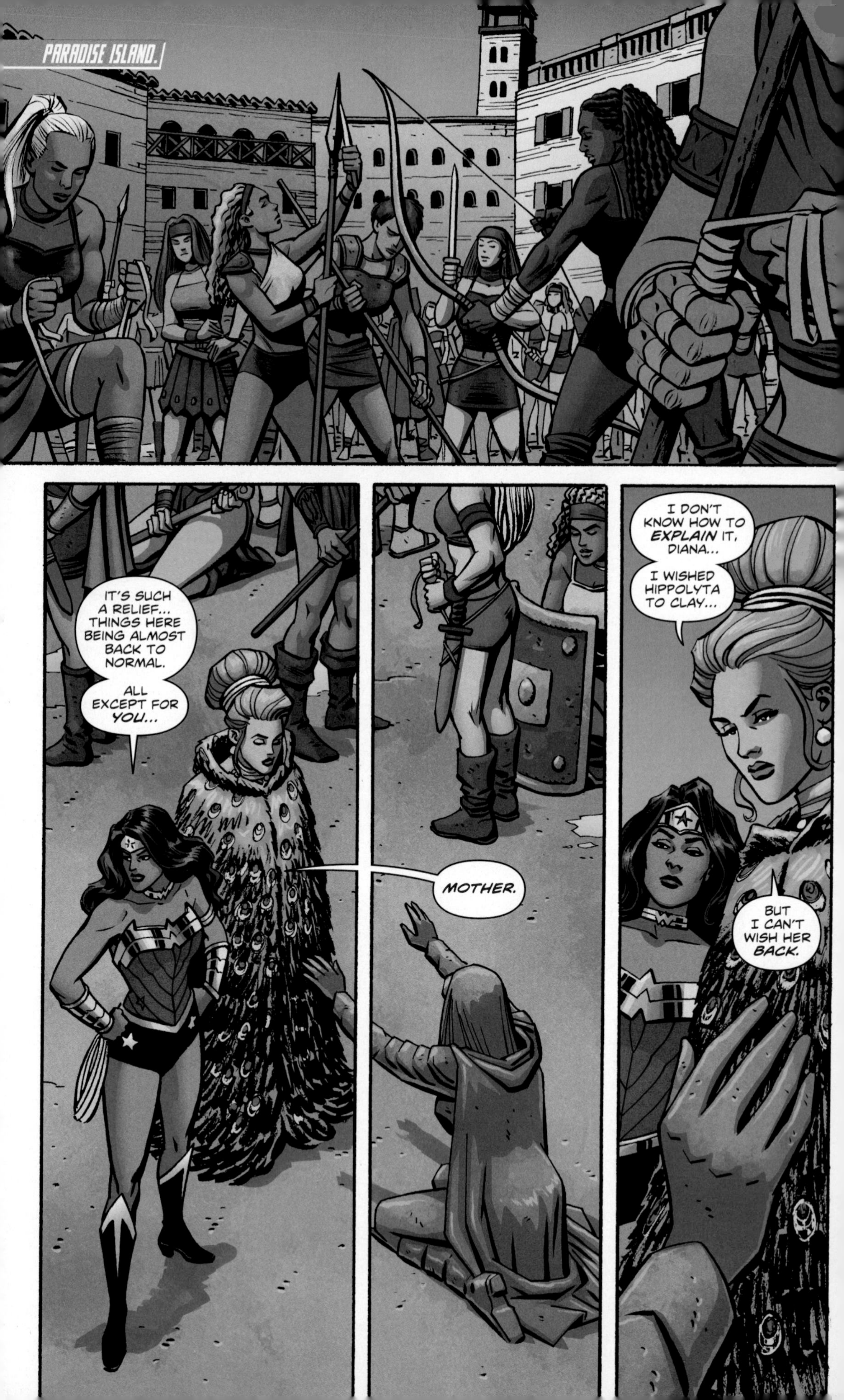
PARADISE ISLAND.
IT'S SUCH A RELIEF... THINGS HERE BEING ALMOST BACK TO NORMAL.
ALL EXCEPT FOR YOU...
MOTHER.
I DON'T KNOW HOW TO EXPLAIN IT, DIANA...
I WISHED HIPPOLYTA TO CLAY...
BUT I CAN'T WISH HER BACK.

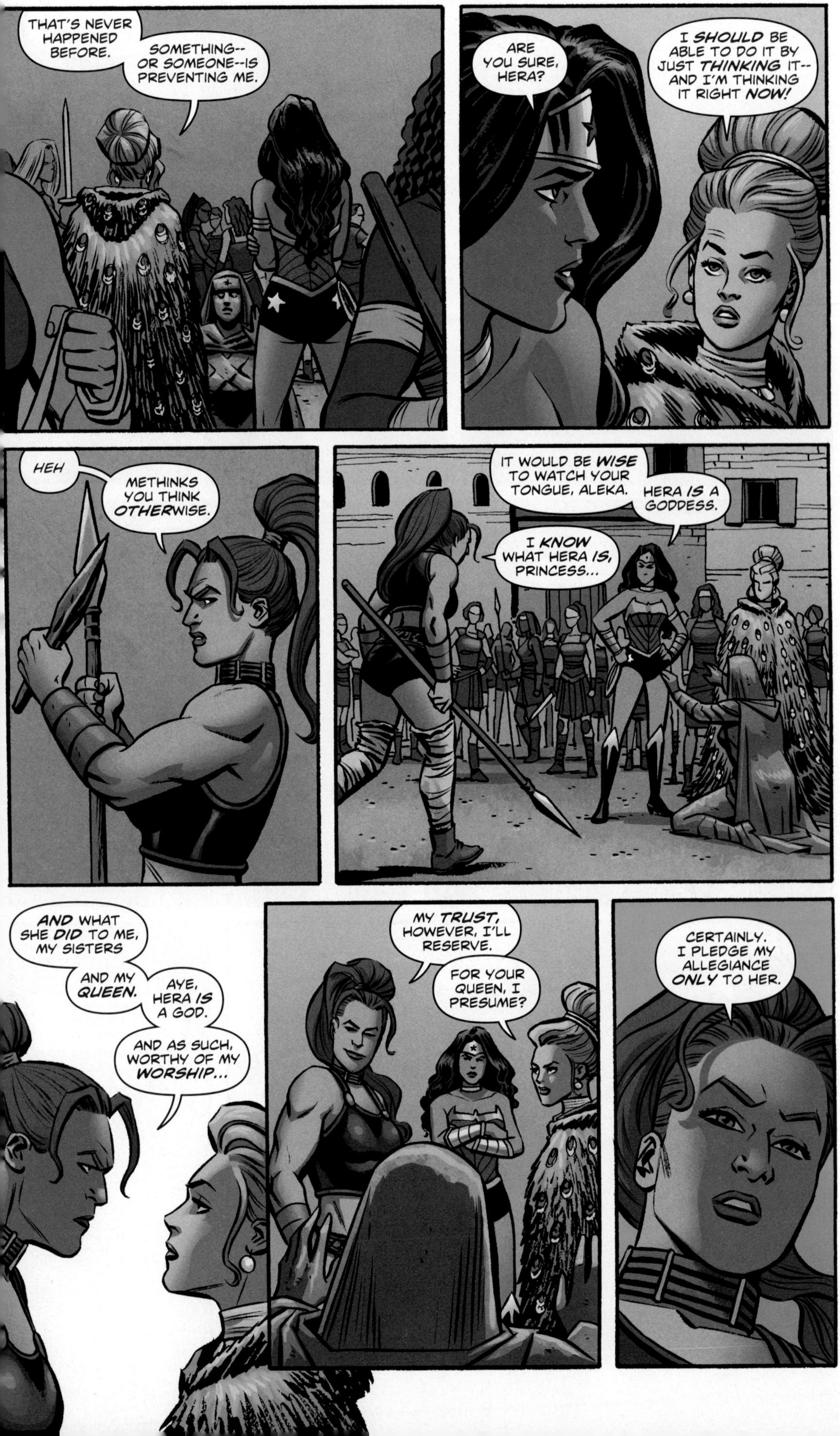

THAT'S NEVER HAPPENED BEFORE.
SOMETHING-- OR SOMEONE--IS PREVENTING ME.
ARE YOU SURE, HERA?
I SHOULD BE ABLE TO DO IT BY JUST THINKING IT-- AND I'M THINKING IT RIGHT NOW!
HEH
METHINKS YOU THINK OTHERWISE.
IT WOULD BE WISE TO WATCH YOUR TONGUE, ALEKA.
HERA IS A GODDESS.
I KNOW WHAT HERA IS, PRINCESS...
AND WHAT SHE DID TO ME, MY SISTERS
AND MY QUEEN.
AYE, HERA IS A GOD.
AND AS SUCH, WORTHY OF MY WORSHIP...
MY TRUST, HOWEVER, I'LL RESERVE.
FOR YOUR QUEEN, I PRESUME?
CERTAINLY. I PLEDGE MY ALLEGIANCE ONLY TO HER.

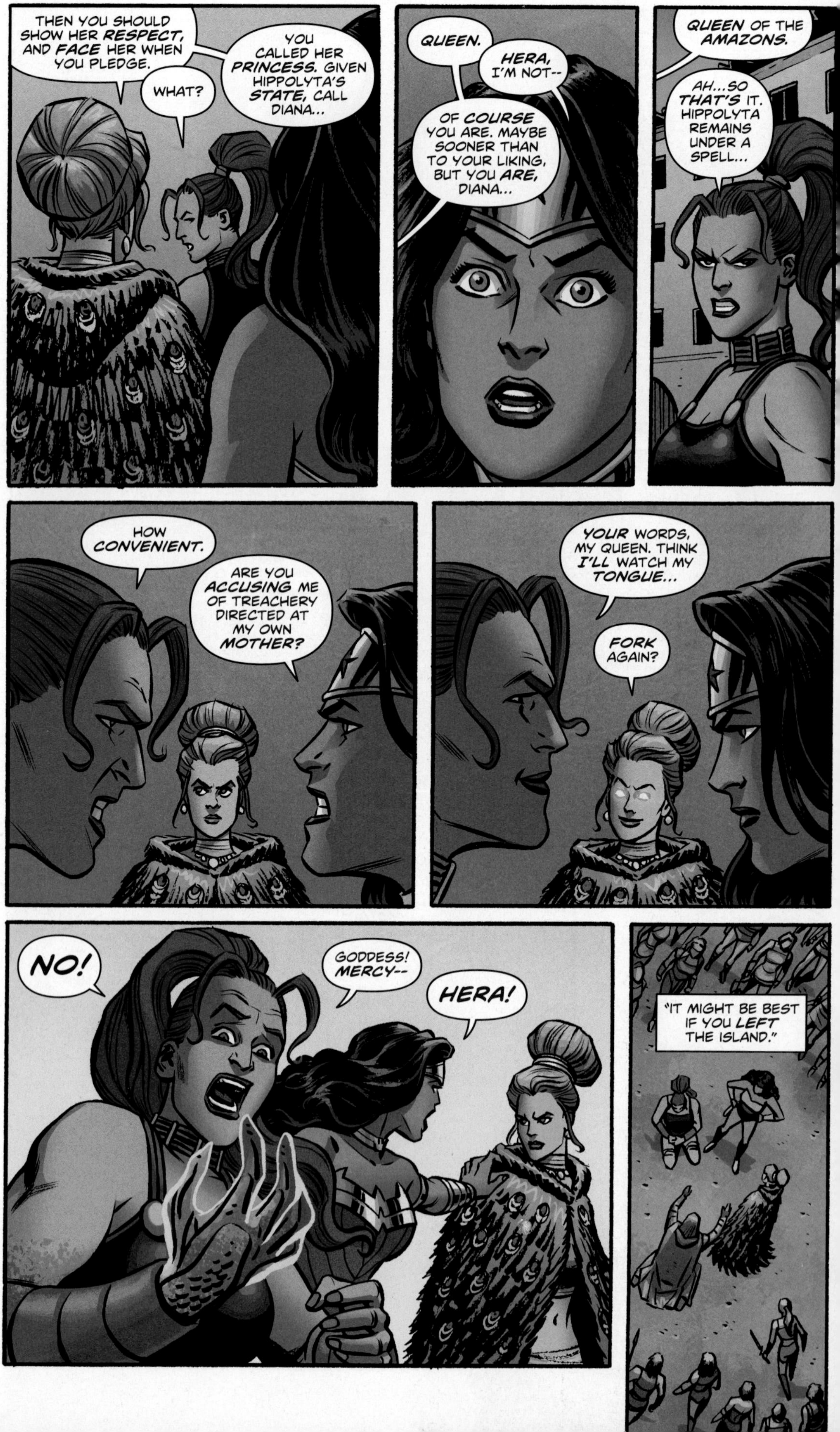
THEN YOU SHOULD SHOW HER *RESPECT*, AND *FACE* HER WHEN YOU PLEDGE.
WHAT?
YOU CALLED HER *PRINCESS*. GIVEN HIPPOLYTA'S *STATE*, CALL DIANA...
QUEEN.
HERA, I'M NOT--
OF *COURSE* YOU ARE. MAYBE SOONER THAN TO YOUR LIKING, BUT YOU *ARE*, DIANA...
QUEEN OF THE *AMAZONS*.
AH...SO *THAT'S* IT. HIPPOLYTA REMAINS UNDER A SPELL...
HOW *CONVENIENT*.
ARE YOU *ACCUSING* ME OF TREACHERY DIRECTED AT MY OWN *MOTHER*?
YOUR WORDS, MY QUEEN. THINK *I'LL* WATCH MY *TONGUE*...
FORK AGAIN?
NO!
GODDESS! *MERCY*--
HERA!
"IT MIGHT BE BEST IF YOU *LEFT* THE ISLAND."

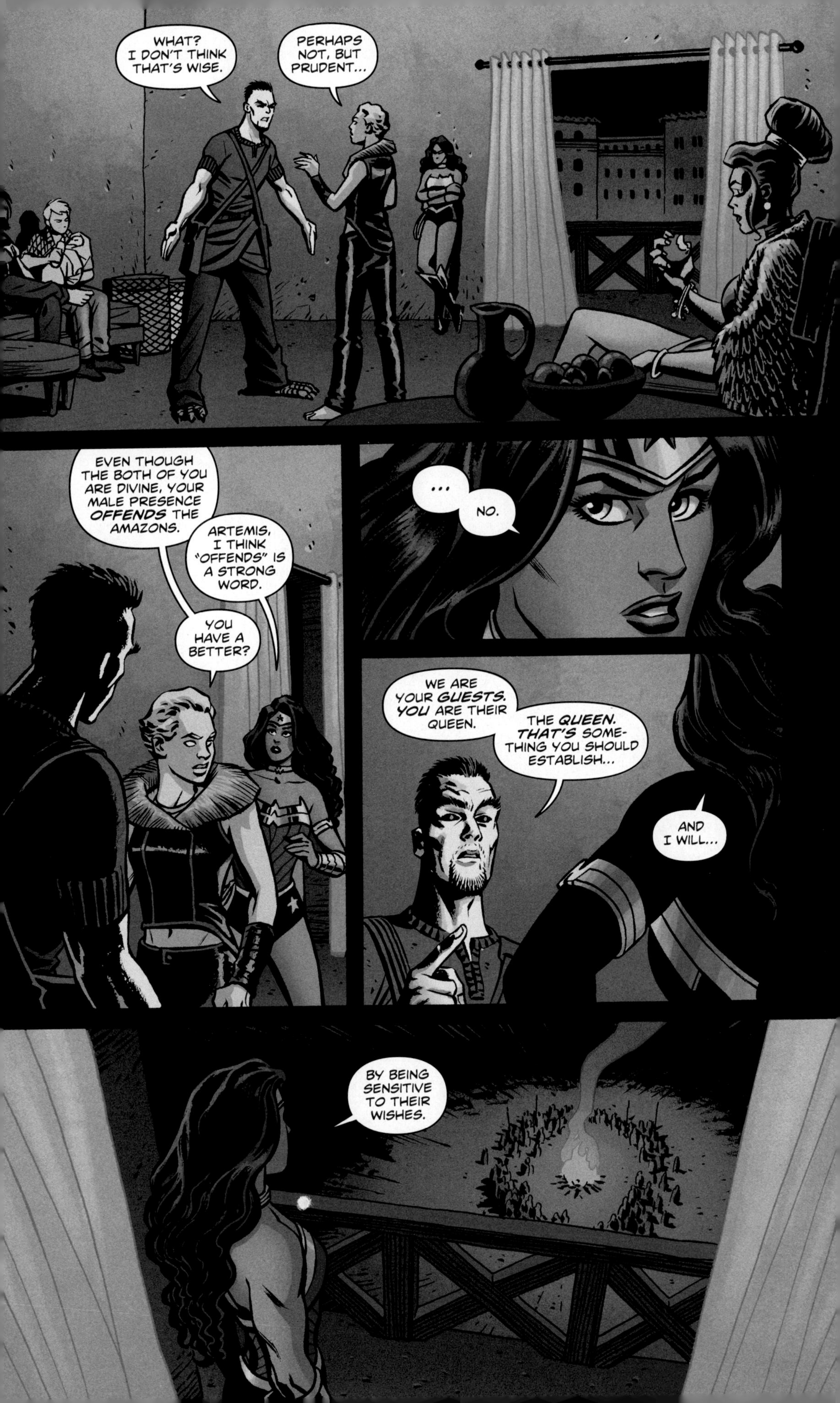
WHAT? I DON'T THINK THAT'S WISE.
PERHAPS NOT, BUT PRUDENT...
EVEN THOUGH THE BOTH OF YOU ARE DIVINE, YOUR MALE PRESENCE OFFENDS THE AMAZONS.
ARTEMIS, I THINK "OFFENDS" IS A STRONG WORD.
YOU HAVE A BETTER?
...
NO.
WE ARE YOUR GUESTS. YOU ARE THEIR QUEEN.
THE QUEEN. THAT'S SOMETHING YOU SHOULD ESTABLISH...
AND I WILL...
BY BEING SENSITIVE TO THEIR WISHES.

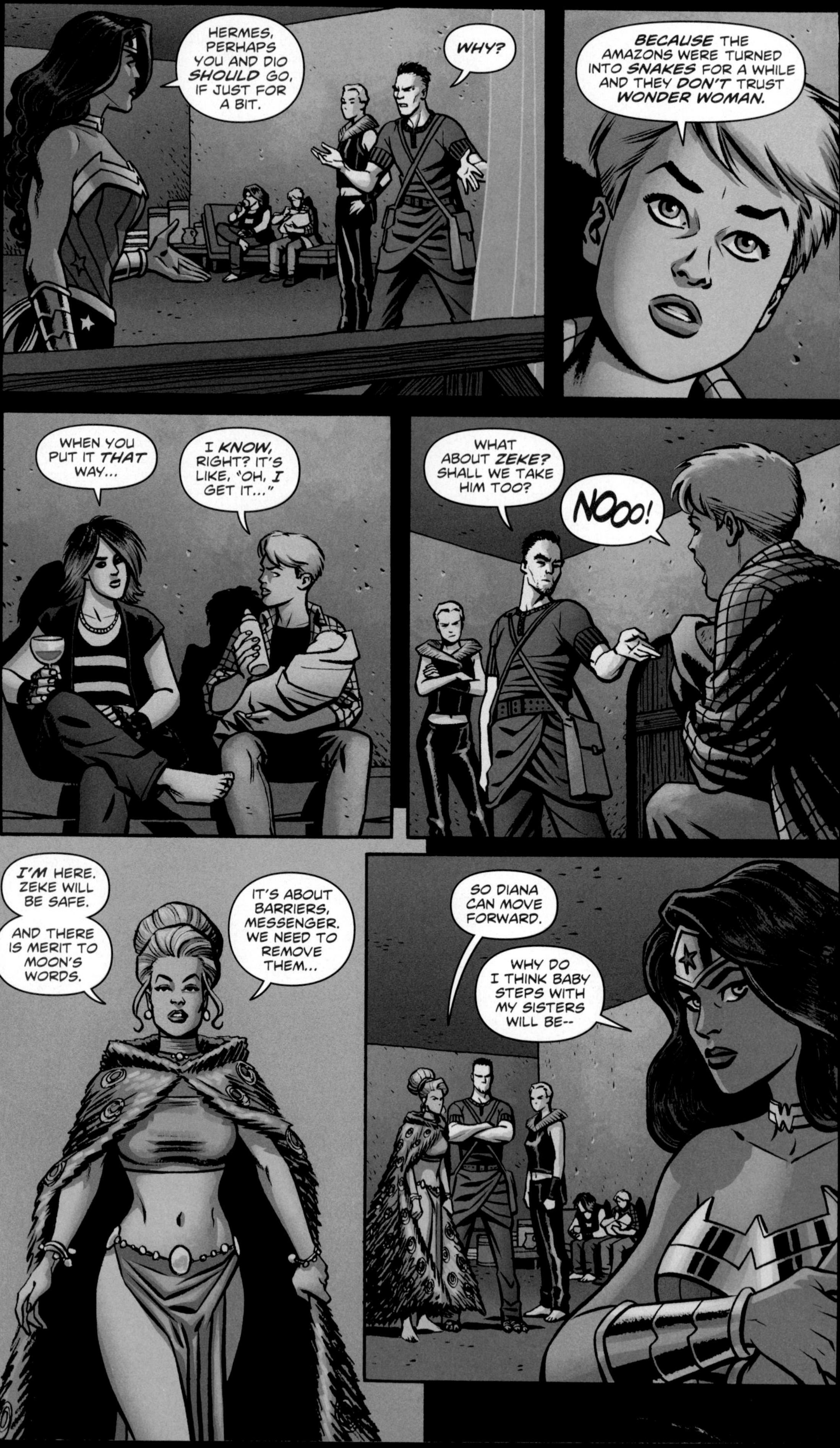
HERMES, PERHAPS YOU AND DIO SHOULD GO, IF JUST FOR A BIT.
WHY?
BECAUSE THE AMAZONS WERE TURNED INTO SNAKES FOR A WHILE AND THEY DON'T TRUST WONDER WOMAN.
WHEN YOU PUT IT THAT WAY...
I KNOW, RIGHT? IT'S LIKE, "OH, I GET IT..."
WHAT ABOUT ZEKE? SHALL WE TAKE HIM TOO?
NOOO!
I'M HERE. ZEKE WILL BE SAFE.
AND THERE IS MERIT TO MOON'S WORDS.
IT'S ABOUT BARRIERS, MESSENGER. WE NEED TO REMOVE THEM...
SO DIANA CAN MOVE FORWARD.
WHY DO I THINK BABY STEPS WITH MY SISTERS WILL BE--

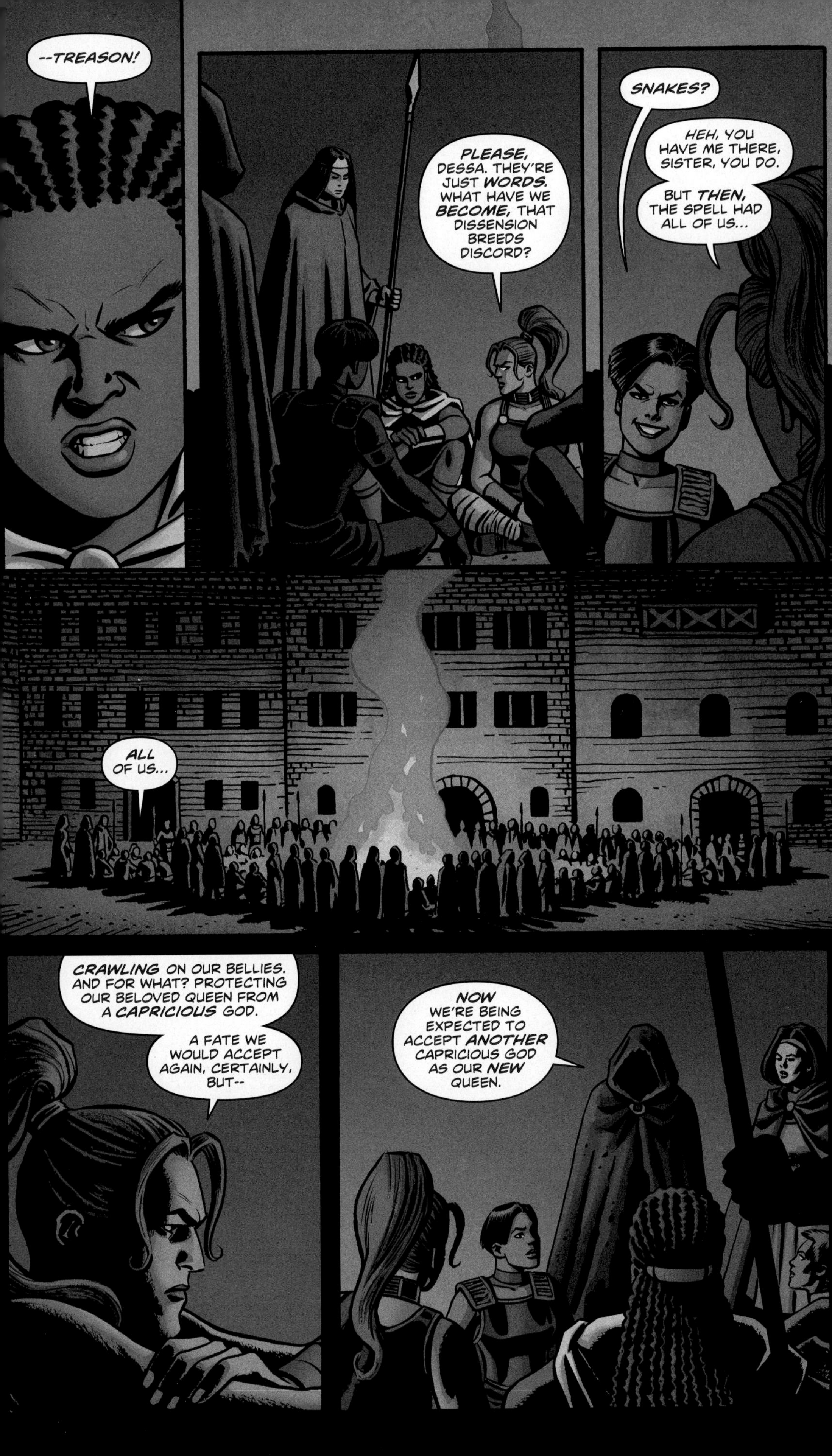
--TREASON!
PLEASE, DESSA. THEY'RE JUST WORDS. WHAT HAVE WE BECOME, THAT DISSENSION BREEDS DISCORD?
SNAKES?
HEH, YOU HAVE ME THERE, SISTER, YOU DO.
BUT THEN, THE SPELL HAD ALL OF US...
ALL OF US...
CRAWLING ON OUR BELLIES. AND FOR WHAT? PROTECTING OUR BELOVED QUEEN FROM A CAPRICIOUS GOD.
A FATE WE WOULD ACCEPT AGAIN, CERTAINLY, BUT--
NOW WE'RE BEING EXPECTED TO ACCEPT ANOTHER CAPRICIOUS GOD AS OUR NEW QUEEN.

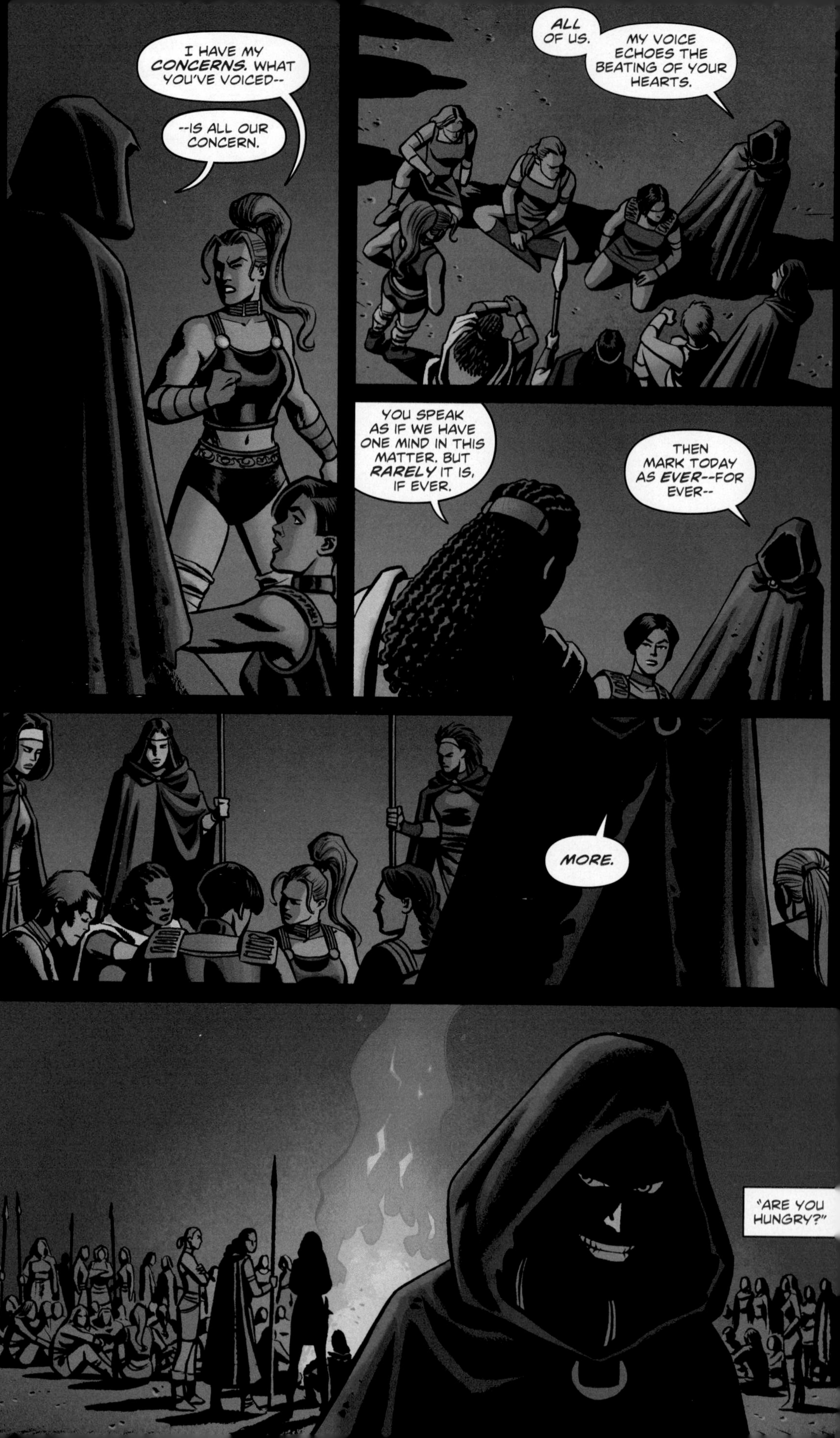
I HAVE MY CONCERNS. WHAT YOU'VE VOICED--
--IS ALL OUR CONCERN.
ALL OF US.
MY VOICE ECHOES THE BEATING OF YOUR HEARTS.
YOU SPEAK AS IF WE HAVE ONE MIND IN THIS MATTER. BUT RARELY IT IS, IF EVER.
THEN MARK TODAY AS EVER--FOR EVER--
MORE.
"ARE YOU HUNGRY?"

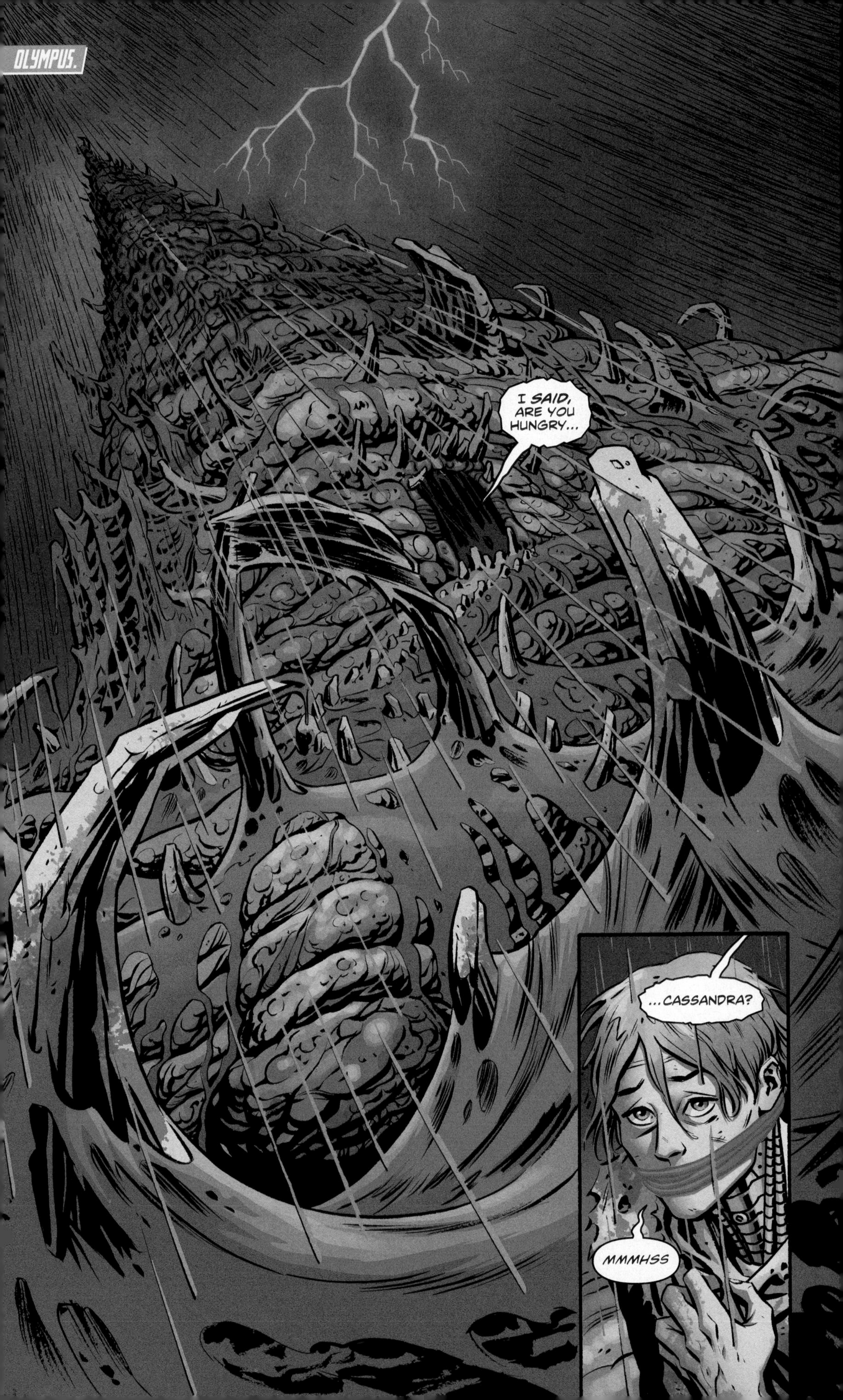
OLYMPUS.
I SAID, ARE YOU HUNGRY...
...CASSANDRA?
MMMHSS

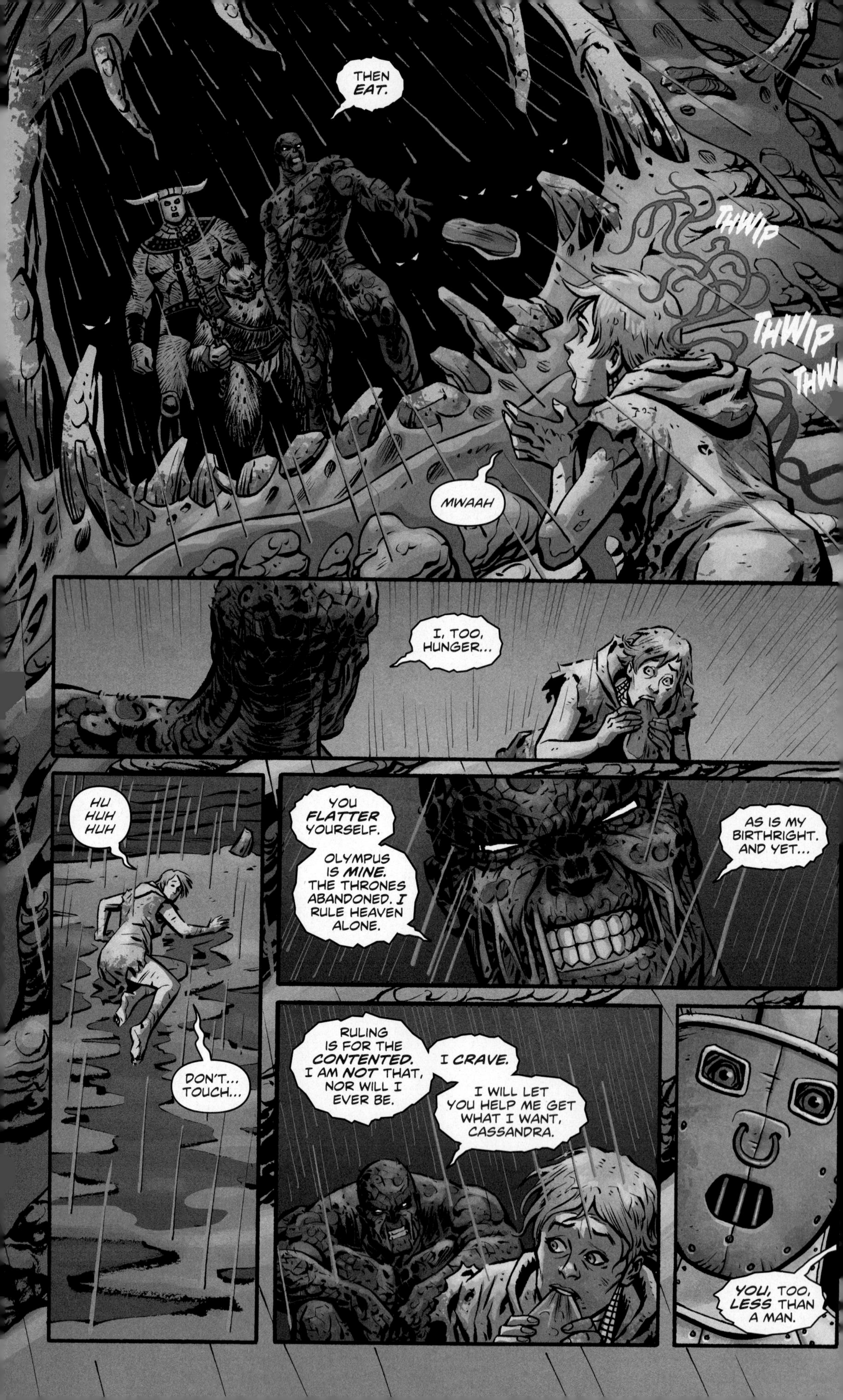
THEN EAT.
THWIP
THWIP
THWI
MWAAH
I, TOO, HUNGER...
HU HUH HUH
DON'T... TOUCH...
YOU FLATTER YOURSELF.
OLYMPUS IS MINE. THE THRONES ABANDONED. I RULE HEAVEN ALONE.
AS IS MY BIRTHRIGHT. AND YET...
RULING IS FOR THE CONTENTED. I AM NOT THAT, NOR WILL I EVER BE.
I CRAVE.
I WILL LET YOU HELP ME GET WHAT I WANT, CASSANDRA.
YOU, TOO, LESS THAN A MAN.

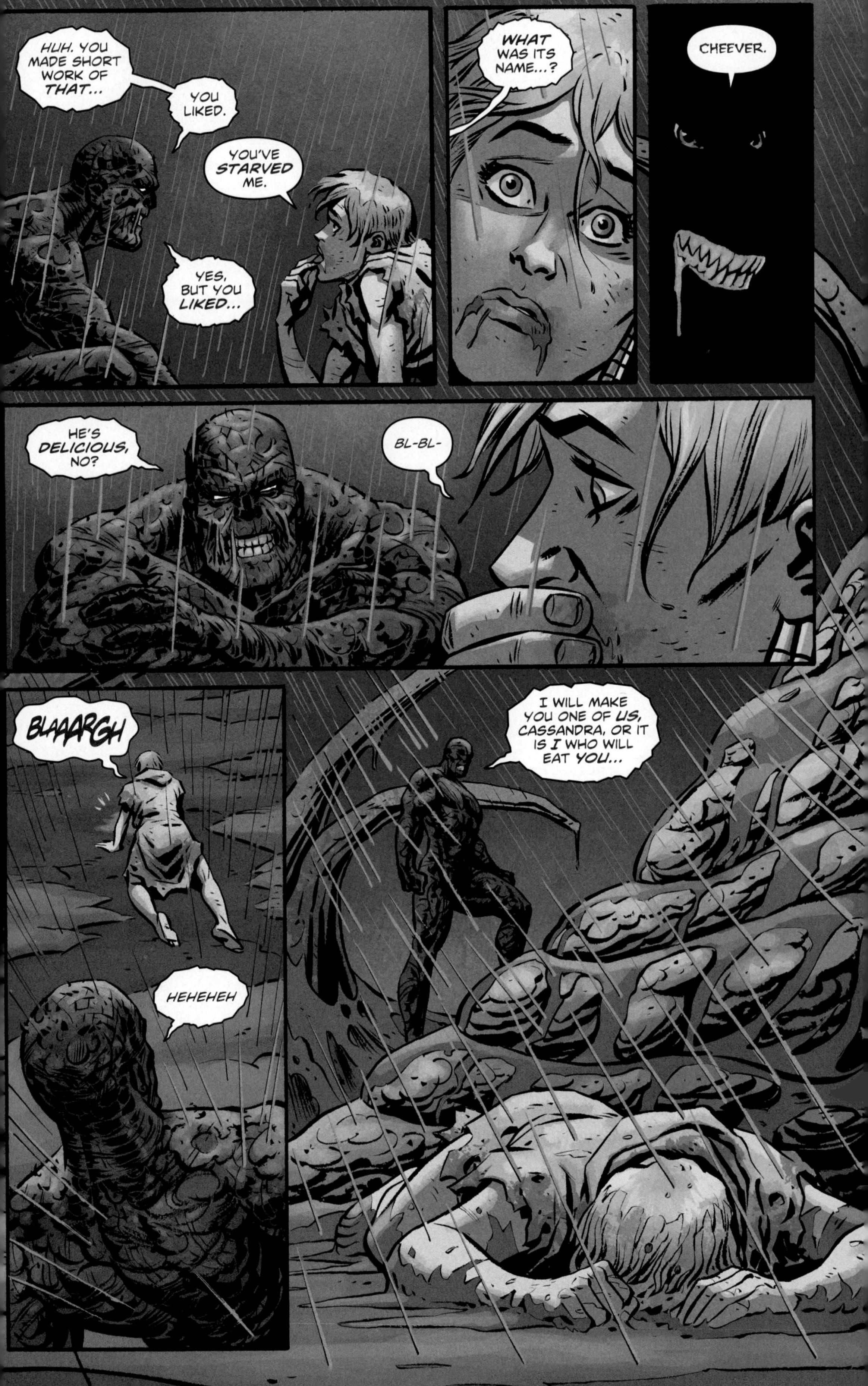
HUH. YOU MADE SHORT WORK OF THAT...
YOU LIKED.
YOU'VE STARVED ME.
YES, BUT YOU LIKED...
WHAT WAS ITS NAME...?
CHEEVER.
HE'S DELICIOUS, NO?
BL-BL-
BLAAARGH
HEHEHEH
I WILL MAKE YOU ONE OF US, CASSANDRA, OR IT IS I WHO WILL EAT YOU...

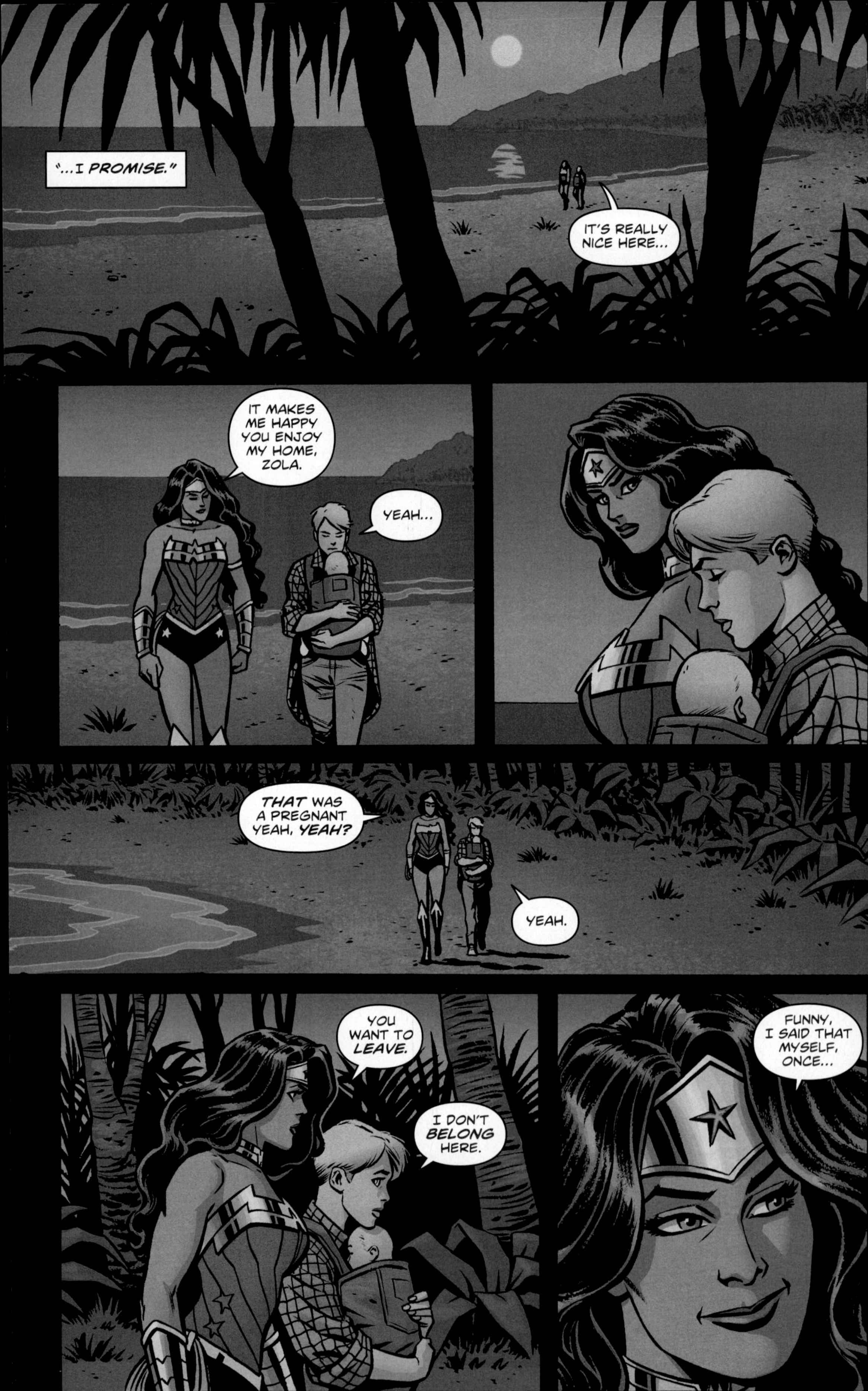
"...I *PROMISE.*"
IT'S REALLY NICE HERE...
IT MAKES ME HAPPY YOU ENJOY MY HOME, ZOLA.
YEAH...
THAT WAS A PREGNANT YEAH, ***YEAH?***
YEAH.
YOU WANT TO *LEAVE.*
I DON'T *BELONG* HERE.
FUNNY, I SAID THAT MYSELF, ONCE...

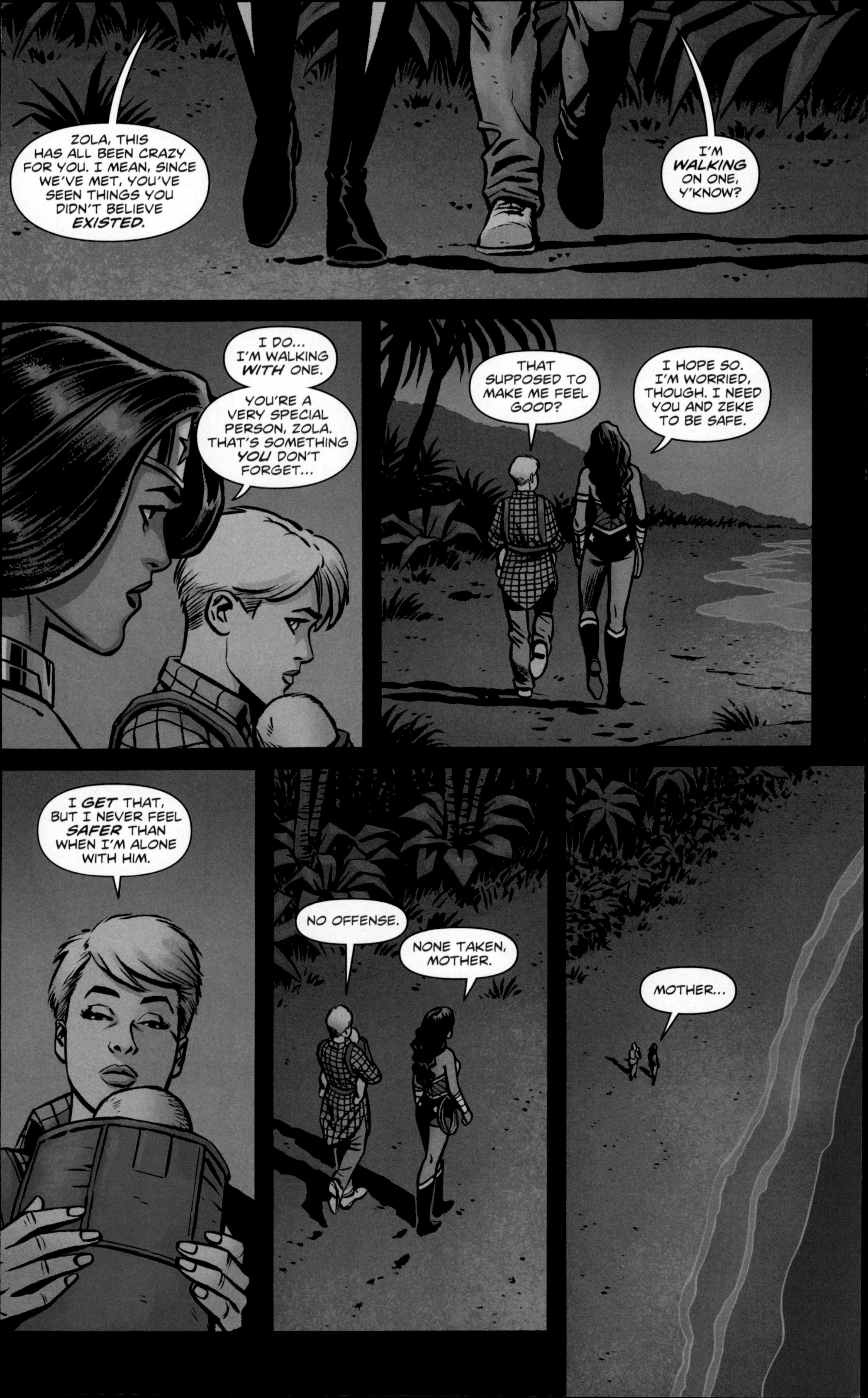
ZOLA, THIS HAS ALL BEEN CRAZY FOR YOU. I MEAN, SINCE WE'VE MET, YOU'VE SEEN THINGS YOU DIDN'T BELIEVE EXISTED.
I'M WALKING ON ONE, Y'KNOW?
I DO... I'M WALKING WITH ONE.
YOU'RE A VERY SPECIAL PERSON, ZOLA. THAT'S SOMETHING YOU DON'T FORGET...
THAT SUPPOSED TO MAKE ME FEEL GOOD?
I HOPE SO. I'M WORRIED, THOUGH. I NEED YOU AND ZEKE TO BE SAFE.
I GET THAT, BUT I NEVER FEEL SAFER THAN WHEN I'M ALONE WITH HIM.
NO OFFENSE.
NONE TAKEN, MOTHER.
MOTHER...

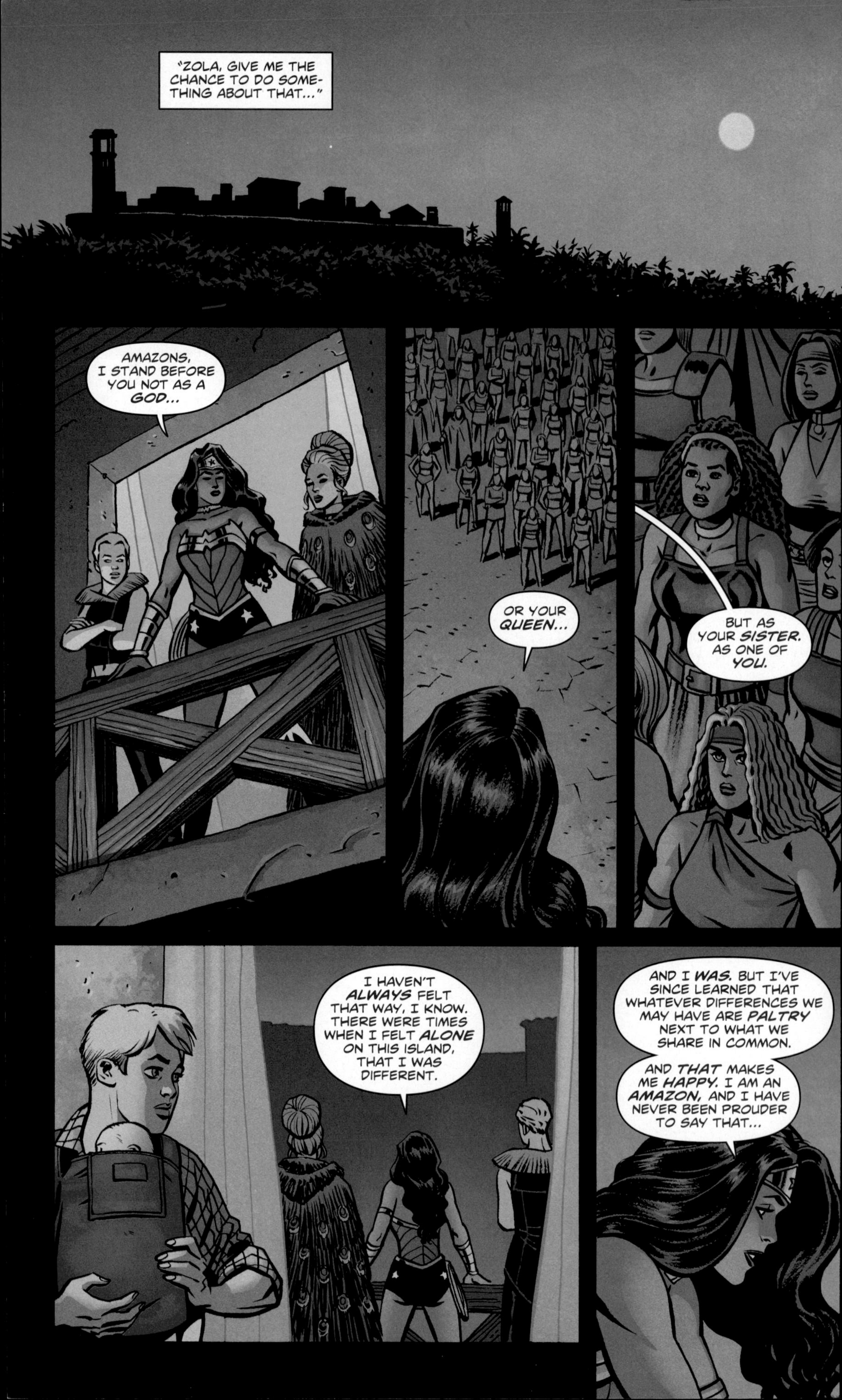
"ZOLA, GIVE ME THE CHANCE TO DO SOMETHING ABOUT THAT..."
AMAZONS, I STAND BEFORE YOU NOT AS A GOD...
OR YOUR QUEEN...
BUT AS YOUR SISTER. AS ONE OF YOU.
I HAVEN'T ALWAYS FELT THAT WAY, I KNOW. THERE WERE TIMES WHEN I FELT ALONE ON THIS ISLAND, THAT I WAS DIFFERENT.
AND I WAS. BUT I'VE SINCE LEARNED THAT WHATEVER DIFFERENCES WE MAY HAVE ARE PALTRY NEXT TO WHAT WE SHARE IN COMMON.
AND THAT MAKES ME HAPPY. I AM AN AMAZON, AND I HAVE NEVER BEEN PROUDER TO SAY THAT...

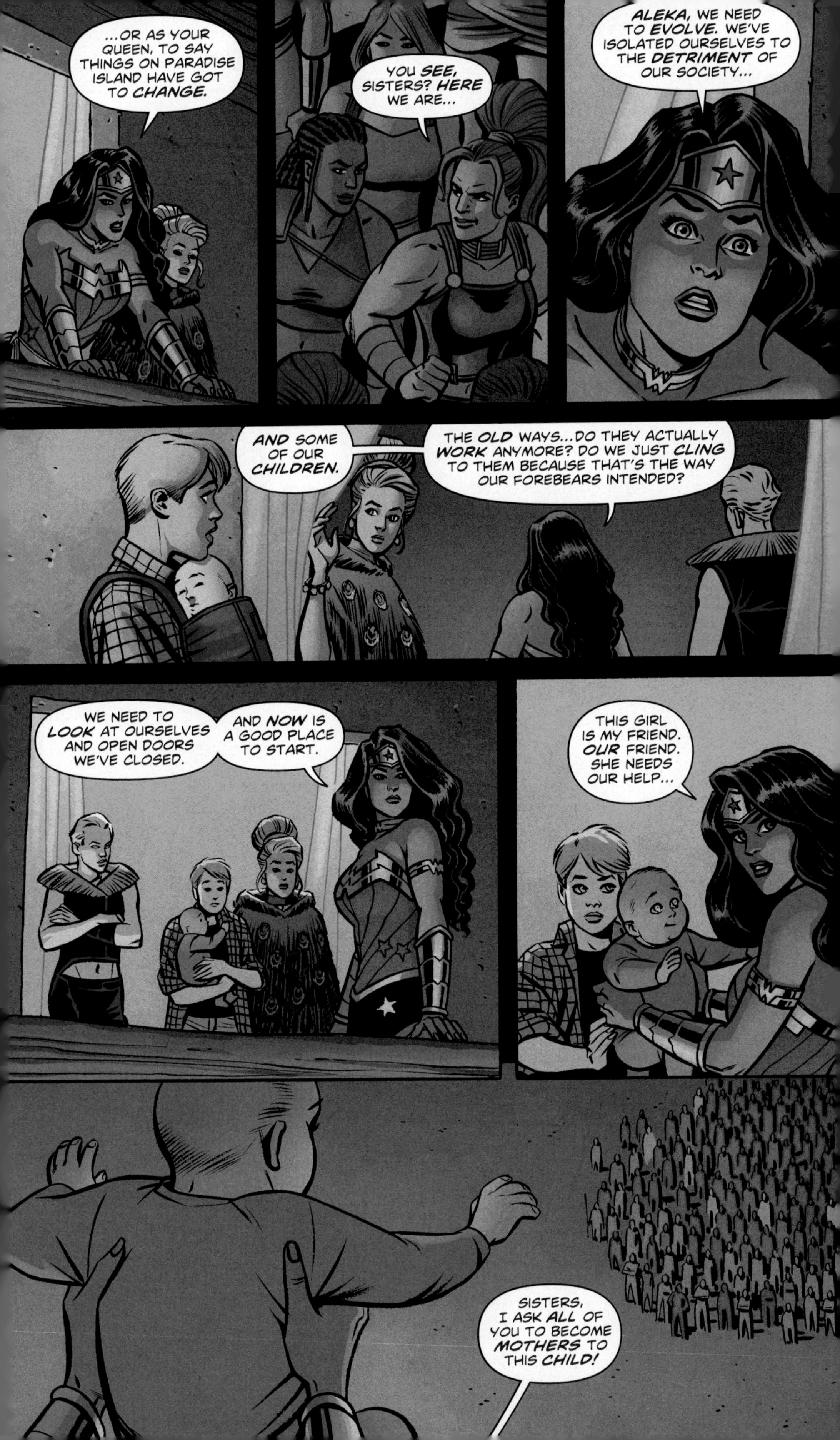
...OR AS YOUR QUEEN, TO SAY THINGS ON PARADISE ISLAND HAVE GOT TO CHANGE.
YOU SEE, SISTERS? HERE WE ARE...
ALEKA, WE NEED TO EVOLVE. WE'VE ISOLATED OURSELVES TO THE DETRIMENT OF OUR SOCIETY...
AND SOME OF OUR CHILDREN.
THE OLD WAYS...DO THEY ACTUALLY WORK ANYMORE? DO WE JUST CLING TO THEM BECAUSE THAT'S THE WAY OUR FOREBEARS INTENDED?
WE NEED TO LOOK AT OURSELVES AND OPEN DOORS WE'VE CLOSED.
AND NOW IS A GOOD PLACE TO START.
THIS GIRL IS MY FRIEND. OUR FRIEND. SHE NEEDS OUR HELP...
SISTERS, I ASK ALL OF YOU TO BECOME MOTHERS TO THIS CHILD!

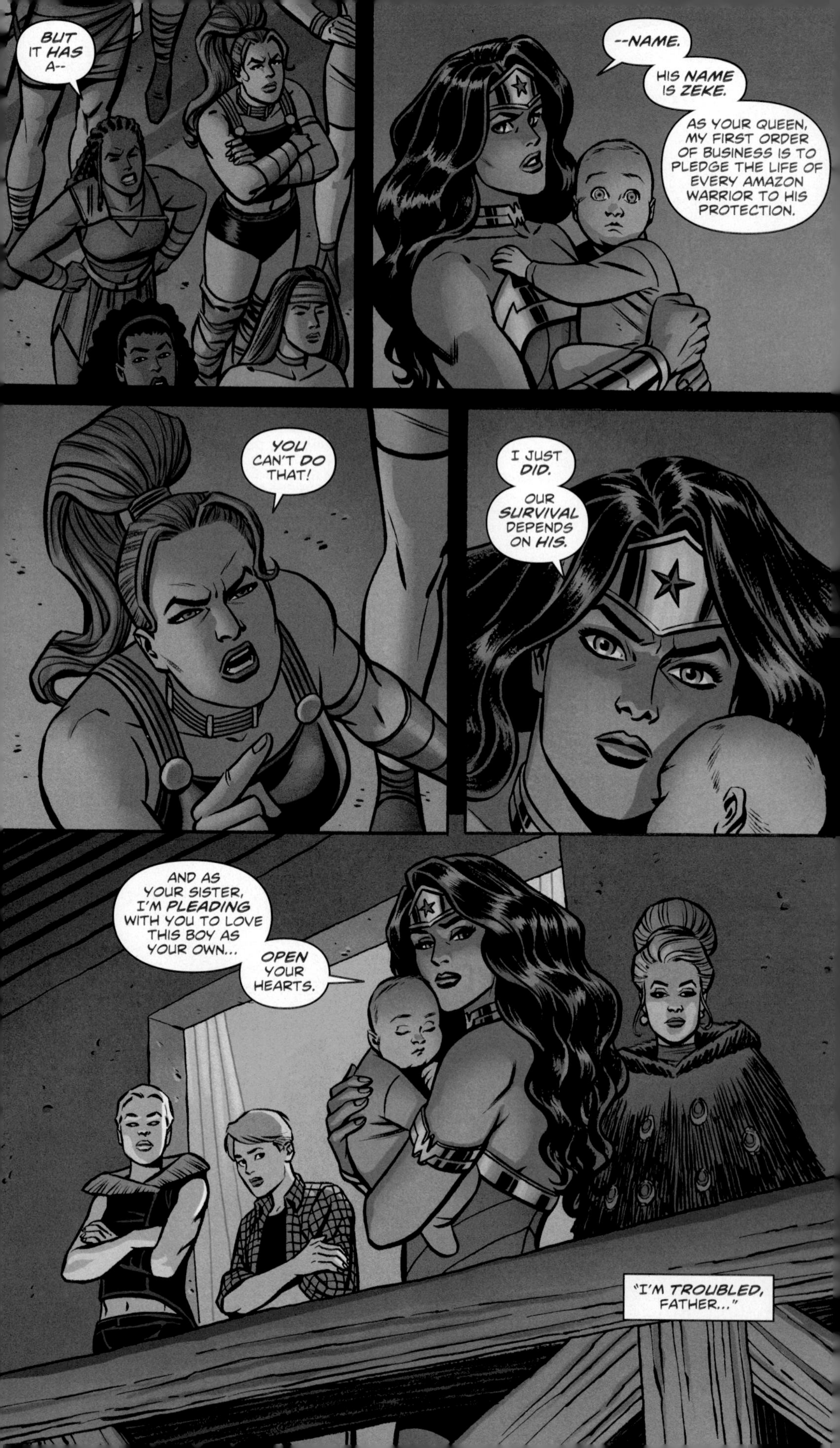
BUT IT HAS A--
--NAME.
HIS NAME IS ZEKE.
AS YOUR QUEEN, MY FIRST ORDER OF BUSINESS IS TO PLEDGE THE LIFE OF EVERY AMAZON WARRIOR TO HIS PROTECTION.
YOU CAN'T DO THAT!
I JUST DID.
OUR SURVIVAL DEPENDS ON HIS.
AND AS YOUR SISTER, I'M PLEADING WITH YOU TO LOVE THIS BOY AS YOUR OWN...
OPEN YOUR HEARTS.
"I'M TROUBLED, FATHER..."

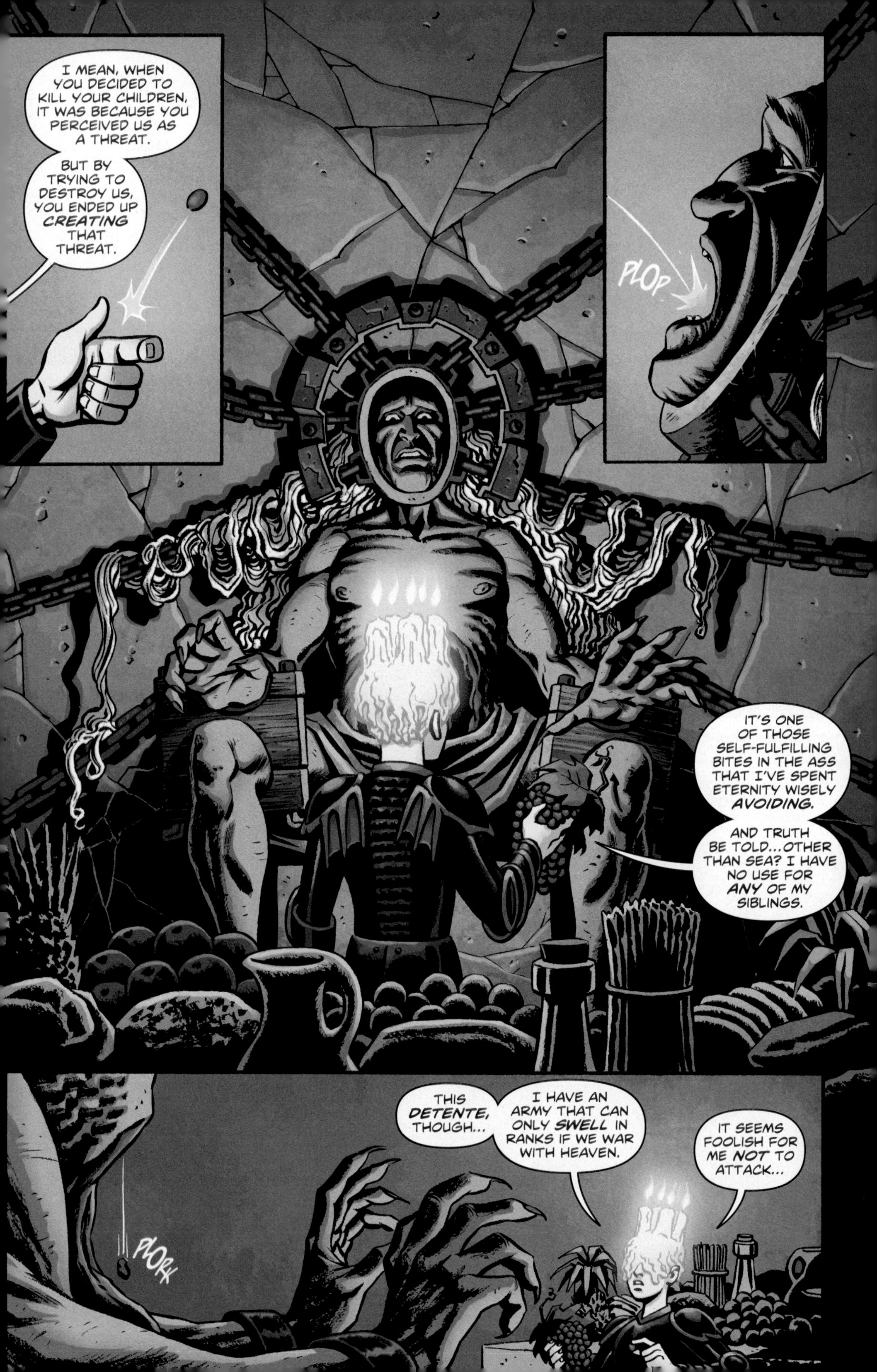
I MEAN, WHEN YOU DECIDED TO KILL YOUR CHILDREN, IT WAS BECAUSE YOU PERCEIVED US AS A THREAT.
BUT BY TRYING TO DESTROY US, YOU ENDED UP *CREATING* THAT THREAT.
PLOP
IT'S ONE OF THOSE SELF-FULFILLING BITES IN THE ASS THAT I'VE SPENT ETERNITY WISELY *AVOIDING.*
AND TRUTH BE TOLD...OTHER THAN SEA? I HAVE NO USE FOR *ANY* OF MY SIBLINGS.
THIS *DETENTE,* THOUGH...
I HAVE AN ARMY THAT CAN ONLY *SWELL* IN RANKS IF WE WAR WITH HEAVEN.
IT SEEMS FOOLISH FOR ME *NOT* TO ATTACK...
PLORK

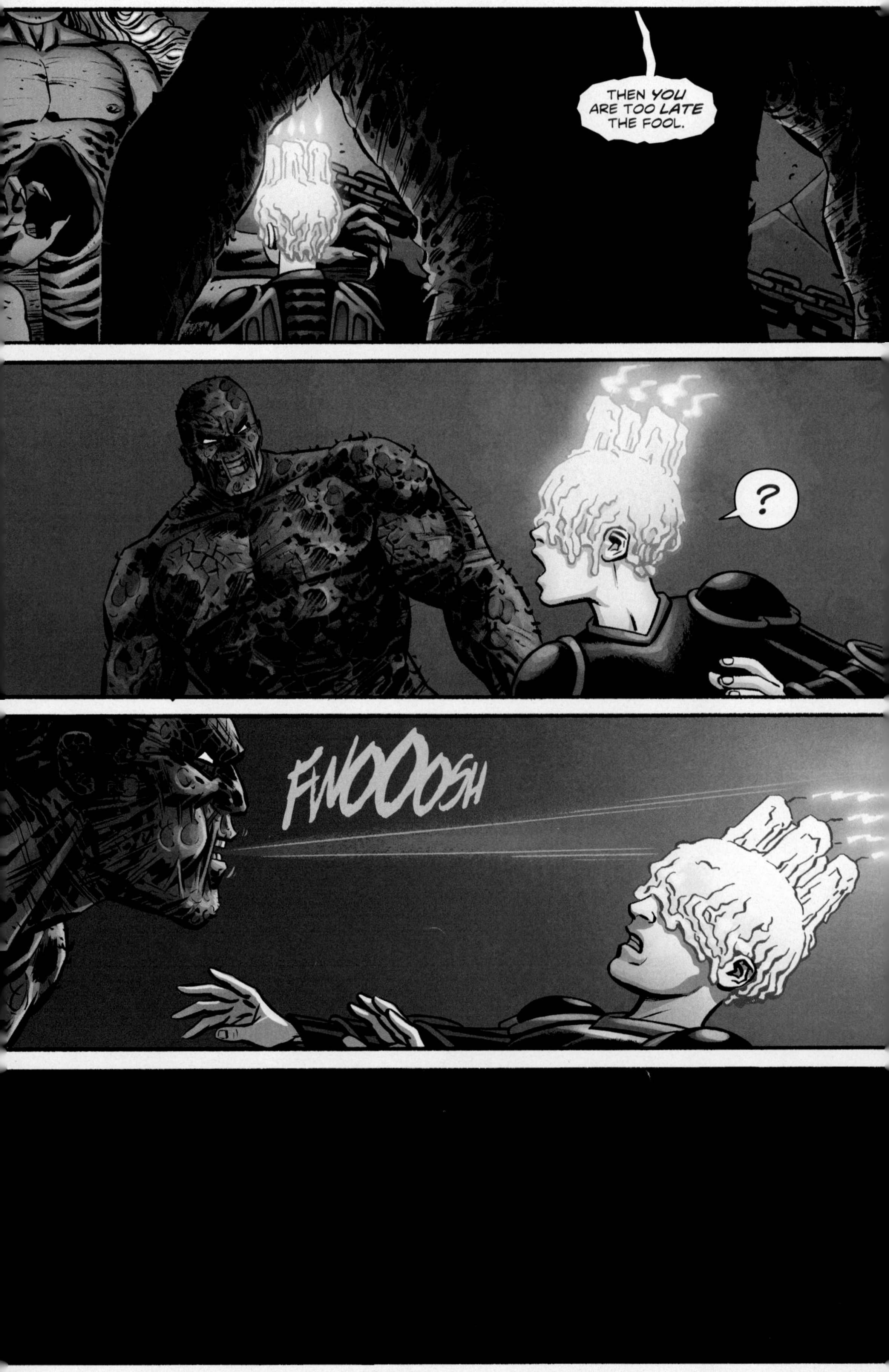
THEN *YOU* ARE TOO *LATE* THE FOOL.
?
FWOOOSH

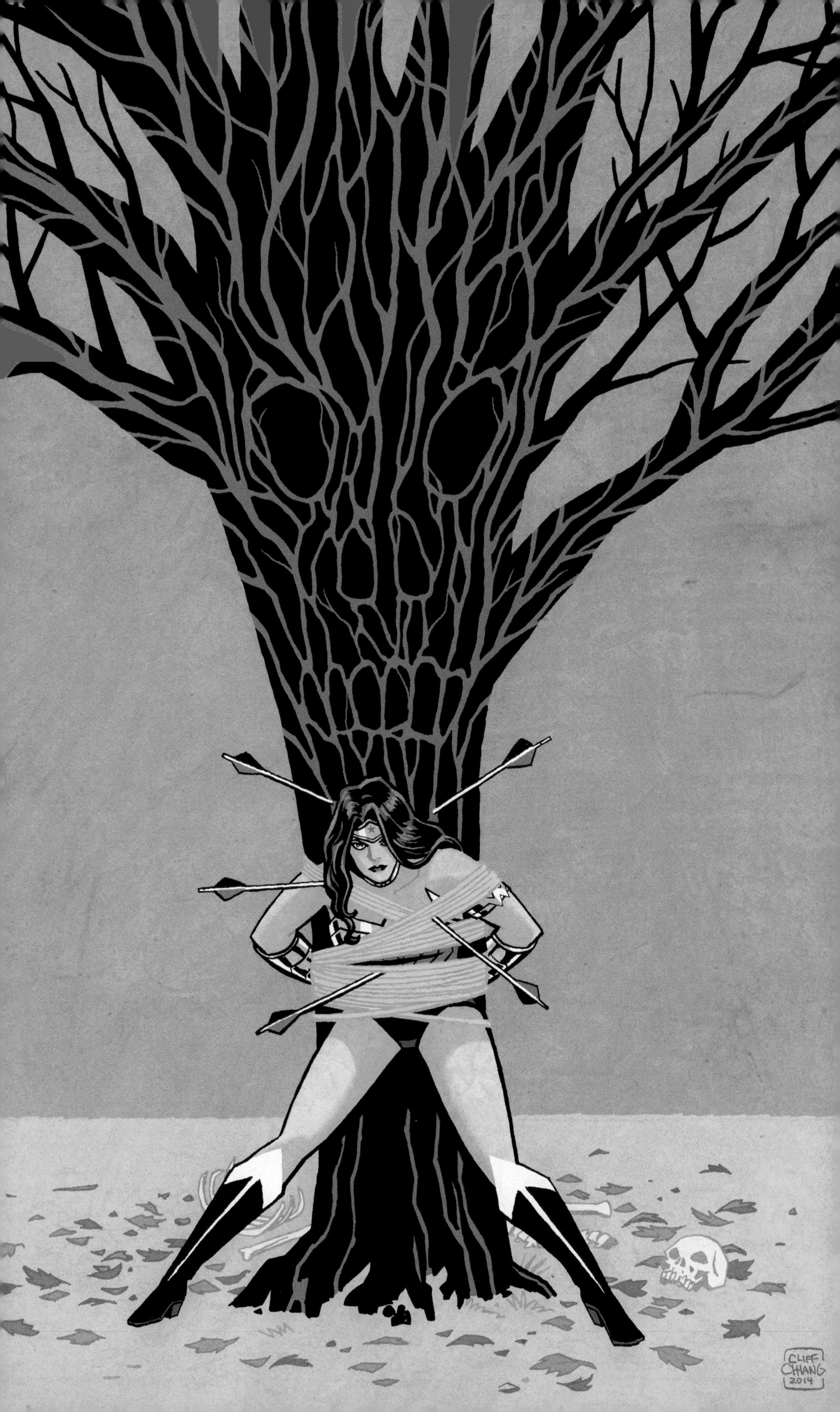
CLIFF
CHIANG
2014

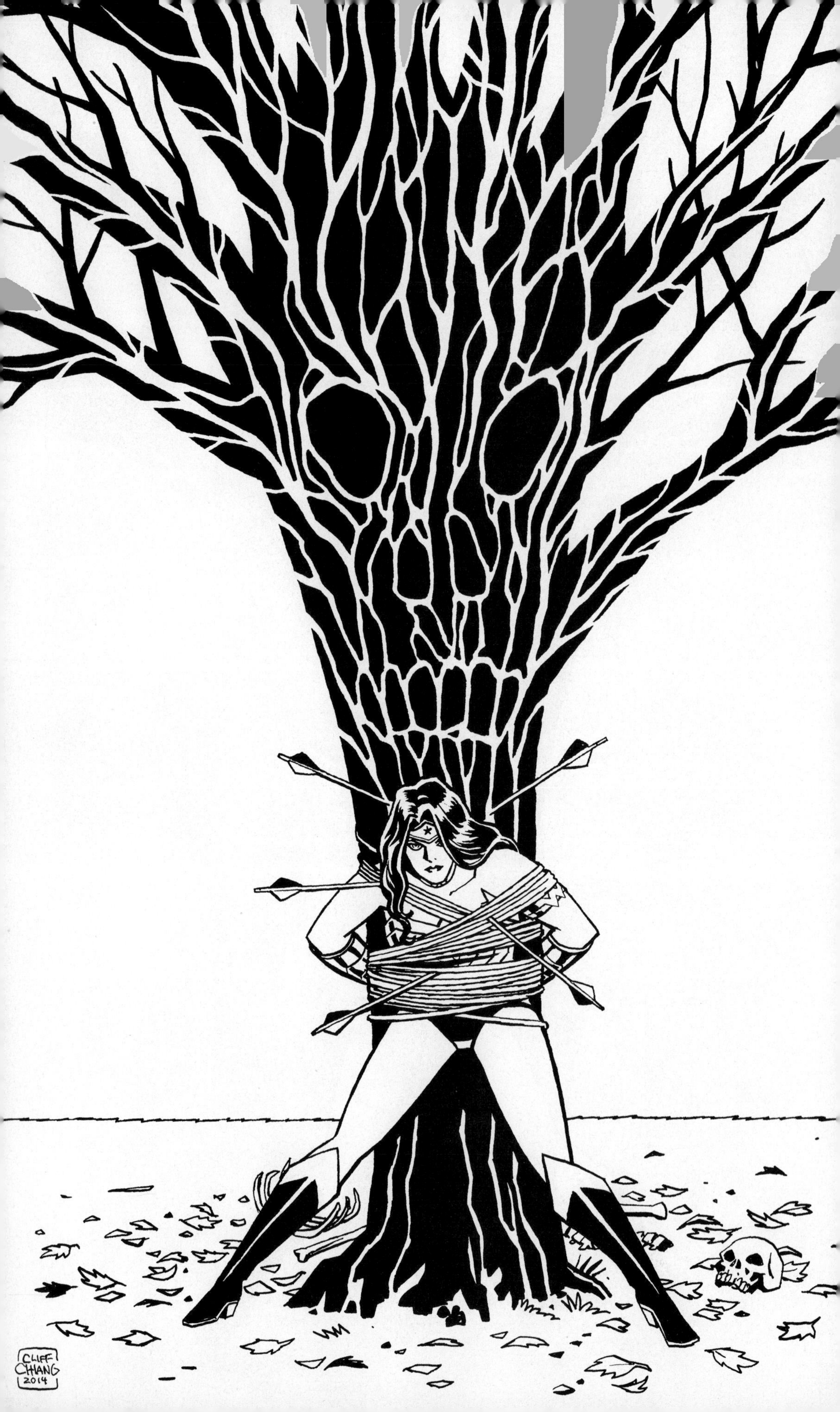
CLIFF
CHIANG
2014

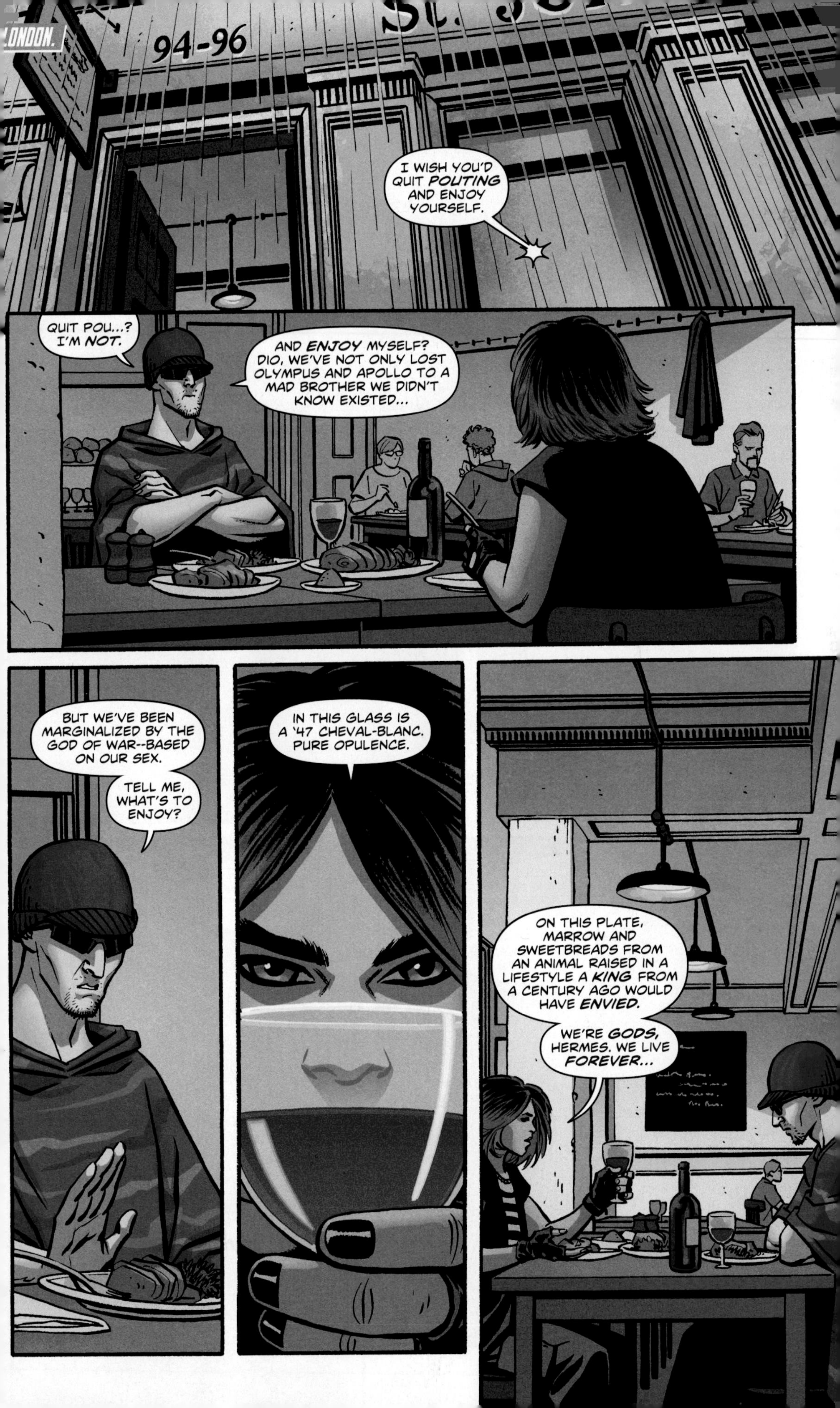
LONDON.
94-96
I WISH YOU'D QUIT POUTING AND ENJOY YOURSELF.
QUIT POU...? I'M NOT.
AND ENJOY MYSELF? DIO, WE'VE NOT ONLY LOST OLYMPUS AND APOLLO TO A MAD BROTHER WE DIDN'T KNOW EXISTED...
BUT WE'VE BEEN MARGINALIZED BY THE GOD OF WAR--BASED ON OUR SEX.
TELL ME, WHAT'S TO ENJOY?
IN THIS GLASS IS A '47 CHEVAL-BLANC. PURE OPULENCE.
ON THIS PLATE, MARROW AND SWEETBREADS FROM AN ANIMAL RAISED IN A LIFESTYLE A KING FROM A CENTURY AGO WOULD HAVE ENVIED.
WE'RE GODS, HERMES. WE LIVE FOREVER...

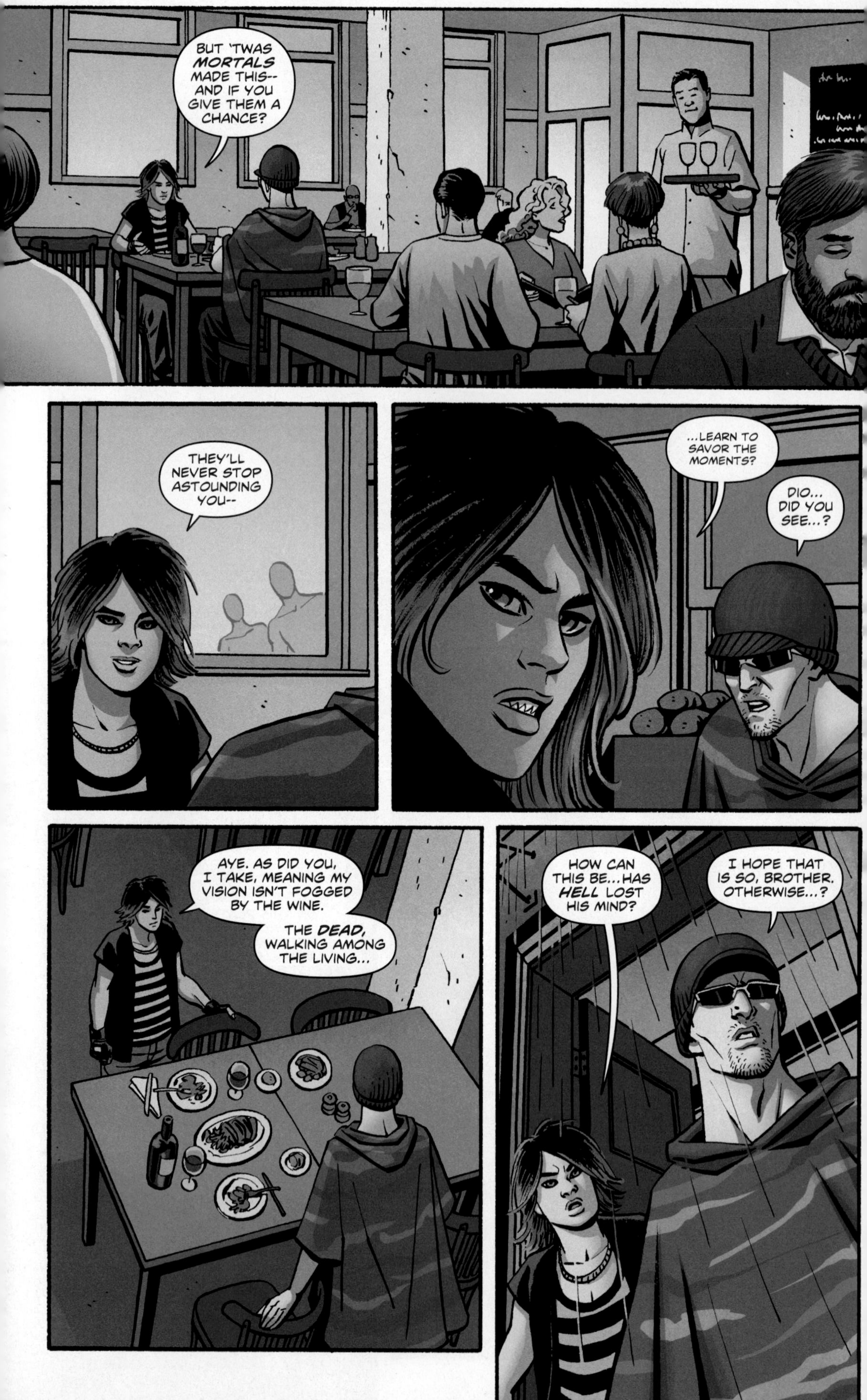

BUT 'TWAS *MORTALS* MADE THIS--AND IF YOU GIVE THEM A CHANCE?
THEY'LL NEVER STOP ASTOUNDING YOU--
...LEARN TO SAVOR THE MOMENTS?
DIO... DID YOU SEE...?
AYE. AS DID YOU, I TAKE, MEANING MY VISION ISN'T FOGGED BY THE WINE.
THE *DEAD,* WALKING AMONG THE LIVING...
HOW CAN THIS BE...HAS *HELL* LOST HIS MIND?
I HOPE THAT IS SO, BROTHER. OTHERWISE...?

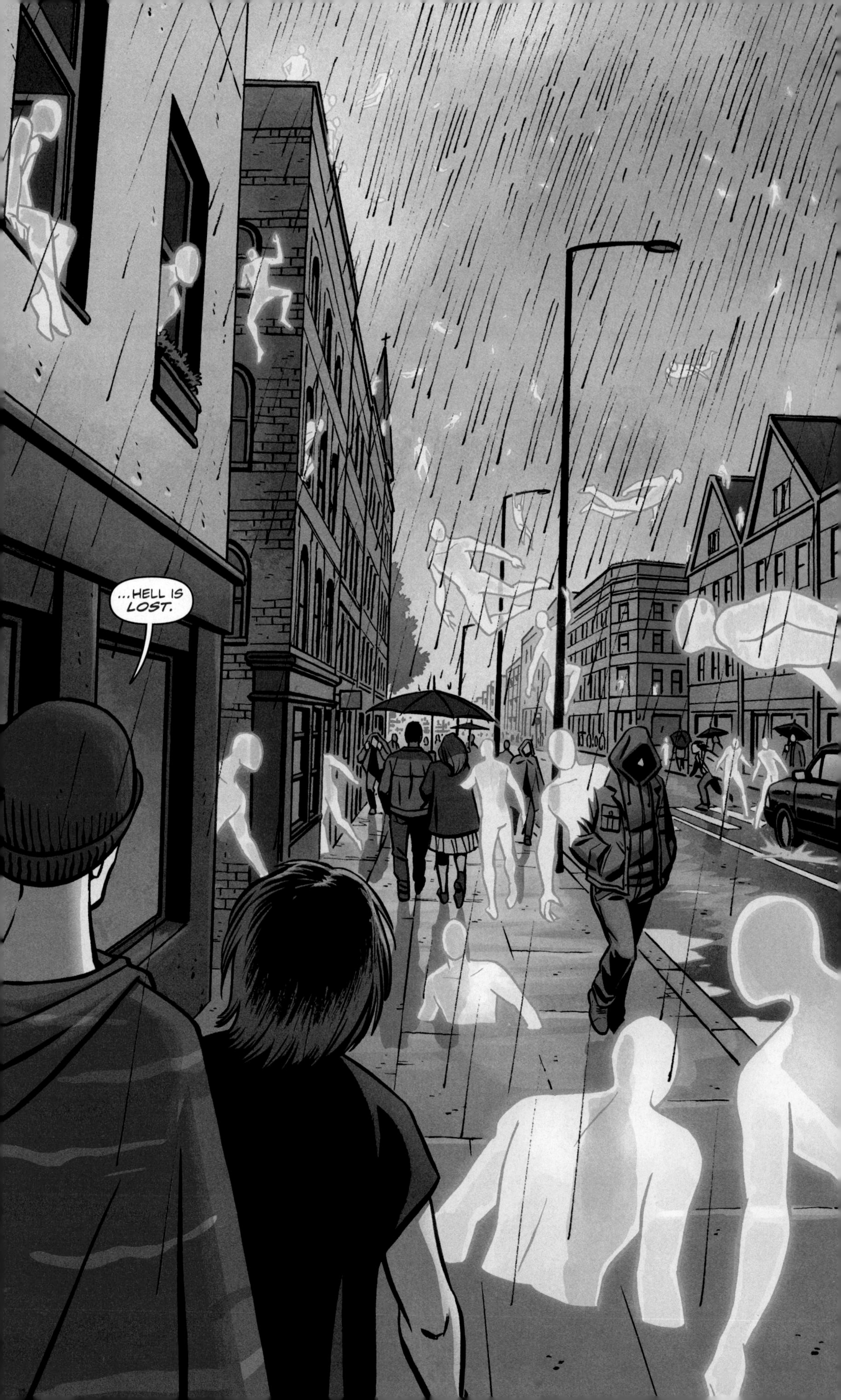
...HELL IS LOST.

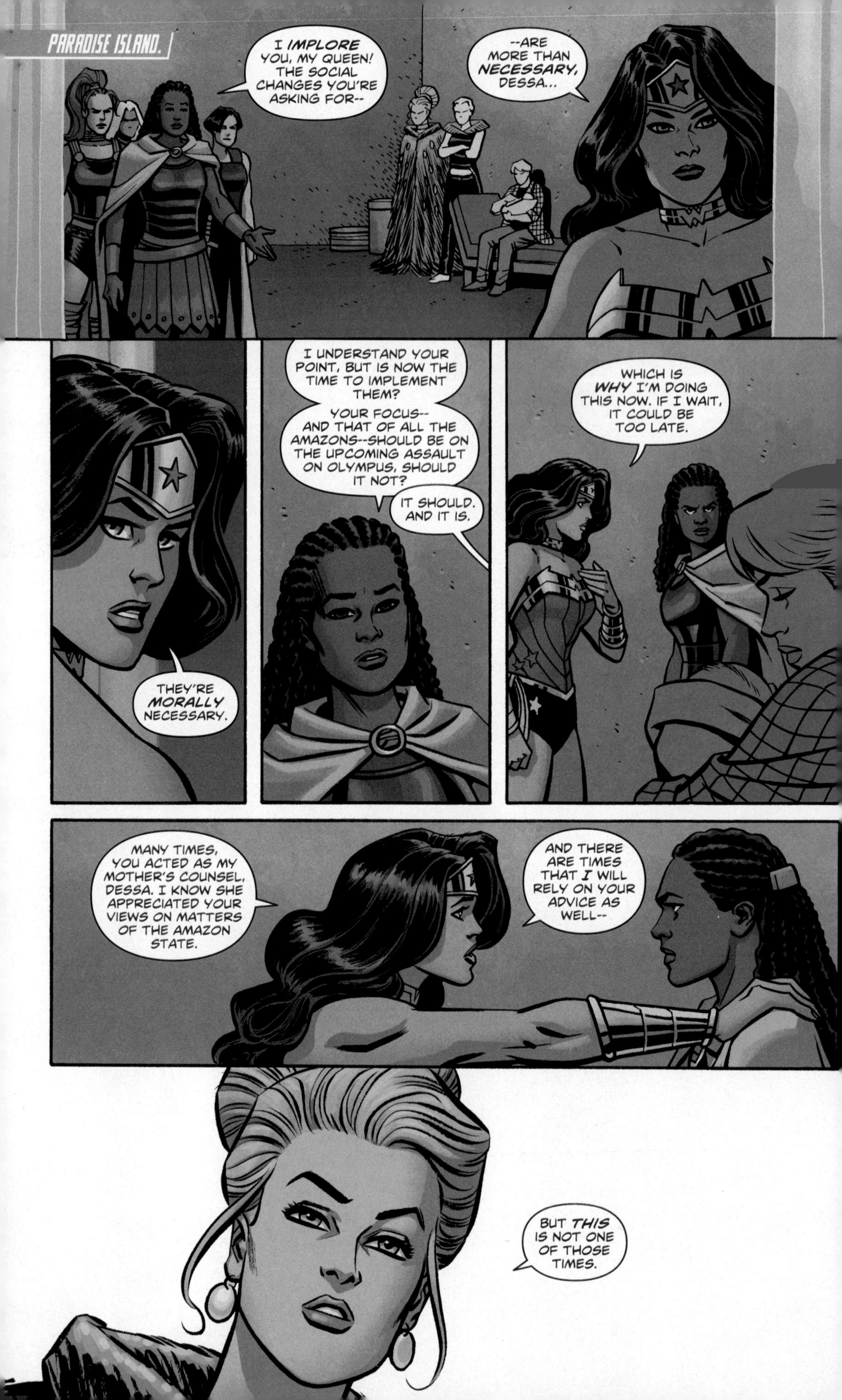
PARADISE ISLAND.
I IMPLORE YOU, MY QUEEN! THE SOCIAL CHANGES YOU'RE ASKING FOR--
--ARE MORE THAN NECESSARY, DESSA...
THEY'RE MORALLY NECESSARY.
I UNDERSTAND YOUR POINT, BUT IS NOW THE TIME TO IMPLEMENT THEM?
YOUR FOCUS-- AND THAT OF ALL THE AMAZONS--SHOULD BE ON THE UPCOMING ASSAULT ON OLYMPUS, SHOULD IT NOT?
IT SHOULD. AND IT IS.
WHICH IS WHY I'M DOING THIS NOW. IF I WAIT, IT COULD BE TOO LATE.
MANY TIMES, YOU ACTED AS MY MOTHER'S COUNSEL, DESSA. I KNOW SHE APPRECIATED YOUR VIEWS ON MATTERS OF THE AMAZON STATE.
AND THERE ARE TIMES THAT I WILL RELY ON YOUR ADVICE AS WELL--
BUT THIS IS NOT ONE OF THOSE TIMES.

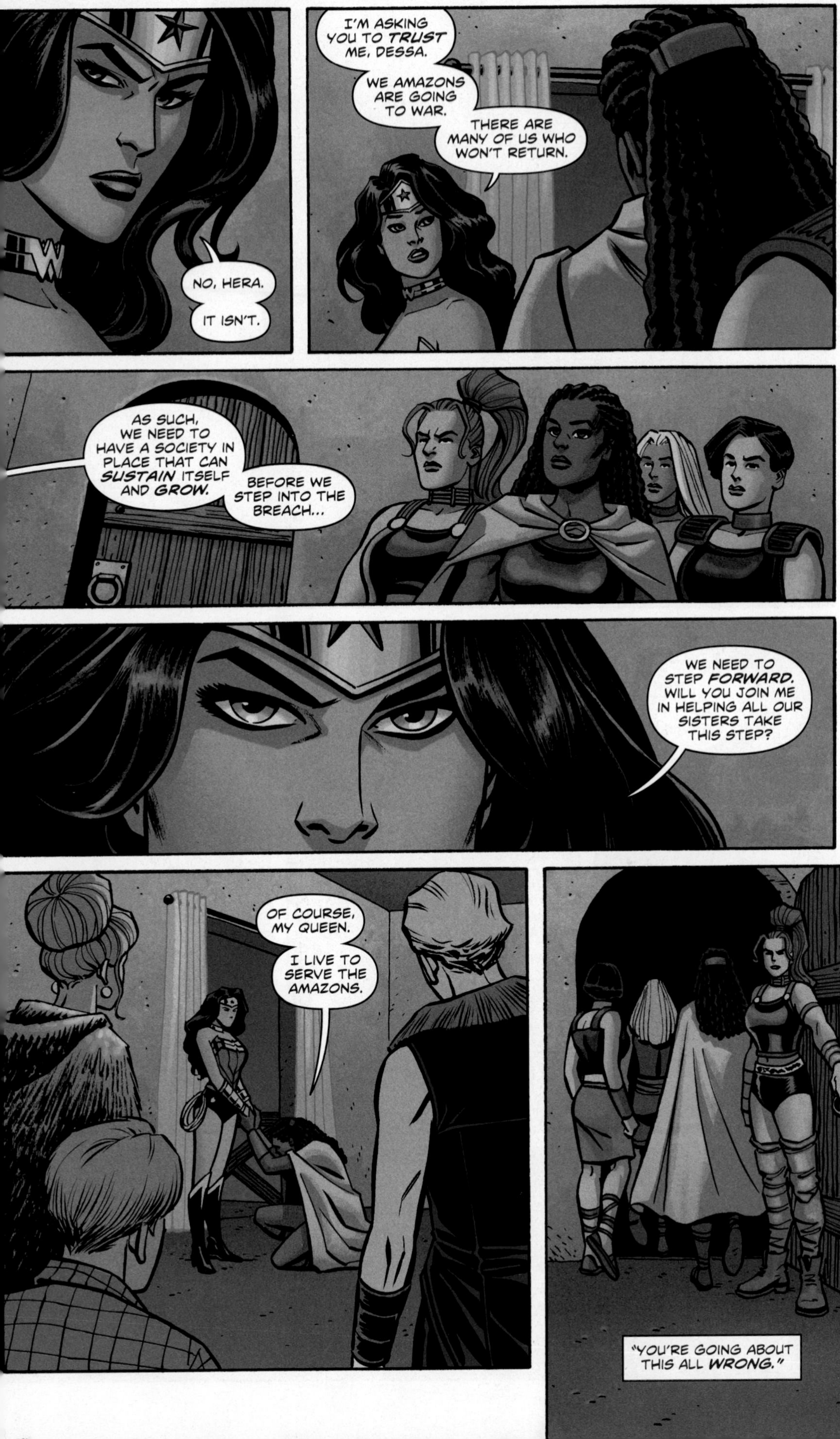
NO, HERA.
IT ISN'T.
I'M ASKING YOU TO TRUST ME, DESSA.
WE AMAZONS ARE GOING TO WAR.
THERE ARE MANY OF US WHO WON'T RETURN.
AS SUCH, WE NEED TO HAVE A SOCIETY IN PLACE THAT CAN SUSTAIN ITSELF AND GROW.
BEFORE WE STEP INTO THE BREACH...
WE NEED TO STEP FORWARD. WILL YOU JOIN ME IN HELPING ALL OUR SISTERS TAKE THIS STEP?
OF COURSE, MY QUEEN.
I LIVE TO SERVE THE AMAZONS.
"YOU'RE GOING ABOUT THIS ALL WRONG."

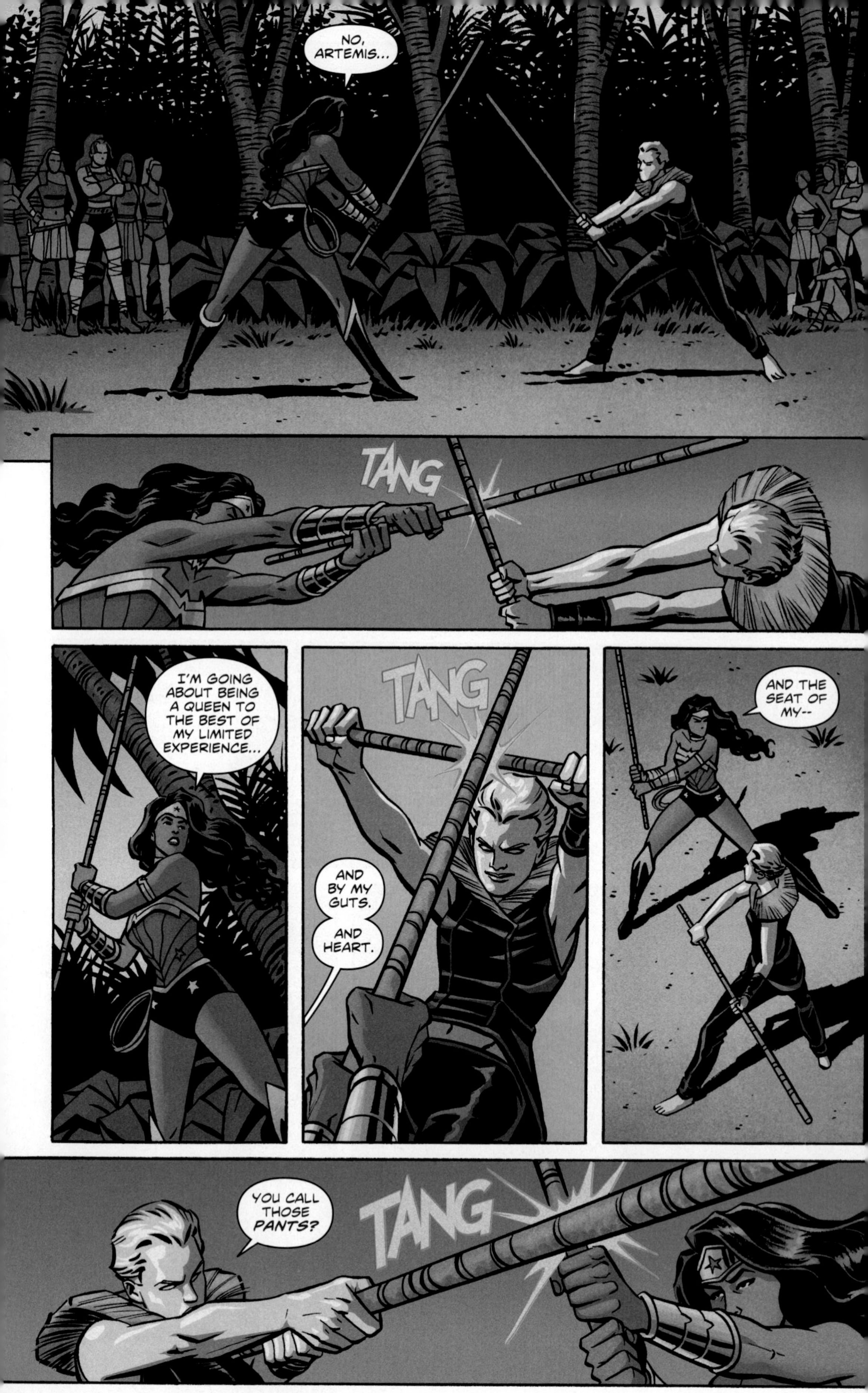
NO, ARTEMIS...
TANG
I'M GOING ABOUT BEING A QUEEN TO THE BEST OF MY LIMITED EXPERIENCE...
TANG
AND BY MY GUTS.
AND HEART.
AND THE SEAT OF MY--
YOU CALL THOSE *PANTS*?
TANG

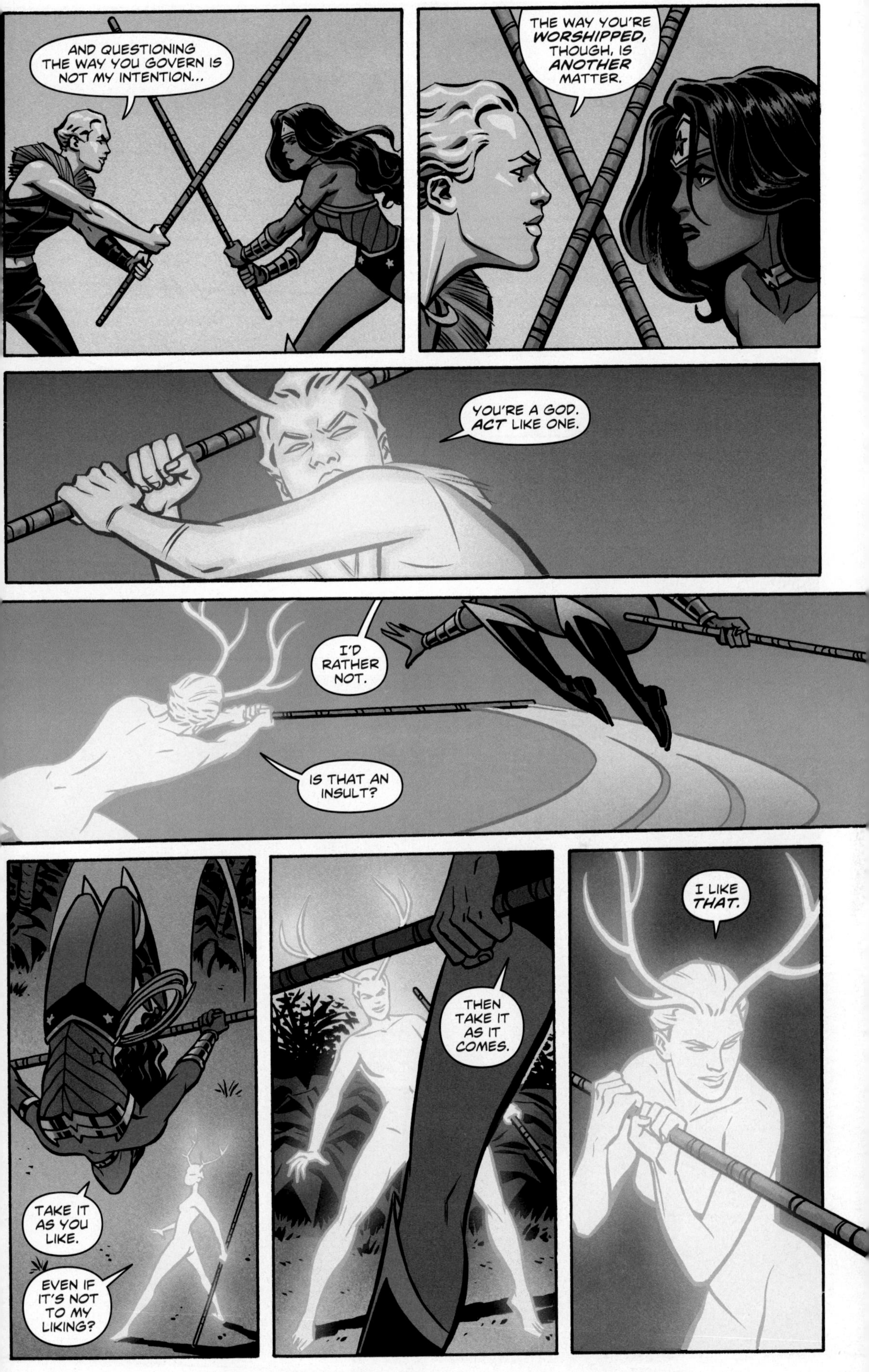
AND QUESTIONING THE WAY YOU GOVERN IS NOT MY INTENTION...
THE WAY YOU'RE WORSHIPPED, THOUGH, IS ANOTHER MATTER.
YOU'RE A GOD. ACT LIKE ONE.
I'D RATHER NOT.
IS THAT AN INSULT?
TAKE IT AS YOU LIKE.
EVEN IF IT'S NOT TO MY LIKING?
THEN TAKE IT AS IT COMES.
I LIKE THAT.

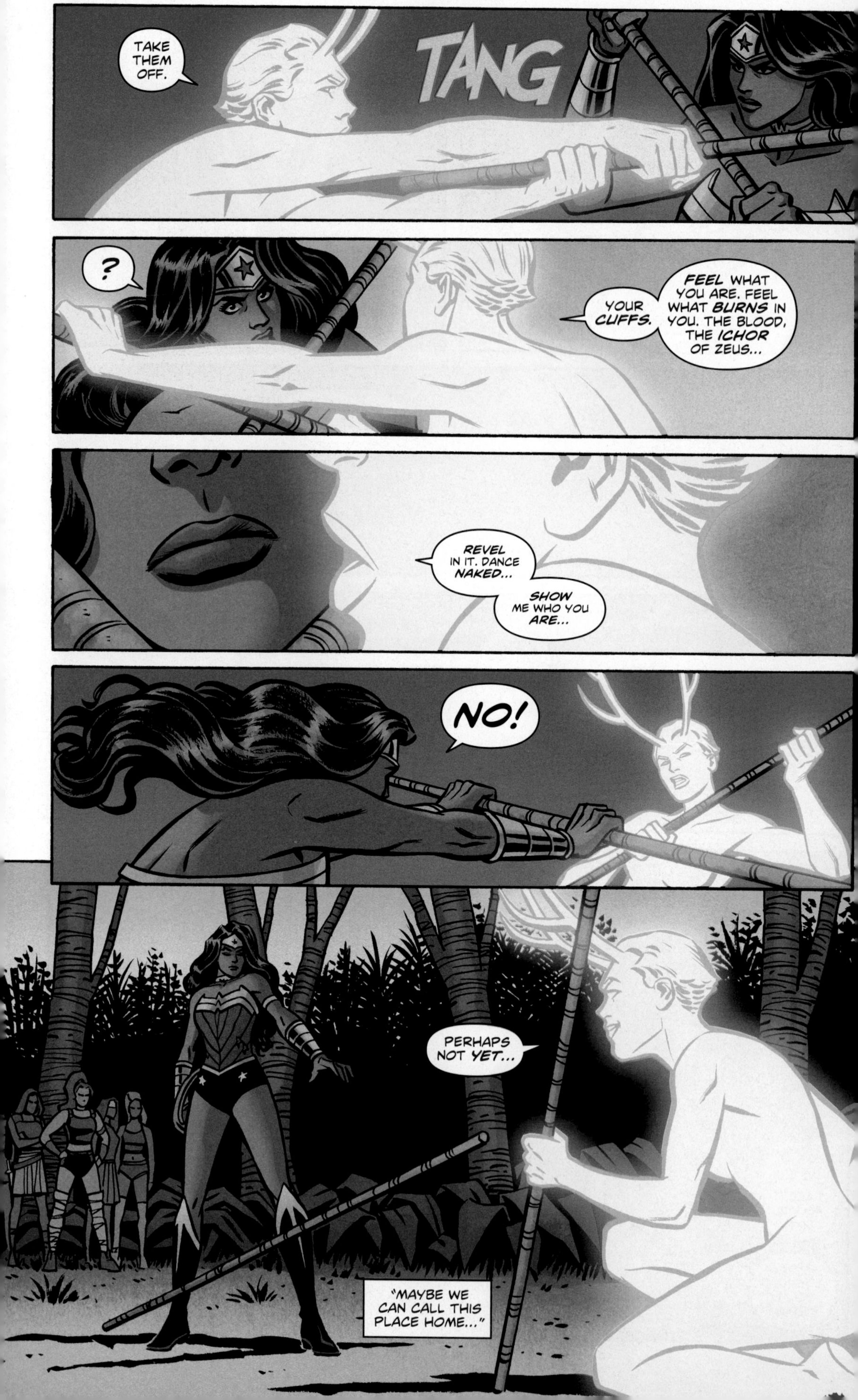
TAKE THEM OFF.
TANG
?
YOUR CUFFS.
FEEL WHAT YOU ARE. FEEL WHAT BURNS IN YOU. THE BLOOD, THE ICHOR OF ZEUS...
REVEL IN IT. DANCE NAKED...
SHOW ME WHO YOU ARE...
NO!
PERHAPS NOT YET...
"MAYBE WE CAN CALL THIS PLACE HOME..."

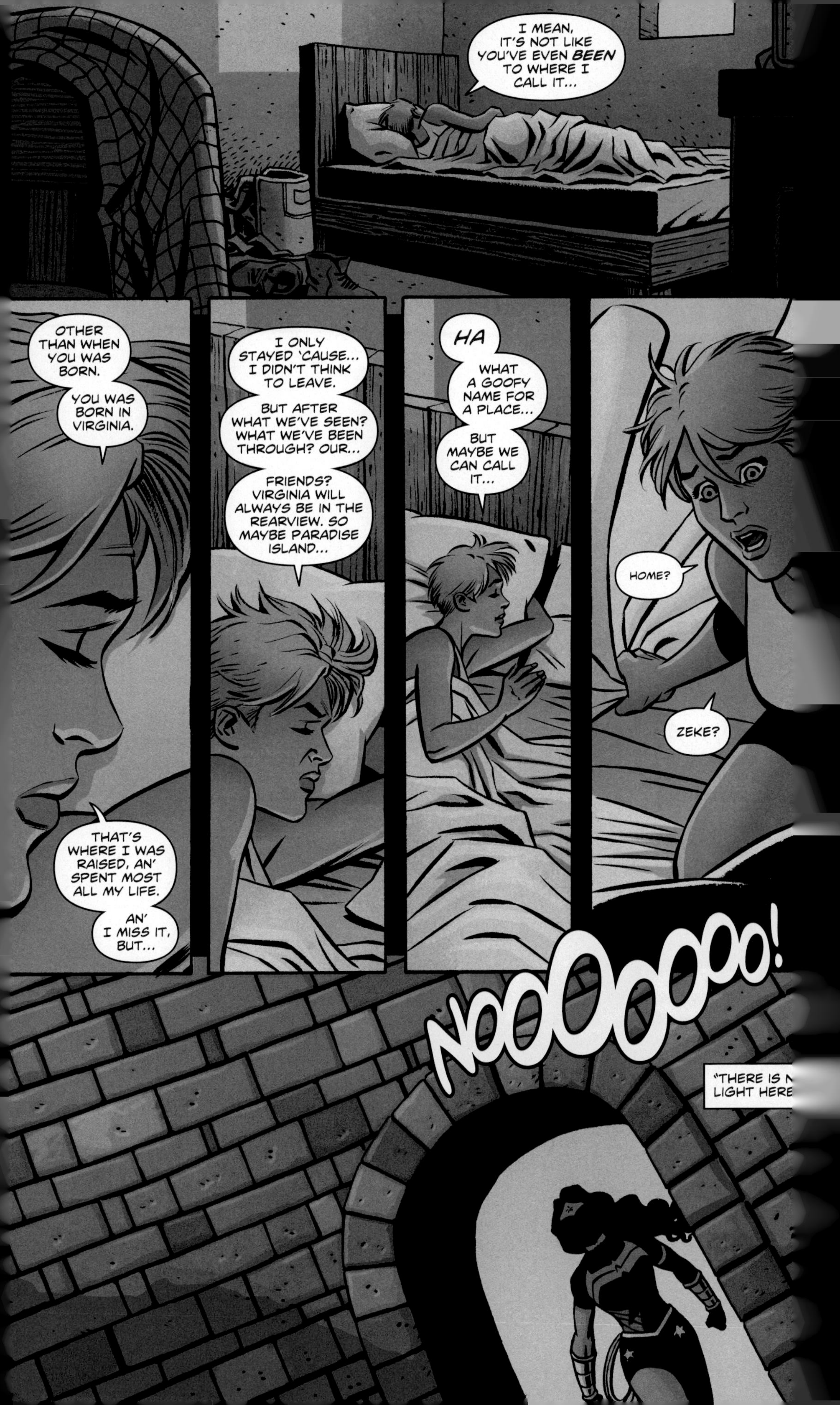
I MEAN, IT'S NOT LIKE YOU'VE EVEN *BEEN* TO WHERE I CALL IT...
OTHER THAN WHEN YOU WAS BORN.
YOU WAS BORN IN VIRGINIA.
THAT'S WHERE I WAS RAISED, AN' SPENT MOST ALL MY LIFE.
AN' I MISS IT, BUT...
I ONLY STAYED 'CAUSE... I DIDN'T THINK TO LEAVE.
BUT AFTER WHAT WE'VE SEEN? WHAT WE'VE BEEN THROUGH? OUR...
FRIENDS? VIRGINIA WILL ALWAYS BE IN THE REARVIEW. SO MAYBE PARADISE ISLAND...
HA
WHAT A GOOFY NAME FOR A PLACE...
BUT MAYBE WE CAN CALL IT...
HOME?
ZEKE?
NOOOOOOO!

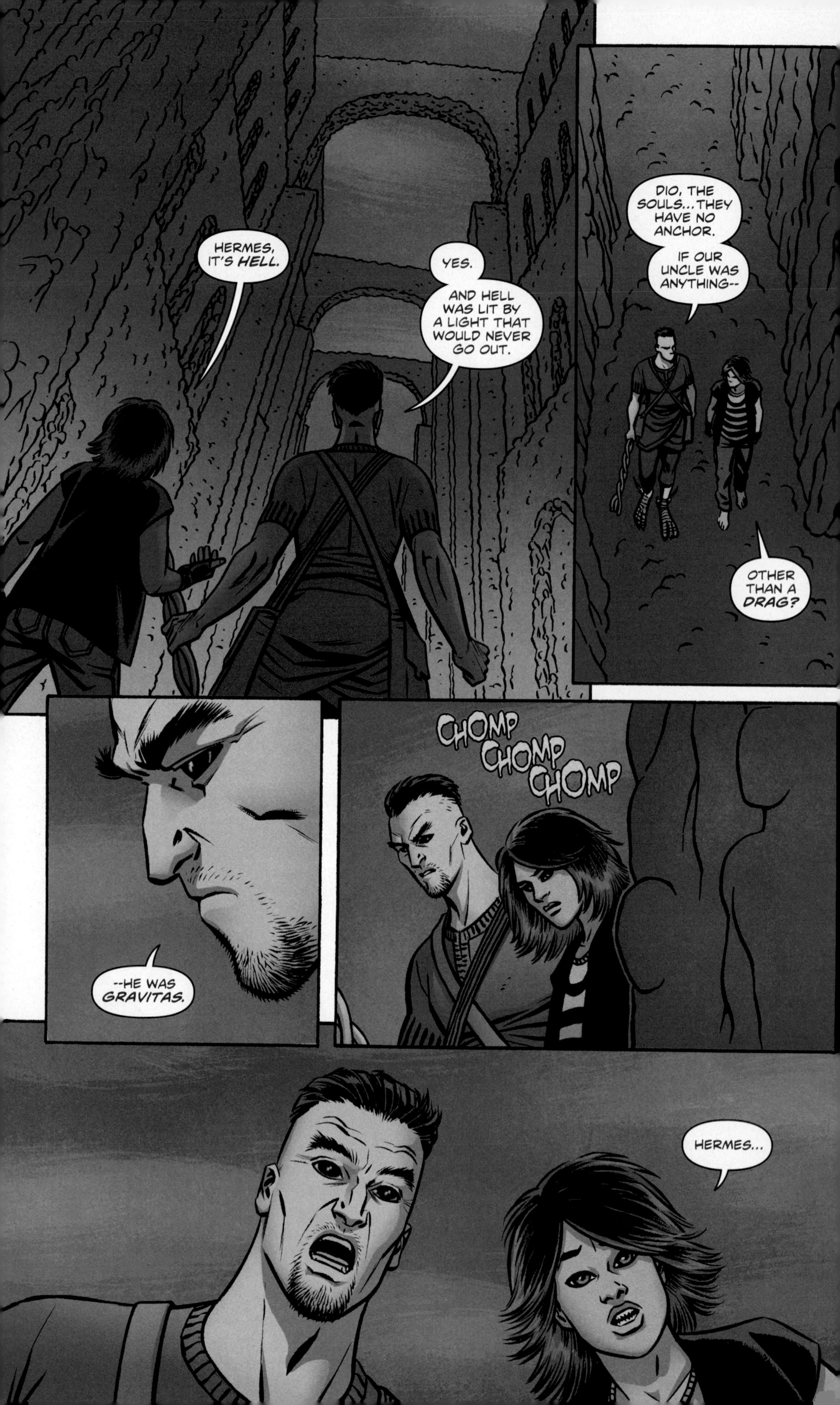
HERMES, IT'S *HELL.*
YES.
AND HELL WAS LIT BY A LIGHT THAT WOULD NEVER GO OUT.
DIO, THE SOULS...THEY HAVE NO ANCHOR.
IF OUR UNCLE WAS ANYTHING--
OTHER THAN A *DRAG?*
--HE WAS *GRAVITAS.*
CHOMP CHOMP CHOMP
HERMES...

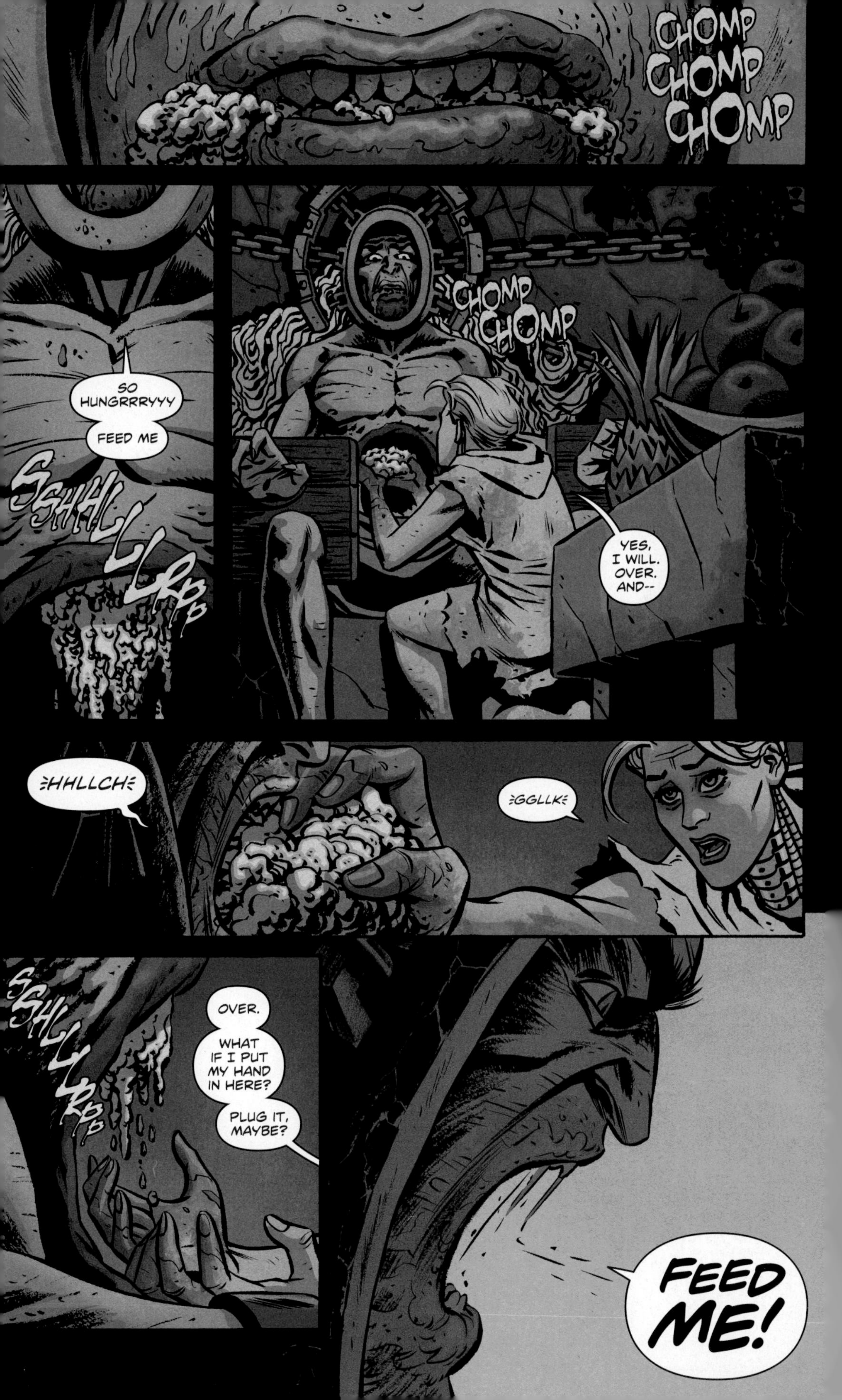
CHOMP CHOMP CHOMP
SO HUNGRRRYYY
FEED ME
SSHHLLLRP
CHOMP CHOMP
YES, I WILL. OVER. AND--
HHLLCH
GGLLK
SSHLLLRP
OVER.
WHAT IF I PUT MY HAND IN HERE?
PLUG IT, MAYBE?
FEED ME!

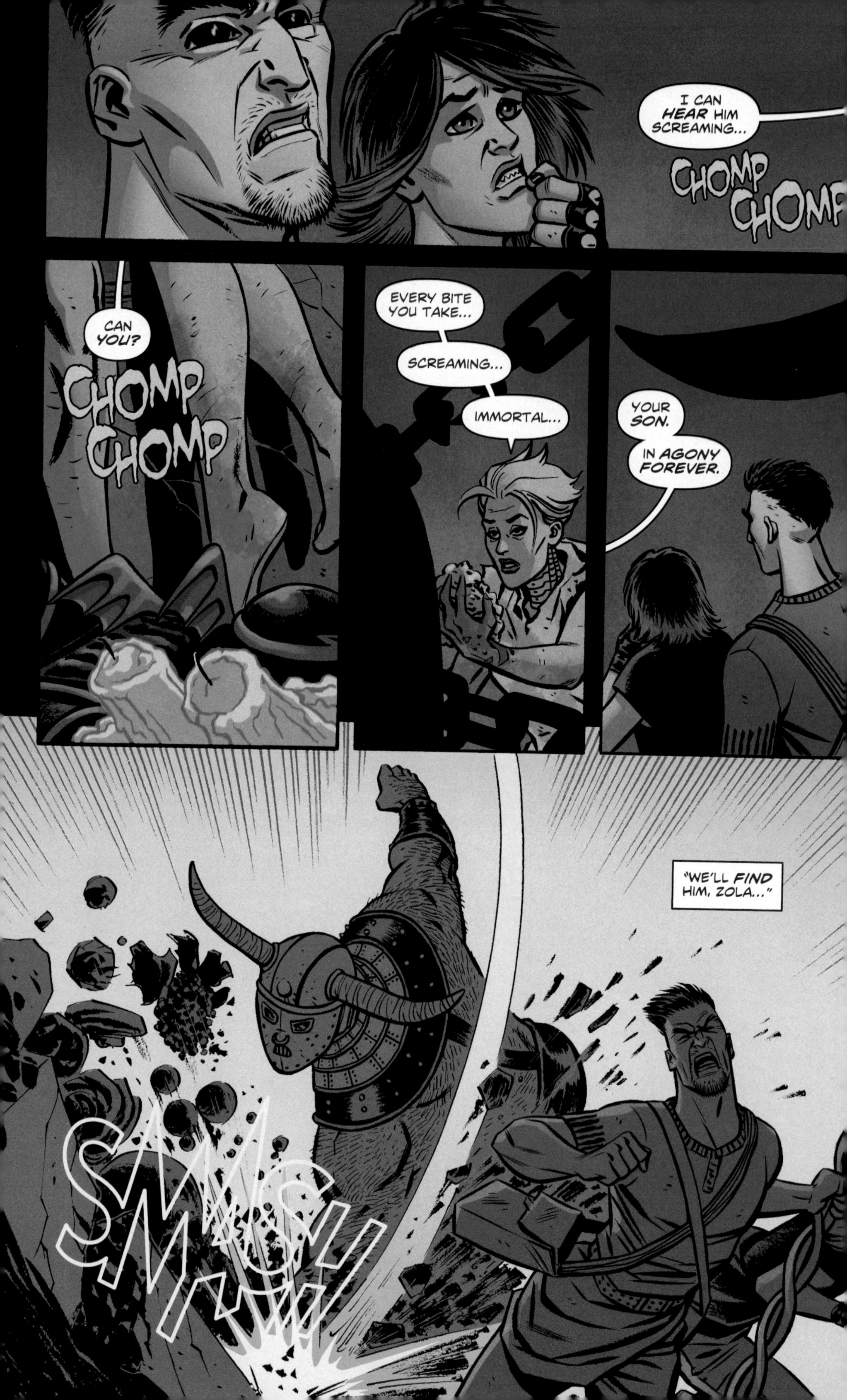
I CAN HEAR HIM SCREAMING...
CHOMP CHOMP
CAN YOU?
CHOMP CHOMP
EVERY BITE YOU TAKE...
SCREAMING...
IMMORTAL...
YOUR SON.
IN AGONY FOREVER.
"WE'LL FIND HIM, ZOLA..."
SMASH

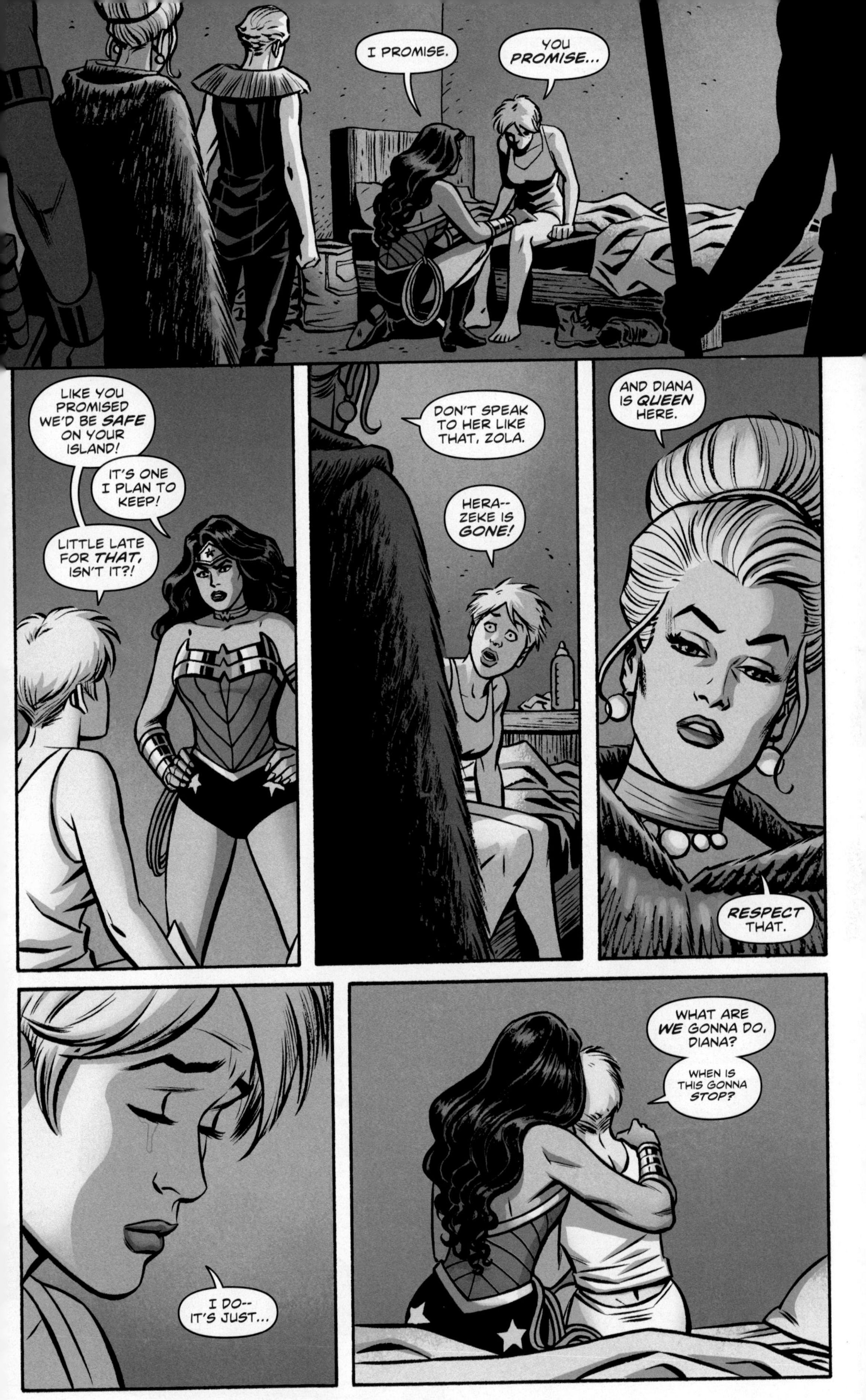
I PROMISE.
YOU PROMISE...
LIKE YOU PROMISED WE'D BE SAFE ON YOUR ISLAND!
IT'S ONE I PLAN TO KEEP!
LITTLE LATE FOR THAT, ISN'T IT?!
DON'T SPEAK TO HER LIKE THAT, ZOLA.
HERA-- ZEKE IS GONE!
AND DIANA IS QUEEN HERE.
RESPECT THAT.
I DO-- IT'S JUST...
WHAT ARE WE GONNA DO, DIANA?
WHEN IS THIS GONNA STOP?

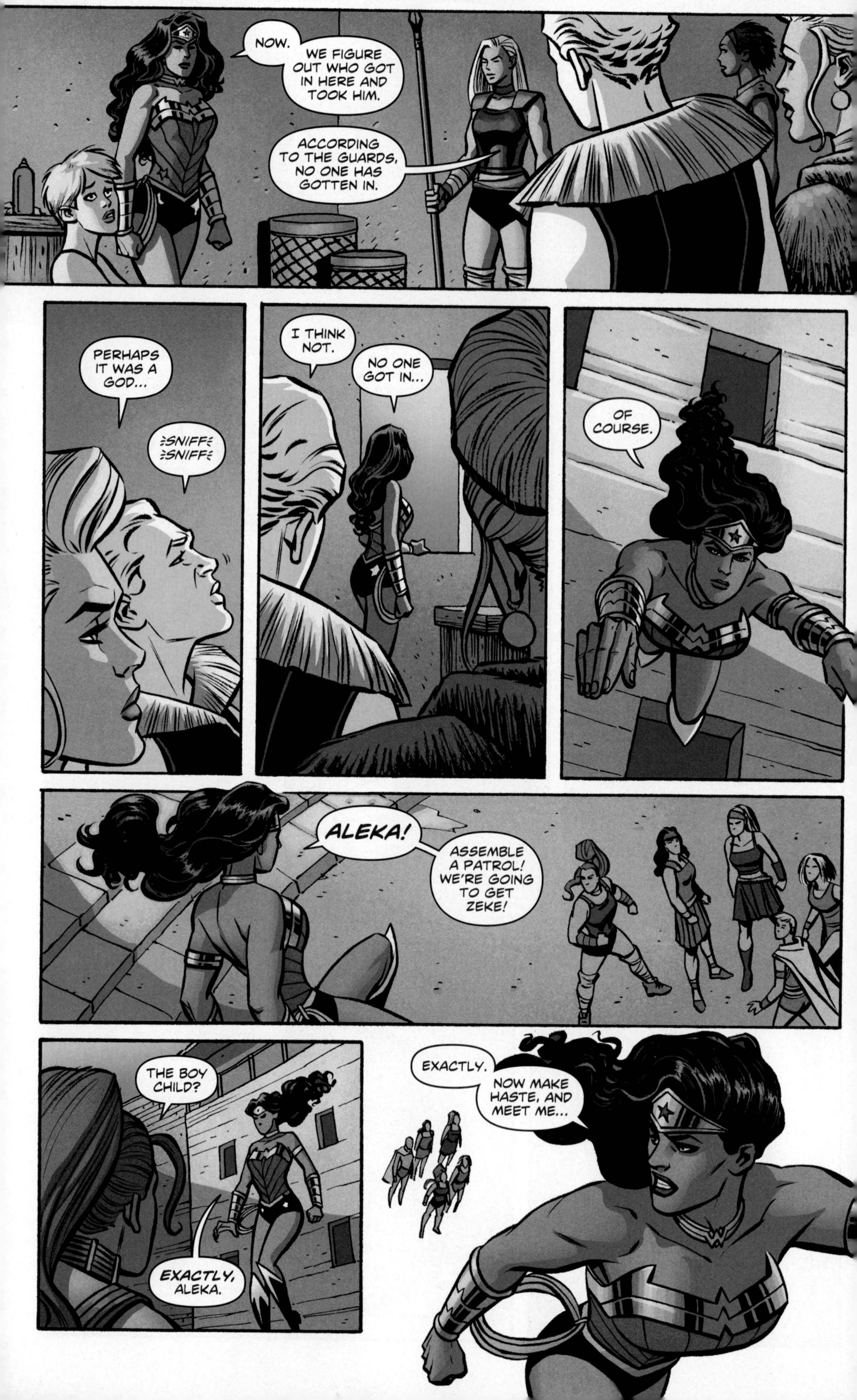

NOW.
WE FIGURE OUT WHO GOT IN HERE AND TOOK HIM.
ACCORDING TO THE GUARDS, NO ONE HAS GOTTEN IN.
PERHAPS IT WAS A GOD...
SNIFF SNIFF
I THINK NOT.
NO ONE GOT IN...
OF COURSE.
ALEKA!
ASSEMBLE A PATROL! WE'RE GOING TO GET ZEKE!
THE BOY CHILD?
EXACTLY, ALEKA.
EXACTLY.
NOW MAKE HASTE, AND MEET ME...

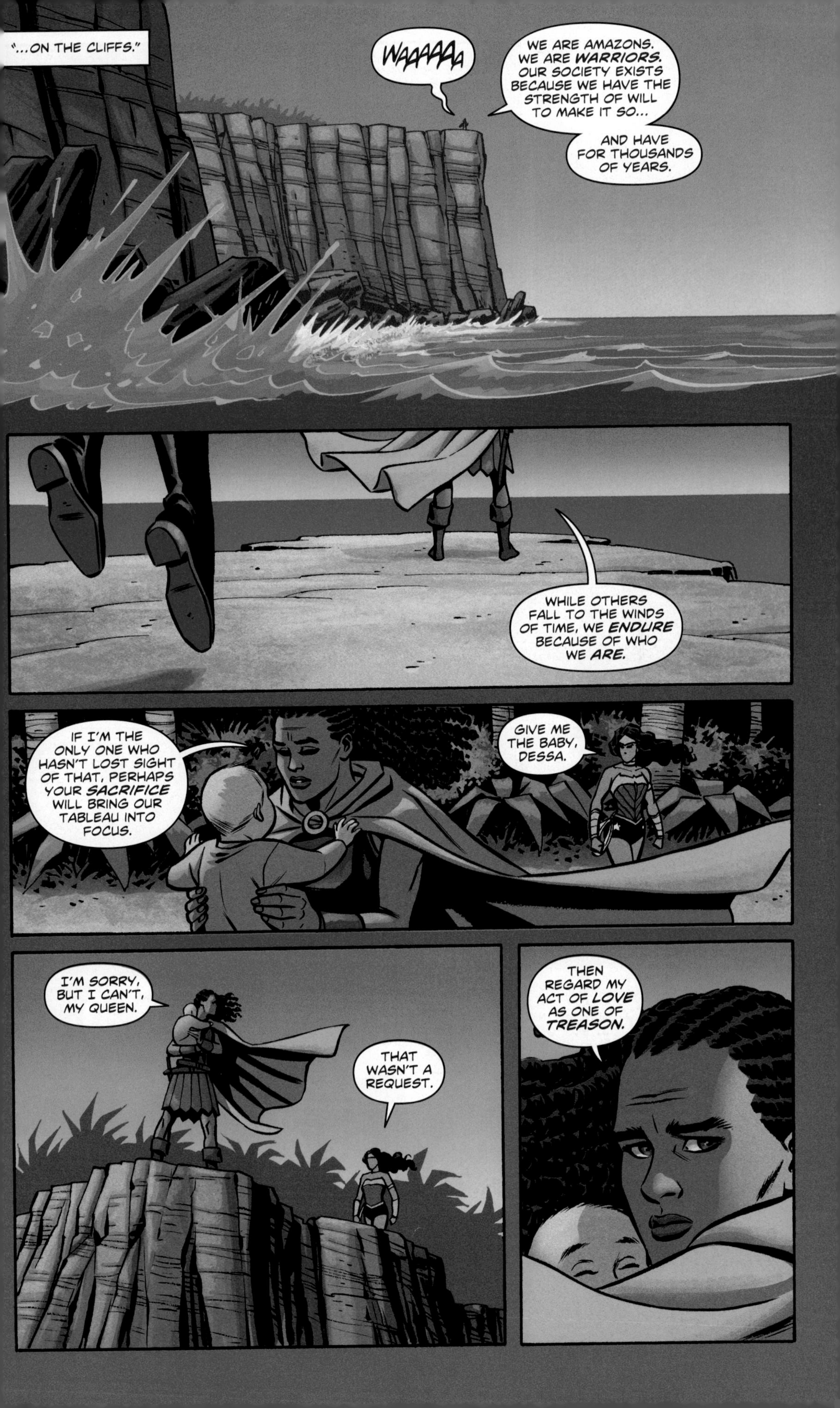
"...ON THE CLIFFS."
WAAAAAA
WE ARE AMAZONS. WE ARE WARRIORS. OUR SOCIETY EXISTS BECAUSE WE HAVE THE STRENGTH OF WILL TO MAKE IT SO...
AND HAVE FOR THOUSANDS OF YEARS.
WHILE OTHERS FALL TO THE WINDS OF TIME, WE ENDURE BECAUSE OF WHO WE ARE.
IF I'M THE ONLY ONE WHO HASN'T LOST SIGHT OF THAT, PERHAPS YOUR SACRIFICE WILL BRING OUR TABLEAU INTO FOCUS.
GIVE ME THE BABY, DESSA.
I'M SORRY, BUT I CAN'T, MY QUEEN.
THAT WASN'T A REQUEST.
THEN REGARD MY ACT OF LOVE AS ONE OF TREASON.

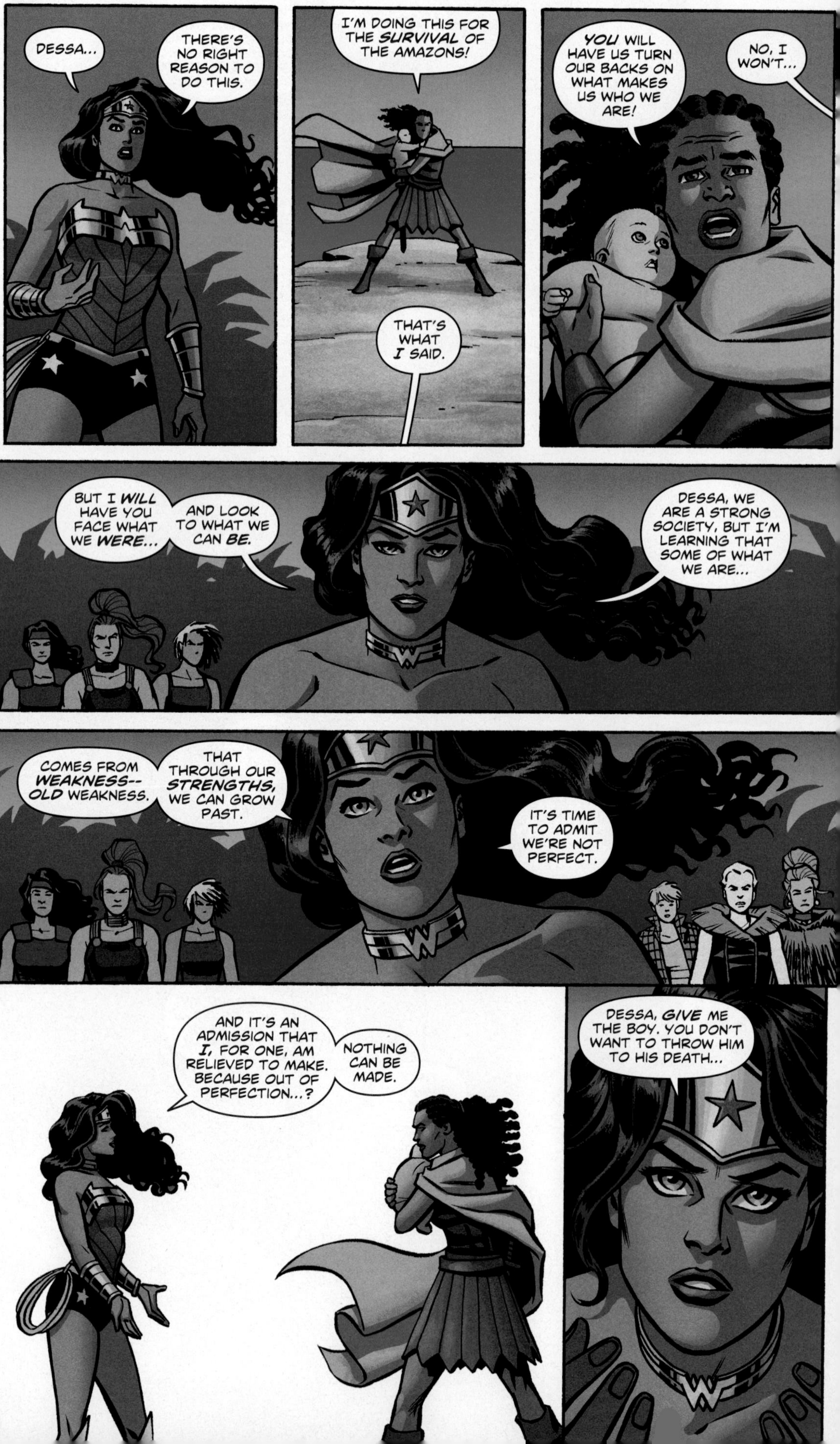

DESSA...
THERE'S NO RIGHT REASON TO DO THIS.
I'M DOING THIS FOR THE SURVIVAL OF THE AMAZONS!
THAT'S WHAT I SAID.
YOU WILL HAVE US TURN OUR BACKS ON WHAT MAKES US WHO WE ARE!
NO, I WON'T...
BUT I WILL HAVE YOU FACE WHAT WE WERE...
AND LOOK TO WHAT WE CAN BE.
DESSA, WE ARE A STRONG SOCIETY, BUT I'M LEARNING THAT SOME OF WHAT WE ARE...
COMES FROM WEAKNESS-- OLD WEAKNESS.
THAT THROUGH OUR STRENGTHS, WE CAN GROW PAST.
IT'S TIME TO ADMIT WE'RE NOT PERFECT.
AND IT'S AN ADMISSION THAT I, FOR ONE, AM RELIEVED TO MAKE. BECAUSE OUT OF PERFECTION...?
NOTHING CAN BE MADE.
DESSA, GIVE ME THE BOY. YOU DON'T WANT TO THROW HIM TO HIS DEATH...

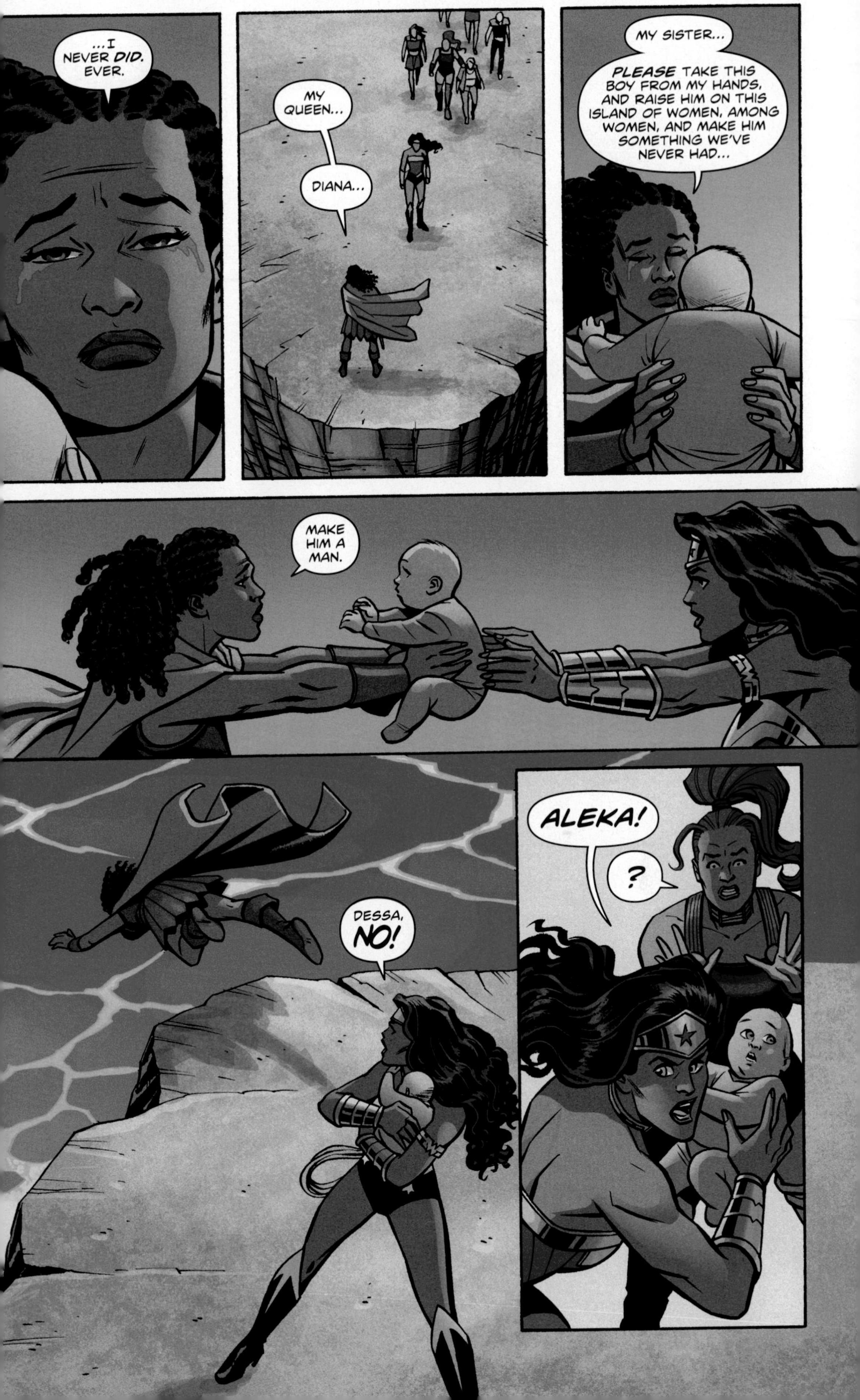
...I NEVER *DID.* EVER.
MY QUEEN...
DIANA...
MY SISTER...
PLEASE TAKE THIS BOY FROM MY HANDS, AND RAISE HIM ON THIS ISLAND OF WOMEN, AMONG WOMEN, AND MAKE HIM SOMETHING WE'VE NEVER HAD...
MAKE HIM A MAN.
DESSA, *NO!*
ALEKA!
?

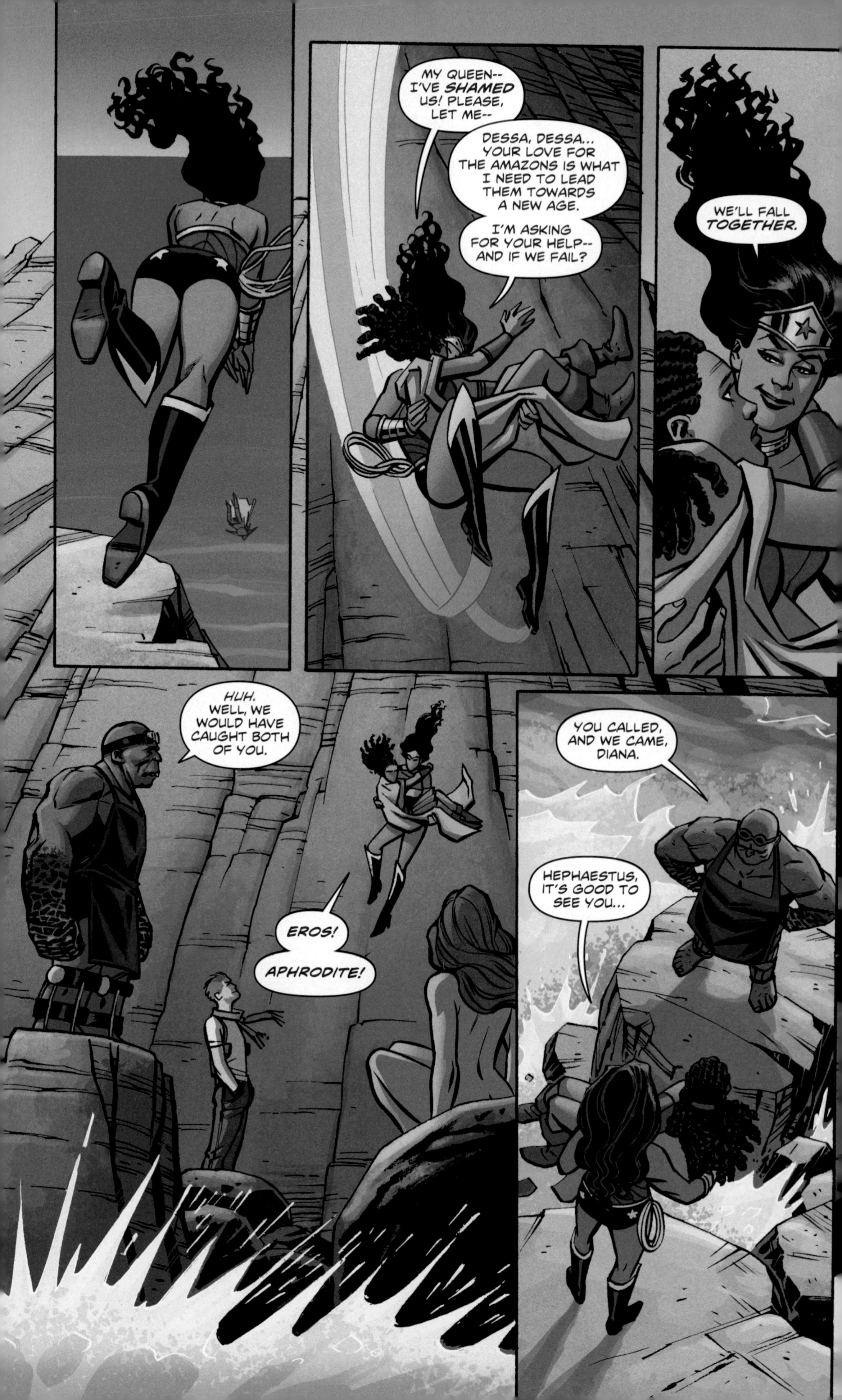

MY QUEEN-- I'VE SHAMED US! PLEASE, LET ME--
DESSA, DESSA... YOUR LOVE FOR THE AMAZONS IS WHAT I NEED TO LEAD THEM TOWARDS A NEW AGE.
I'M ASKING FOR YOUR HELP-- AND IF WE FAIL?
WE'LL FALL TOGETHER.
HUH. WELL, WE WOULD HAVE CAUGHT BOTH OF YOU.
EROS!
APHRODITE!
YOU CALLED, AND WE CAME, DIANA.
HEPHAESTUS, IT'S GOOD TO SEE YOU...

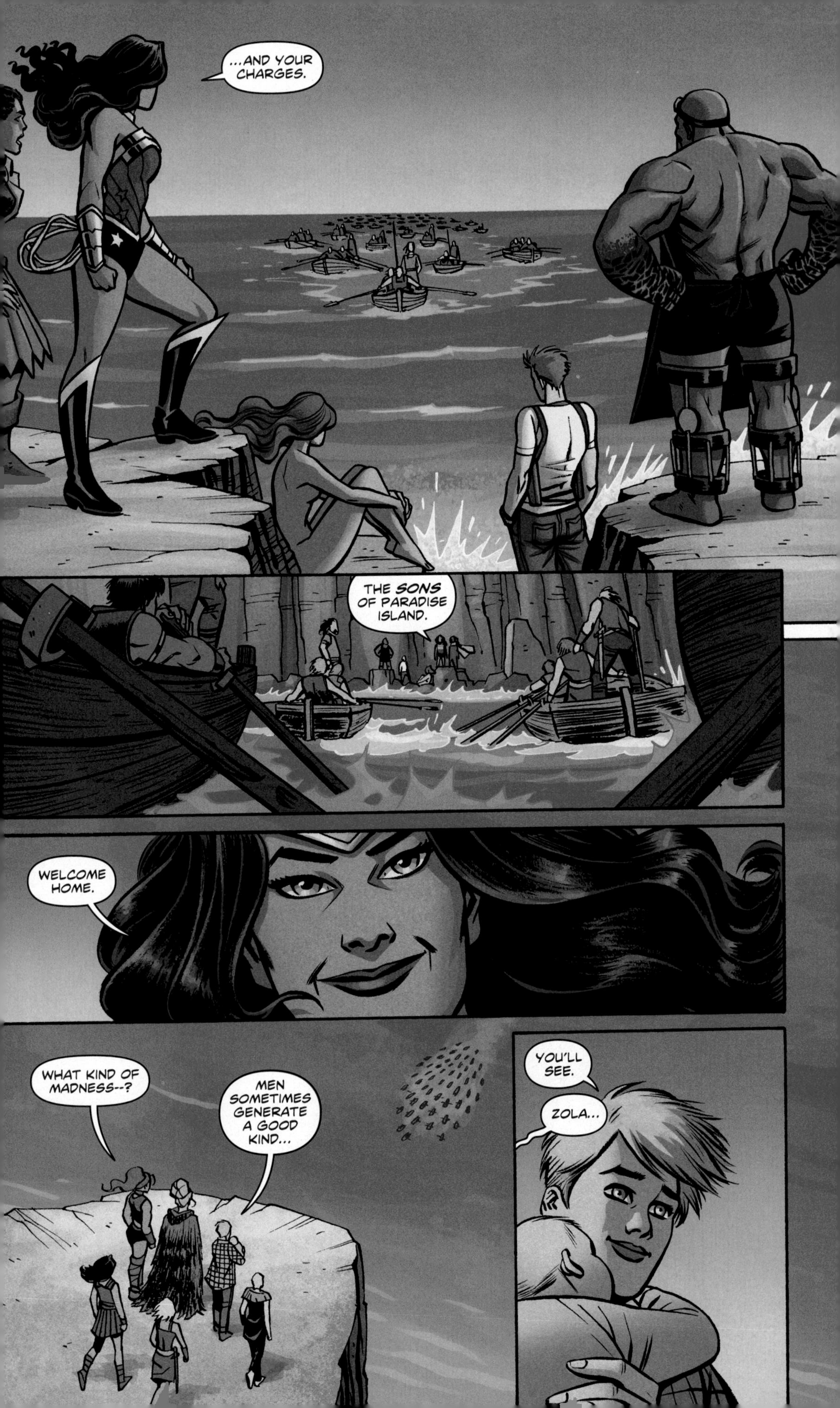
...AND YOUR CHARGES.
THE SONS OF PARADISE ISLAND.
WELCOME HOME.
WHAT KIND OF MADNESS--?
MEN SOMETIMES GENERATE A GOOD KIND...
YOU'LL SEE.
ZOLA...

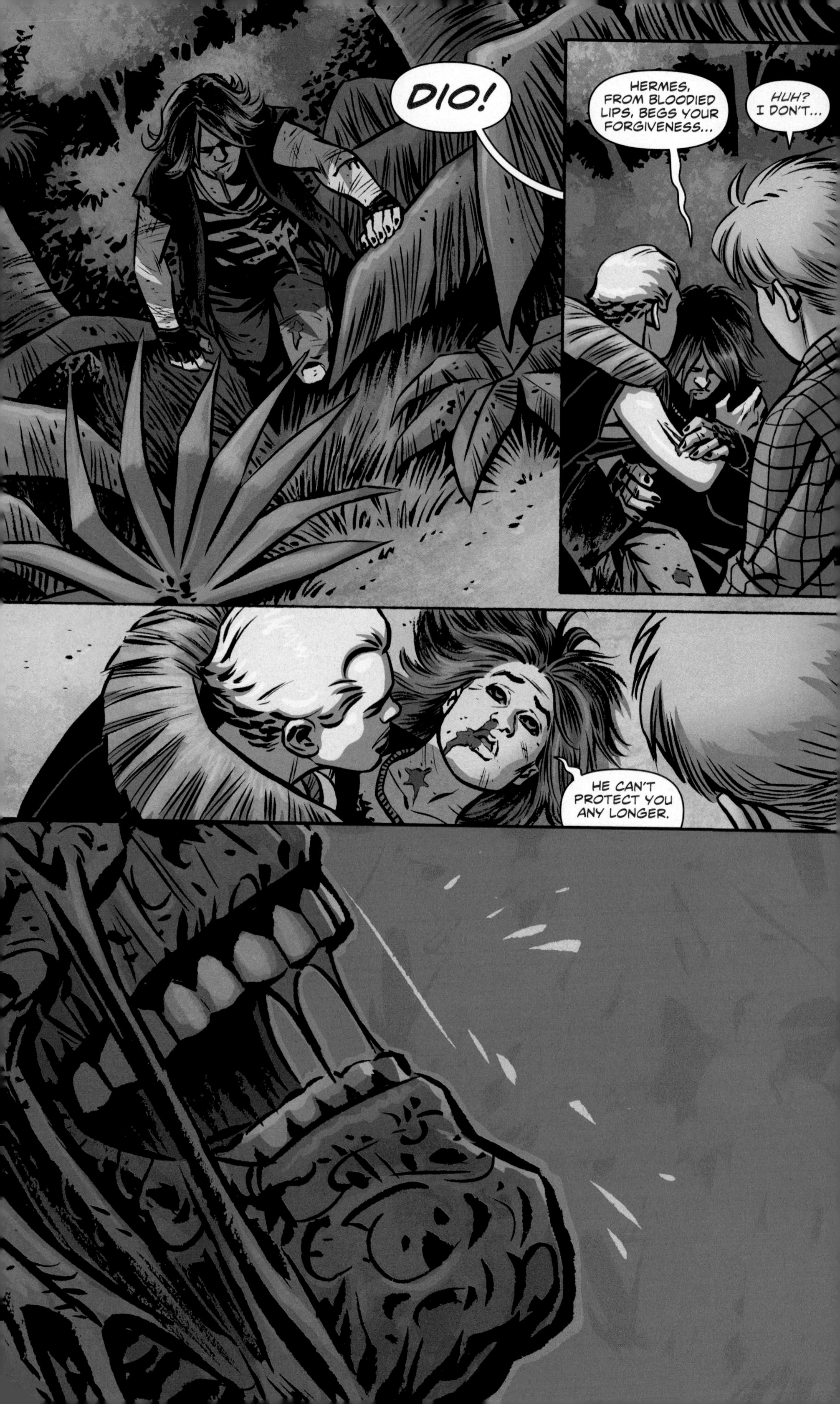

DIO!
HERMES, FROM BLOODIED LIPS, BEGS YOUR FORGIVENESS...
HUH? I DON'T...
HE CAN'T PROTECT YOU ANY LONGER.

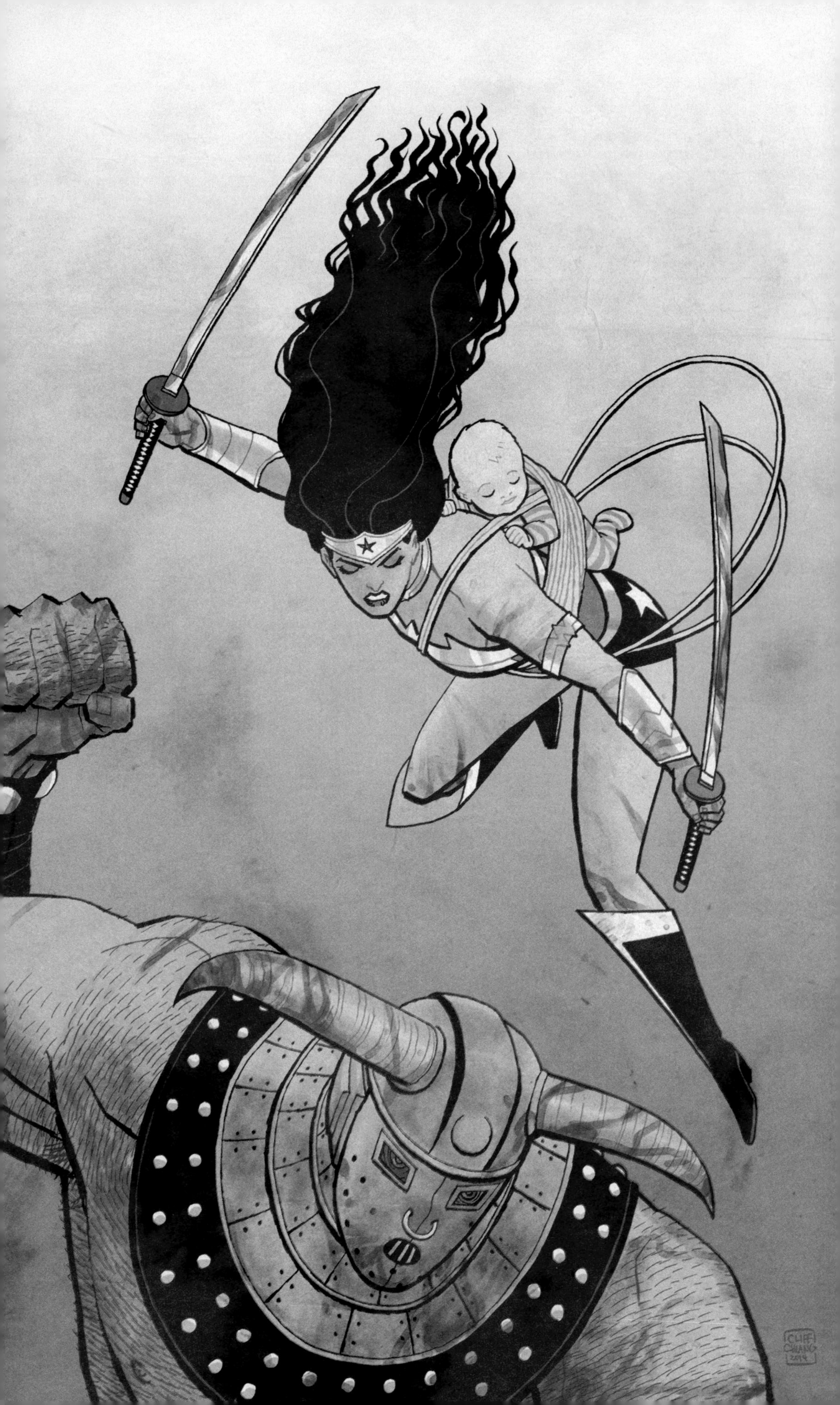
CLIFF
CHIANG
2014

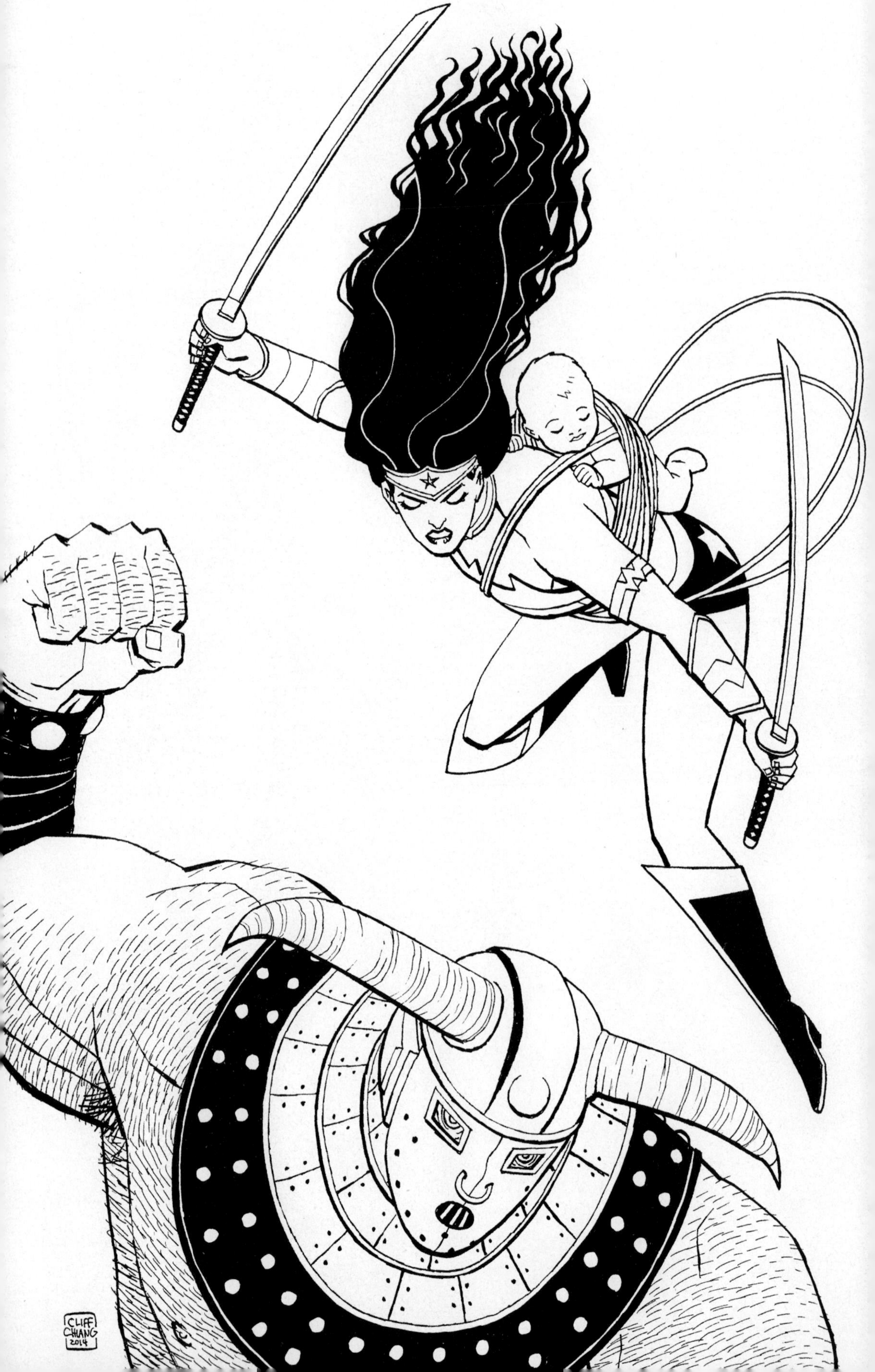
CLIFF CHIANG 2014

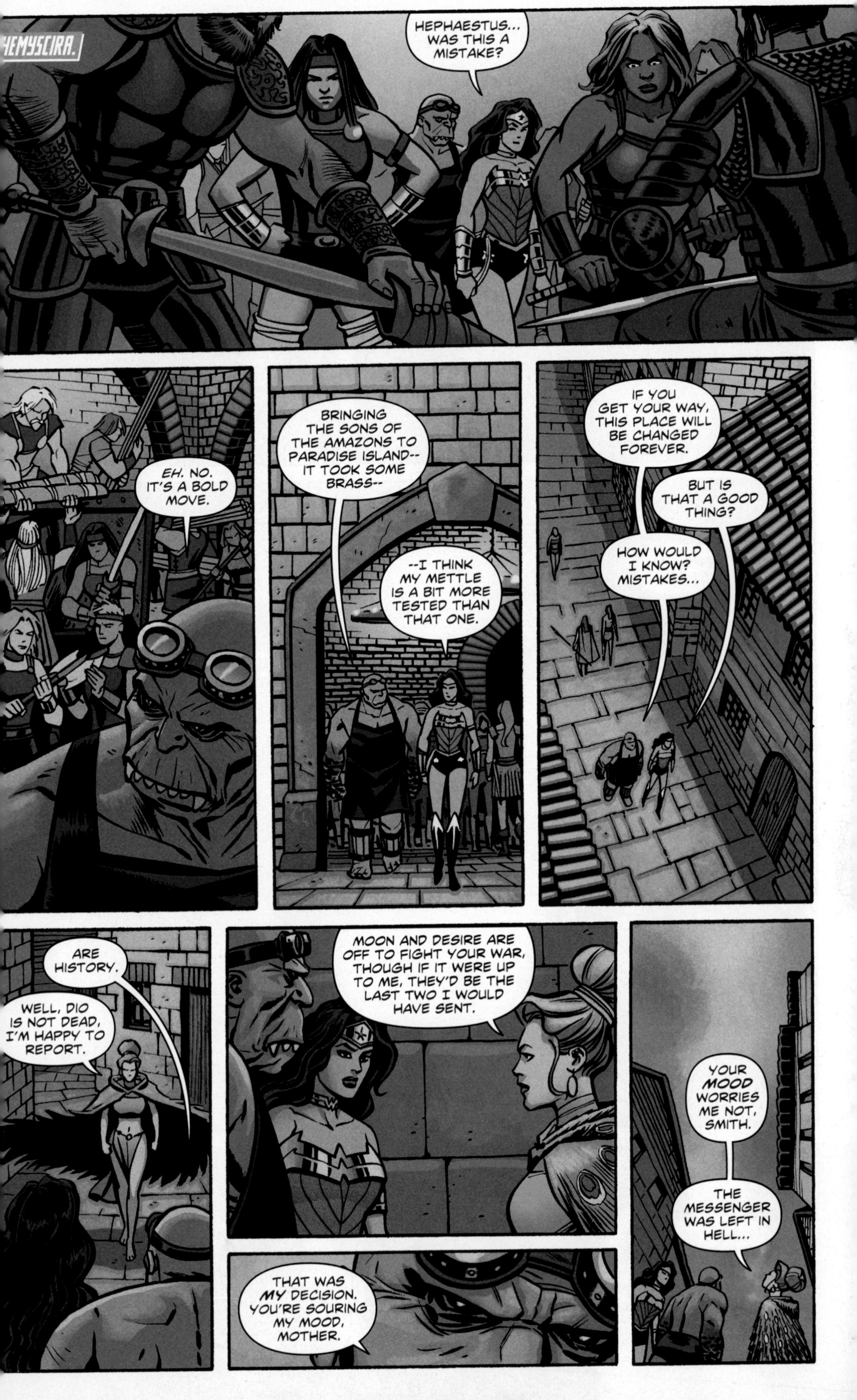
HEMYSCIRA.
HEPHAESTUS... WAS THIS A MISTAKE?
EH. NO. IT'S A BOLD MOVE.
BRINGING THE SONS OF THE AMAZONS TO PARADISE ISLAND-- IT TOOK SOME BRASS--
--I THINK MY METTLE IS A BIT MORE TESTED THAN THAT ONE.
IF YOU GET YOUR WAY, THIS PLACE WILL BE CHANGED FOREVER.
BUT IS THAT A GOOD THING?
HOW WOULD I KNOW? MISTAKES...
ARE HISTORY.
WELL, DIO IS NOT DEAD, I'M HAPPY TO REPORT.
MOON AND DESIRE ARE OFF TO FIGHT YOUR WAR, THOUGH IF IT WERE UP TO ME, THEY'D BE THE LAST TWO I WOULD HAVE SENT.
THAT WAS *MY* DECISION. YOU'RE SOURING MY MOOD, MOTHER.
YOUR *MOOD* WORRIES ME NOT, SMITH.
THE MESSENGER WAS LEFT IN HELL...

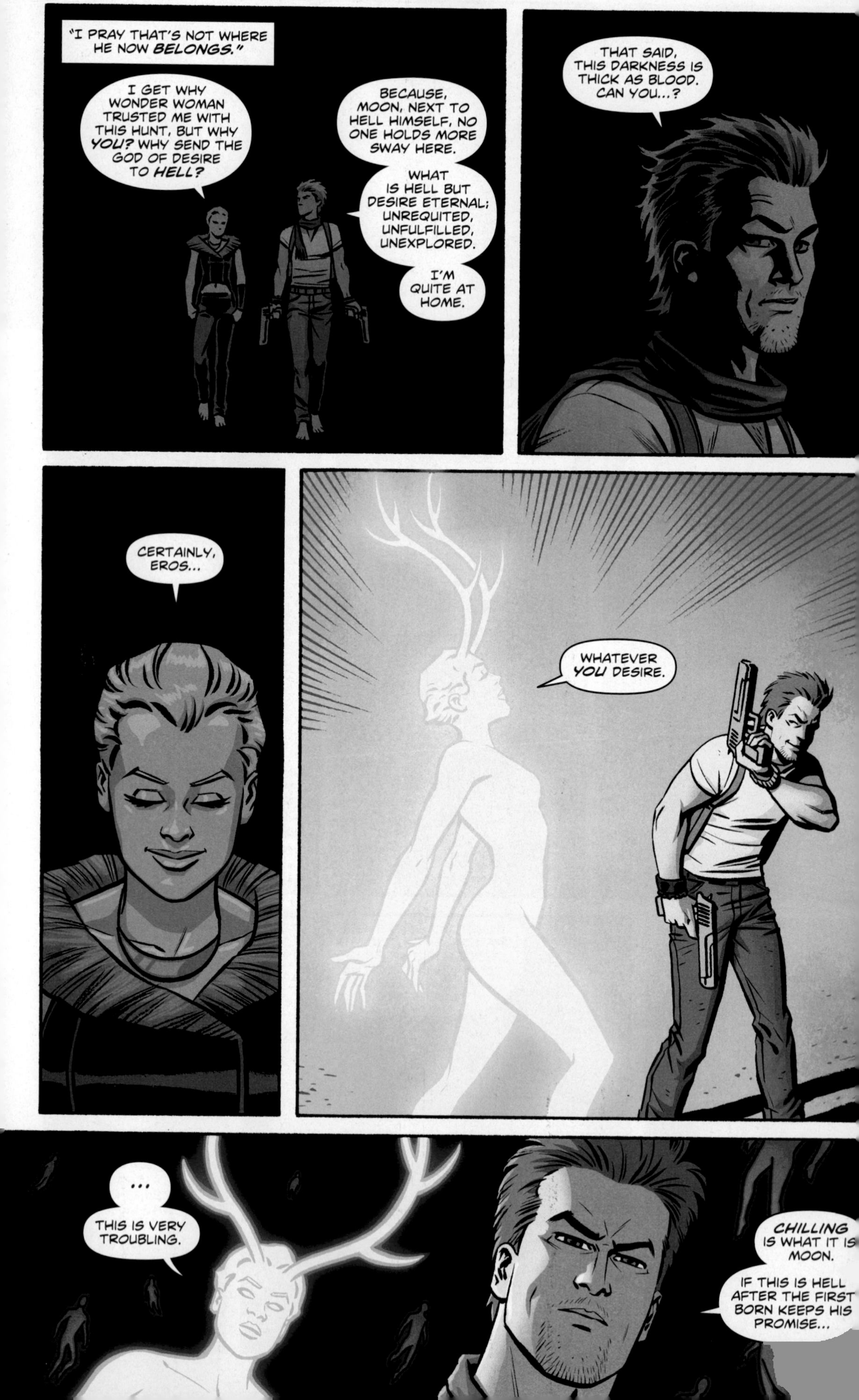
"I PRAY THAT'S NOT WHERE HE NOW BELONGS."
I GET WHY WONDER WOMAN TRUSTED ME WITH THIS HUNT, BUT WHY YOU? WHY SEND THE GOD OF DESIRE TO HELL?
BECAUSE, MOON, NEXT TO HELL HIMSELF, NO ONE HOLDS MORE SWAY HERE.
WHAT IS HELL BUT DESIRE ETERNAL; UNREQUITED, UNFULFILLED, UNEXPLORED.
I'M QUITE AT HOME.
THAT SAID, THIS DARKNESS IS THICK AS BLOOD. CAN YOU...?
CERTAINLY, EROS...
WHATEVER YOU DESIRE.
...
THIS IS VERY TROUBLING.
CHILLING IS WHAT IT IS MOON.
IF THIS IS HELL AFTER THE FIRST BORN KEEPS HIS PROMISE...

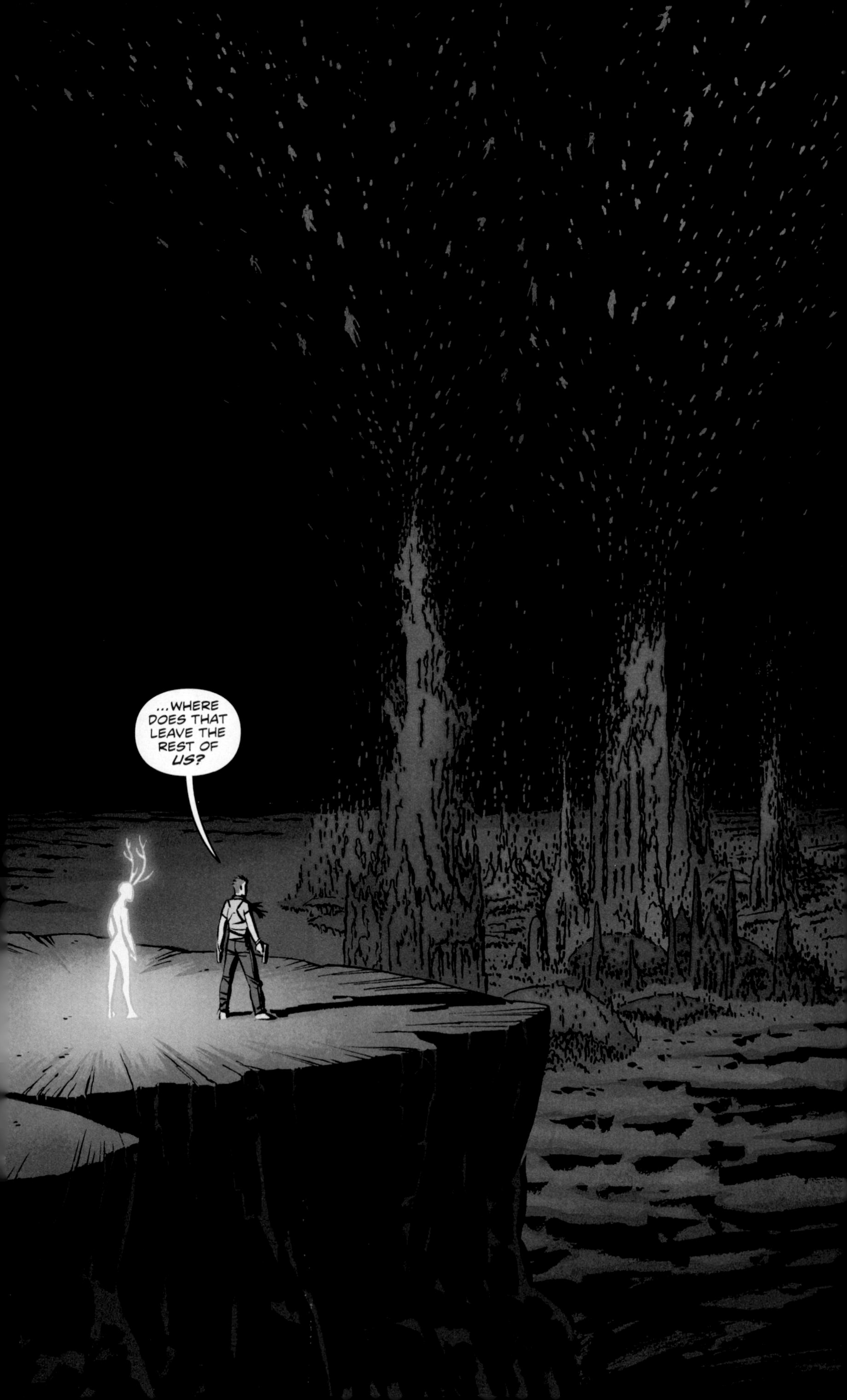
...WHERE DOES THAT LEAVE THE REST OF US?

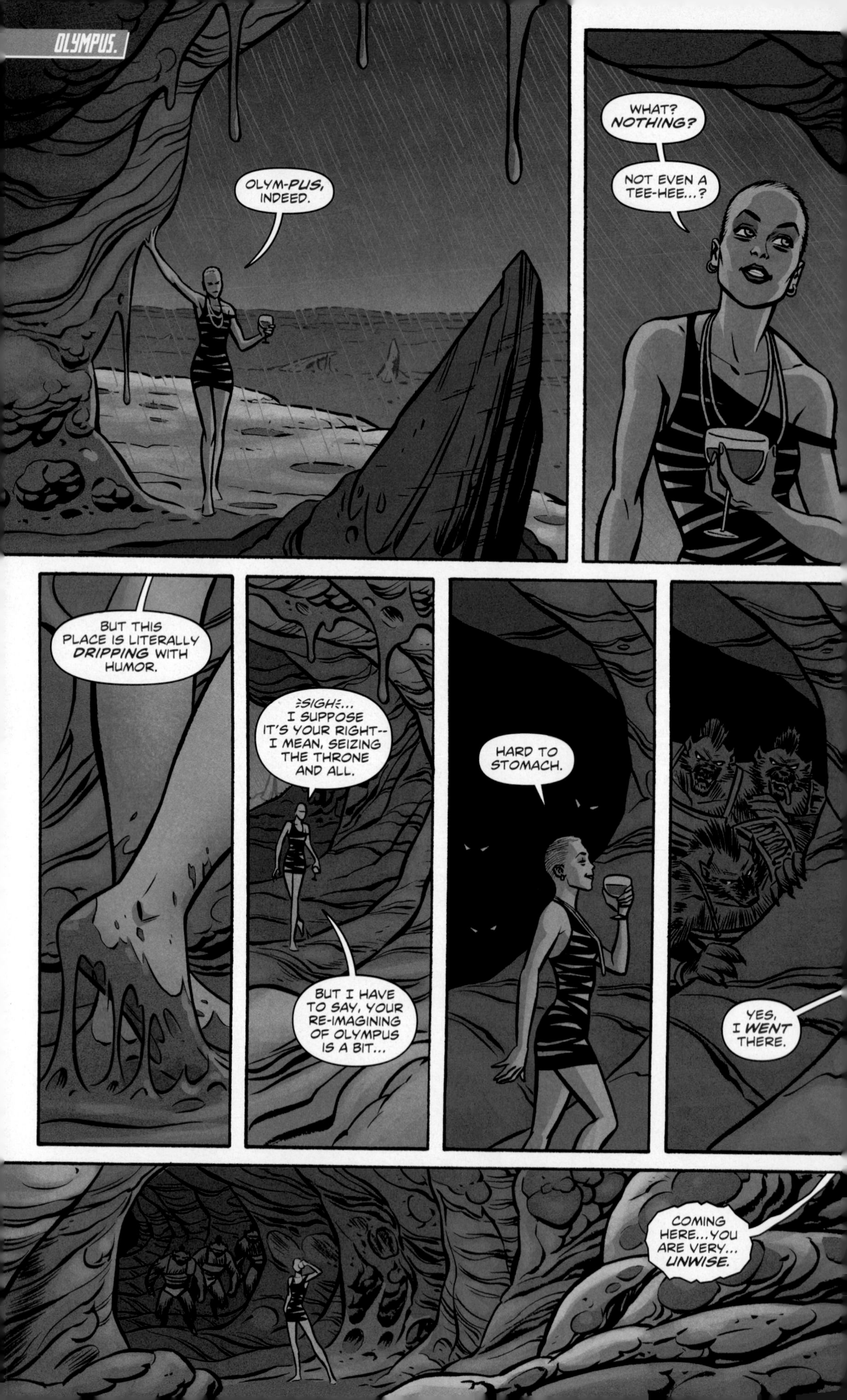
OLYMPUS.
OLYM-PUS, INDEED.
WHAT? NOTHING?
NOT EVEN A TEE-HEE...?
BUT THIS PLACE IS LITERALLY DRIPPING WITH HUMOR.
SIGH... I SUPPOSE IT'S YOUR RIGHT-- I MEAN, SEIZING THE THRONE AND ALL.
BUT I HAVE TO SAY, YOUR RE-IMAGINING OF OLYMPUS IS A BIT...
HARD TO STOMACH.
YES, I WENT THERE.
COMING HERE...YOU ARE VERY... UNWISE.

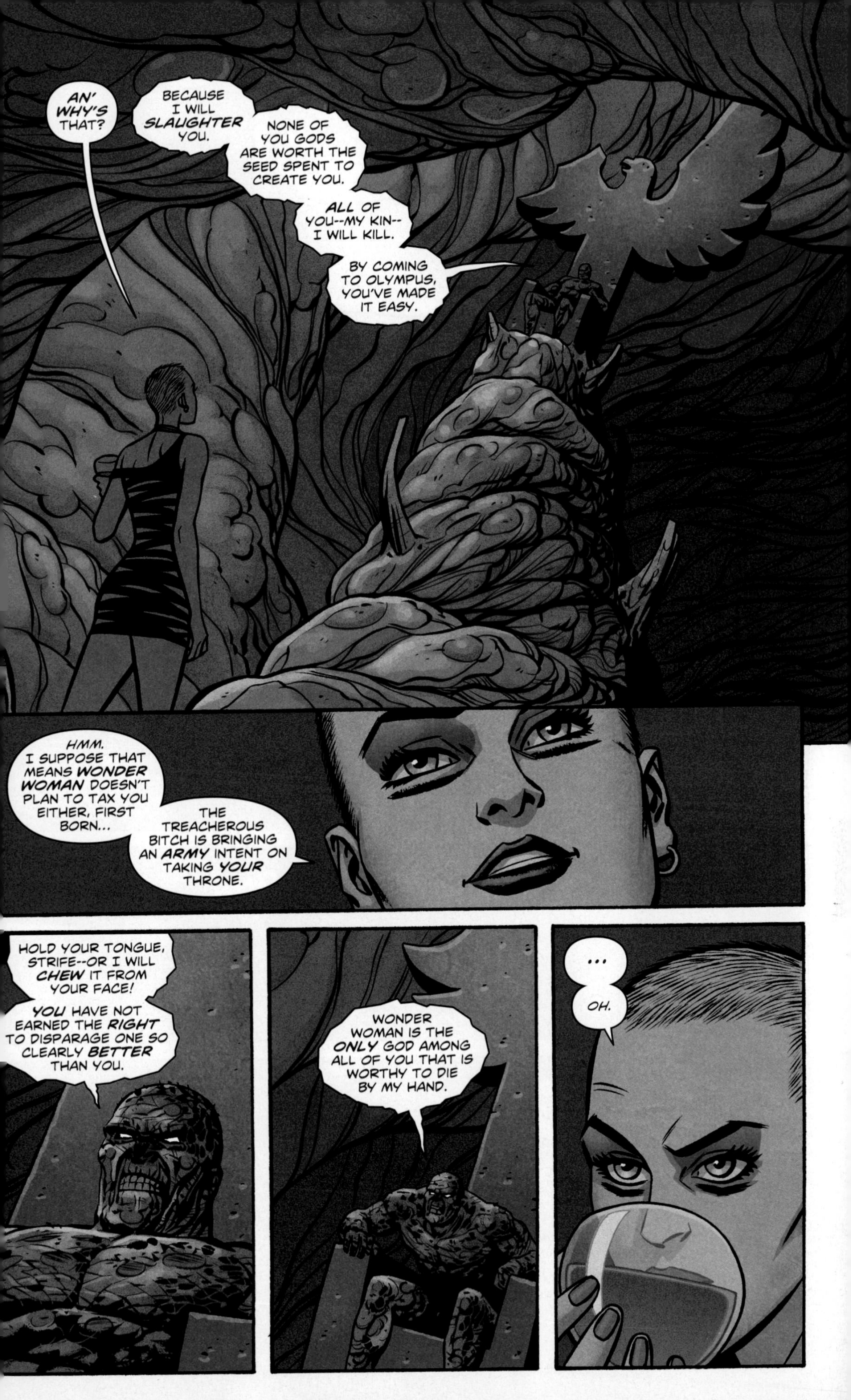
AN' WHY'S THAT?
BECAUSE I WILL SLAUGHTER YOU.
NONE OF YOU GODS ARE WORTH THE SEED SPENT TO CREATE YOU.
ALL OF YOU--MY KIN-- I WILL KILL.
BY COMING TO OLYMPUS, YOU'VE MADE IT EASY.
HMM. I SUPPOSE THAT MEANS WONDER WOMAN DOESN'T PLAN TO TAX YOU EITHER, FIRST BORN...
THE TREACHEROUS BITCH IS BRINGING AN ARMY INTENT ON TAKING YOUR THRONE.
HOLD YOUR TONGUE, STRIFE--OR I WILL CHEW IT FROM YOUR FACE!
YOU HAVE NOT EARNED THE RIGHT TO DISPARAGE ONE SO CLEARLY BETTER THAN YOU.
WONDER WOMAN IS THE ONLY GOD AMONG ALL OF YOU THAT IS WORTHY TO DIE BY MY HAND.
...
OH.

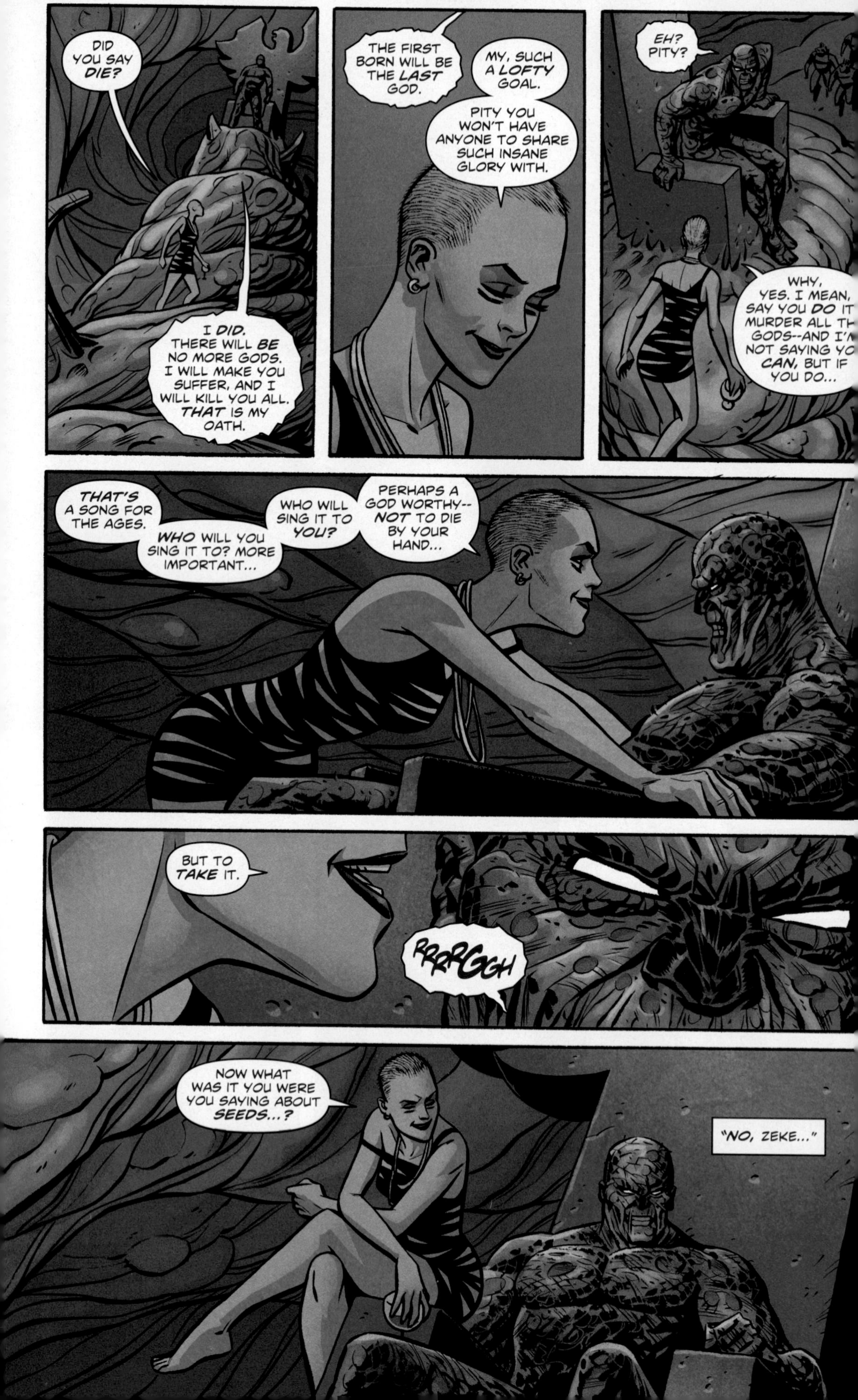
DID YOU SAY DIE?
I DID. THERE WILL BE NO MORE GODS. I WILL MAKE YOU SUFFER, AND I WILL KILL YOU ALL. THAT IS MY OATH.
THE FIRST BORN WILL BE THE LAST GOD.
MY, SUCH A LOFTY GOAL.
PITY YOU WON'T HAVE ANYONE TO SHARE SUCH INSANE GLORY WITH.
EH? PITY?
WHY, YES. I MEAN, SAY YOU DO IT MURDER ALL TH GODS--AND I'M NOT SAYING YO CAN, BUT IF YOU DO...
THAT'S A SONG FOR THE AGES.
WHO WILL YOU SING IT TO? MORE IMPORTANT...
WHO WILL SING IT TO YOU?
PERHAPS A GOD WORTHY-- NOT TO DIE BY YOUR HAND...
BUT TO TAKE IT.
RRRRGGH
NOW WHAT WAS IT YOU WERE YOU SAYING ABOUT SEEDS...?
"NO, ZEKE..."

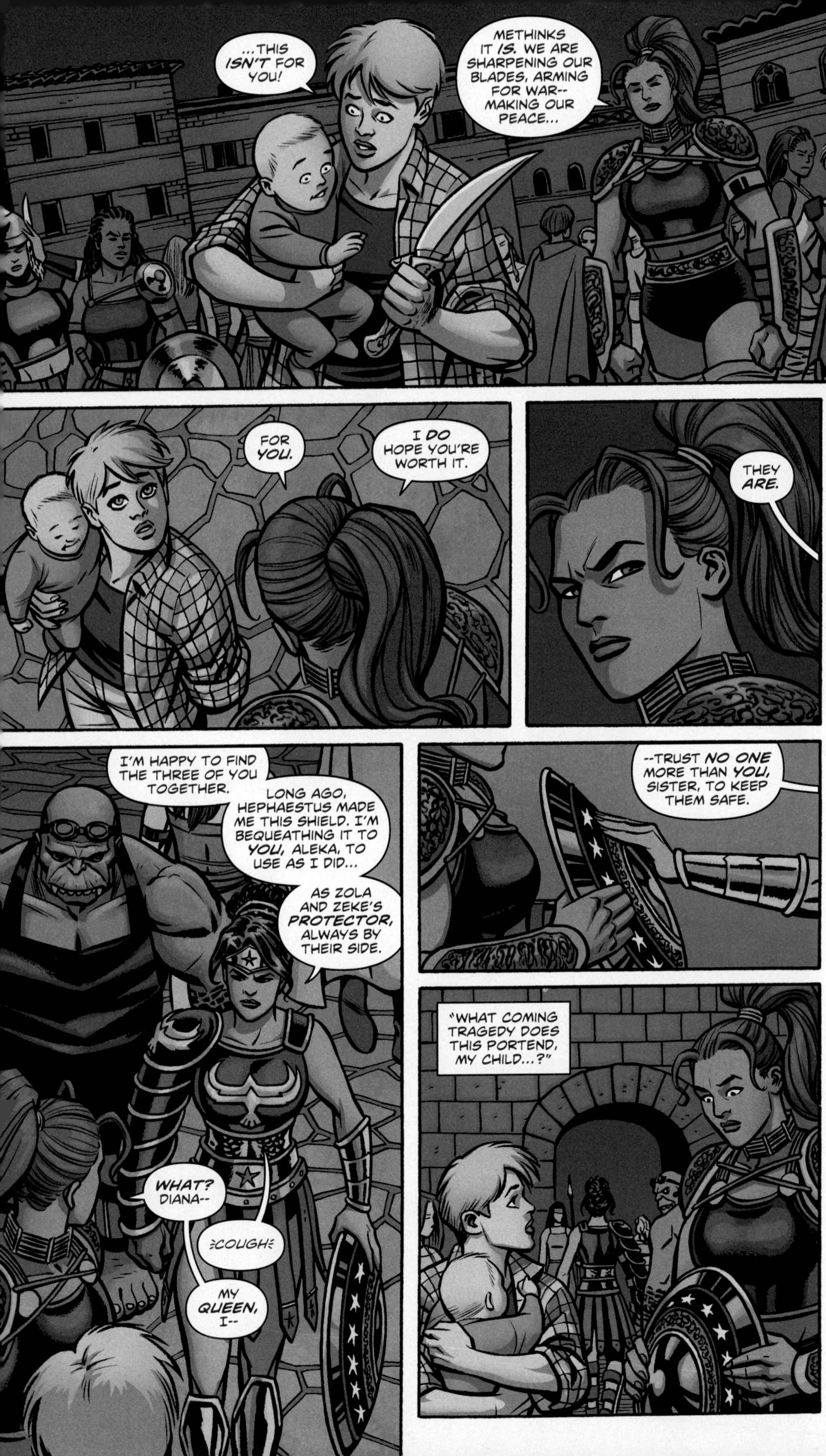
...THIS ISN'T FOR YOU!
METHINKS IT IS. WE ARE SHARPENING OUR BLADES, ARMING FOR WAR-- MAKING OUR PEACE...
FOR YOU.
I DO HOPE YOU'RE WORTH IT.
THEY ARE.
I'M HAPPY TO FIND THE THREE OF YOU TOGETHER.
LONG AGO, HEPHAESTUS MADE ME THIS SHIELD. I'M BEQUEATHING IT TO YOU, ALEKA, TO USE AS I DID...
AS ZOLA AND ZEKE'S PROTECTOR, ALWAYS BY THEIR SIDE.
WHAT? DIANA--
COUGH
MY QUEEN, I--
--TRUST NO ONE MORE THAN YOU, SISTER, TO KEEP THEM SAFE.
"WHAT COMING TRAGEDY DOES THIS PORTEND, MY CHILD...?"

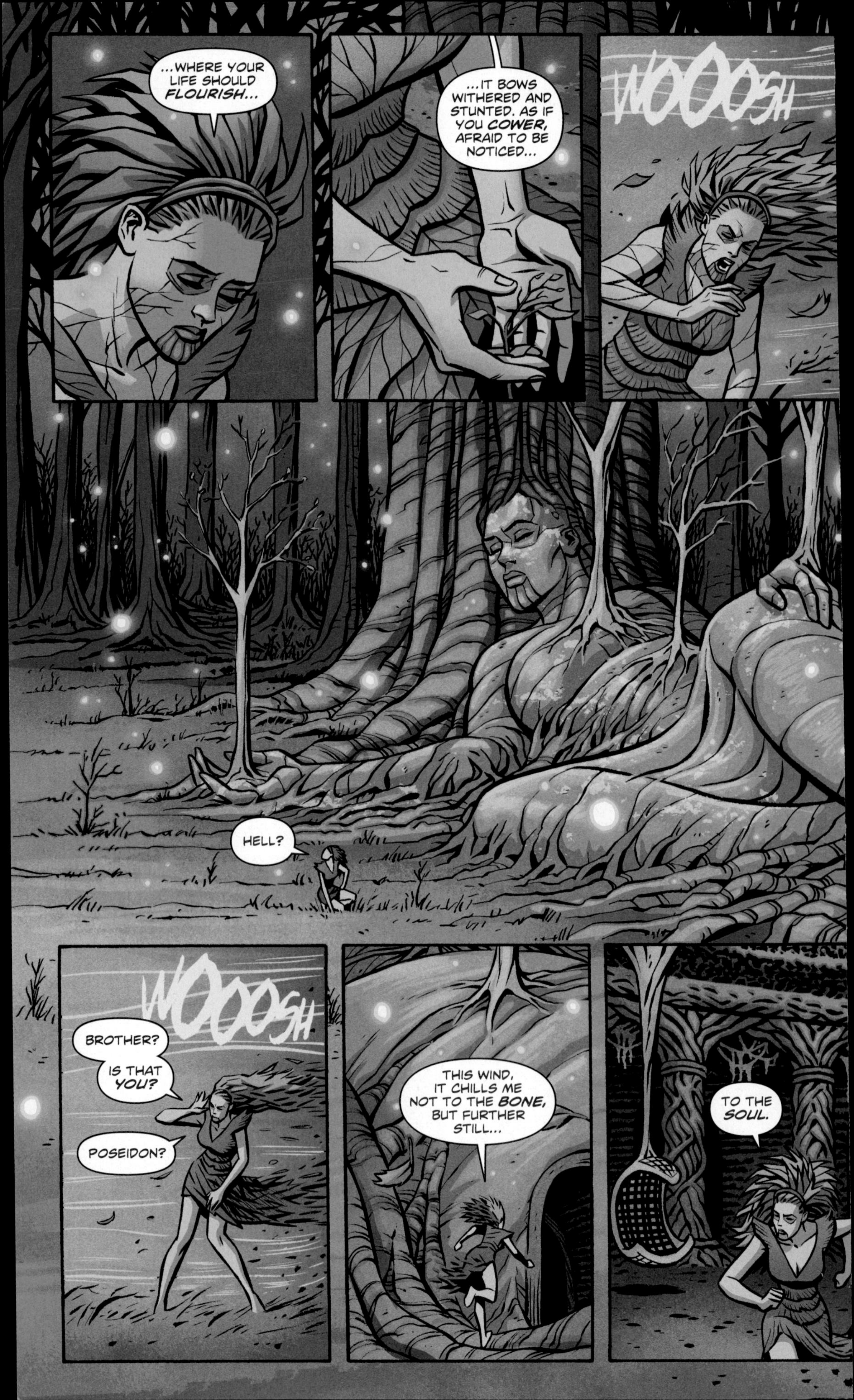
...WHERE YOUR LIFE SHOULD FLOURISH...
...IT BOWS WITHERED AND STUNTED. AS IF YOU COWER, AFRAID TO BE NOTICED...
WOOOSH
HELL?
WOOOSH
BROTHER?
IS THAT YOU?
POSEIDON?
THIS WIND, IT CHILLS ME NOT TO THE BONE, BUT FURTHER STILL...
TO THE SOUL.

HERMES!

KERRUNCH
KRUNCH

MESSENGER! ARE YOU--

SORRY, HARVEST.

SO VERY, VERY SORRY.

DON'T KILL THE MESSENGER!

DON'T KILL THE MESSENGER!

KILL THE MESSANGEE!

IN THE NAME OF MY MASTER!

FUMP

SNCCTH TCHH

I MAY SNUFF YOU BOTH.

WASTED *TIME,* HARVEST QUEEN! MY MASTER *CAN'T* BE KILLED...

AND *I* CAN'T BE--

CAUGHT?

THIS IS *MY* REALM, INVADER.

AND HERE, WE DEAL WITH PESTS...

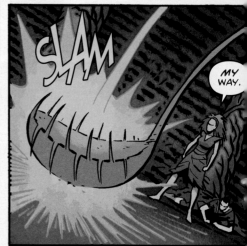

SLAM

MY WAY.

NOOO! LET ME GO!

I WAS *ONLY* DOING WHAT THE MASTER *ASKED* OF ME!

I'M AFRAID IT'S TOO LATE FOR THAT, PEST. CONSIDER THE LASHES THAT BIND YOU...

LINKS IN THE *FOOD* CHAIN.

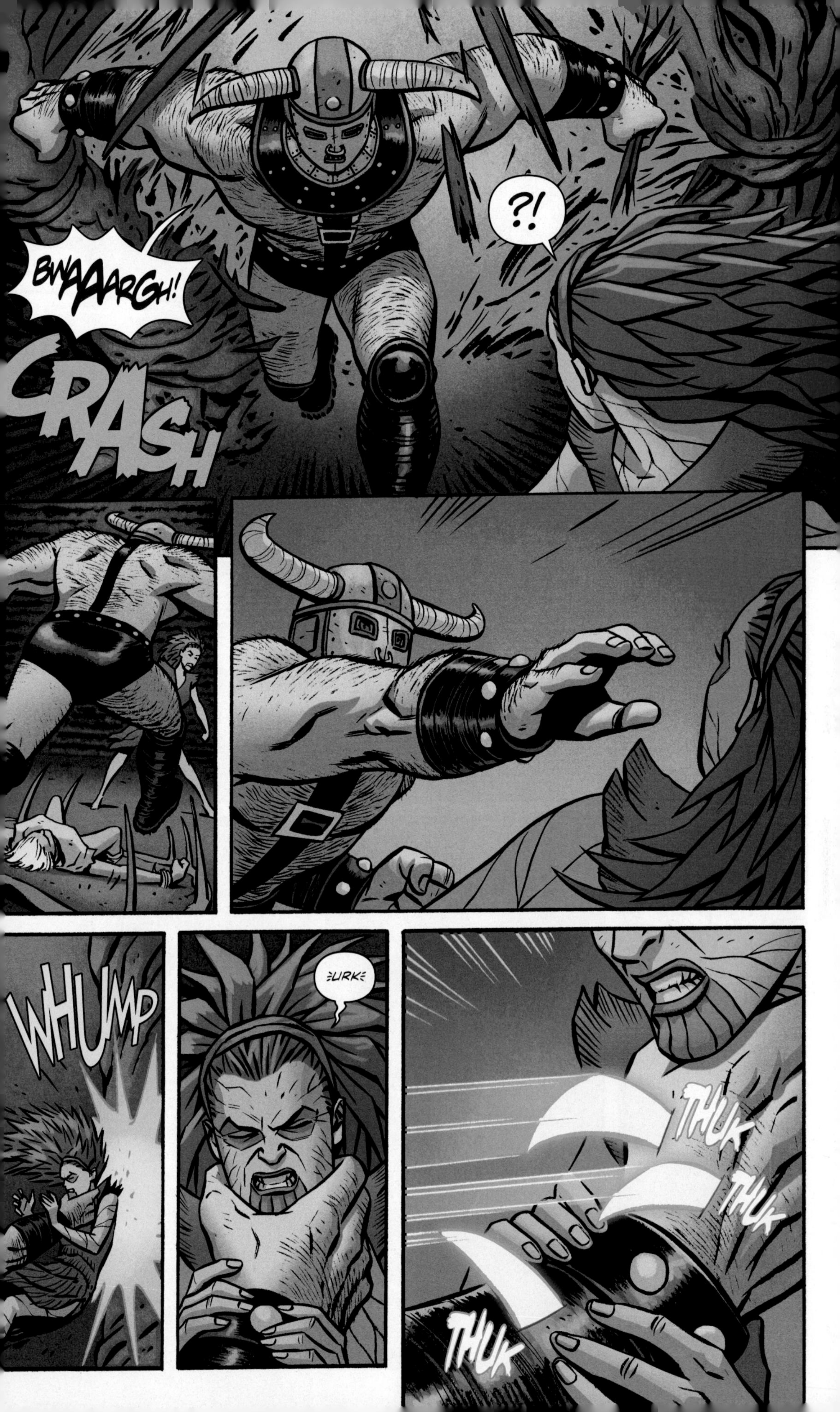
?!
BWAAARGH!
CRASH
WHUMP
URK
THUK
THUK
THUK

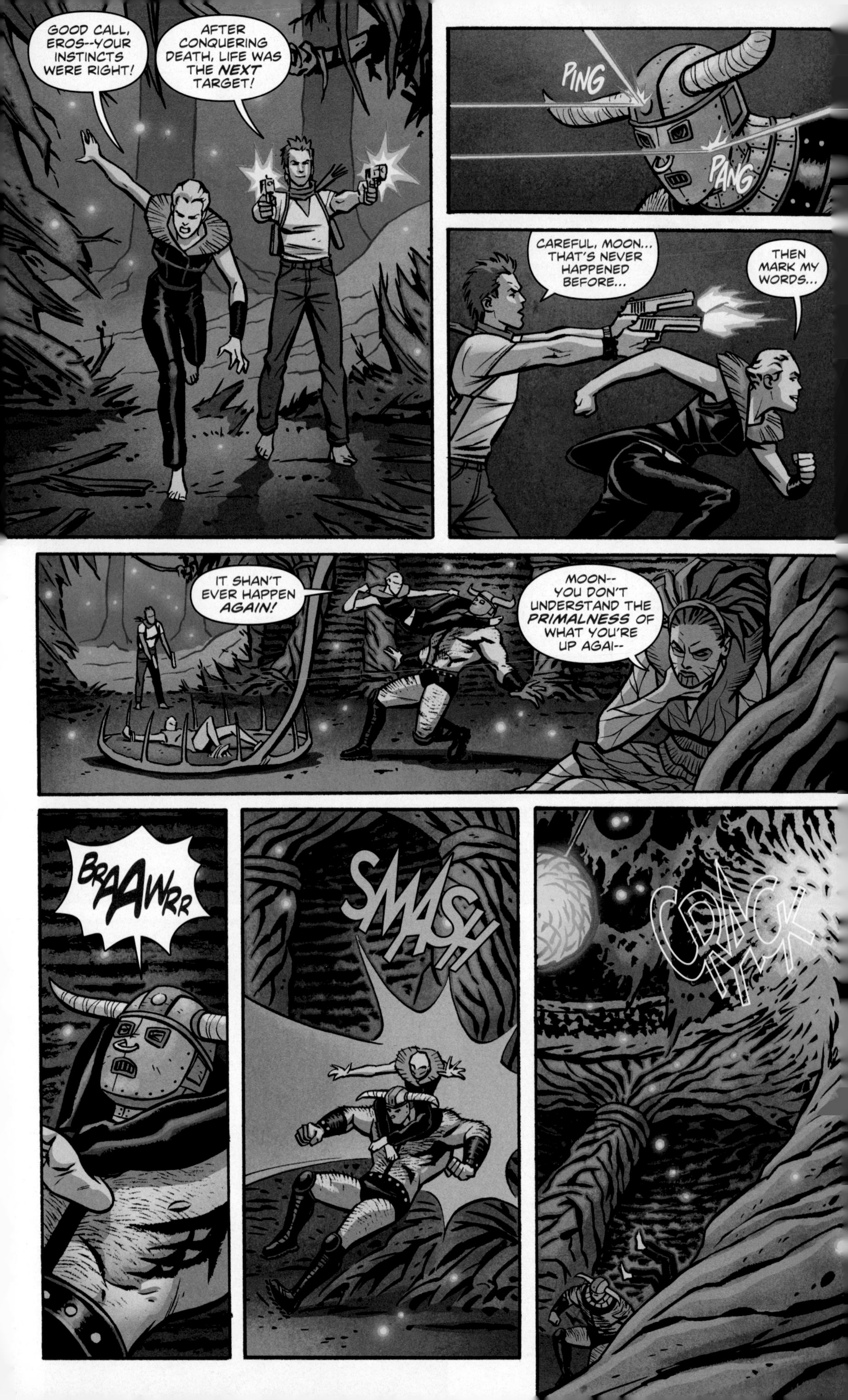
GOOD CALL, EROS--YOUR INSTINCTS WERE RIGHT!
AFTER CONQUERING DEATH, LIFE WAS THE NEXT TARGET!
PING
PANG
CAREFUL, MOON... THAT'S NEVER HAPPENED BEFORE...
THEN MARK MY WORDS...
IT SHAN'T EVER HAPPEN AGAIN!
MOON-- YOU DON'T UNDERSTAND THE PRIMALNESS OF WHAT YOU'RE UP AGAI--
BRAAWRR
SMASH

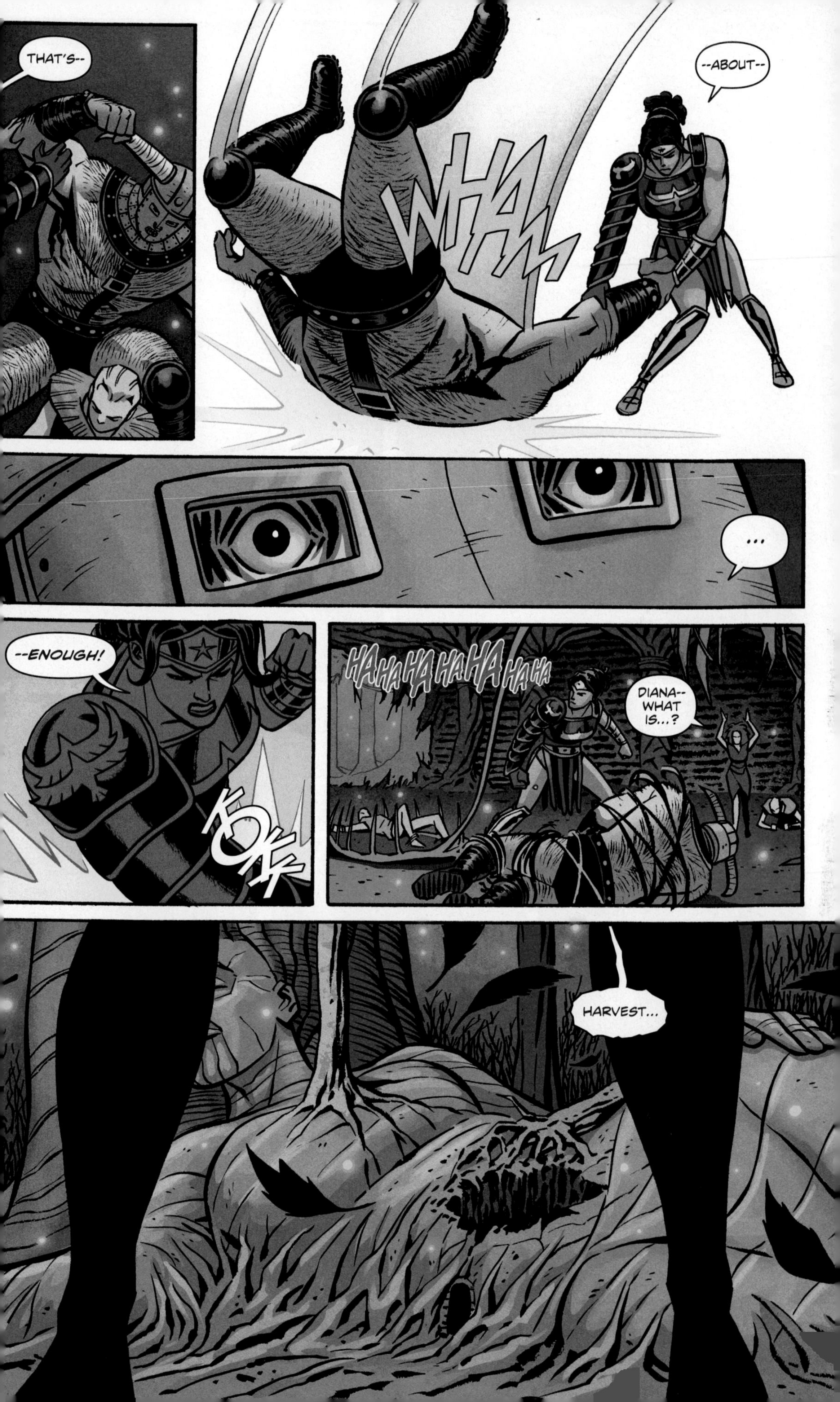

THAT'S--
--ABOUT--
WHAM
...
--ENOUGH!
KOKK
HAHAHAHAHAHAHAHA
DIANA-- WHAT IS...?
HARVEST...

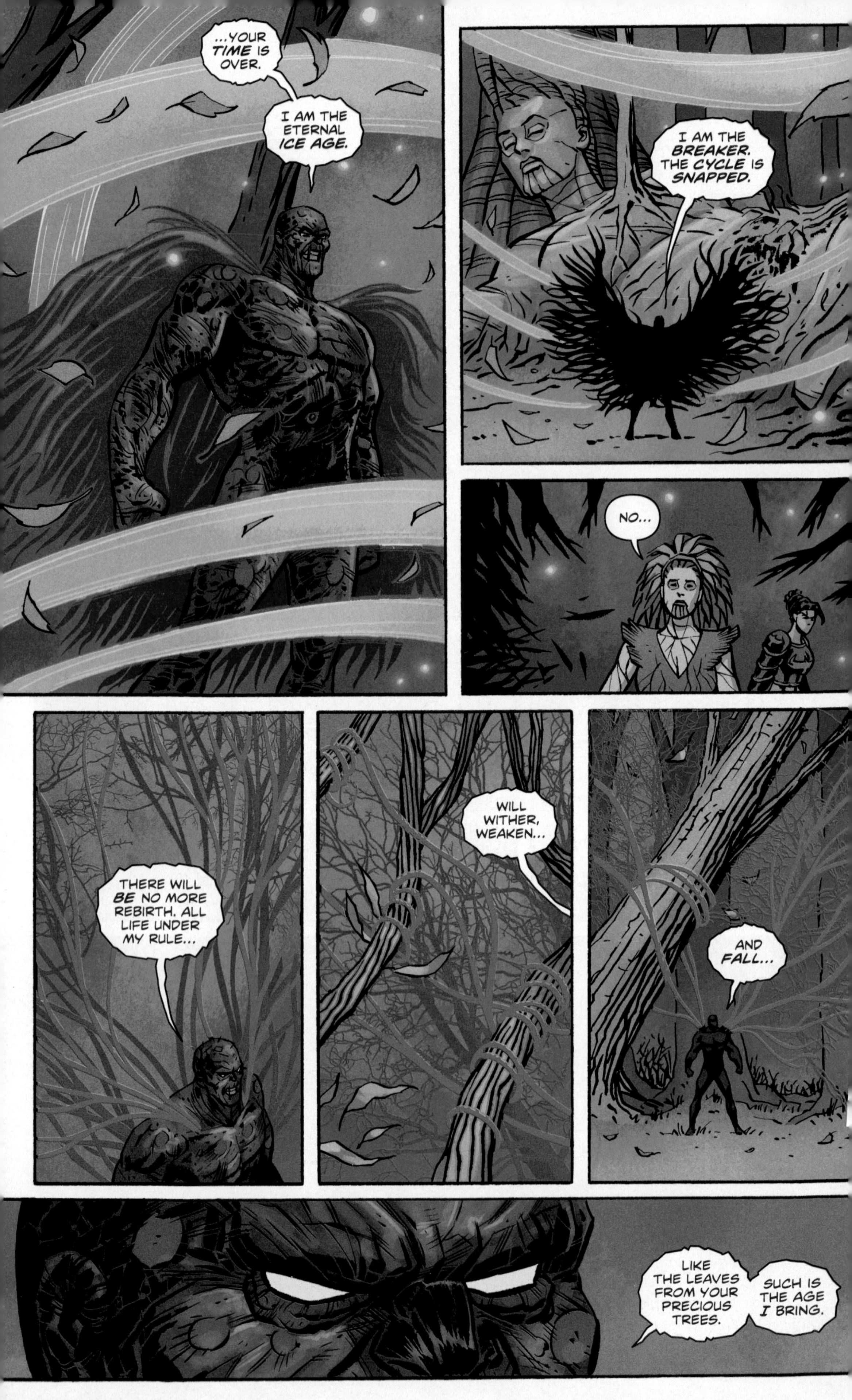

...YOUR TIME IS OVER.
I AM THE ETERNAL ICE AGE.
I AM THE BREAKER. THE CYCLE IS SNAPPED.
NO...
THERE WILL BE NO MORE REBIRTH. ALL LIFE UNDER MY RULE...
WILL WITHER, WEAKEN...
AND FALL...
LIKE THE LEAVES FROM YOUR PRECIOUS TREES.
SUCH IS THE AGE I BRING.

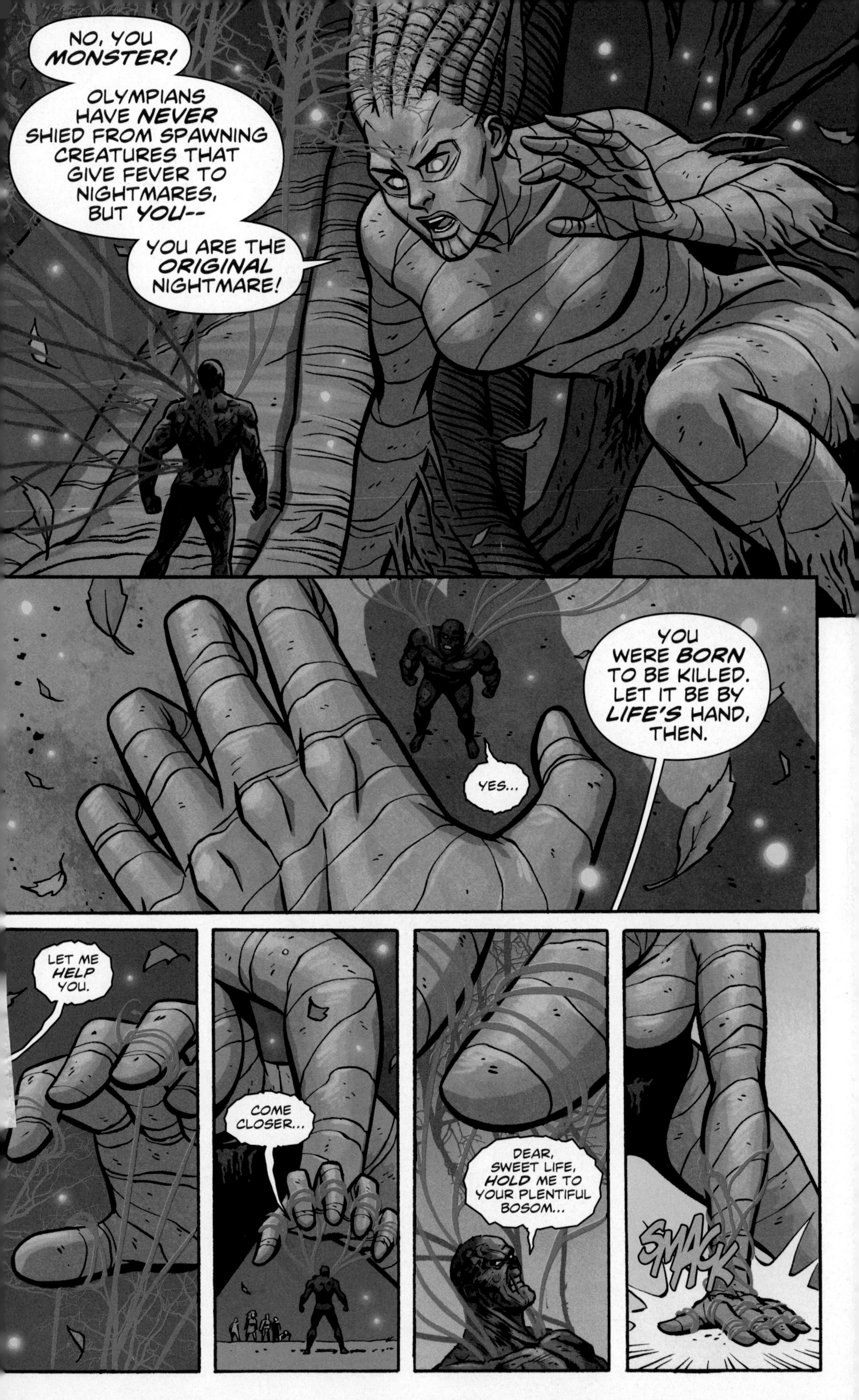
NO, YOU MONSTER!
OLYMPIANS HAVE NEVER SHIED FROM SPAWNING CREATURES THAT GIVE FEVER TO NIGHTMARES, BUT YOU--
YOU ARE THE ORIGINAL NIGHTMARE!
YOU WERE BORN TO BE KILLED. LET IT BE BY LIFE'S HAND, THEN.
YES...
LET ME HELP YOU.
COME CLOSER...
DEAR, SWEET LIFE, HOLD ME TO YOUR PLENTIFUL BOSOM...
SMACK

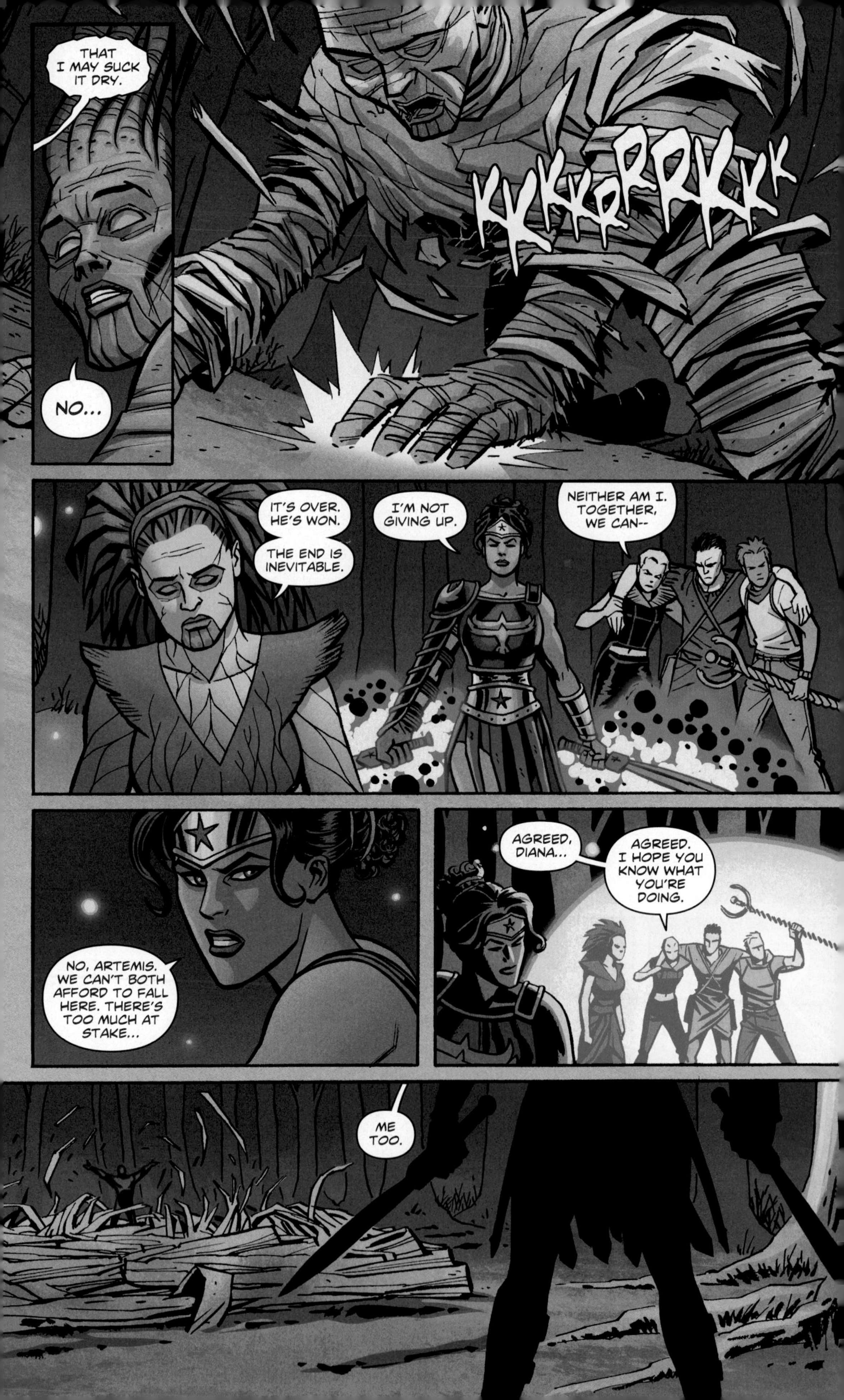
THAT I MAY SUCK IT DRY.
KKKKRRKKK
NO...
IT'S OVER. HE'S WON.
THE END IS INEVITABLE.
I'M NOT GIVING UP.
NEITHER AM I. TOGETHER, WE CAN--
NO, ARTEMIS. WE CAN'T BOTH AFFORD TO FALL HERE. THERE'S TOO MUCH AT STAKE...
AGREED, DIANA...
AGREED. I HOPE YOU KNOW WHAT YOU'RE DOING.
ME TOO.

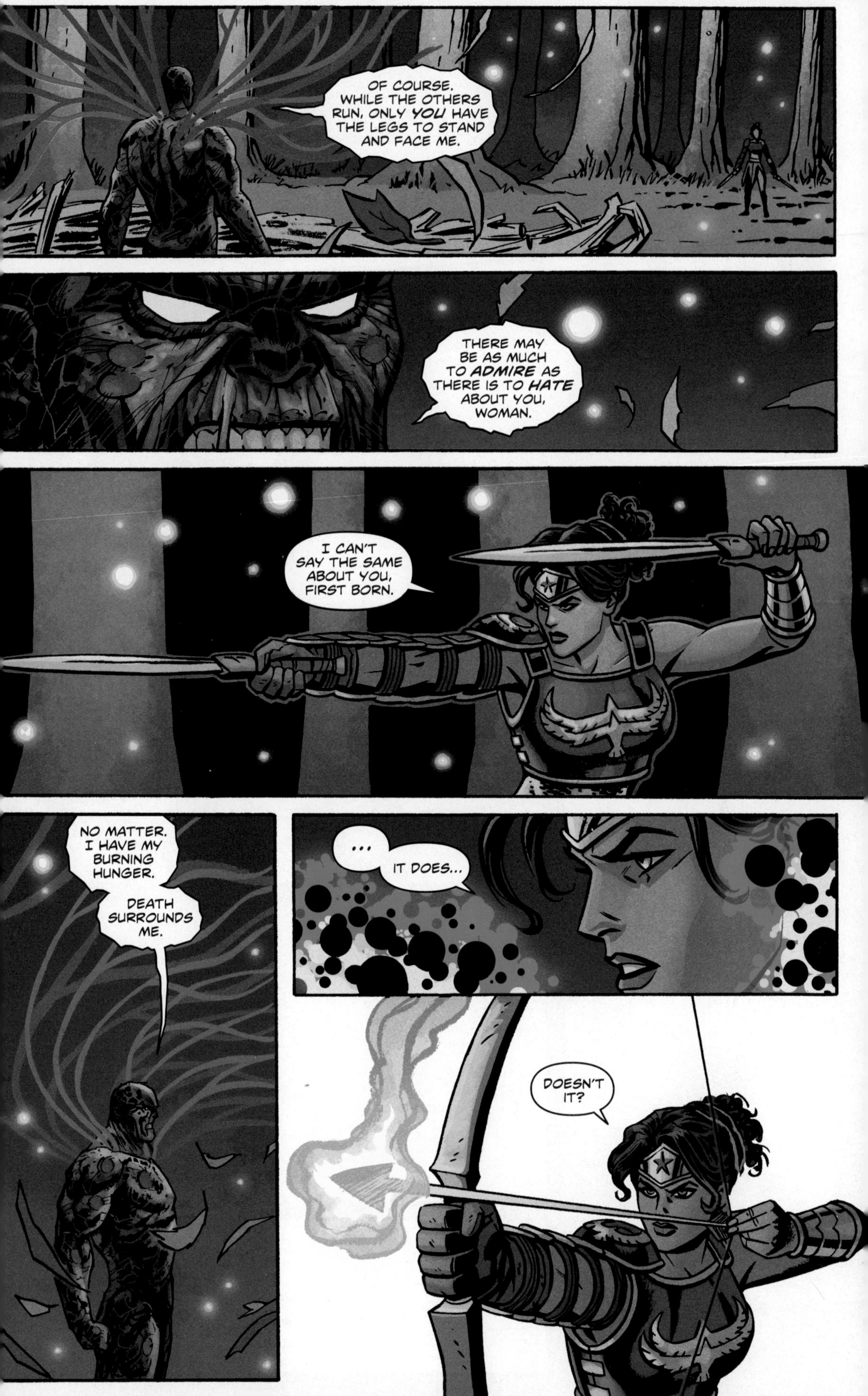
OF COURSE. WHILE THE OTHERS RUN, ONLY YOU HAVE THE LEGS TO STAND AND FACE ME.
THERE MAY BE AS MUCH TO ADMIRE AS THERE IS TO HATE ABOUT YOU, WOMAN.
I CAN'T SAY THE SAME ABOUT YOU, FIRST BORN.
NO MATTER. I HAVE MY BURNING HUNGER.
DEATH SURROUNDS ME.
...
IT DOES...
DOESN'T IT?

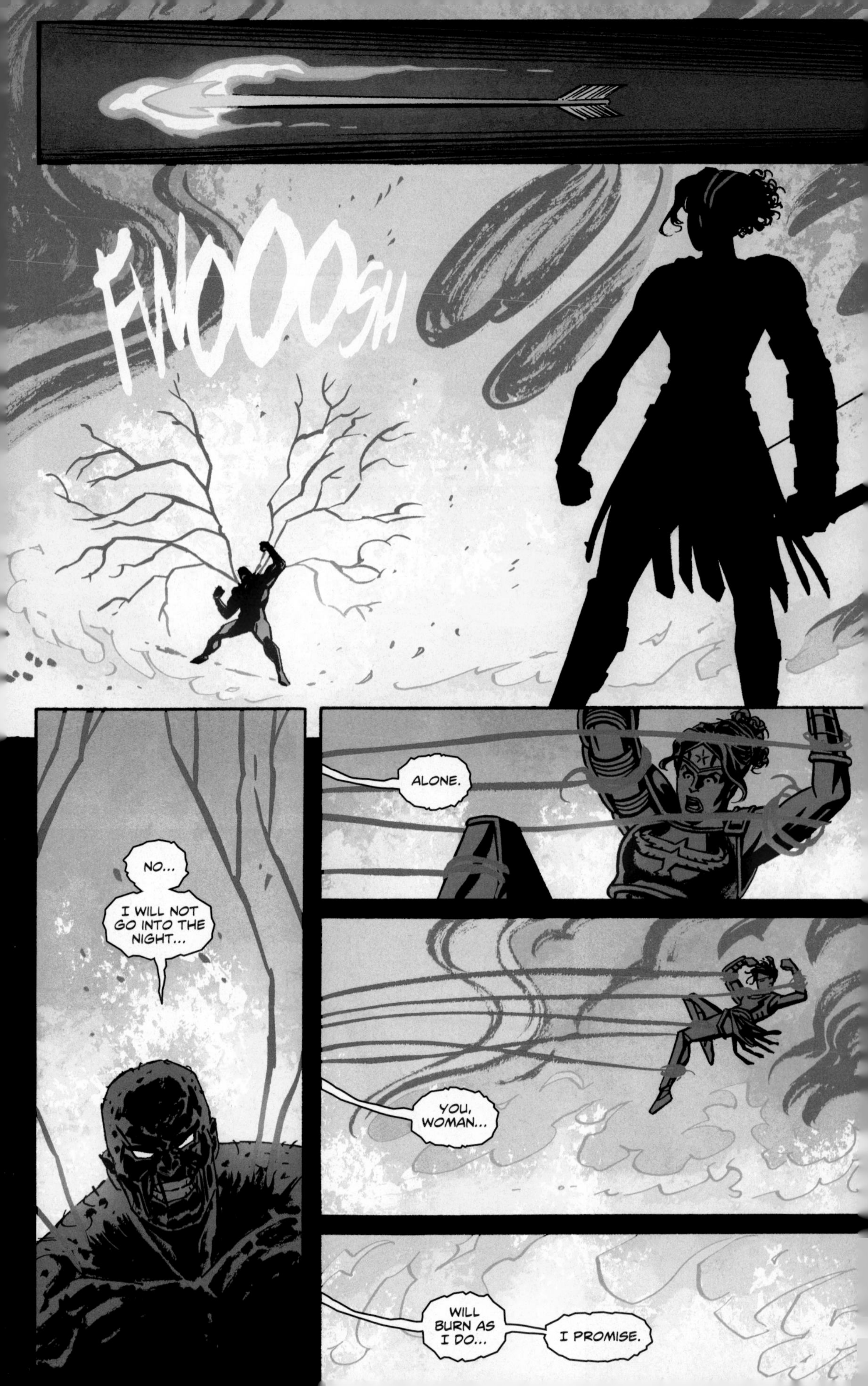
FWOOOSH
ALONE.
NO...
I WILL NOT GO INTO THE NIGHT...
YOU, WOMAN...
WILL BURN AS I DO...
I PROMISE.

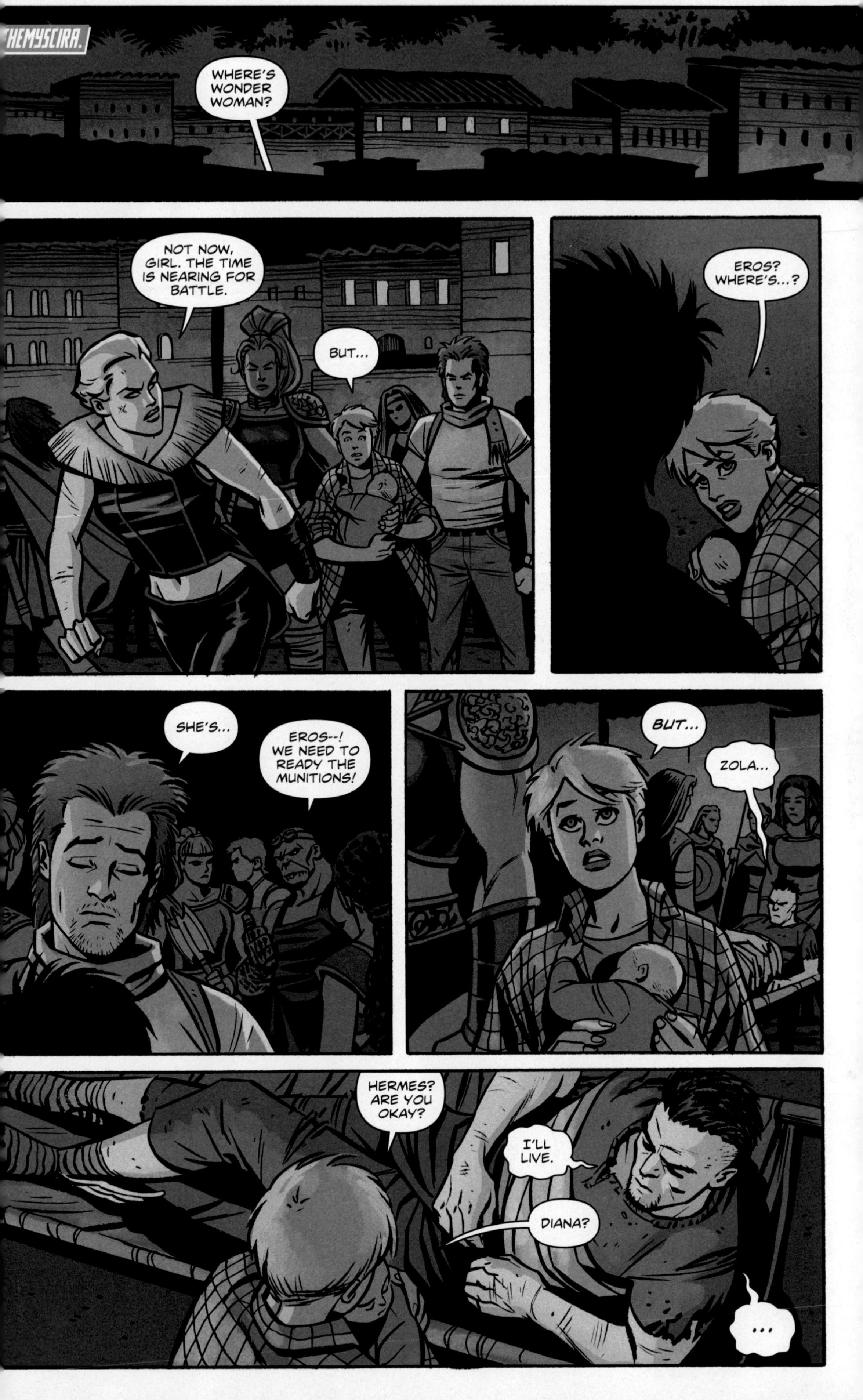
THEMYSCIRA.
WHERE'S WONDER WOMAN?
NOT NOW, GIRL. THE TIME IS NEARING FOR BATTLE.
BUT...
EROS? WHERE'S...?
SHE'S...
EROS--! WE NEED TO READY THE MUNITIONS!
BUT...
ZOLA...
HERMES? ARE YOU OKAY?
I'LL LIVE.
DIANA?
...

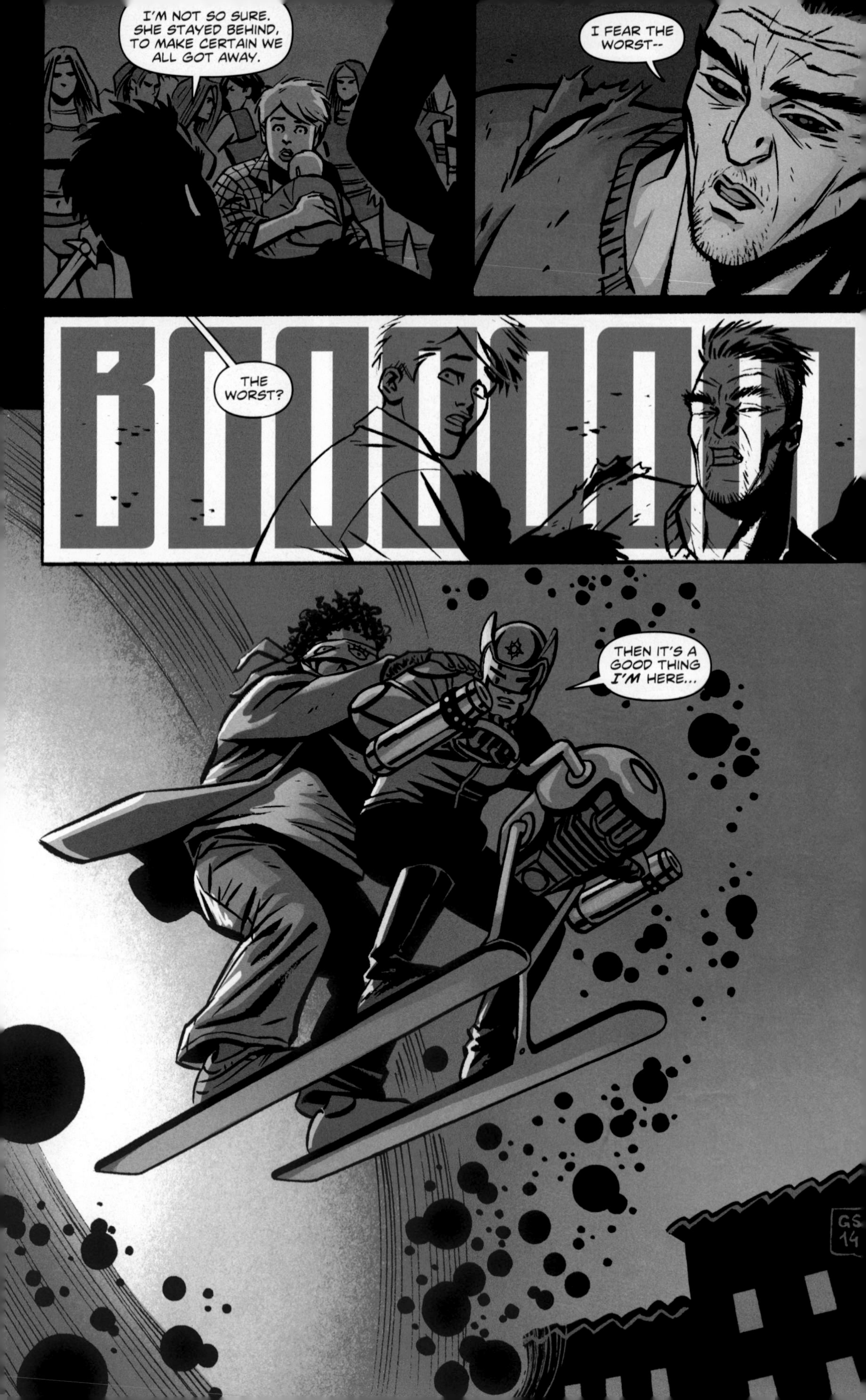

I'M NOT SO SURE. SHE STAYED BEHIND, TO MAKE CERTAIN WE ALL GOT AWAY.
I FEAR THE WORST--
THE WORST?
THEN IT'S A GOOD THING I'M HERE...
GS 14

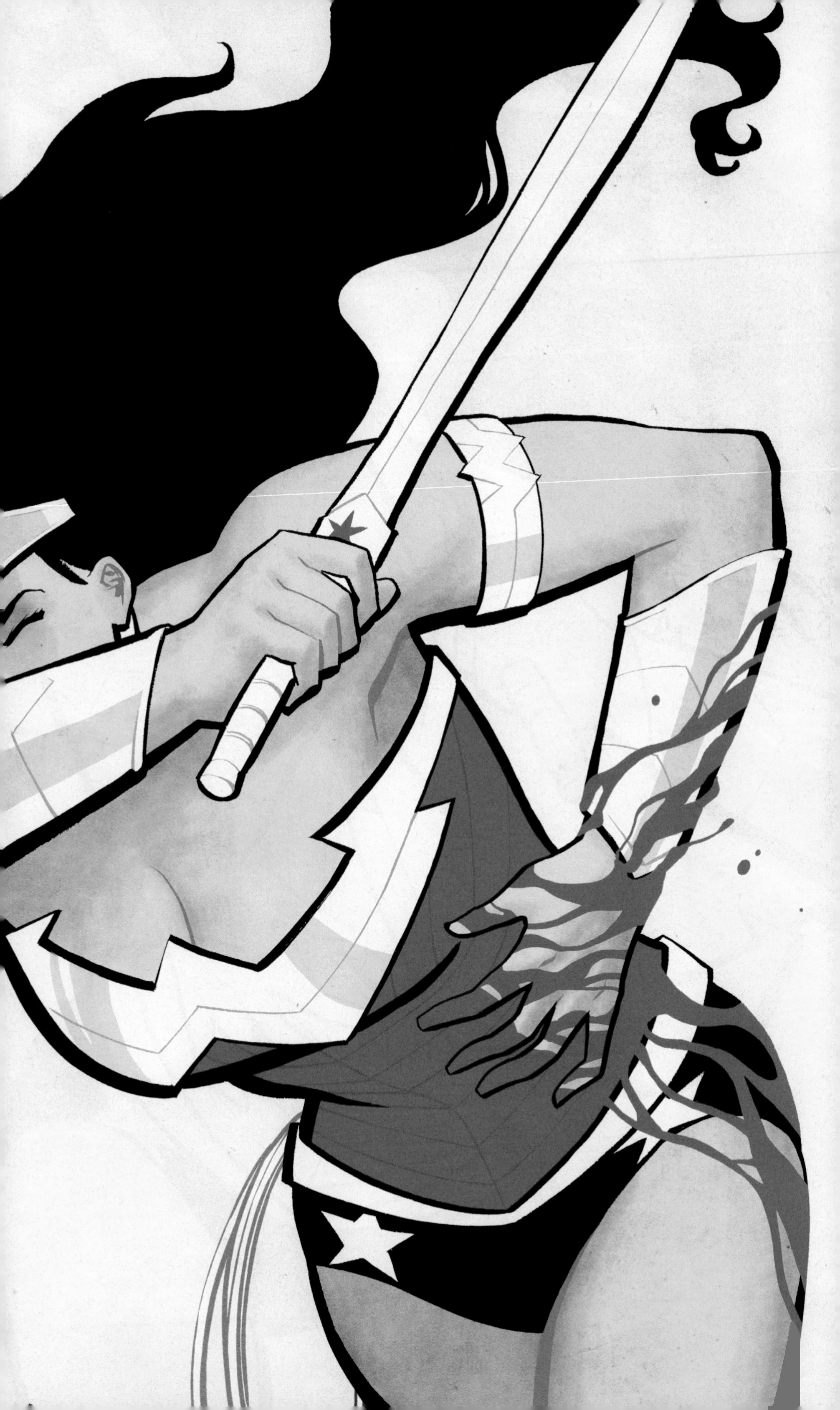

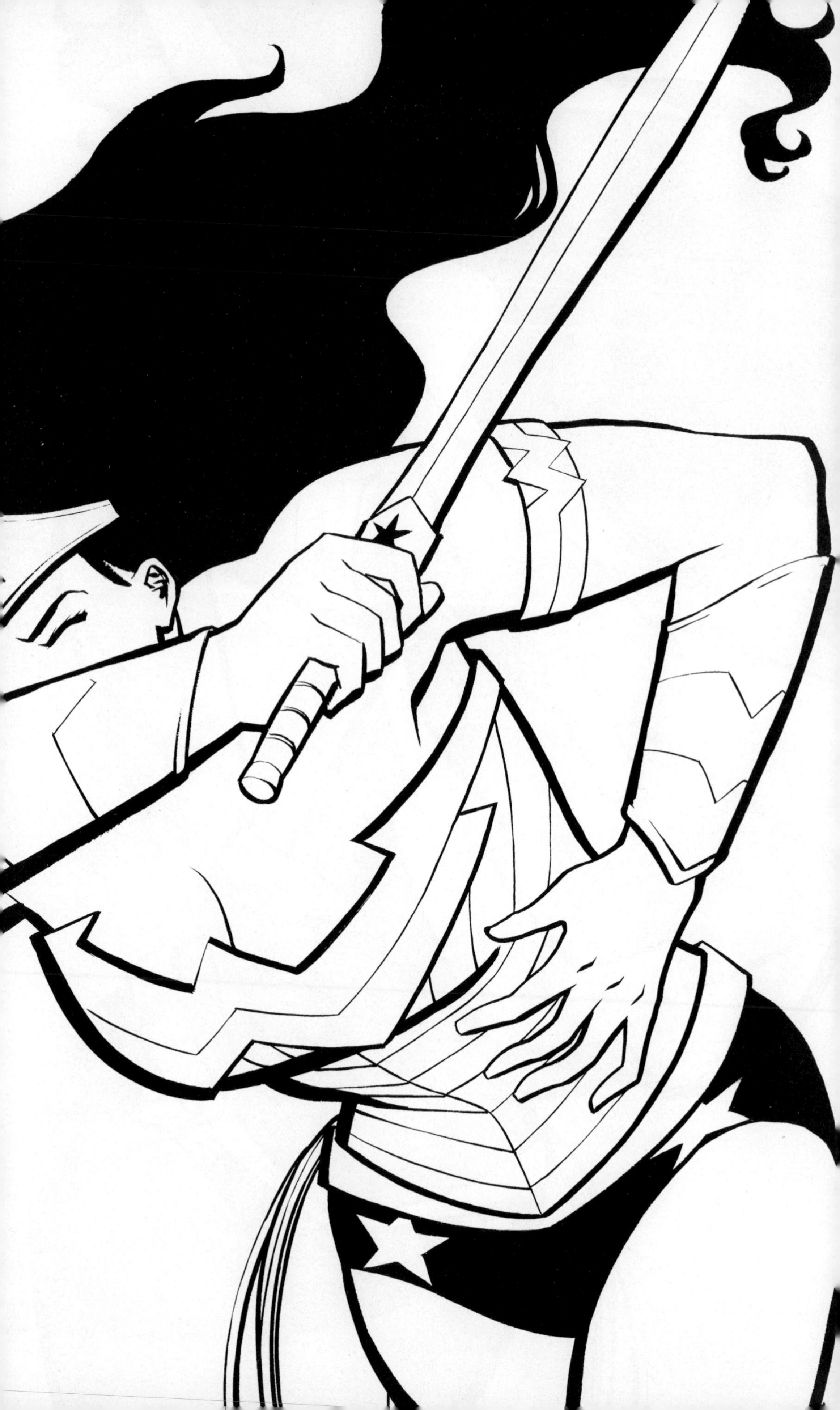

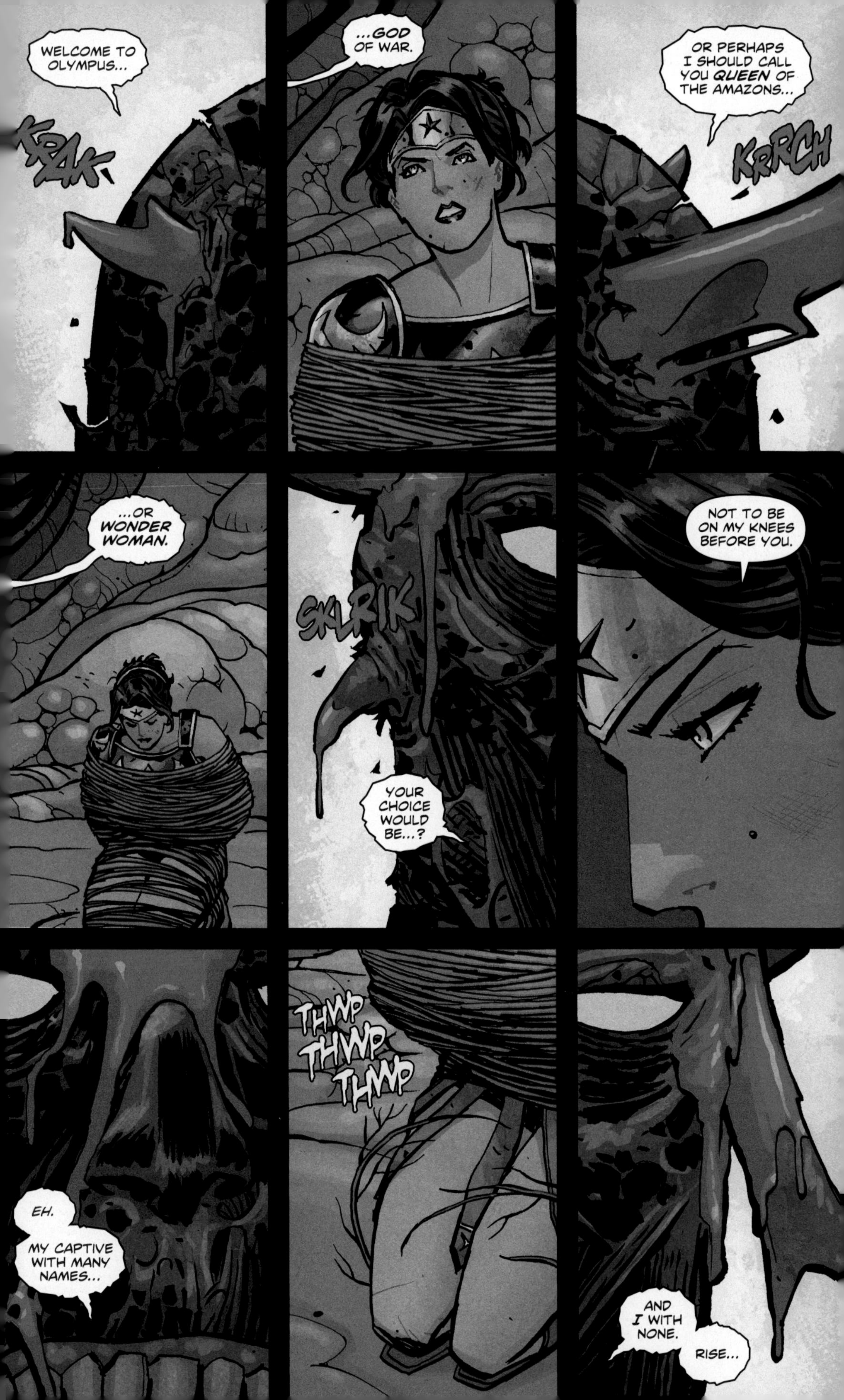
WELCOME TO OLYMPUS...
KRAK
...GOD OF WAR.
OR PERHAPS I SHOULD CALL YOU QUEEN OF THE AMAZONS...
KRRCH
...OR WONDER WOMAN.
SKLRIK
YOUR CHOICE WOULD BE...?
NOT TO BE ON MY KNEES BEFORE YOU.
EH.
MY CAPTIVE WITH MANY NAMES...
THWP THWP THWP
AND I WITH NONE.
RISE...

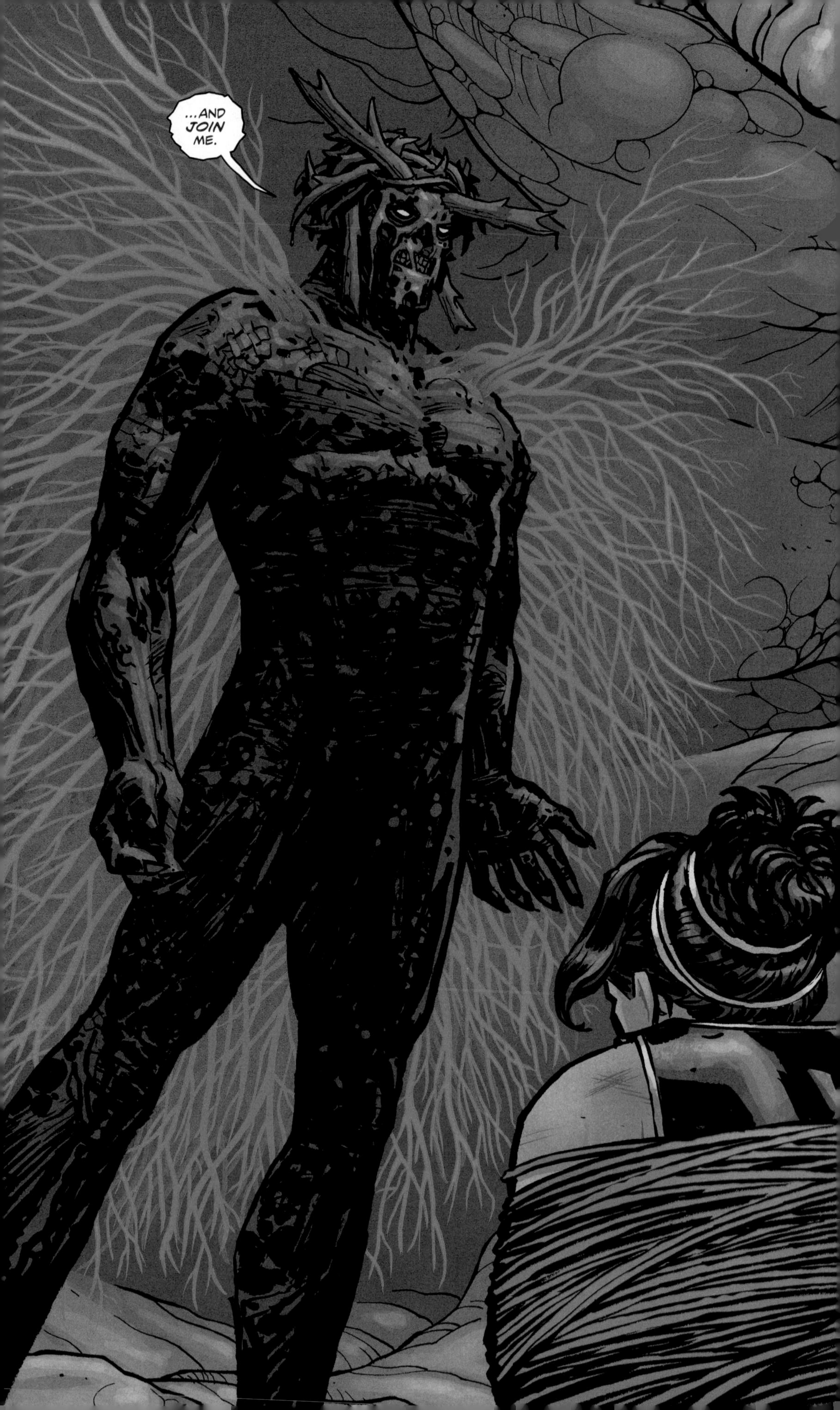
...AND JOIN ME.

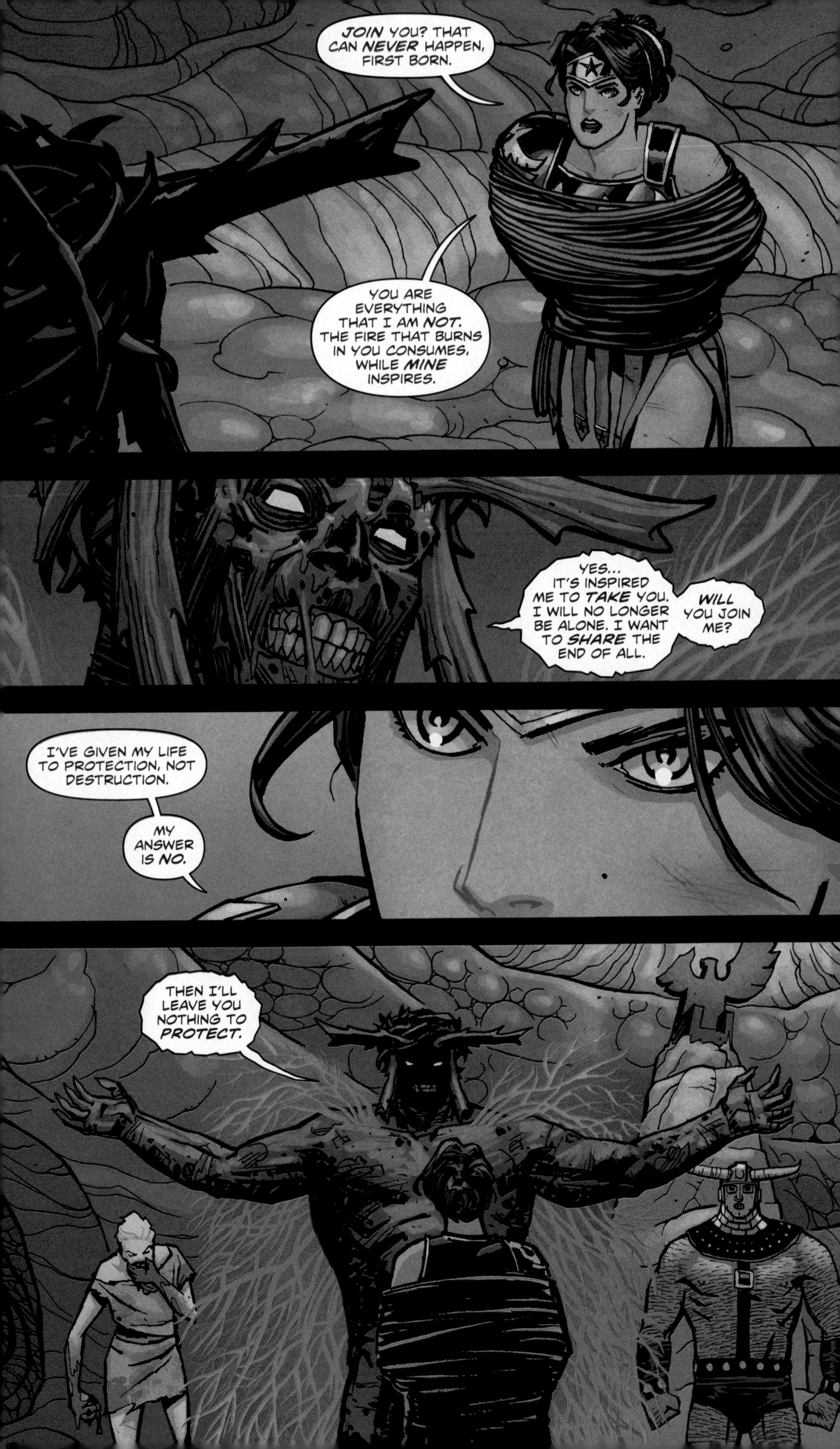
JOIN YOU? THAT CAN NEVER HAPPEN, FIRST BORN.
YOU ARE EVERYTHING THAT I AM NOT. THE FIRE THAT BURNS IN YOU CONSUMES, WHILE MINE INSPIRES.
YES... IT'S INSPIRED ME TO TAKE YOU. I WILL NO LONGER BE ALONE. I WANT TO SHARE THE END OF ALL.
WILL YOU JOIN ME?
I'VE GIVEN MY LIFE TO PROTECTION, NOT DESTRUCTION.
MY ANSWER IS NO.
THEN I'LL LEAVE YOU NOTHING TO PROTECT.

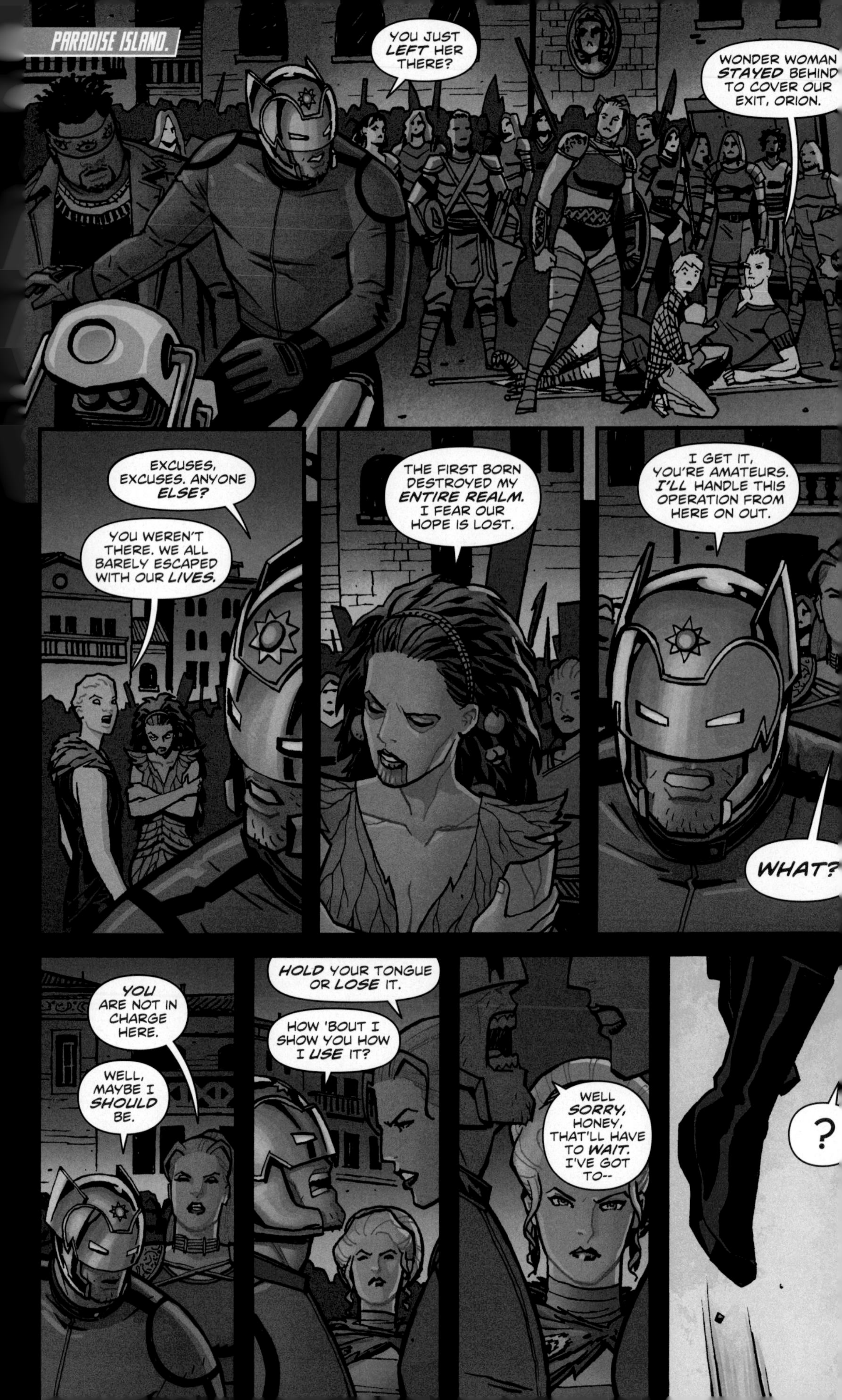

PARADISE ISLAND.
YOU JUST LEFT HER THERE?
WONDER WOMAN STAYED BEHIND TO COVER OUR EXIT, ORION.
EXCUSES, EXCUSES. ANYONE ELSE?
YOU WEREN'T THERE. WE ALL BARELY ESCAPED WITH OUR LIVES.
THE FIRST BORN DESTROYED MY ENTIRE REALM. I FEAR OUR HOPE IS LOST.
I GET IT, YOU'RE AMATEURS. I'LL HANDLE THIS OPERATION FROM HERE ON OUT.
WHAT?
YOU ARE NOT IN CHARGE HERE.
WELL, MAYBE I SHOULD BE.
HOLD YOUR TONGUE OR LOSE IT.
HOW 'BOUT I SHOW YOU HOW I USE IT?
WELL SORRY, HONEY, THAT'LL HAVE TO WAIT. I'VE GOT TO--
?

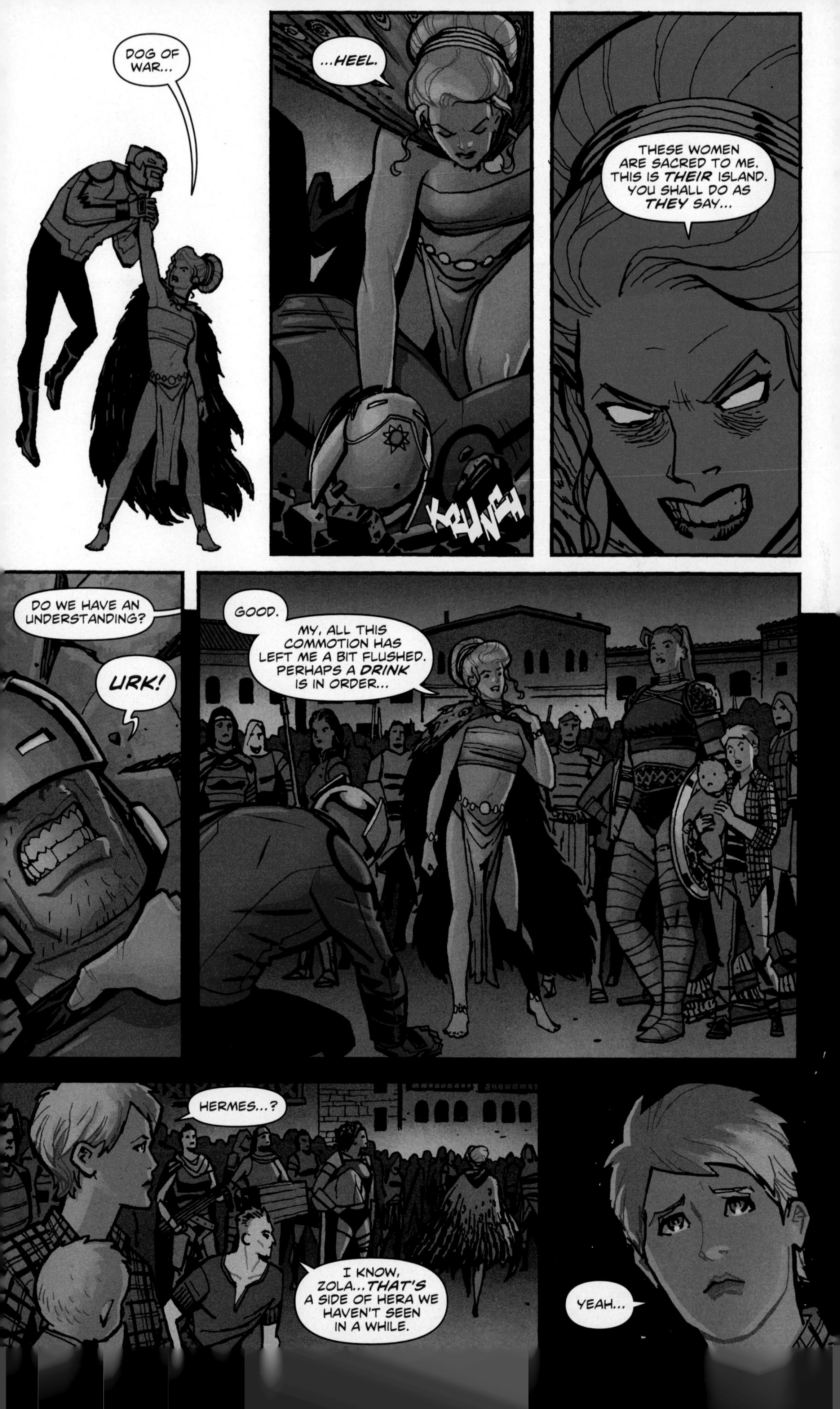
DOG OF WAR...
...HEEL.
KRUNCH
THESE WOMEN ARE SACRED TO ME. THIS IS THEIR ISLAND. YOU SHALL DO AS THEY SAY...
DO WE HAVE AN UNDERSTANDING?
URK!
GOOD.
MY, ALL THIS COMMOTION HAS LEFT ME A BIT FLUSHED. PERHAPS A DRINK IS IN ORDER...
HERMES...?
I KNOW, ZOLA...THAT'S A SIDE OF HERA WE HAVEN'T SEEN IN A WHILE.
YEAH...

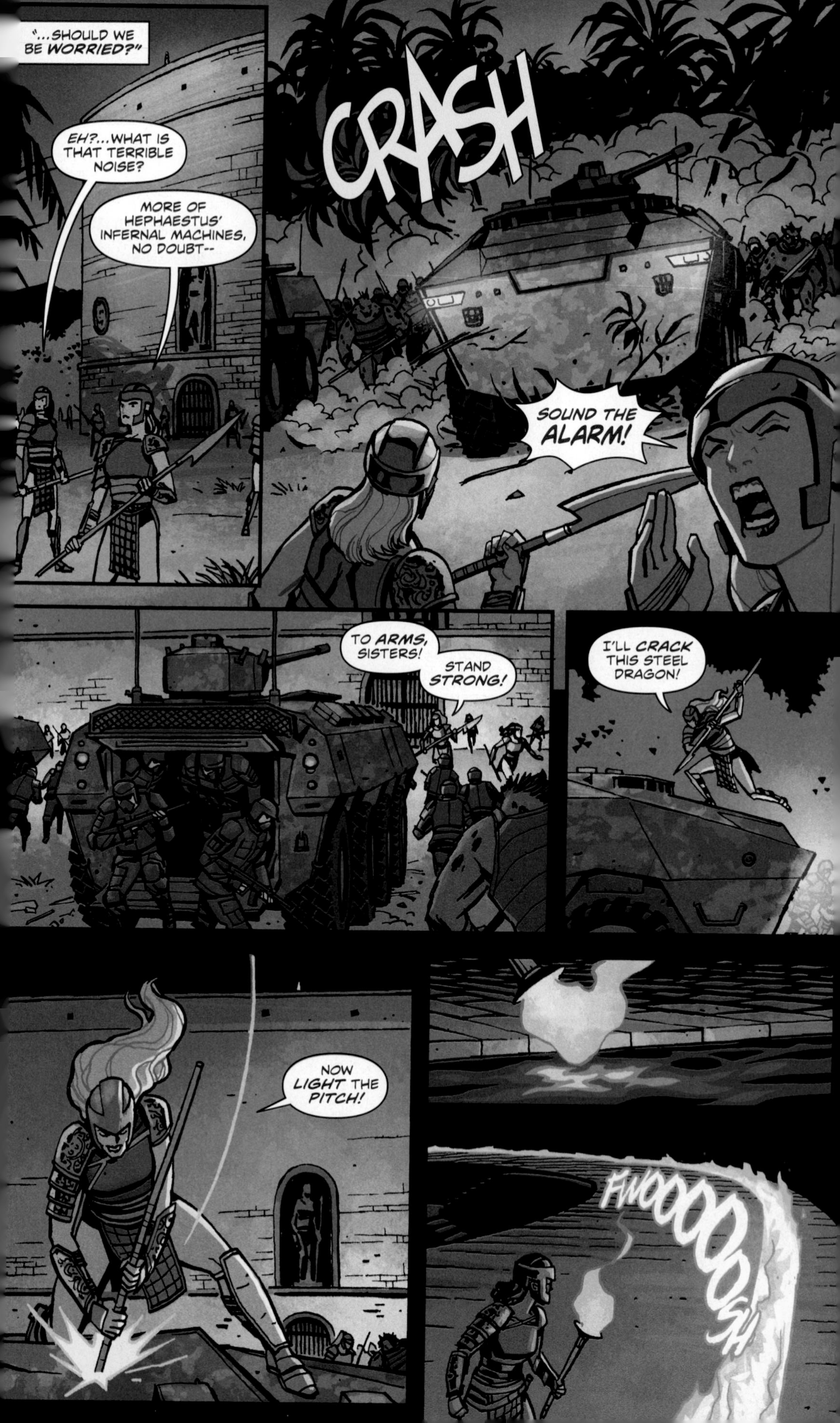
"...SHOULD WE BE WORRIED?"
EH?...WHAT IS THAT TERRIBLE NOISE?
MORE OF HEPHAESTUS' INFERNAL MACHINES, NO DOUBT--
CRASH
SOUND THE ALARM!
TO ARMS, SISTERS!
STAND STRONG!
I'LL CRACK THIS STEEL DRAGON!
NOW LIGHT THE PITCH!
FWOOOOOOSH

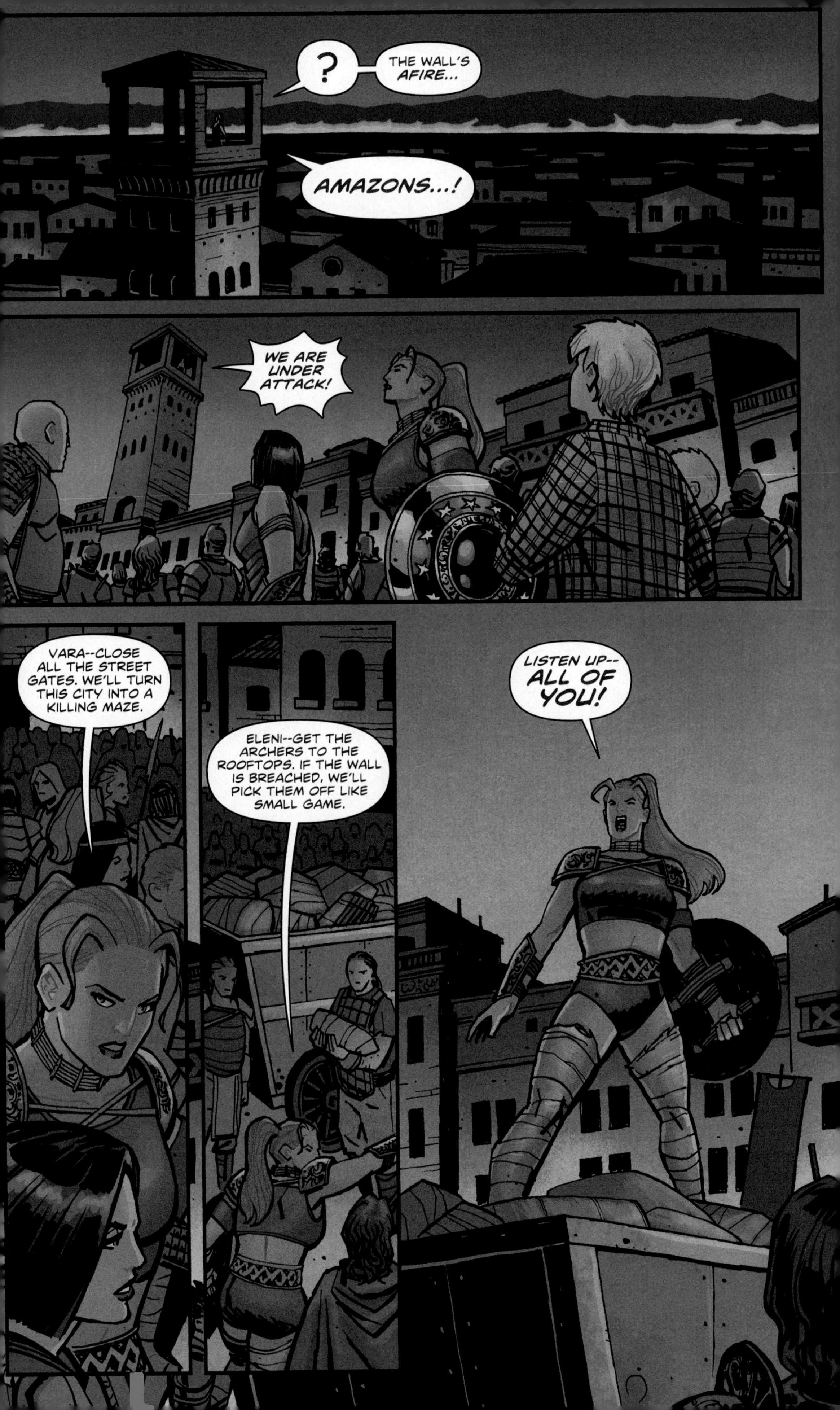
?
THE WALL'S AFIRE...
AMAZONS...!
WE ARE UNDER ATTACK!
VARA--CLOSE ALL THE STREET GATES. WE'LL TURN THIS CITY INTO A KILLING MAZE.
ELENI--GET THE ARCHERS TO THE ROOFTOPS. IF THE WALL IS BREACHED, WE'LL PICK THEM OFF LIKE SMALL GAME.
LISTEN UP-- ALL OF YOU!

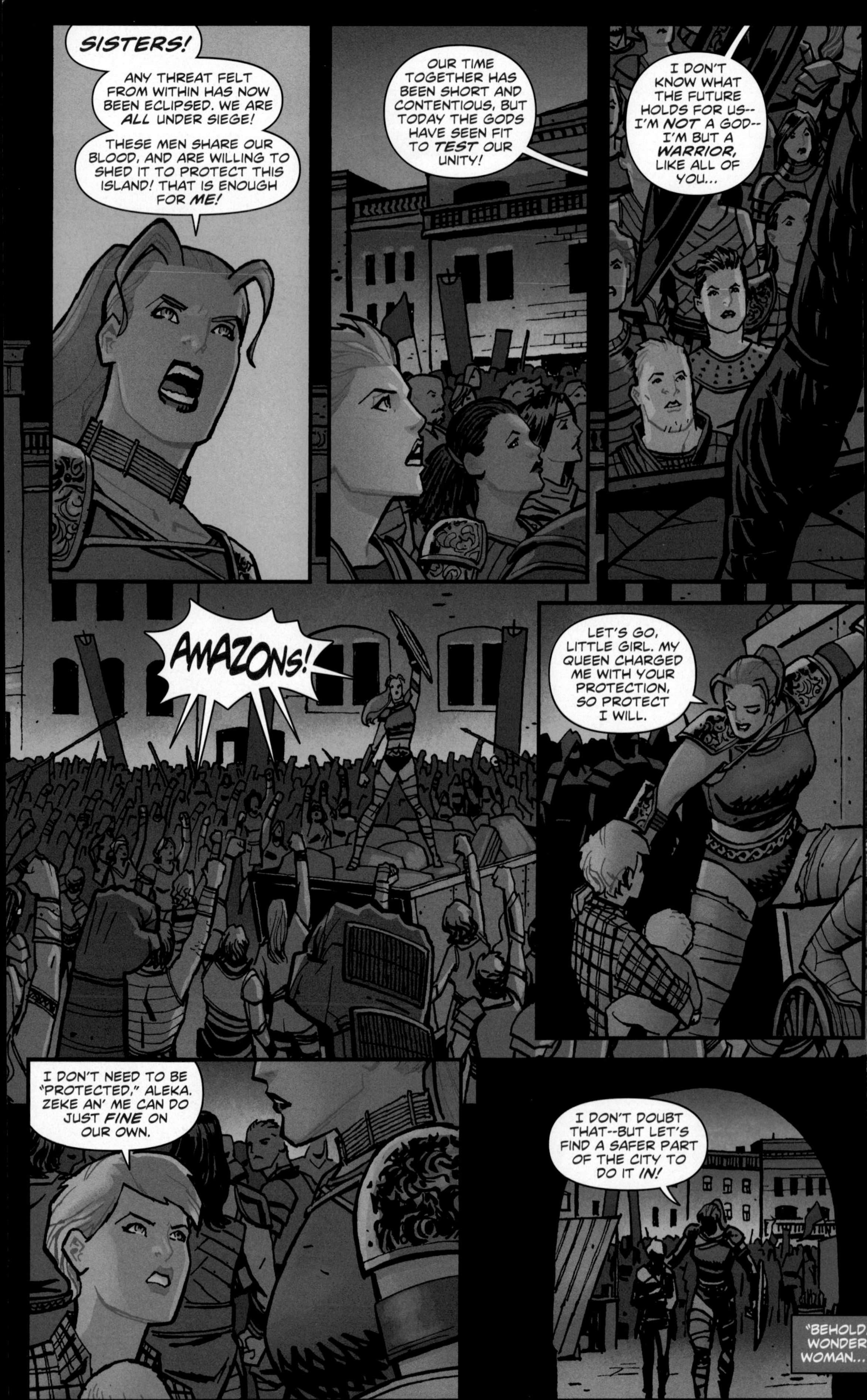
SISTERS!
ANY THREAT FELT FROM WITHIN HAS NOW BEEN ECLIPSED. WE ARE ALL UNDER SIEGE!
THESE MEN SHARE OUR BLOOD, AND ARE WILLING TO SHED IT TO PROTECT THIS ISLAND! THAT IS ENOUGH FOR ME!
OUR TIME TOGETHER HAS BEEN SHORT AND CONTENTIOUS, BUT TODAY THE GODS HAVE SEEN FIT TO TEST OUR UNITY!
I DON'T KNOW WHAT THE FUTURE HOLDS FOR US-- I'M NOT A GOD-- I'M BUT A WARRIOR, LIKE ALL OF YOU...
AMAZONS!
LET'S GO, LITTLE GIRL. MY QUEEN CHARGED ME WITH YOUR PROTECTION, SO PROTECT I WILL.
I DON'T NEED TO BE "PROTECTED," ALEKA. ZEKE AN' ME CAN DO JUST FINE ON OUR OWN.
I DON'T DOUBT THAT--BUT LET'S FIND A SAFER PART OF THE CITY TO DO IT IN!
"BEHOLD WONDER WOMAN...

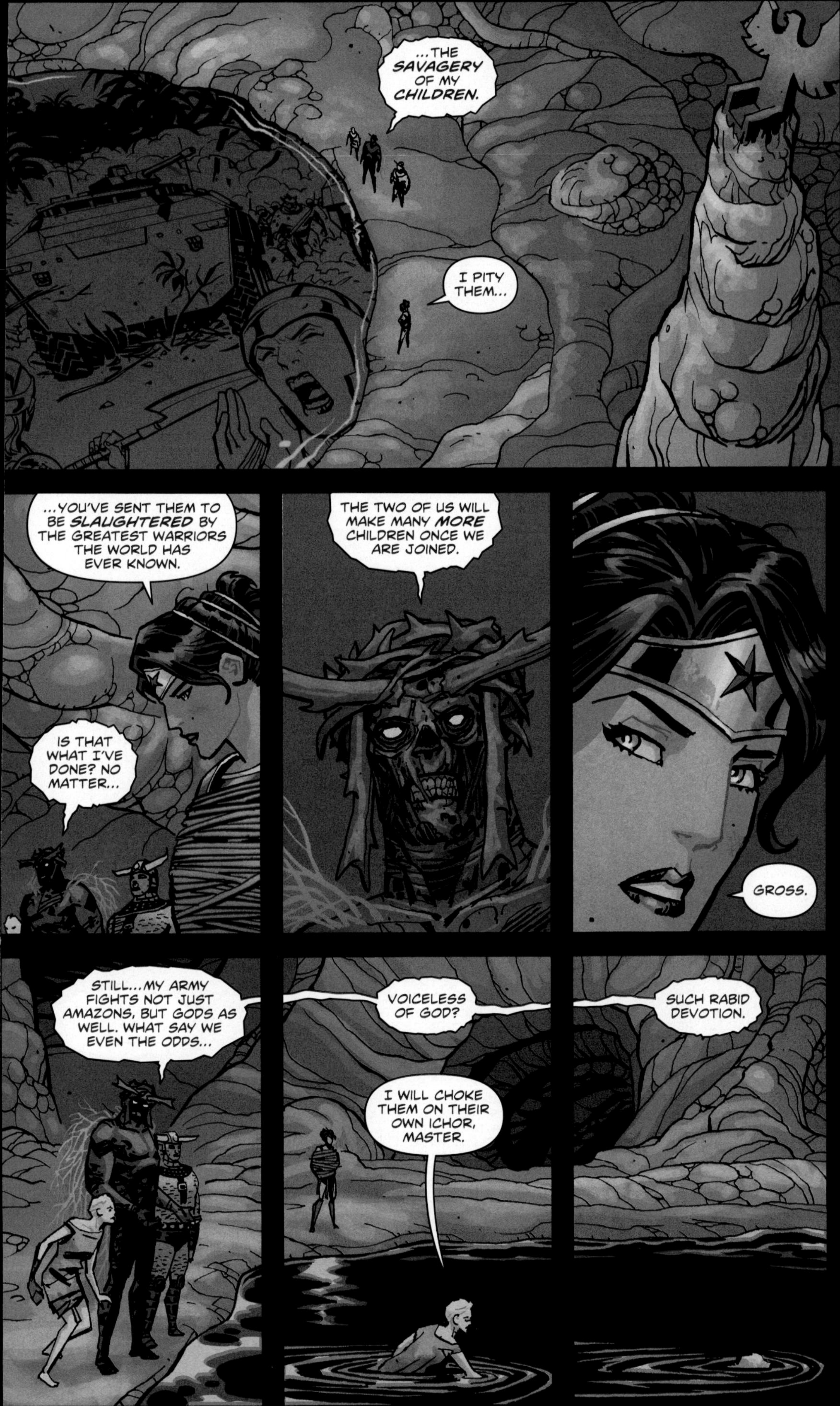
...THE SAVAGERY OF MY CHILDREN.
I PITY THEM...
...YOU'VE SENT THEM TO BE SLAUGHTERED BY THE GREATEST WARRIORS THE WORLD HAS EVER KNOWN.
IS THAT WHAT I'VE DONE? NO MATTER...
THE TWO OF US WILL MAKE MANY MORE CHILDREN ONCE WE ARE JOINED.
GROSS.
STILL...MY ARMY FIGHTS NOT JUST AMAZONS, BUT GODS AS WELL. WHAT SAY WE EVEN THE ODDS...
VOICELESS OF GOD?
SUCH RABID DEVOTION.
I WILL CHOKE THEM ON THEIR OWN ICHOR, MASTER.

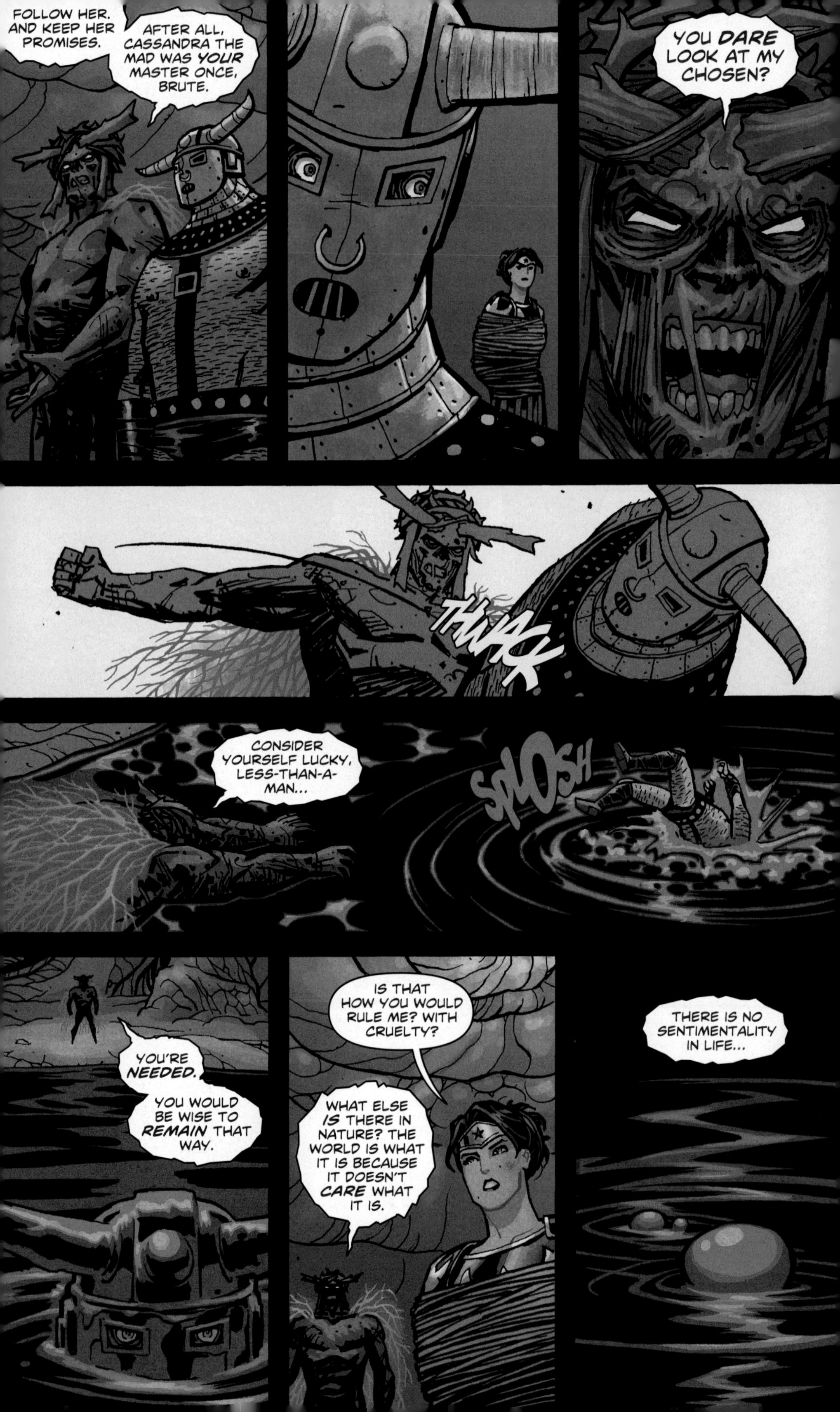
FOLLOW HER. AND KEEP HER PROMISES.
AFTER ALL, CASSANDRA THE MAD WAS YOUR MASTER ONCE, BRUTE.
YOU DARE LOOK AT MY CHOSEN?
THWACK
CONSIDER YOURSELF LUCKY, LESS-THAN-A-MAN...
SPLOSH
YOU'RE NEEDED.
YOU WOULD BE WISE TO REMAIN THAT WAY.
IS THAT HOW YOU WOULD RULE ME? WITH CRUELTY?
WHAT ELSE IS THERE IN NATURE? THE WORLD IS WHAT IT IS BECAUSE IT DOESN'T CARE WHAT IT IS.
THERE IS NO SENTIMENTALITY IN LIFE...

"...NO, SENTIMENTALITY IS FOR THE *LIVING*."

IT WILL NEVER MAKE SENSE TO ME, MESSENGER...

WHAT'S THAT, DIO?

THEIR INCONSOLABLE RUSH TO DEATH.

"I MEAN, BEING ALIVE--IT'S THE *ABSOLUTE* THING THEY CAN BE..."

"YET, THEY TOO OFTEN TAKE IT FOR GRANTED..."

"AND WANTONLY, I MIGHT ADD."

THEY DON'T SAVOR IT.

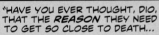

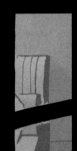
HMM...

"HAVE YOU EVER THOUGHT, DIO, THAT THE *REASON* THEY NEED TO GET SO CLOSE TO DEATH...

"IS TO *FEEL* LIFE?"

"THE MORTALS, I MEAN."

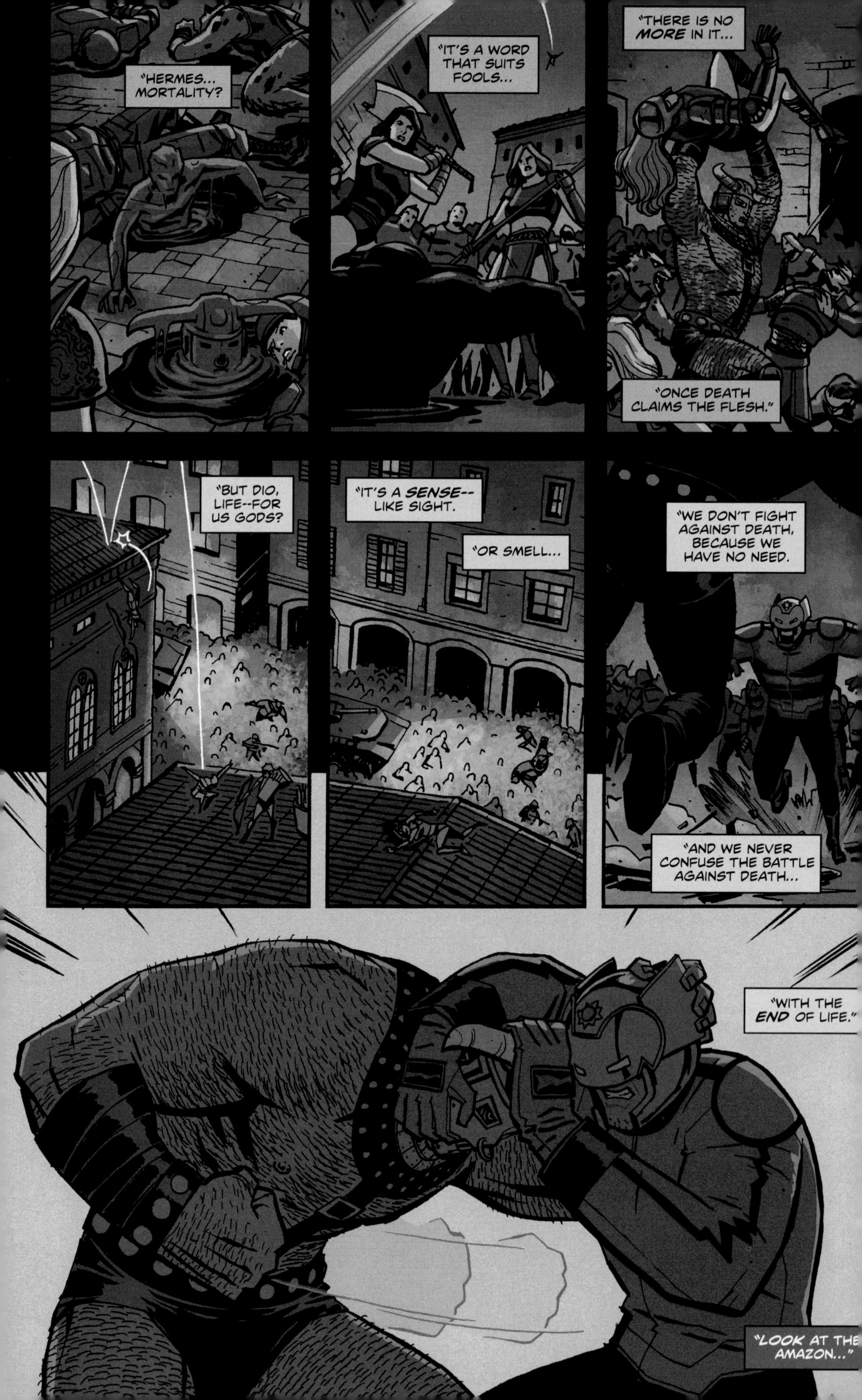
"HERMES... MORTALITY?
"IT'S A WORD THAT SUITS FOOLS...
"THERE IS NO MORE IN IT...
"ONCE DEATH CLAIMS THE FLESH."
"BUT DIO, LIFE--FOR US GODS?
"IT'S A SENSE-- LIKE SIGHT.
"OR SMELL...
"WE DON'T FIGHT AGAINST DEATH, BECAUSE WE HAVE NO NEED.
"AND WE NEVER CONFUSE THE BATTLE AGAINST DEATH...
"WITH THE END OF LIFE."
"LOOK AT THE AMAZON..."

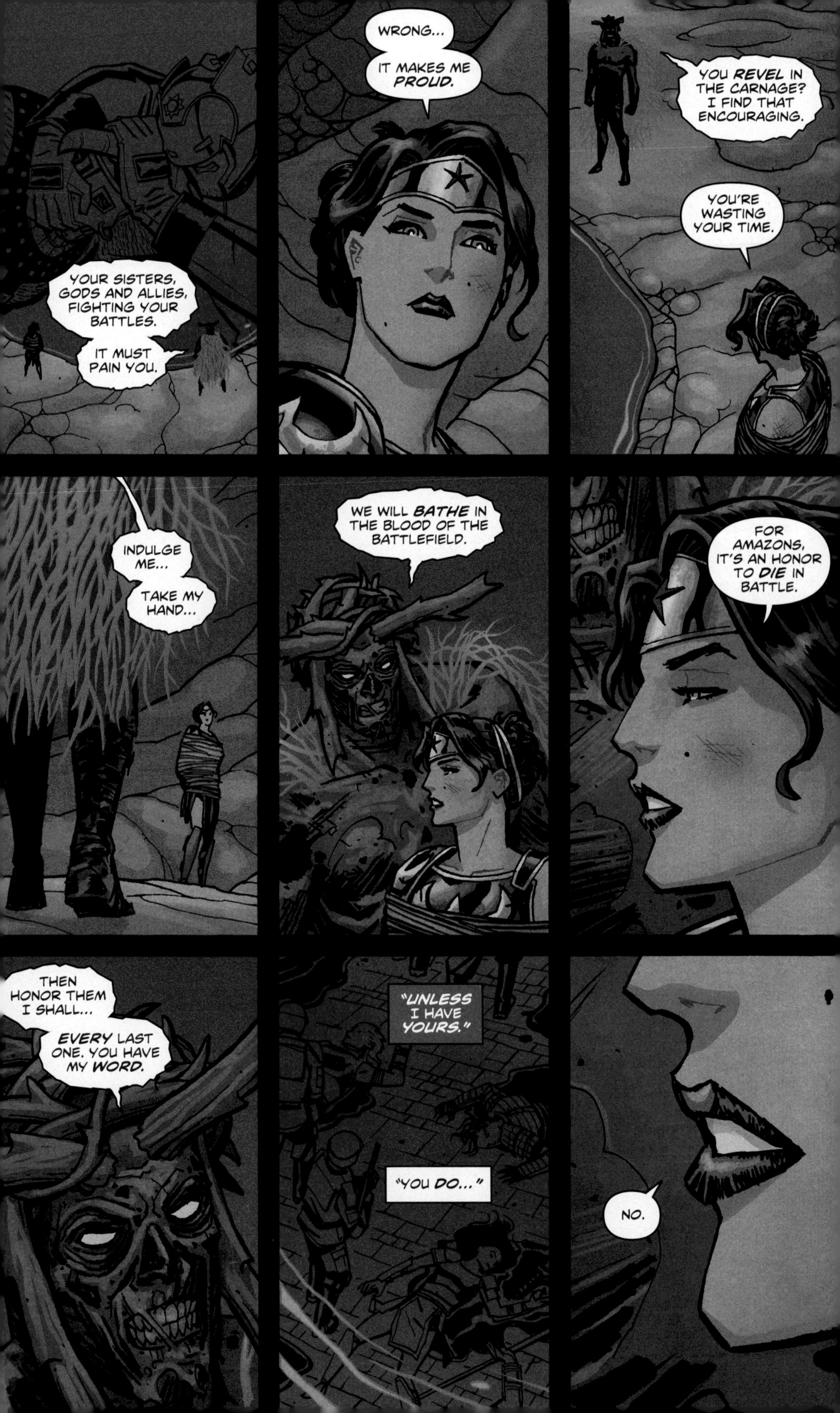
YOUR SISTERS, GODS AND ALLIES, FIGHTING YOUR BATTLES.
IT MUST PAIN YOU.
WRONG...
IT MAKES ME PROUD.
YOU REVEL IN THE CARNAGE? I FIND THAT ENCOURAGING.
YOU'RE WASTING YOUR TIME.
INDULGE ME...
TAKE MY HAND...
WE WILL BATHE IN THE BLOOD OF THE BATTLEFIELD.
FOR AMAZONS, IT'S AN HONOR TO DIE IN BATTLE.
THEN HONOR THEM I SHALL...
EVERY LAST ONE. YOU HAVE MY WORD.
"UNLESS I HAVE YOURS."
"YOU DO..."
NO.

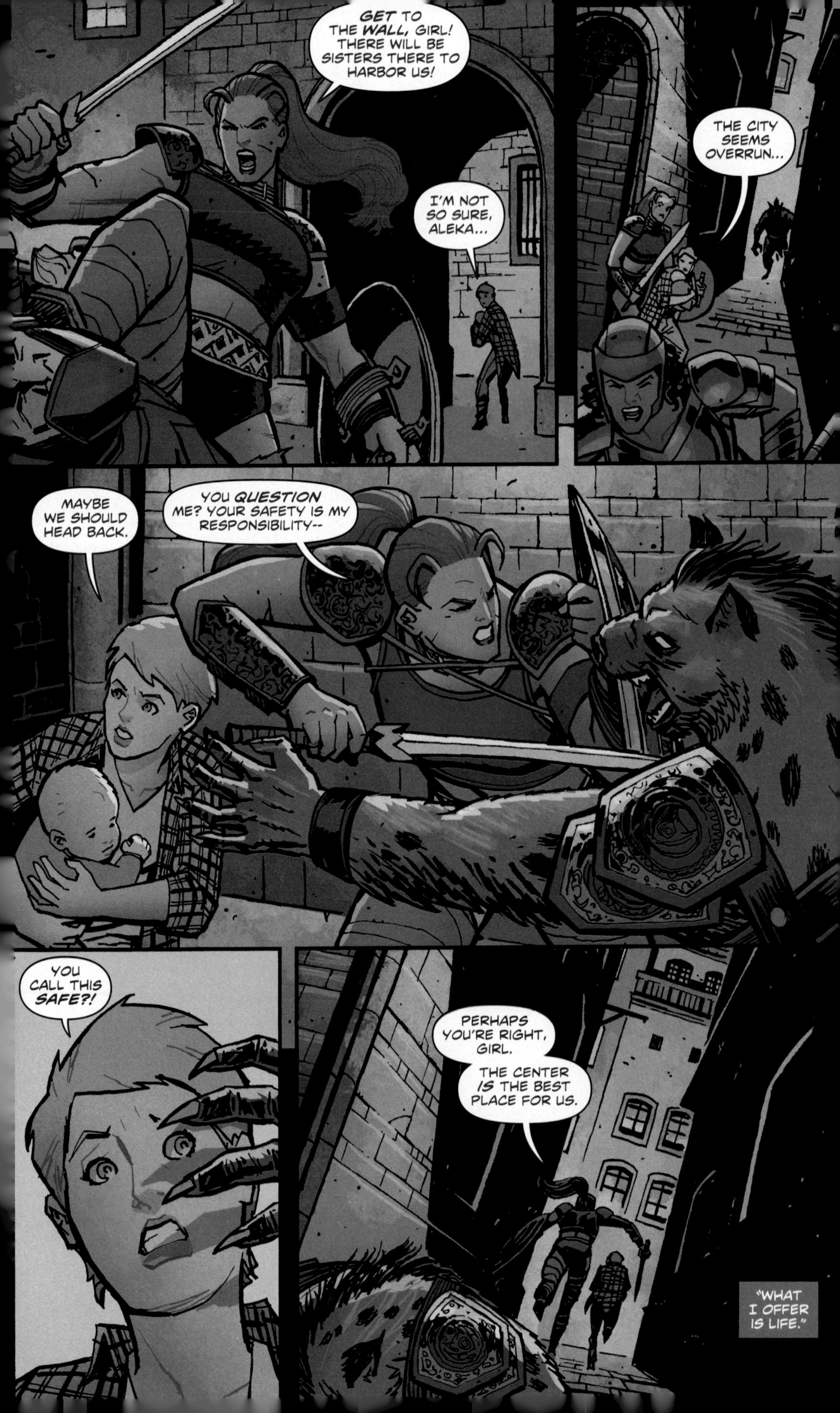
GET TO THE WALL, GIRL! THERE WILL BE SISTERS THERE TO HARBOR US!
I'M NOT SO SURE, ALEKA...
THE CITY SEEMS OVERRUN...
MAYBE WE SHOULD HEAD BACK.
YOU QUESTION ME? YOUR SAFETY IS MY RESPONSIBILITY--
YOU CALL THIS SAFE?!
PERHAPS YOU'RE RIGHT, GIRL.
THE CENTER IS THE BEST PLACE FOR US.
"WHAT I OFFER IS LIFE."

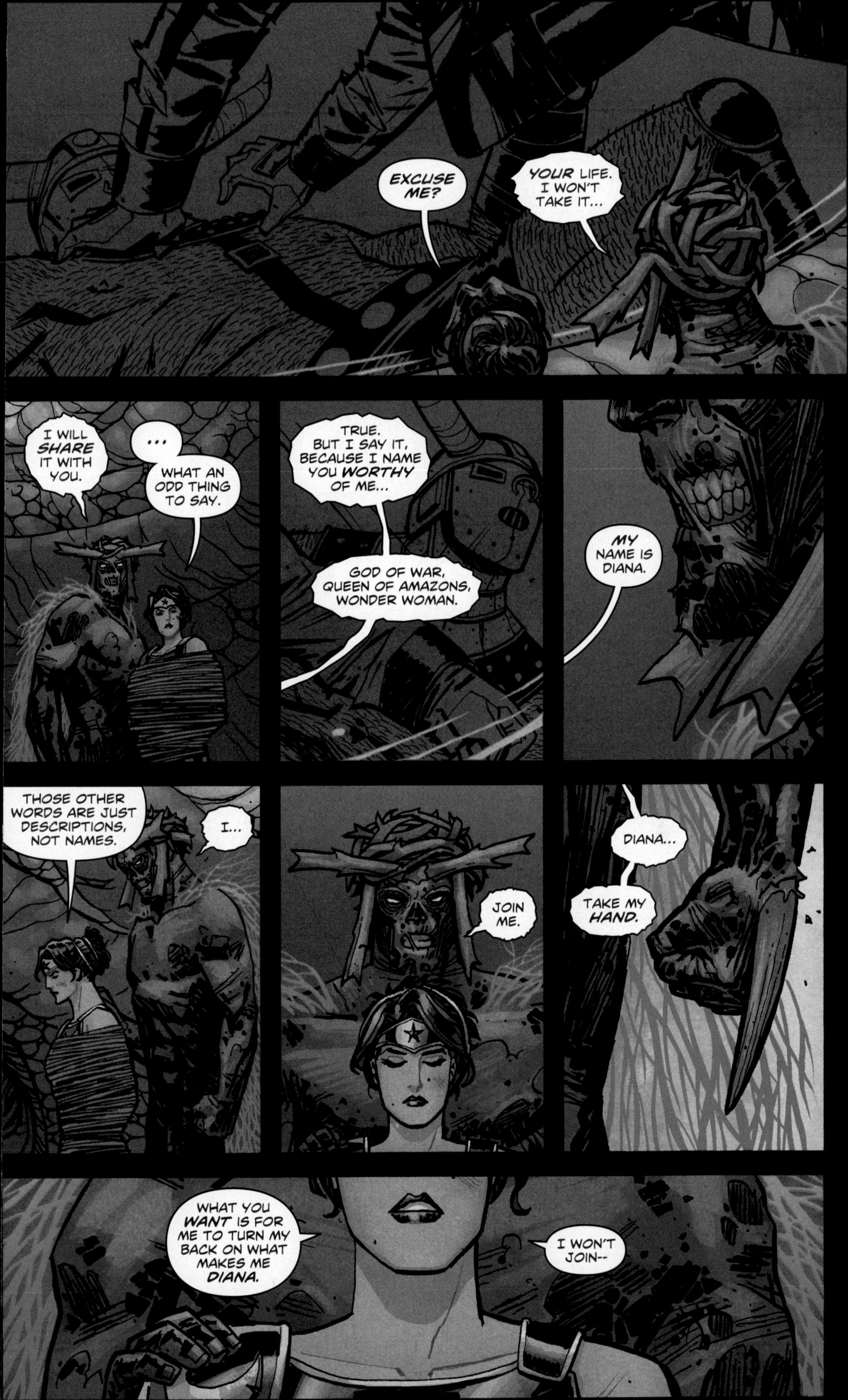
EXCUSE ME?
YOUR LIFE. I WON'T TAKE IT...
I WILL SHARE IT WITH YOU.
...
WHAT AN ODD THING TO SAY.
TRUE. BUT I SAY IT, BECAUSE I NAME YOU WORTHY OF ME...
GOD OF WAR, QUEEN OF AMAZONS, WONDER WOMAN.
MY NAME IS DIANA.
THOSE OTHER WORDS ARE JUST DESCRIPTIONS, NOT NAMES.
I...
JOIN ME.
DIANA...
TAKE MY HAND.
WHAT YOU WANT IS FOR ME TO TURN MY BACK ON WHAT MAKES ME DIANA.
I WON'T JOIN--

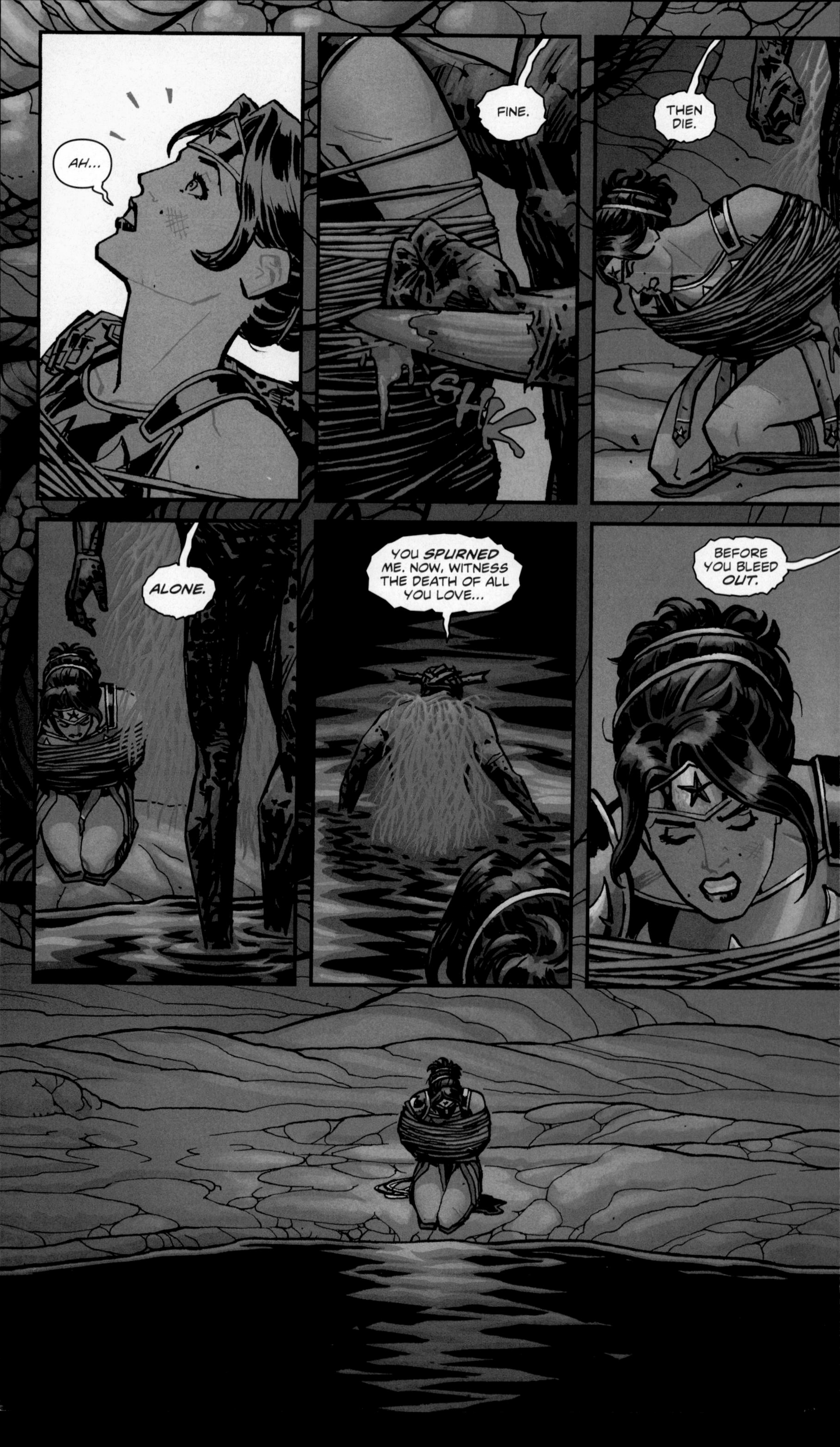
AH...
FINE.
SHK
THEN DIE.
ALONE.
YOU SPURNED ME. NOW, WITNESS THE DEATH OF ALL YOU LOVE...
BEFORE YOU BLEED OUT.

=HUFF=

ENOUGH... OF THIS...

BEAST, *TELL* THE DEVIL THAT SPAWNED YOU...

...THE NAME OF THE GOD THAT *SLEW* YOU...

I AM ORI--

SHK

...

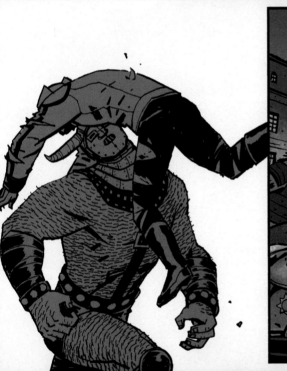

KILL THEM ALL.

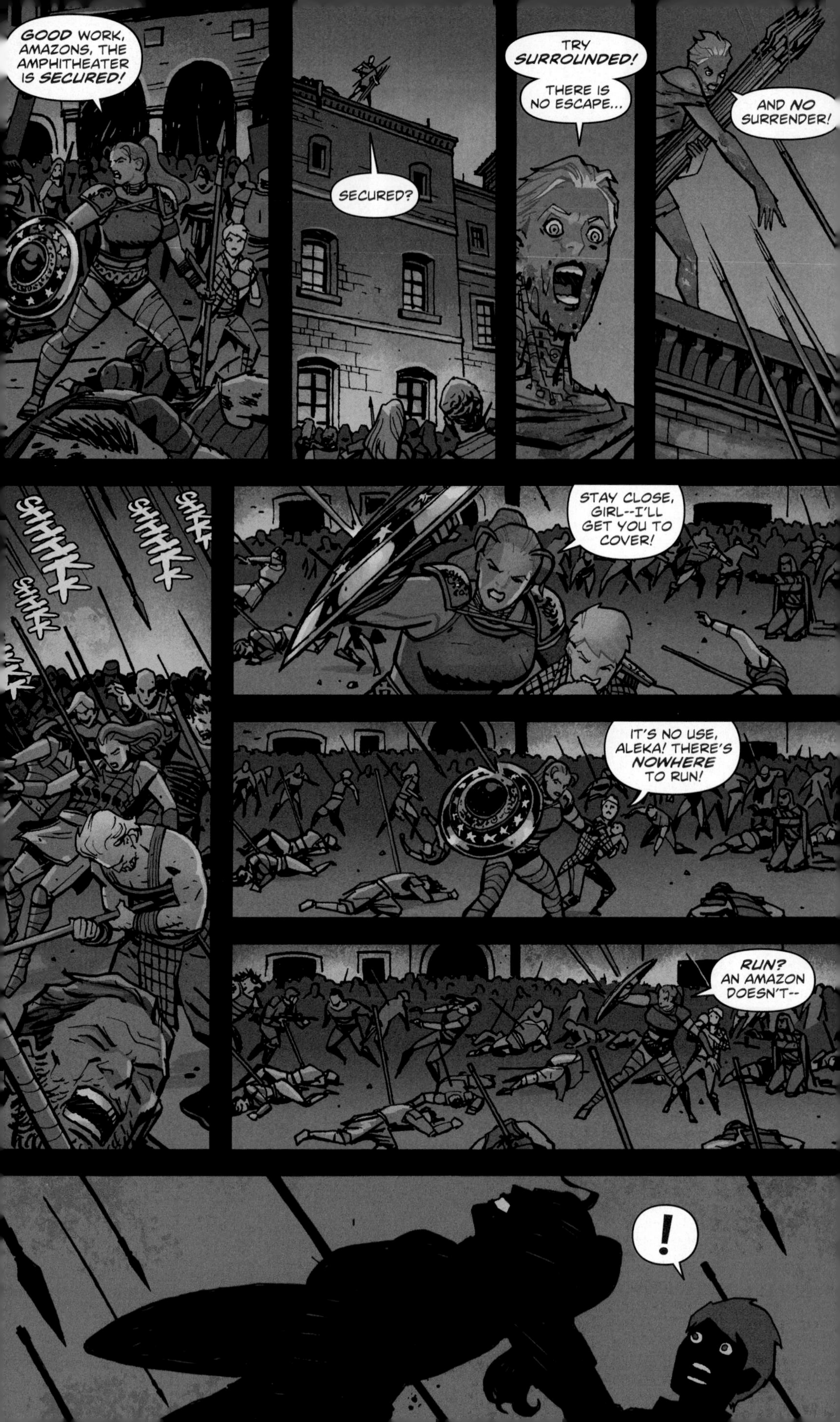
GOOD WORK, AMAZONS, THE AMPHITHEATER IS SECURED!
SECURED?
TRY SURROUNDED!
THERE IS NO ESCAPE...
AND NO SURRENDER!
SHHHKK
SHHHKK
SHHK
SHHHK
STAY CLOSE, GIRL--I'LL GET YOU TO COVER!
IT'S NO USE, ALEKA! THERE'S NOWHERE TO RUN!
RUN? AN AMAZON DOESN'T--
!

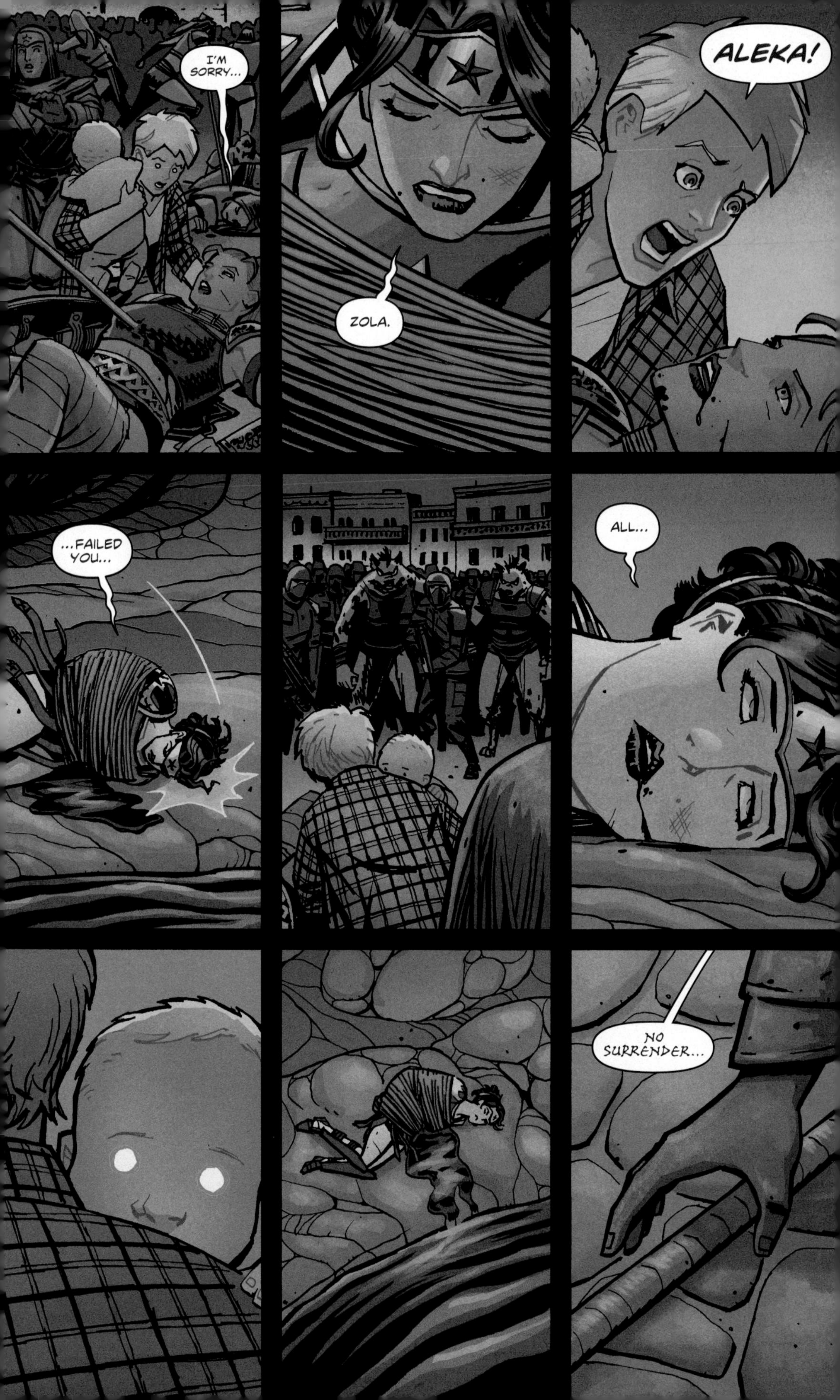
I'M SORRY...
ZOLA.
ALEKA!
...FAILED YOU...
ALL...
NO SURRENDER...

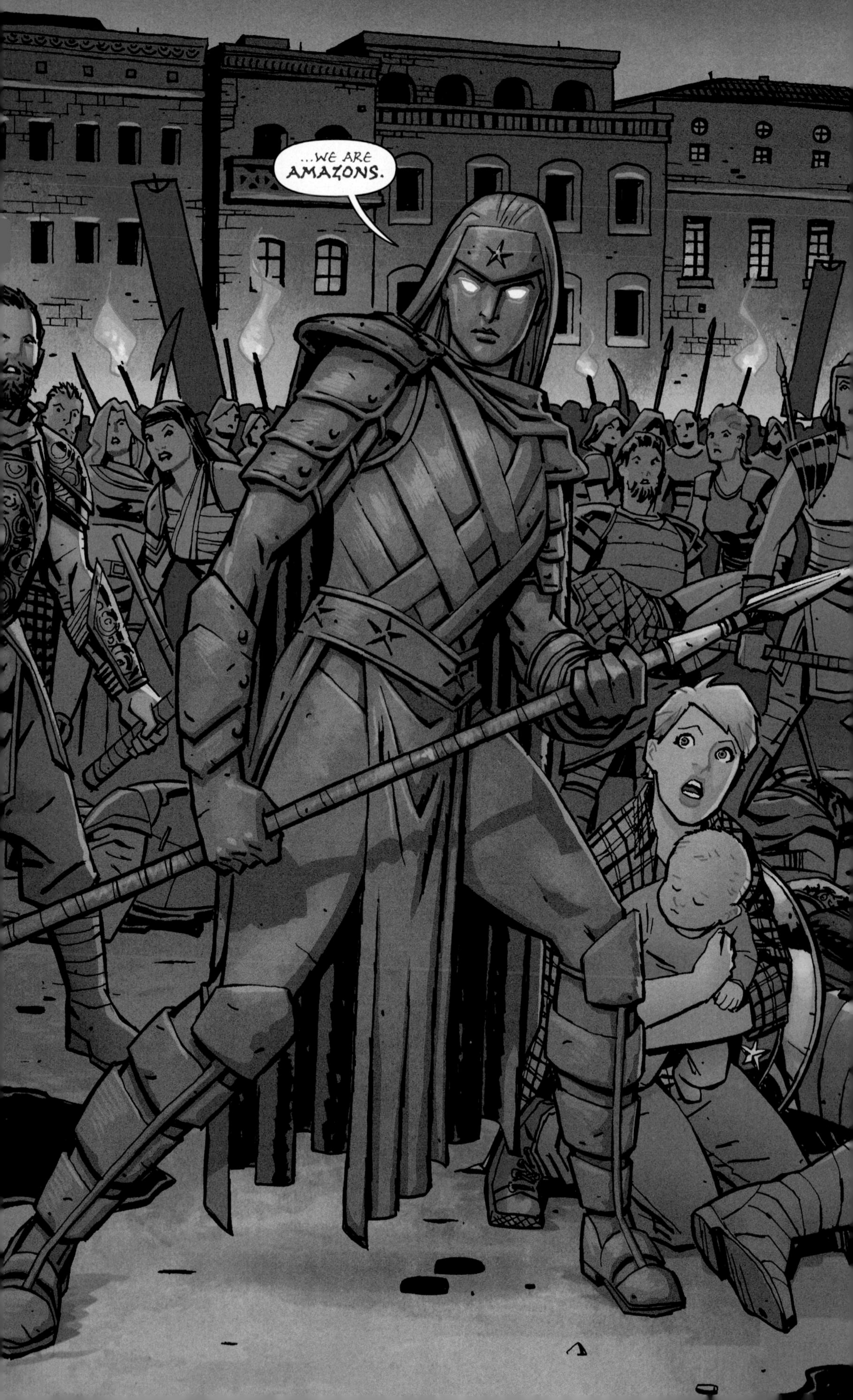
...WE ARE AMAZONS.

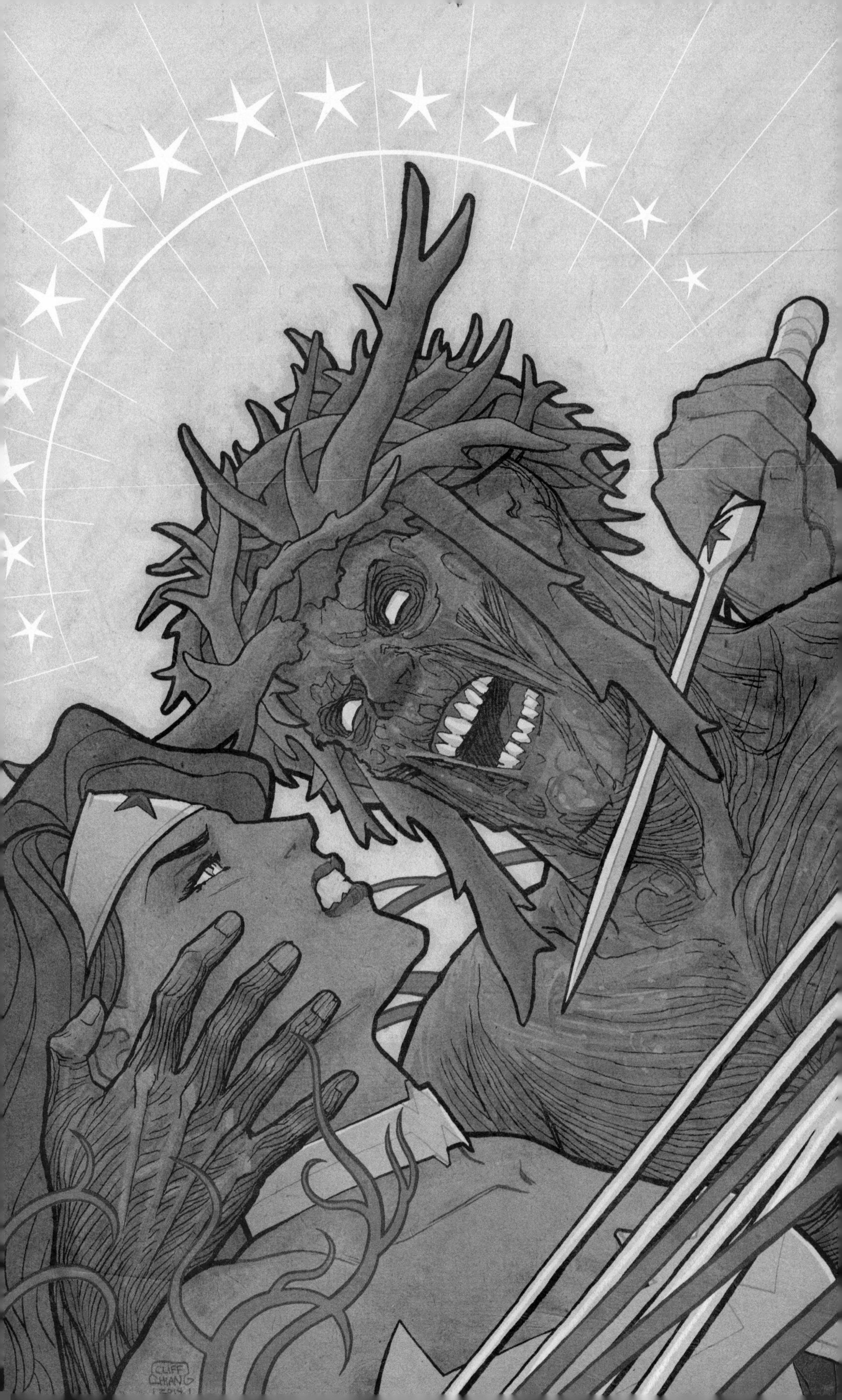
CLIFF CHIANG
2014

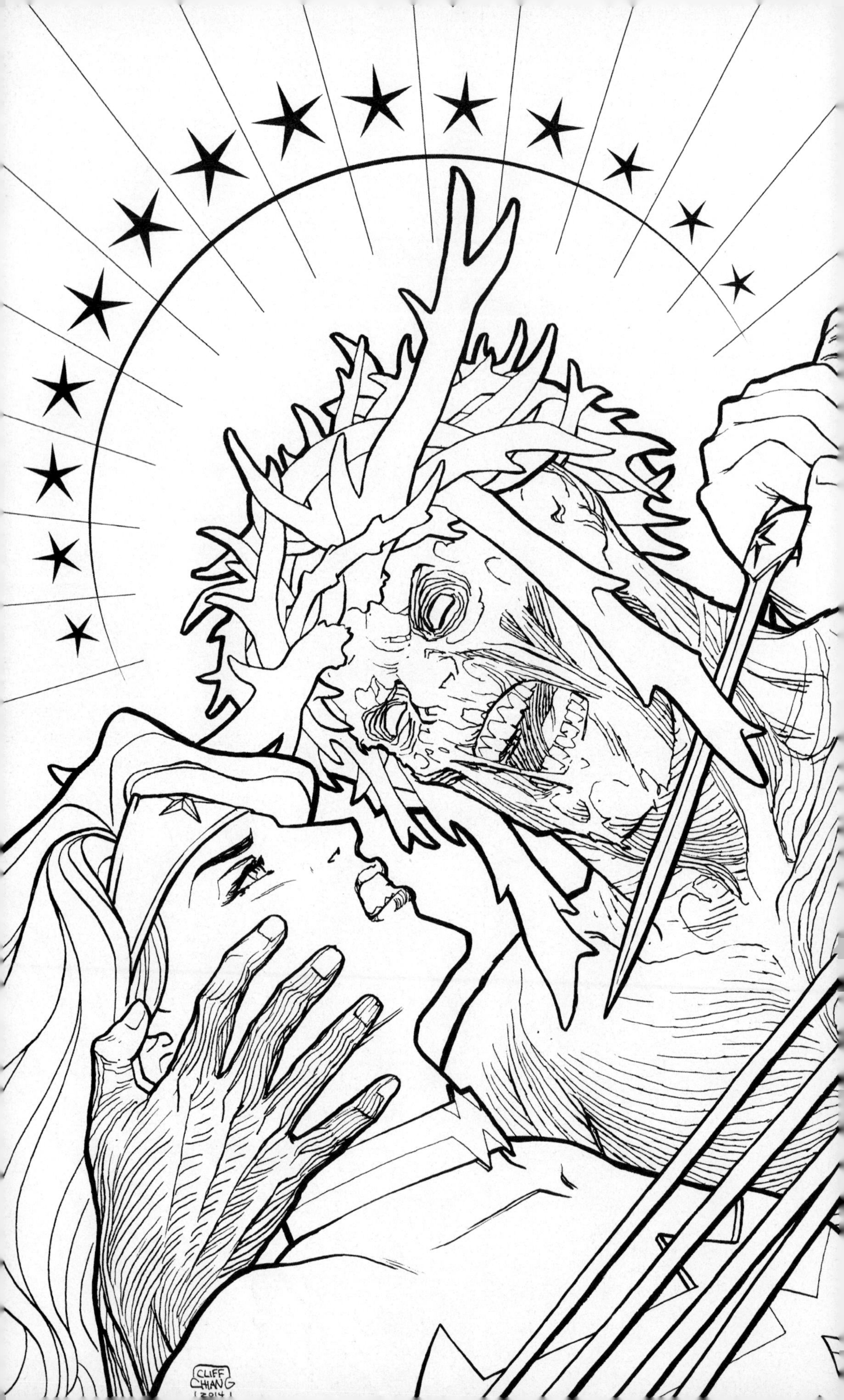
CLIFF CHIANG
2014

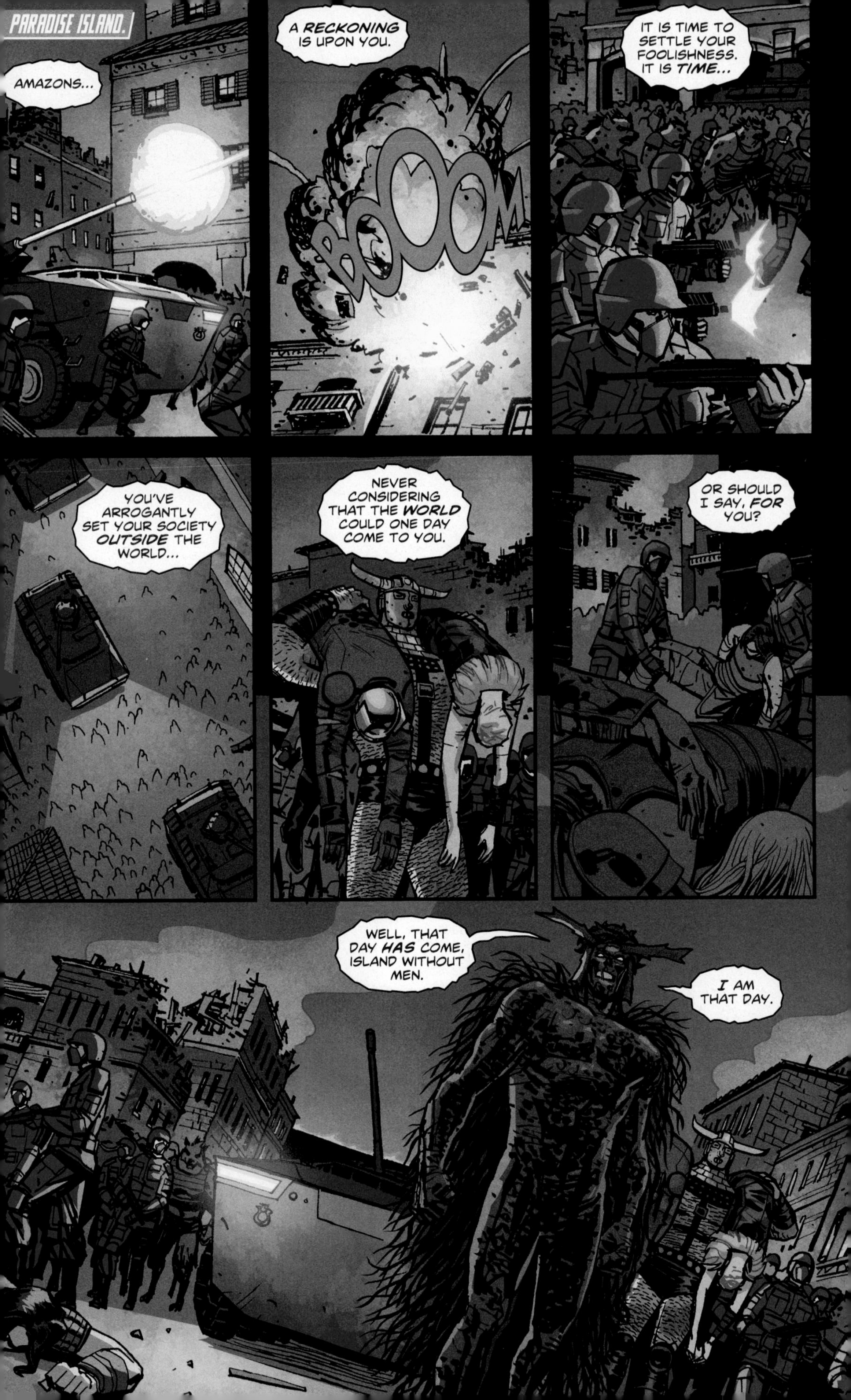
PARADISE ISLAND.
AMAZONS...
A RECKONING IS UPON YOU.
BOOOOM
IT IS TIME TO SETTLE YOUR FOOLISHNESS. IT IS TIME...
YOU'VE ARROGANTLY SET YOUR SOCIETY OUTSIDE THE WORLD...
NEVER CONSIDERING THAT THE WORLD COULD ONE DAY COME TO YOU.
OR SHOULD I SAY, FOR YOU?
WELL, THAT DAY HAS COME, ISLAND WITHOUT MEN.
I AM THAT DAY.

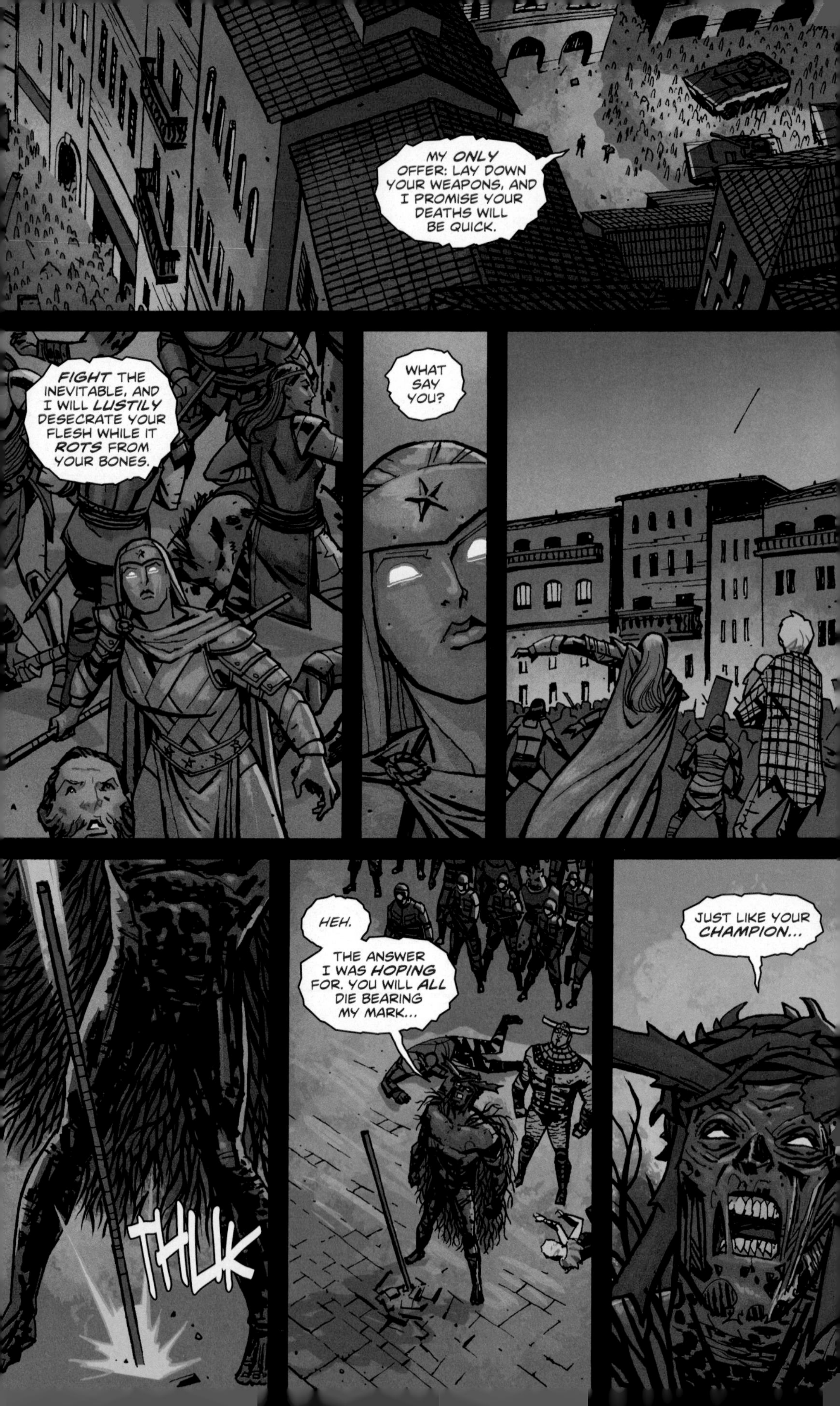
MY ONLY OFFER: LAY DOWN YOUR WEAPONS, AND I PROMISE YOUR DEATHS WILL BE QUICK.
FIGHT THE INEVITABLE, AND I WILL LUSTILY DESECRATE YOUR FLESH WHILE IT ROTS FROM YOUR BONES.
WHAT SAY YOU?
THUK
HEH.
THE ANSWER I WAS HOPING FOR. YOU WILL ALL DIE BEARING MY MARK...
JUST LIKE YOUR CHAMPION...

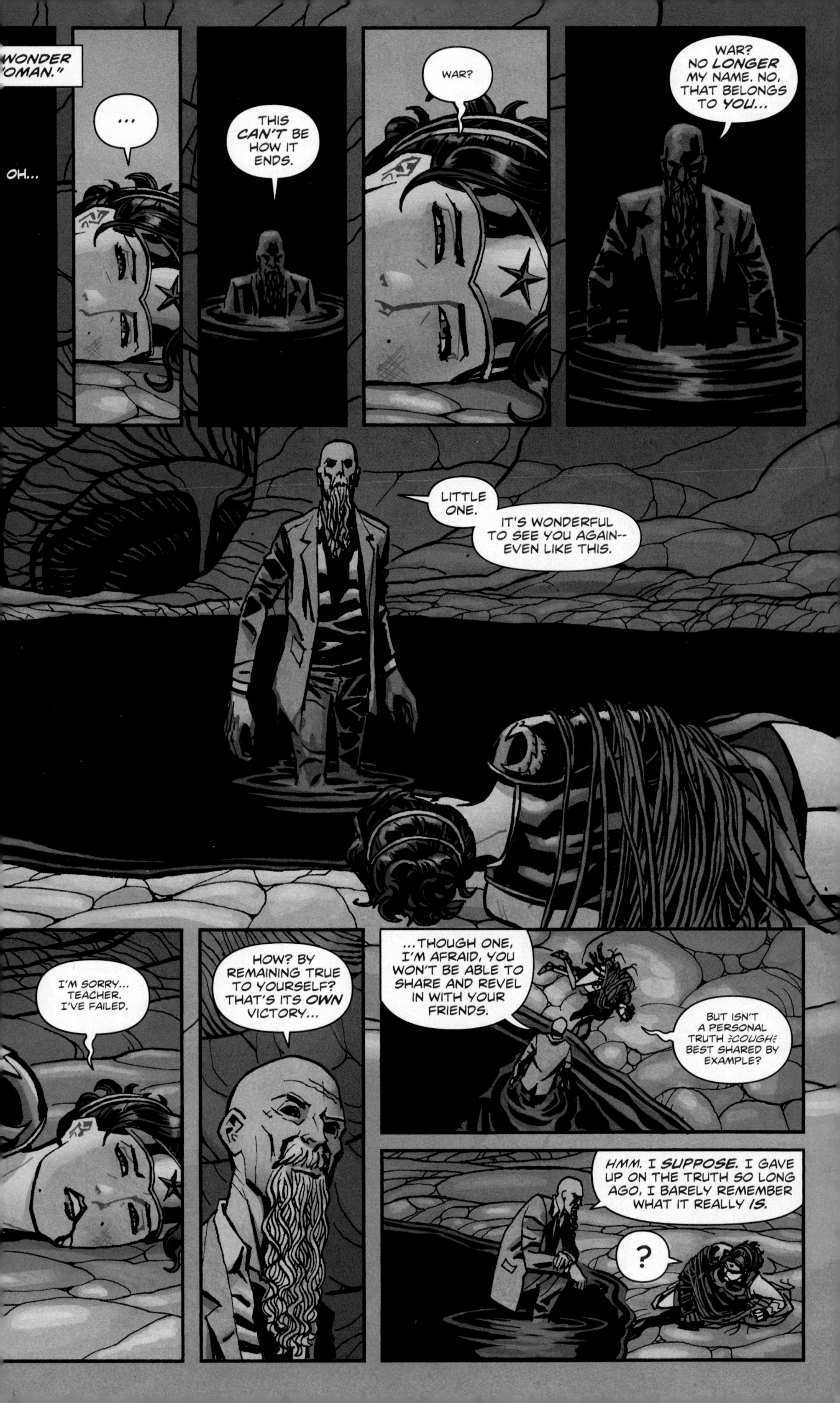

WONDER WOMAN."
OH...
...
THIS CAN'T BE HOW IT ENDS.
WAR?
WAR? NO LONGER MY NAME. NO, THAT BELONGS TO YOU...
LITTLE ONE.
IT'S WONDERFUL TO SEE YOU AGAIN-- EVEN LIKE THIS.
I'M SORRY... TEACHER. I'VE FAILED.
HOW? BY REMAINING TRUE TO YOURSELF? THAT'S ITS OWN VICTORY...
...THOUGH ONE, I'M AFRAID, YOU WON'T BE ABLE TO SHARE AND REVEL IN WITH YOUR FRIENDS.
BUT ISN'T A PERSONAL TRUTH ≈COUGH≈ BEST SHARED BY EXAMPLE?
HMM. I SUPPOSE. I GAVE UP ON THE TRUTH SO LONG AGO, I BARELY REMEMBER WHAT IT REALLY IS.
?

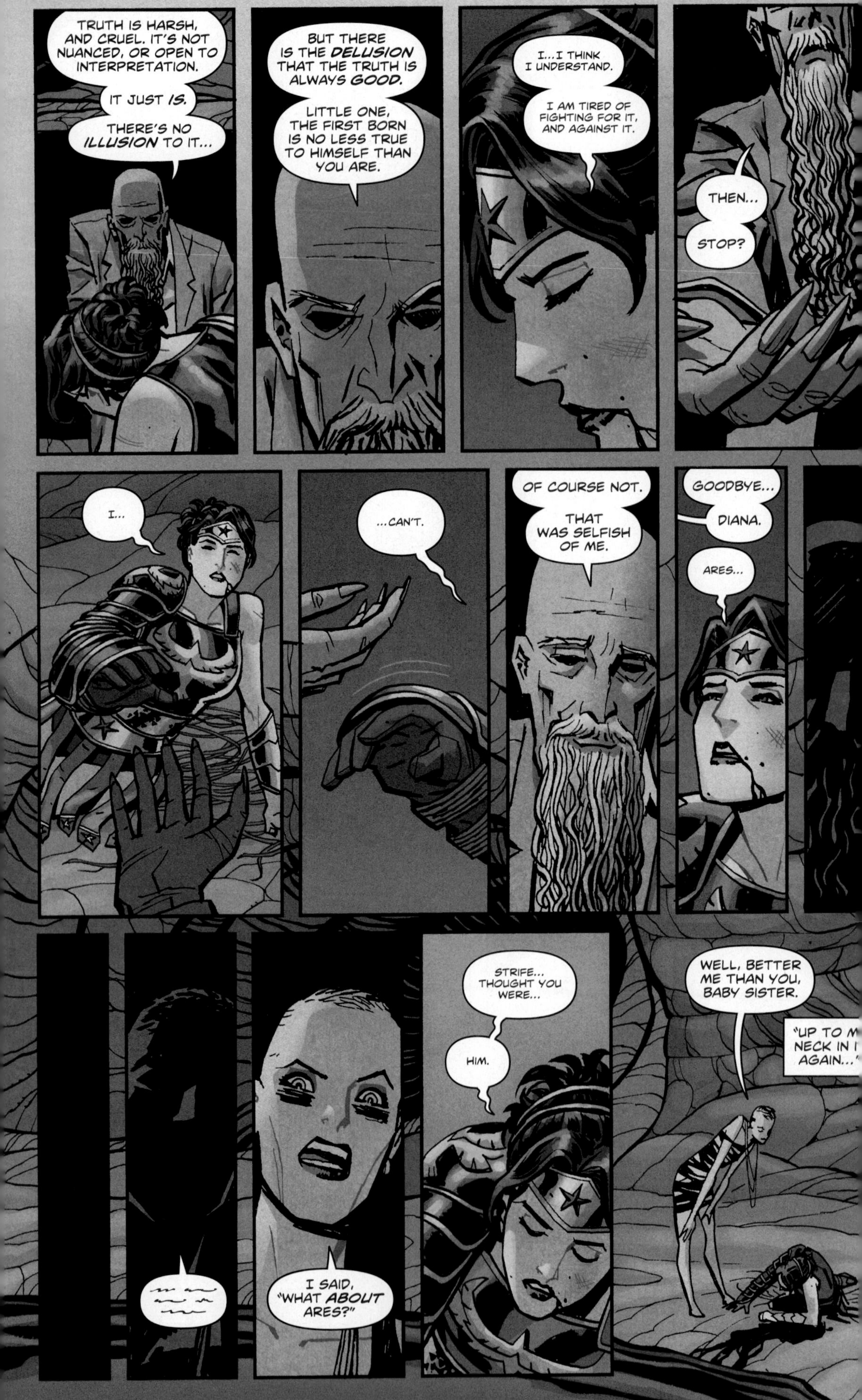
TRUTH IS HARSH, AND CRUEL. IT'S NOT NUANCED, OR OPEN TO INTERPRETATION.
IT JUST *IS.*
THERE'S NO *ILLUSION* TO IT...
BUT THERE IS THE *DELUSION* THAT THE TRUTH IS ALWAYS *GOOD.*
LITTLE ONE, THE FIRST BORN IS NO LESS TRUE TO HIMSELF THAN YOU ARE.
I...I THINK I UNDERSTAND.
I AM TIRED OF FIGHTING FOR IT, AND AGAINST IT.
THEN...
STOP?
I...
...CAN'T.
OF COURSE NOT.
THAT WAS SELFISH OF ME.
GOODBYE...
DIANA.
ARES...
I SAID, "WHAT *ABOUT* ARES?"
STRIFE... THOUGHT YOU WERE...
HIM.
WELL, BETTER ME THAN YOU, BABY SISTER.
"UP TO M NECK IN I AGAIN..."

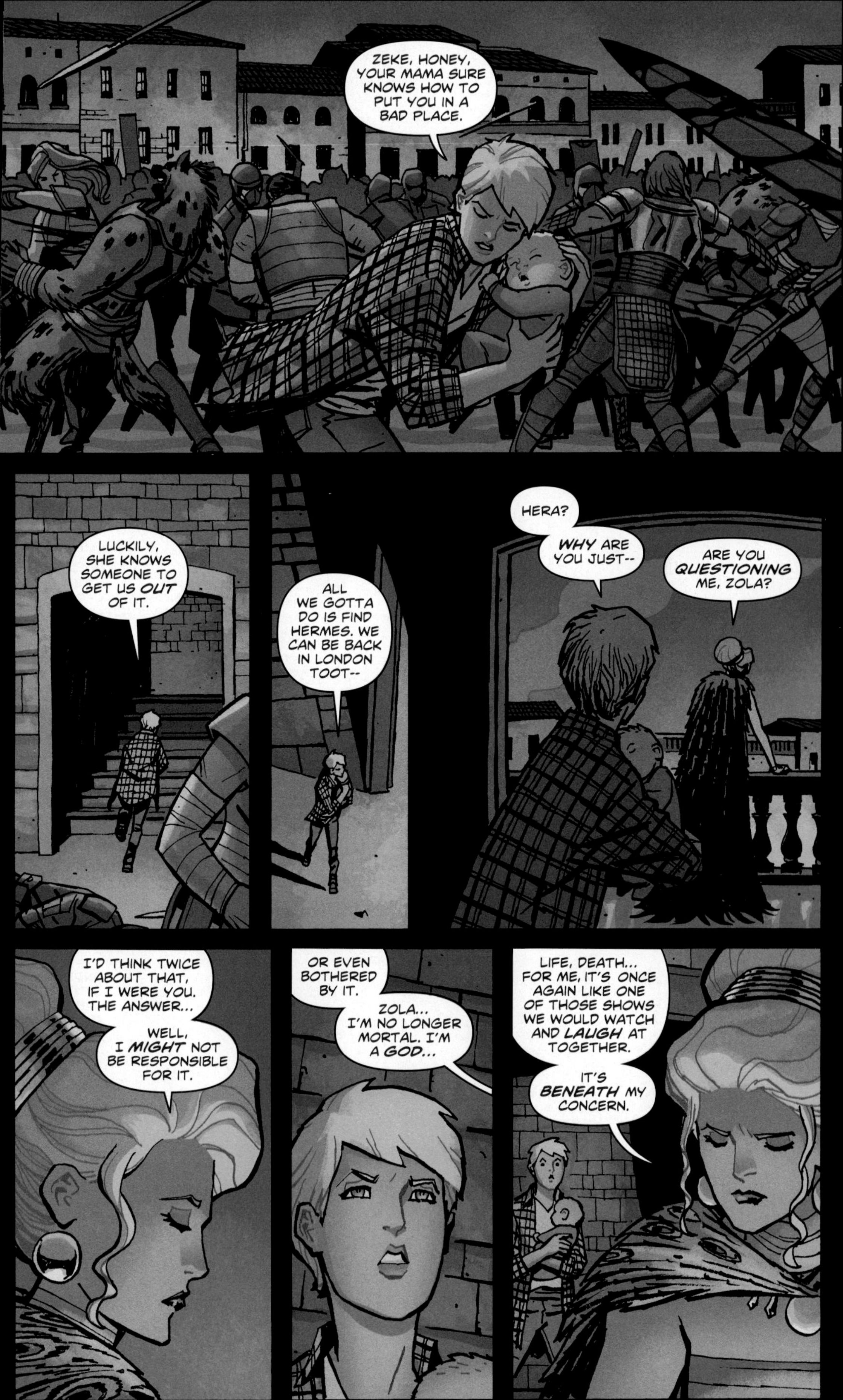
ZEKE, HONEY, YOUR MAMA SURE KNOWS HOW TO PUT YOU IN A BAD PLACE.
LUCKILY, SHE KNOWS SOMEONE TO GET US OUT OF IT.
ALL WE GOTTA DO IS FIND HERMES. WE CAN BE BACK IN LONDON TOOT--
HERA?
WHY ARE YOU JUST--
ARE YOU QUESTIONING ME, ZOLA?
I'D THINK TWICE ABOUT THAT, IF I WERE YOU. THE ANSWER...
WELL, I MIGHT NOT BE RESPONSIBLE FOR IT.
OR EVEN BOTHERED BY IT.
ZOLA... I'M NO LONGER MORTAL. I'M A GOD...
LIFE, DEATH... FOR ME, IT'S ONCE AGAIN LIKE ONE OF THOSE SHOWS WE WOULD WATCH AND LAUGH AT TOGETHER.
IT'S BENEATH MY CONCERN.

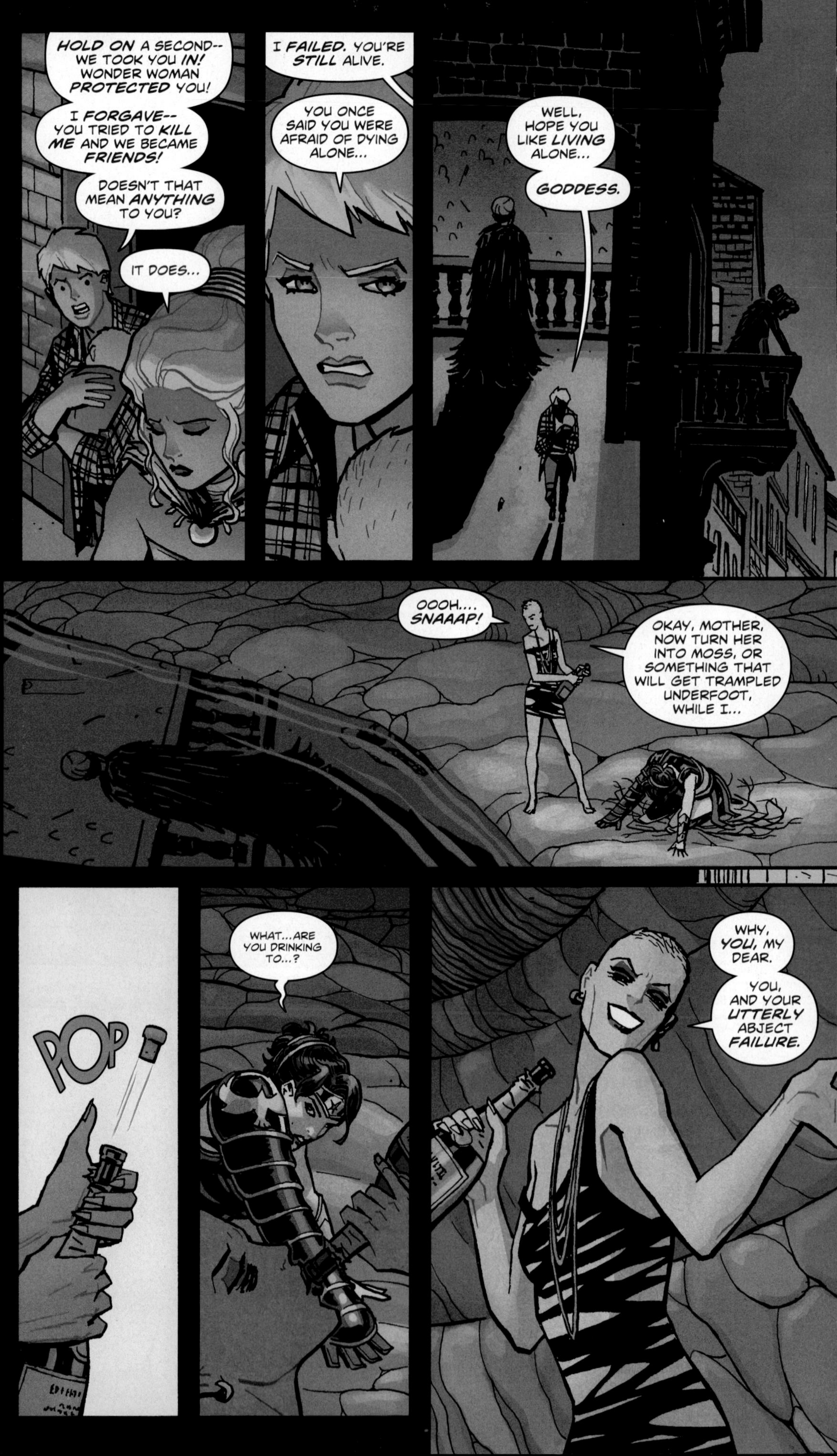
HOLD ON A SECOND-- WE TOOK YOU IN! WONDER WOMAN PROTECTED YOU!
I FORGAVE-- YOU TRIED TO KILL ME AND WE BECAME FRIENDS!
DOESN'T THAT MEAN ANYTHING TO YOU?
IT DOES...
I FAILED. YOU'RE STILL ALIVE.
YOU ONCE SAID YOU WERE AFRAID OF DYING ALONE...
WELL, HOPE YOU LIKE LIVING ALONE...
GODDESS.
OOOH.... SNAAAP!
OKAY, MOTHER, NOW TURN HER INTO MOSS, OR SOMETHING THAT WILL GET TRAMPLED UNDERFOOT, WHILE I...
POP
WHAT...ARE YOU DRINKING TO...?
WHY, YOU, MY DEAR.
YOU, AND YOUR UTTERLY ABJECT FAILURE.

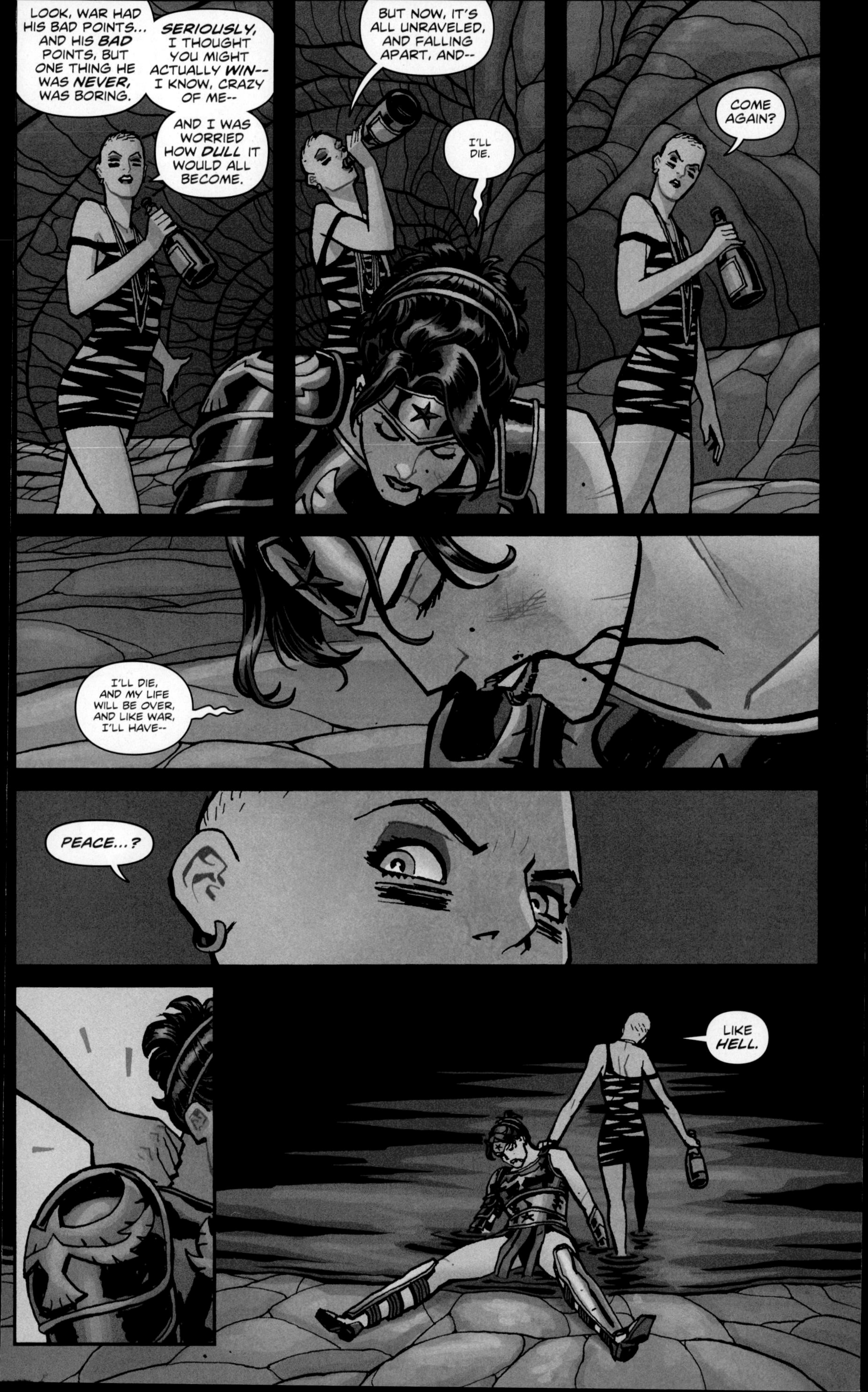
LOOK, WAR HAD HIS BAD POINTS... AND HIS *BAD* POINTS, BUT ONE THING HE WAS *NEVER*, WAS BORING.
SERIOUSLY, I THOUGHT YOU MIGHT ACTUALLY *WIN*-- I KNOW, CRAZY OF ME--
AND I WAS WORRIED HOW *DULL* IT WOULD ALL BECOME.
BUT NOW, IT'S ALL UNRAVELED, AND FALLING APART, AND--
I'LL DIE.
COME AGAIN?
I'LL DIE, AND MY LIFE WILL BE OVER, AND LIKE WAR, I'LL HAVE--
PEACE...?
LIKE *HELL.*

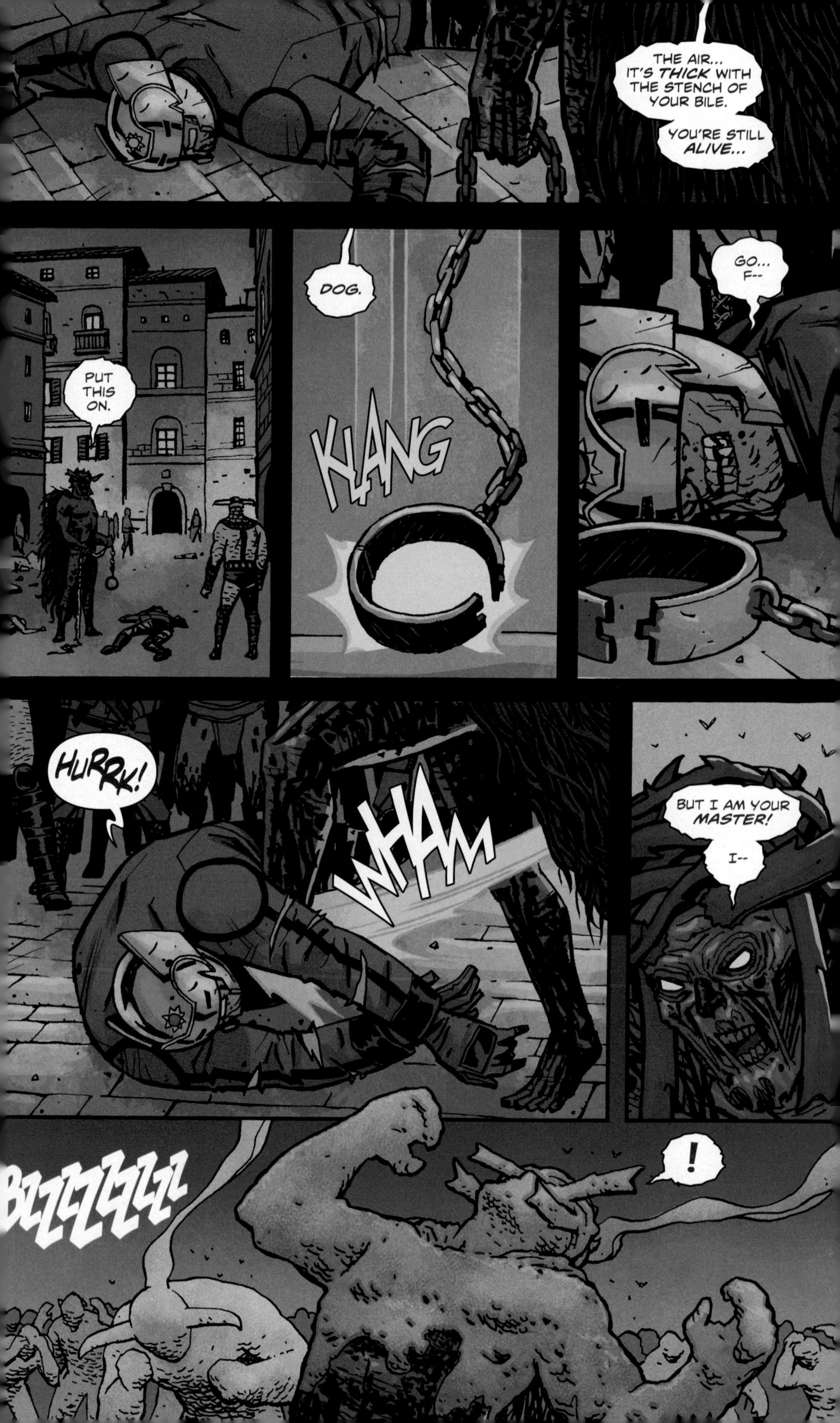
THE AIR... IT'S THICK WITH THE STENCH OF YOUR BILE.
YOU'RE STILL ALIVE...
PUT THIS ON.
DOG.
KLANG
GO... F--
HURRK!
WHAM
BUT I AM YOUR MASTER!
I--
BZZZZZZZZ
!

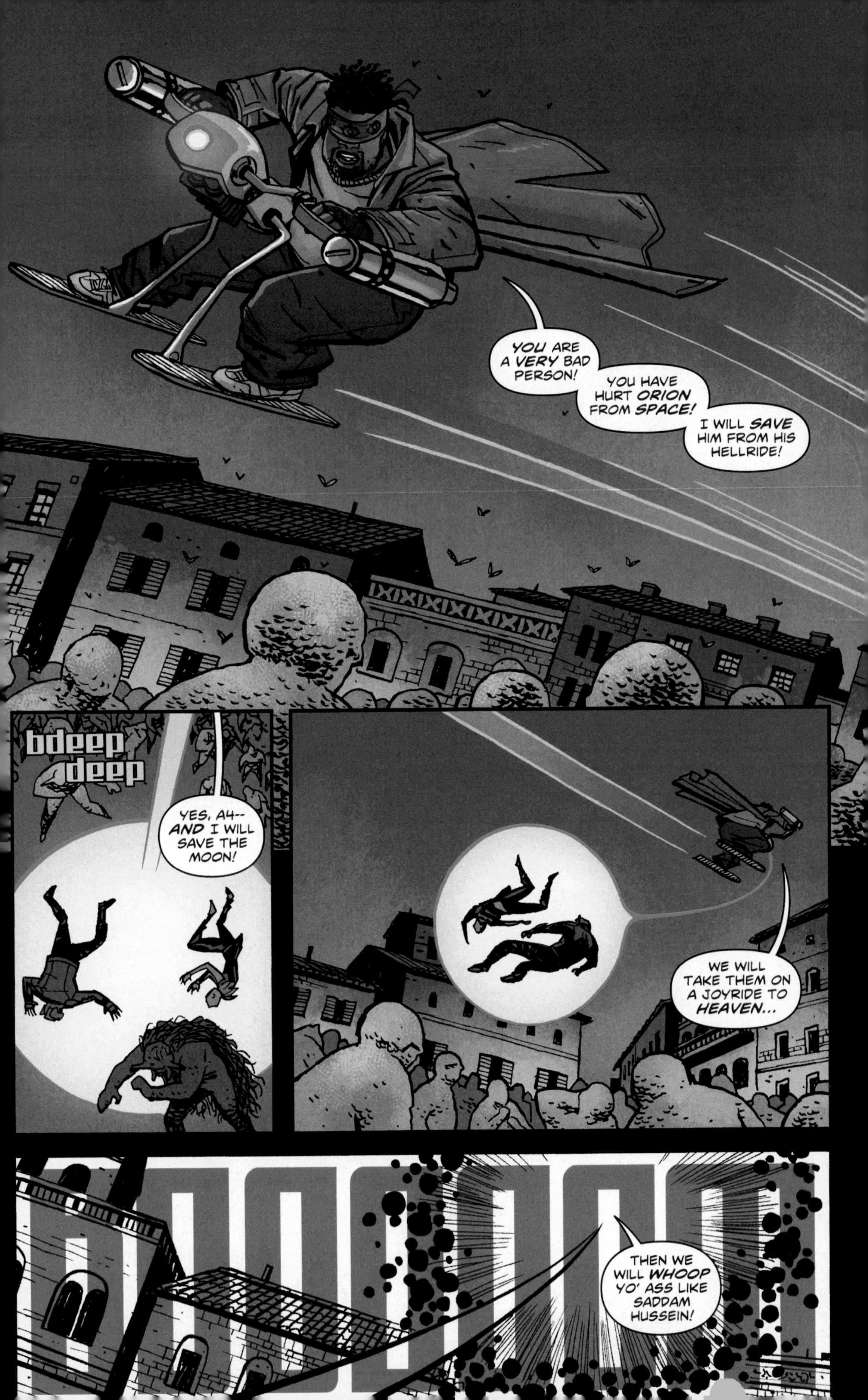
YOU ARE A VERY BAD PERSON!
YOU HAVE HURT ORION FROM SPACE!
I WILL SAVE HIM FROM HIS HELLRIDE!
bdeep deep
YES, A4-- AND I WILL SAVE THE MOON!
WE WILL TAKE THEM ON A JOYRIDE TO HEAVEN...
THEN WE WILL WHOOP YO' ASS LIKE SADDAM HUSSEIN!

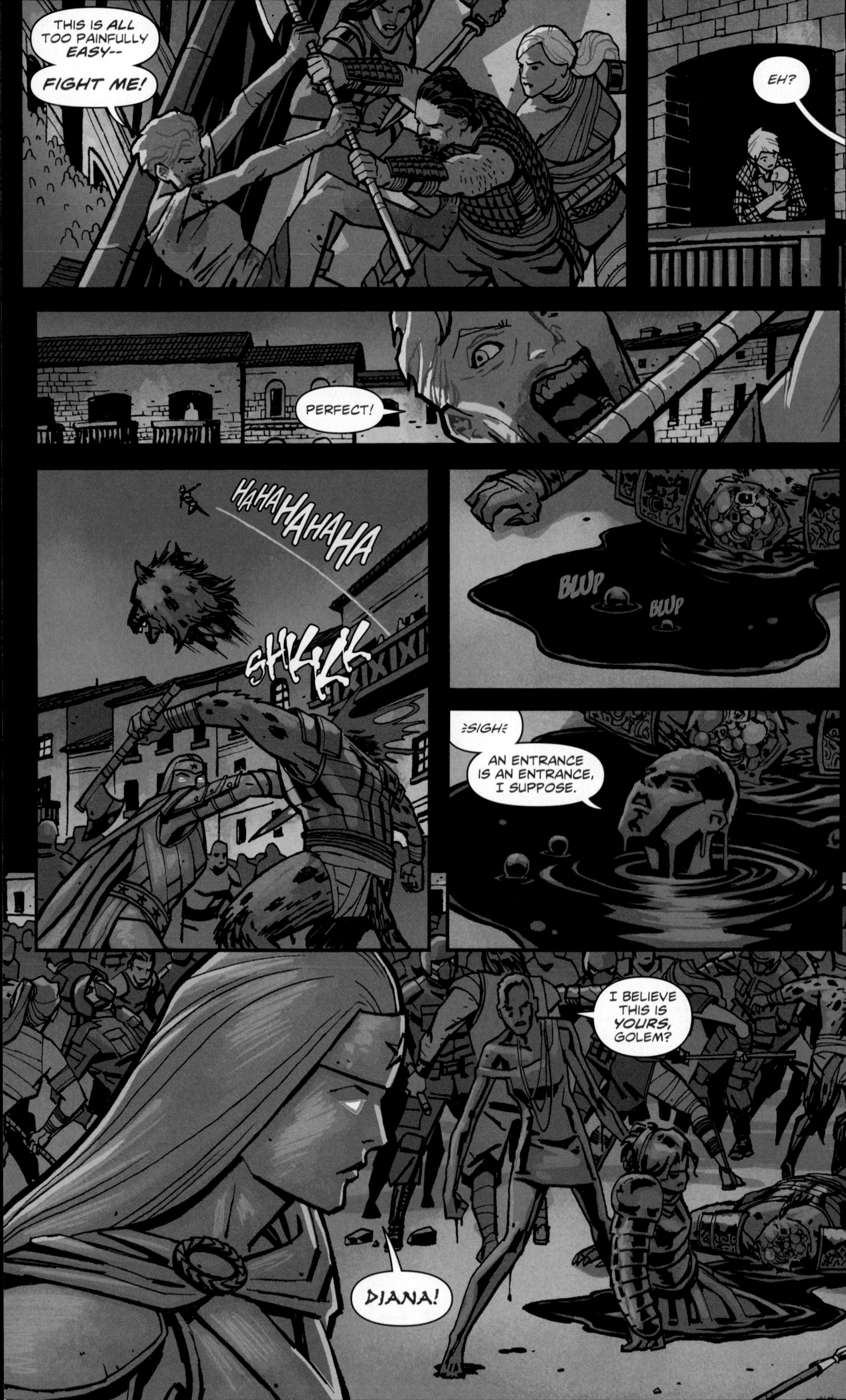
THIS IS ALL TOO PAINFULLY EASY--
FIGHT ME!
EH?
PERFECT!
HAHAHAHAHAHA
SHLLK
BLUP
BLUP
SIGH
AN ENTRANCE IS AN ENTRANCE, I SUPPOSE.
I BELIEVE THIS IS YOURS, GOLEM?
DIANA!

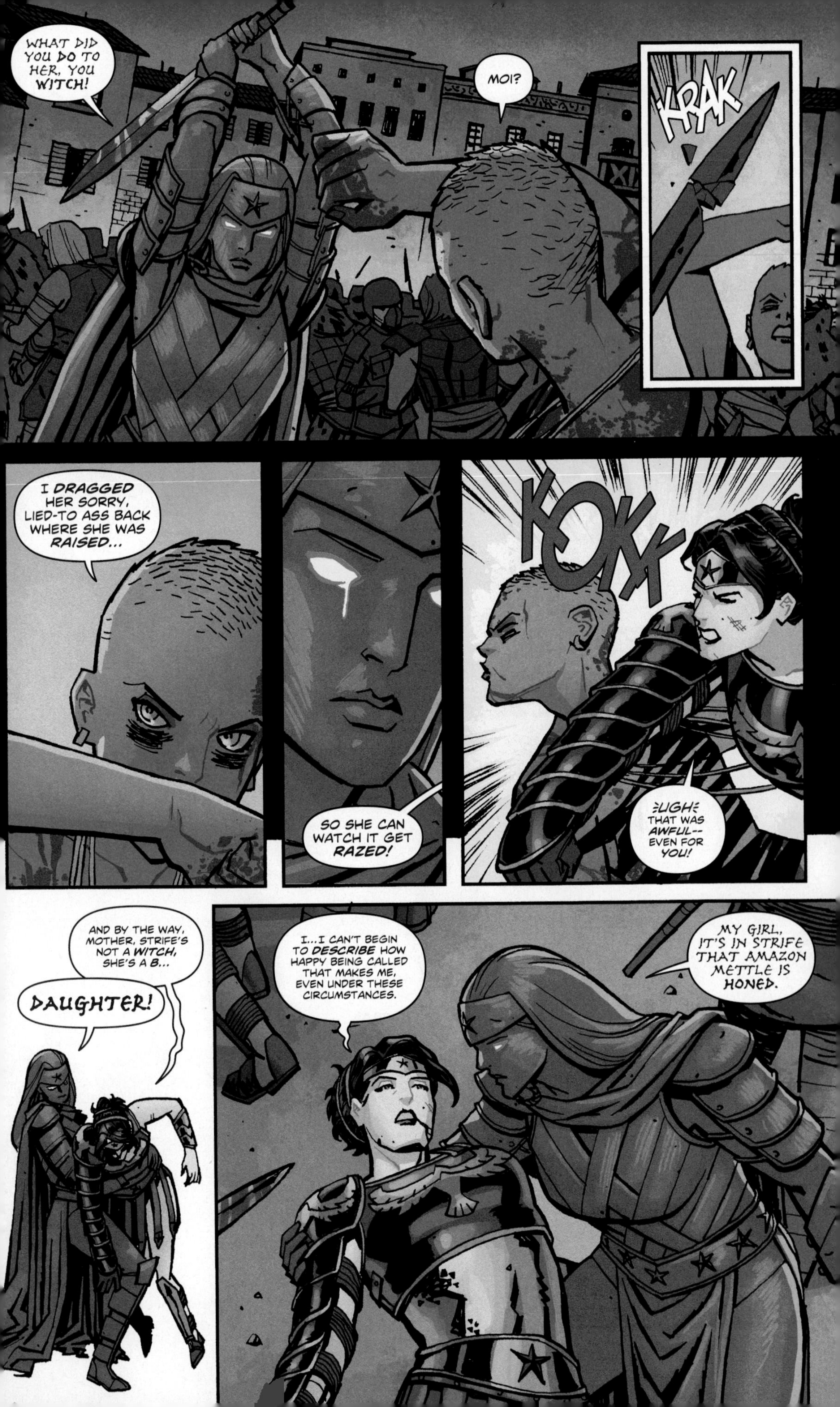
WHAT DID YOU DO TO HER, YOU WITCH!
MOI?
KRAK
I DRAGGED HER SORRY, LIED-TO ASS BACK WHERE SHE WAS RAISED...
SO SHE CAN WATCH IT GET RAZED!
KOKK
UGH THAT WAS AWFUL-- EVEN FOR YOU!
AND BY THE WAY, MOTHER, STRIFE'S NOT A WITCH, SHE'S A B...
DAUGHTER!
I...I CAN'T BEGIN TO DESCRIBE HOW HAPPY BEING CALLED THAT MAKES ME, EVEN UNDER THESE CIRCUMSTANCES.
MY GIRL, IT'S IN STRIFE THAT AMAZON METTLE IS HONED.

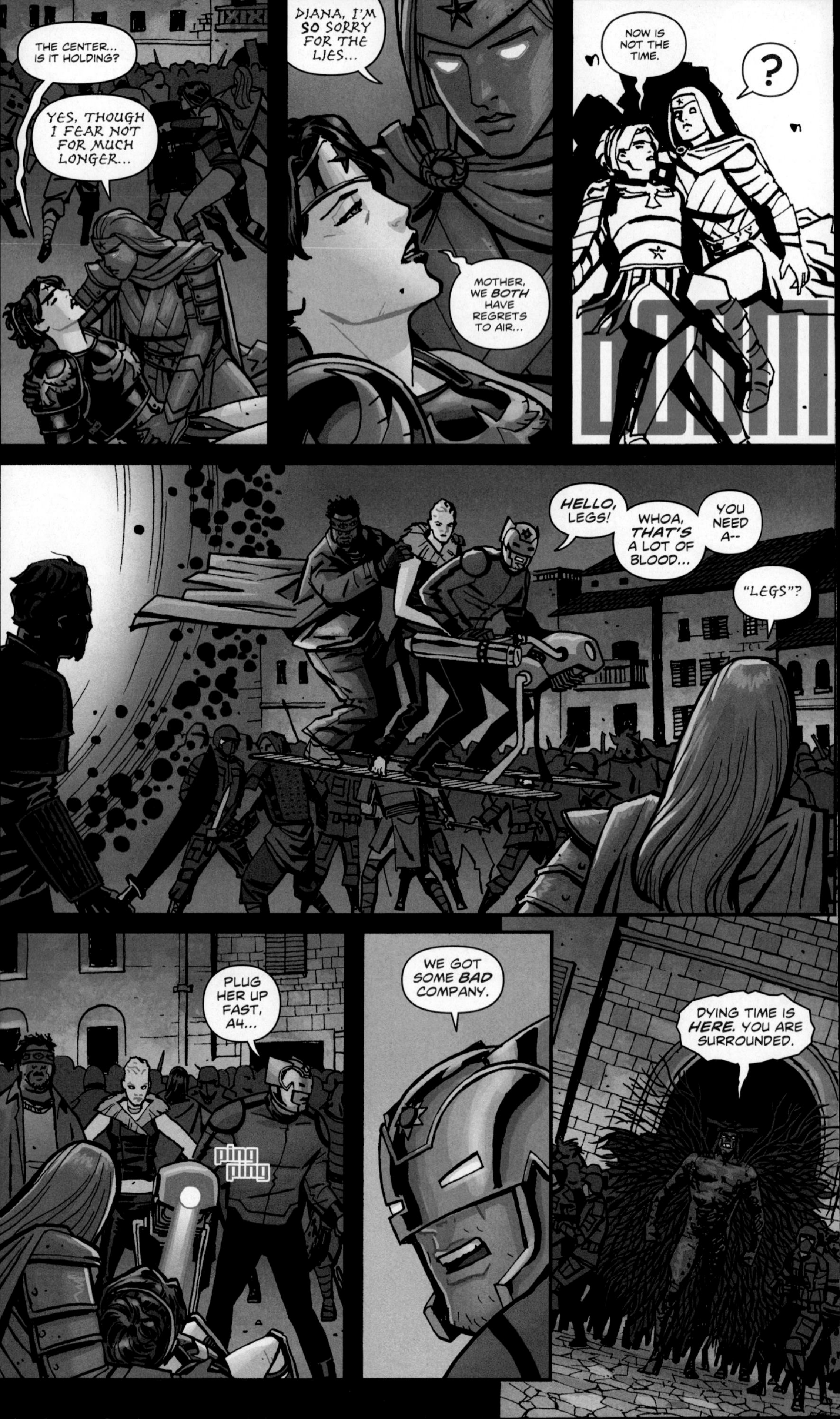
THE CENTER... IS IT HOLDING?
YES, THOUGH I FEAR NOT FOR MUCH LONGER...
DIANA, I'M SO SORRY FOR THE LIES...
MOTHER, WE BOTH HAVE REGRETS TO AIR...
NOW IS NOT THE TIME.
?
HELLO, LEGS!
WHOA, THAT'S A LOT OF BLOOD...
YOU NEED A--
"LEGS"?
PLUG HER UP FAST, A4...
ping ping
WE GOT SOME BAD COMPANY.
DYING TIME IS HERE. YOU ARE SURROUNDED.

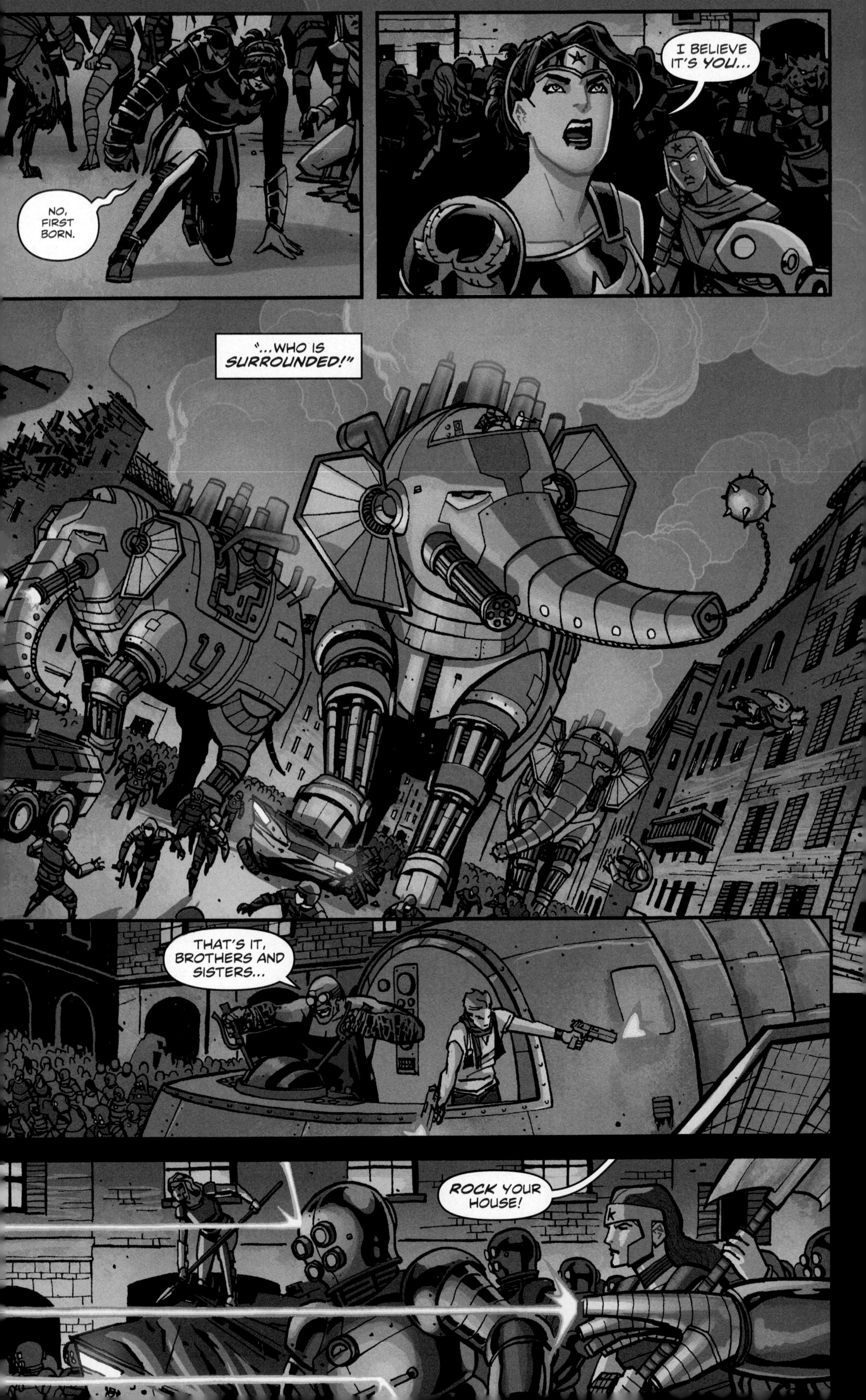
NO, FIRST BORN.
I BELIEVE IT'S YOU...
"...WHO IS SURROUNDED!"
THAT'S IT, BROTHERS AND SISTERS...
ROCK YOUR HOUSE!

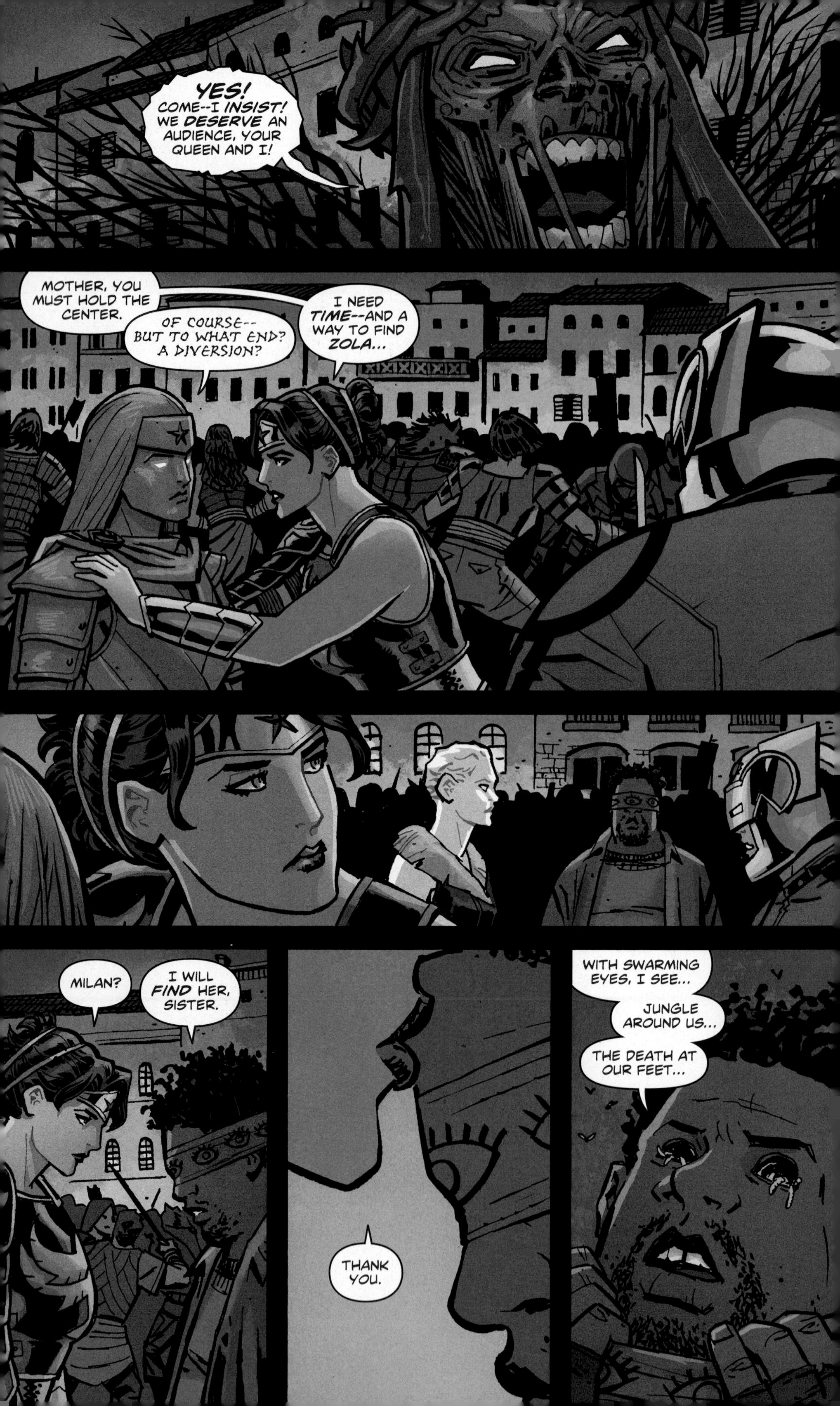
YES! COME--I INSIST! WE DESERVE AN AUDIENCE, YOUR QUEEN AND I!
MOTHER, YOU MUST HOLD THE CENTER.
OF COURSE-- BUT TO WHAT END? A DIVERSION?
I NEED TIME--AND A WAY TO FIND ZOLA...
MILAN?
I WILL FIND HER, SISTER.
THANK YOU.
WITH SWARMING EYES, I SEE...
JUNGLE AROUND US...
THE DEATH AT OUR FEET...

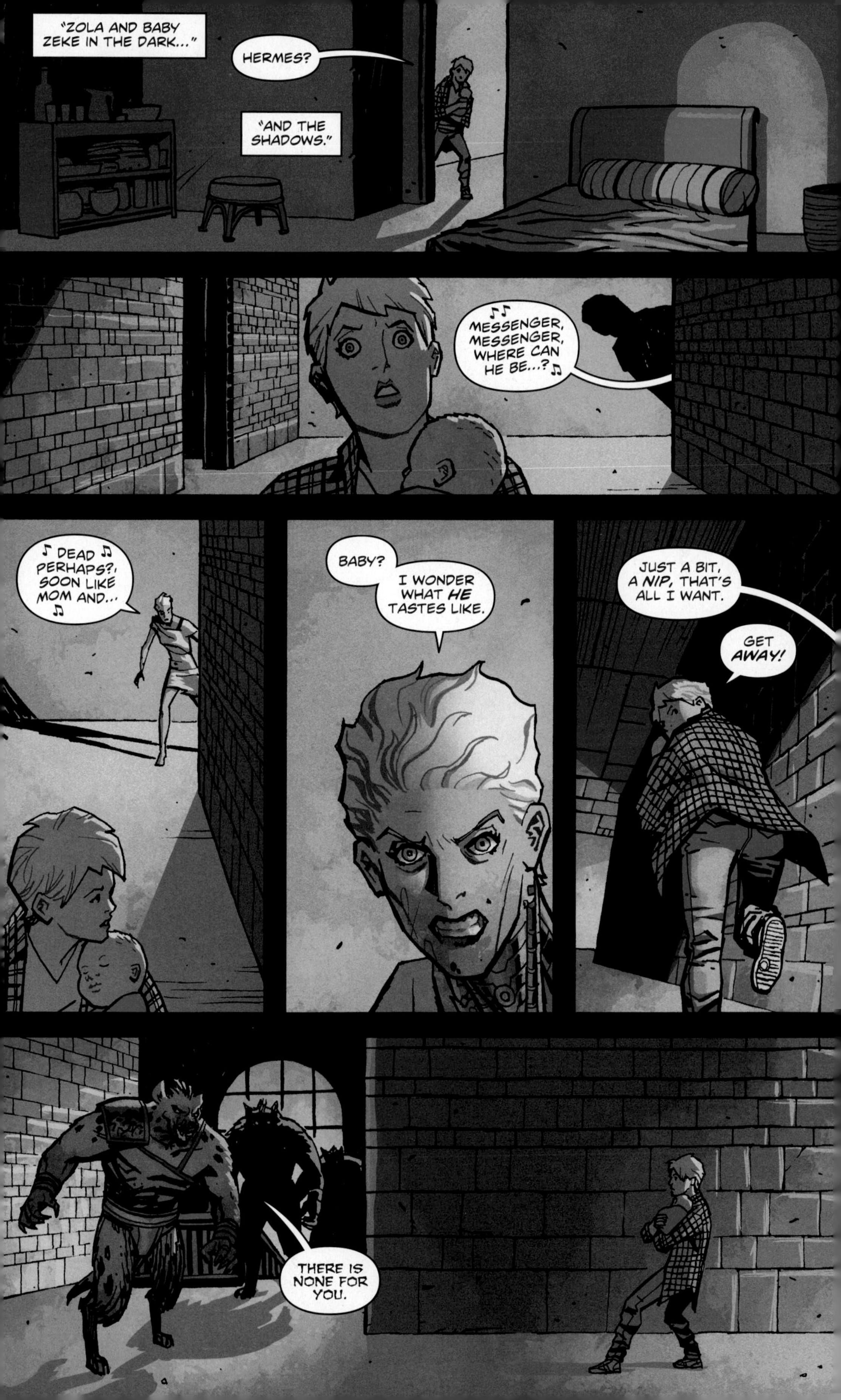
"ZOLA AND BABY ZEKE IN THE DARK..."
HERMES?
"AND THE SHADOWS."
♪♪ MESSENGER, MESSENGER, WHERE CAN HE BE...? ♫
♪ DEAD ♫ PERHAPS?, SOON LIKE MOM AND... ♫
BABY?
I WONDER WHAT *HE* TASTES LIKE.
JUST A BIT, A *NIP*, THAT'S ALL I WANT.
GET *AWAY!*
THERE IS NONE FOR YOU.

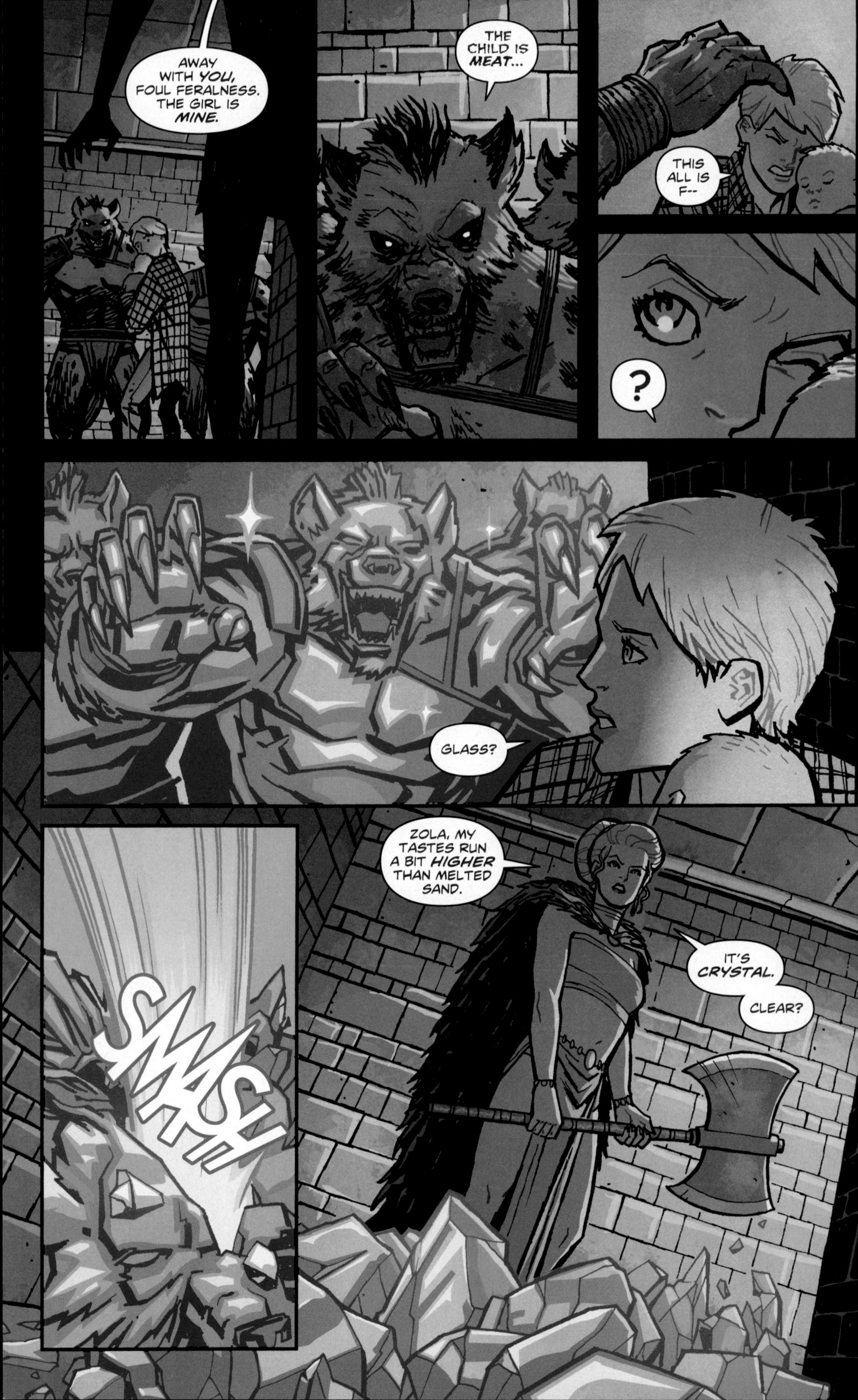
AWAY WITH YOU, FOUL FERALNESS. THE GIRL IS MINE.
THE CHILD IS MEAT...
THIS ALL IS F--
?
GLASS?
ZOLA, MY TASTES RUN A BIT HIGHER THAN MELTED SAND.
IT'S CRYSTAL.
CLEAR?
SMASH

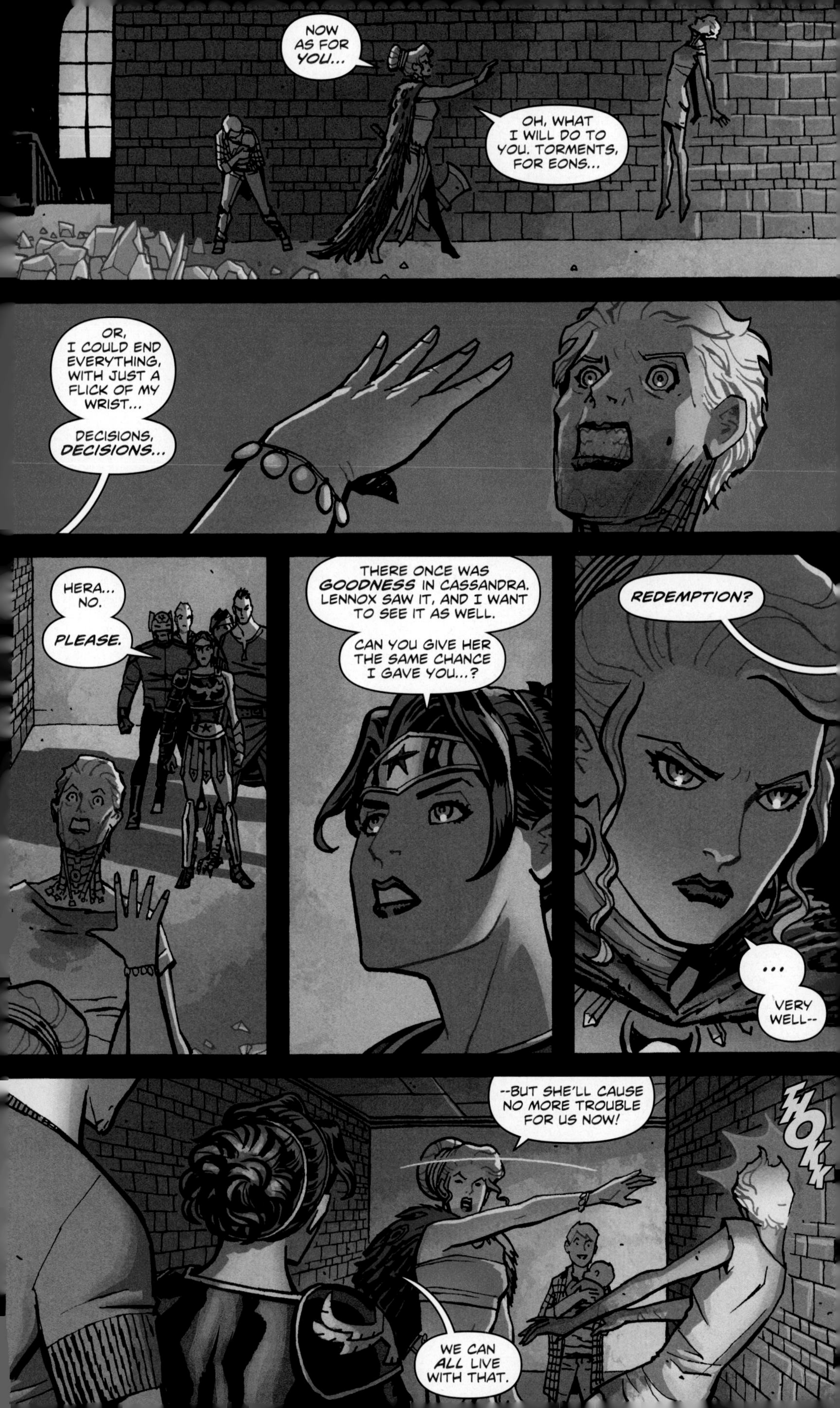
NOW AS FOR YOU...
OH, WHAT I WILL DO TO YOU. TORMENTS, FOR EONS...
OR, I COULD END EVERYTHING, WITH JUST A FLICK OF MY WRIST...
DECISIONS, DECISIONS...
HERA... NO.
PLEASE.
THERE ONCE WAS GOODNESS IN CASSANDRA. LENNOX SAW IT, AND I WANT TO SEE IT AS WELL.
CAN YOU GIVE HER THE SAME CHANCE I GAVE YOU...?
REDEMPTION?
...
VERY WELL--
--BUT SHE'LL CAUSE NO MORE TROUBLE FOR US NOW!
THOKK
WE CAN ALL LIVE WITH THAT.

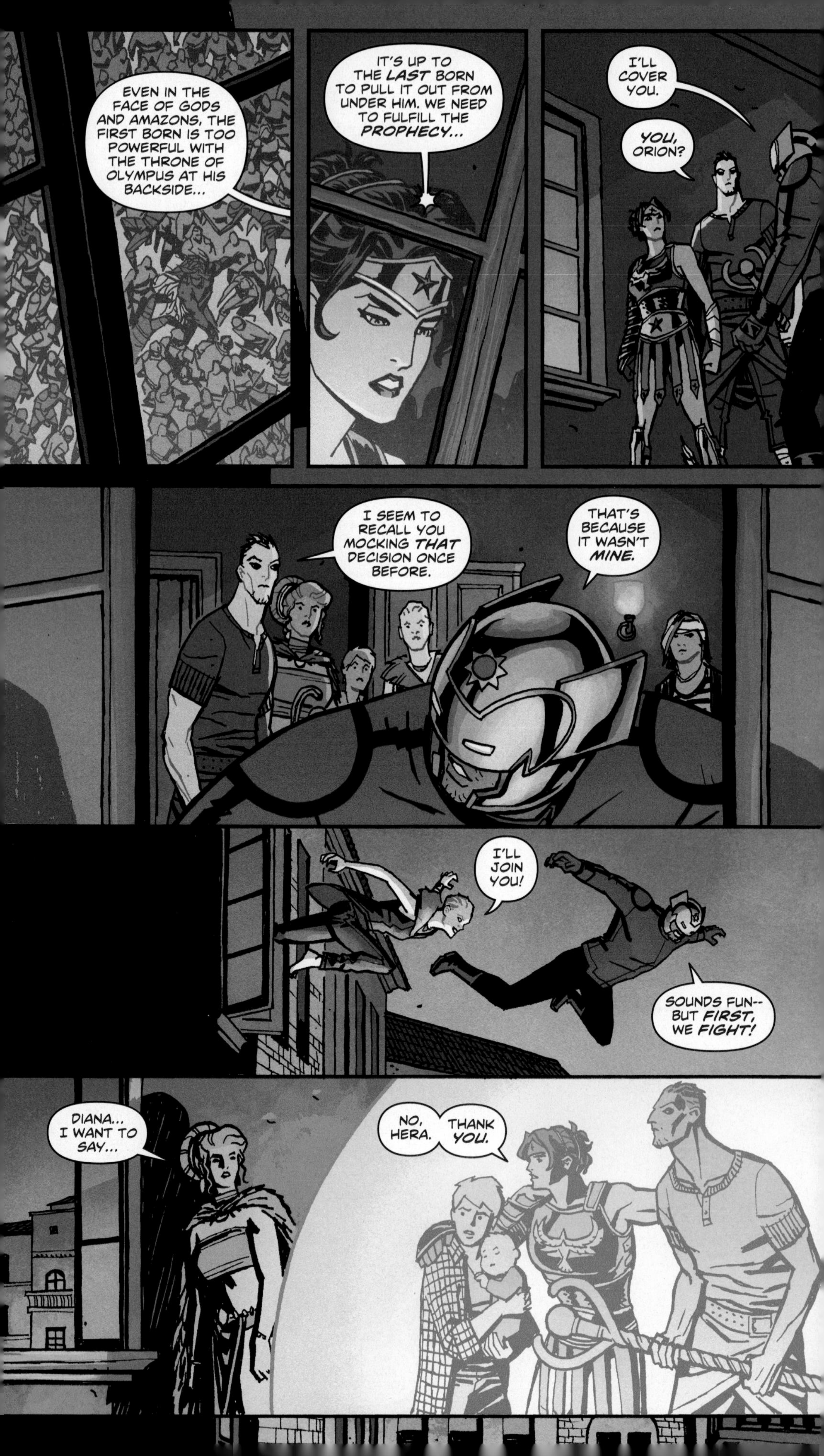
EVEN IN THE FACE OF GODS AND AMAZONS, THE FIRST BORN IS TOO POWERFUL WITH THE THRONE OF OLYMPUS AT HIS BACKSIDE...
IT'S UP TO THE LAST BORN TO PULL IT OUT FROM UNDER HIM. WE NEED TO FULFILL THE PROPHECY...
I'LL COVER YOU.
YOU, ORION?
I SEEM TO RECALL YOU MOCKING THAT DECISION ONCE BEFORE.
THAT'S BECAUSE IT WASN'T MINE.
I'LL JOIN YOU!
SOUNDS FUN-- BUT FIRST, WE FIGHT!
DIANA... I WANT TO SAY...
NO, HERA.
THANK YOU.

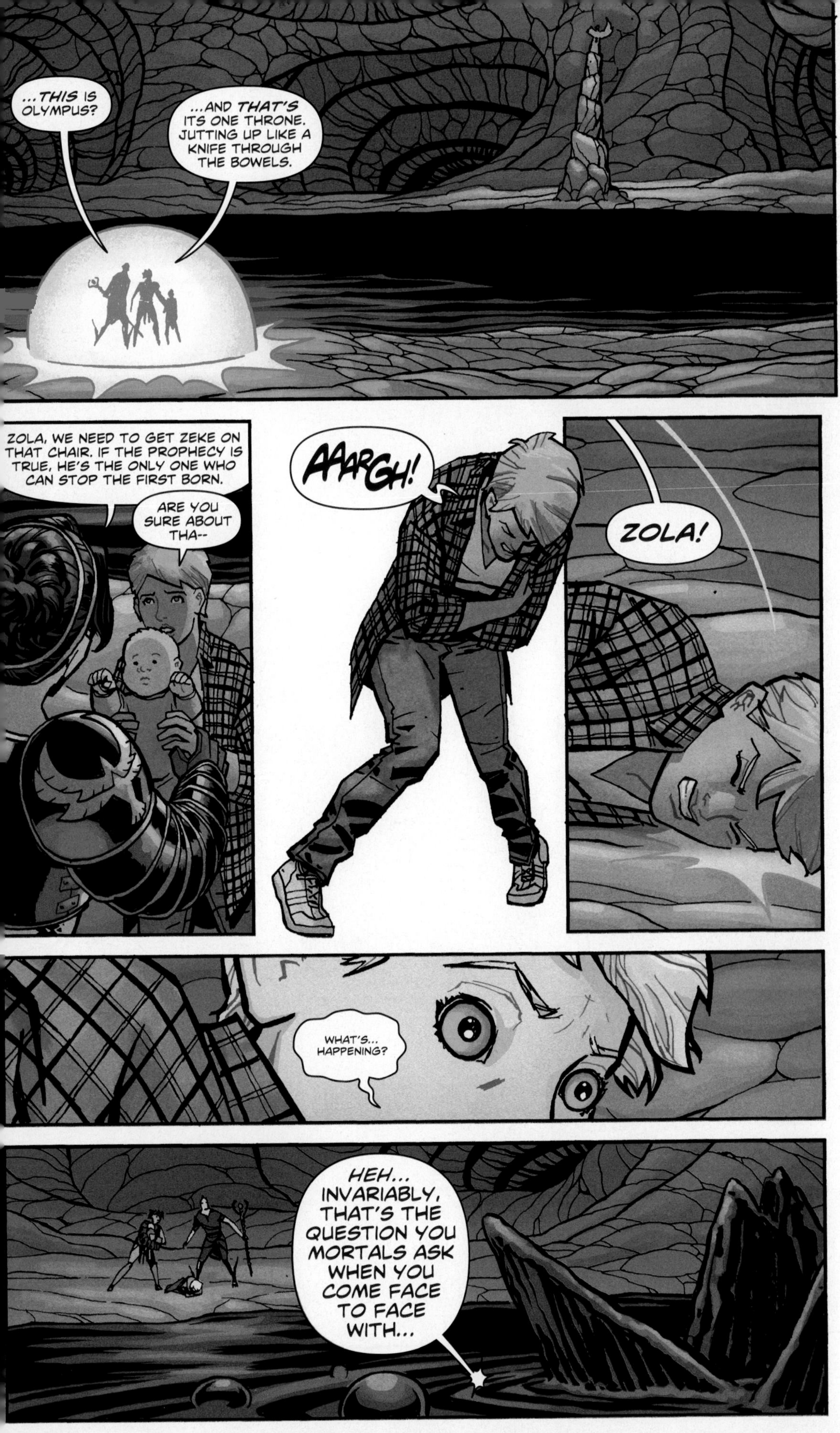
...THIS IS OLYMPUS?
...AND THAT'S ITS ONE THRONE. JUTTING UP LIKE A KNIFE THROUGH THE BOWELS.
ZOLA, WE NEED TO GET ZEKE ON THAT CHAIR. IF THE PROPHECY IS TRUE, HE'S THE ONLY ONE WHO CAN STOP THE FIRST BORN.
ARE YOU SURE ABOUT THA--
AAARGH!
ZOLA!
WHAT'S... HAPPENING?
HEH... INVARIABLY, THAT'S THE QUESTION YOU MORTALS ASK WHEN YOU COME FACE TO FACE WITH...

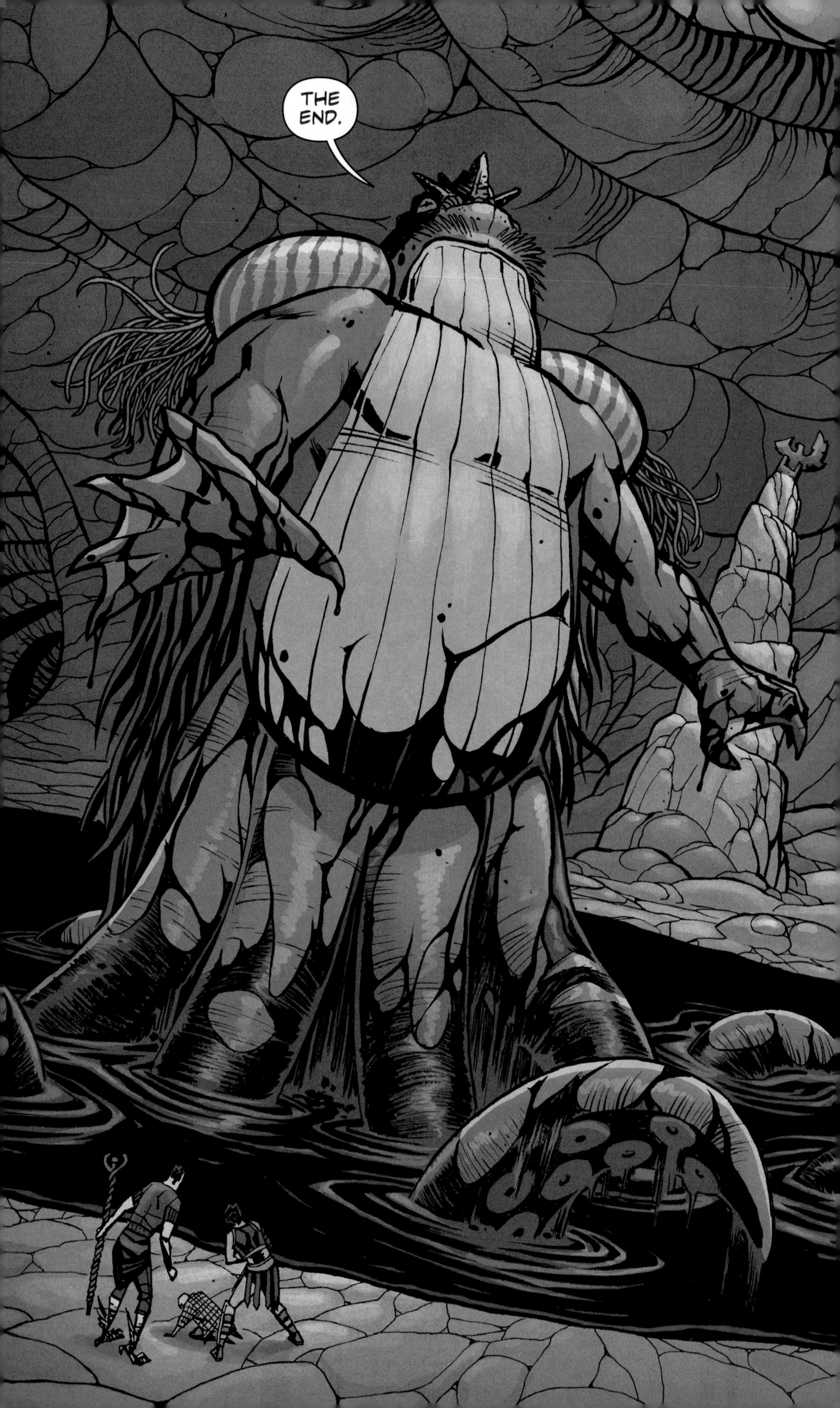
THE END.

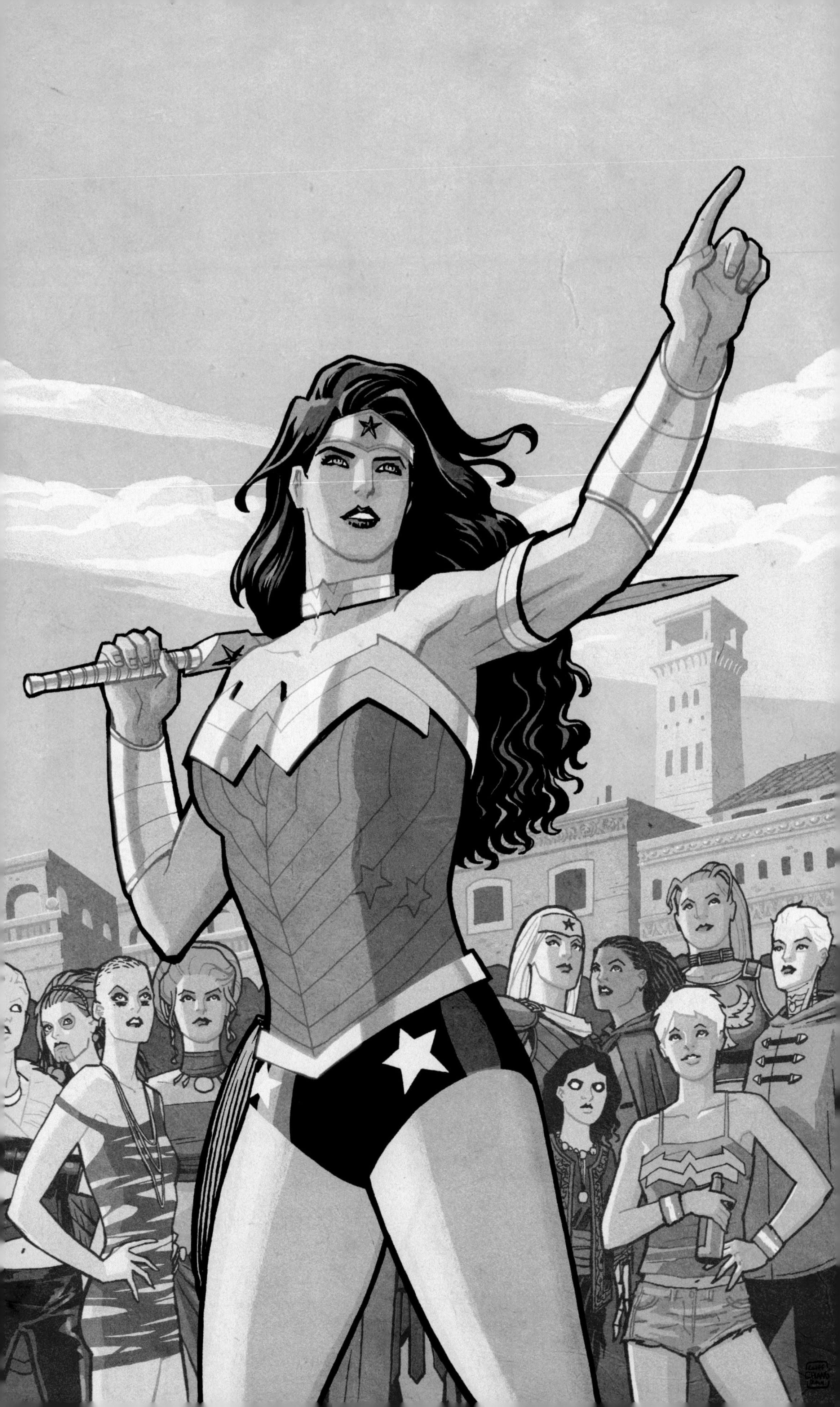

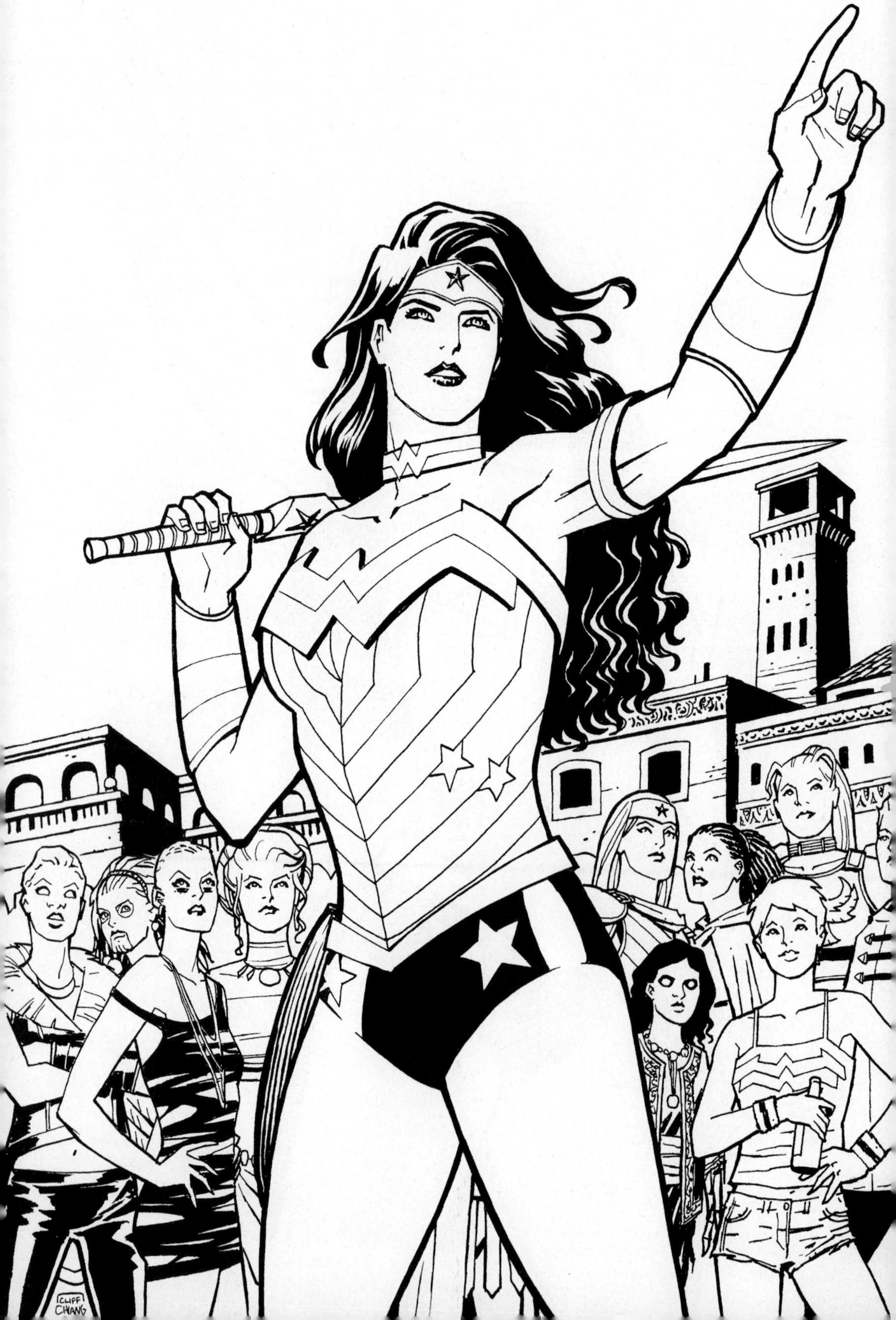
CLIFF CHIANG

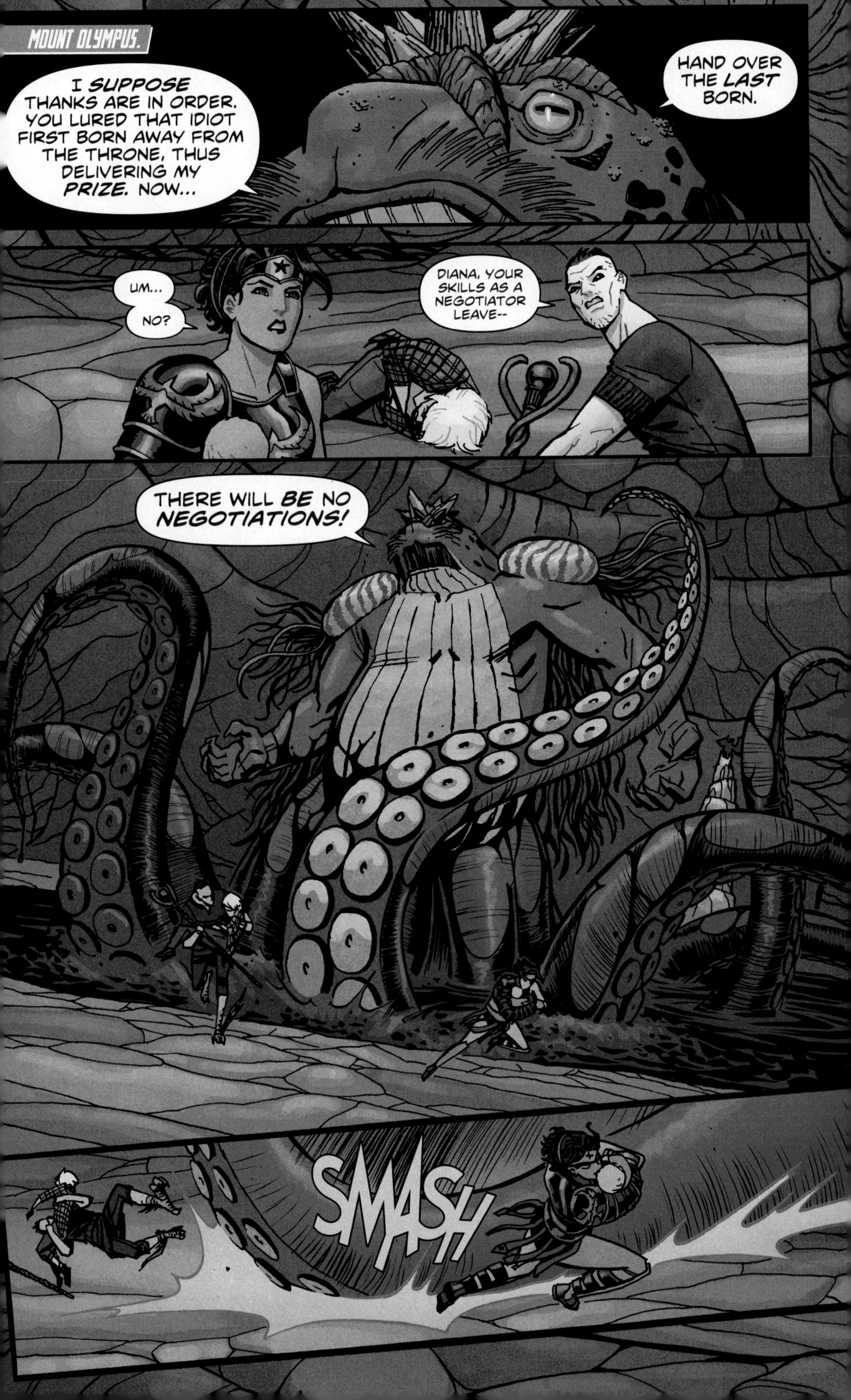

MOUNT OLYMPUS.
I SUPPOSE THANKS ARE IN ORDER. YOU LURED THAT IDIOT FIRST BORN AWAY FROM THE THRONE, THUS DELIVERING MY PRIZE. NOW...
HAND OVER THE LAST BORN.
UM...
NO?
DIANA, YOUR SKILLS AS A NEGOTIATOR LEAVE--
THERE WILL BE NO NEGOTIATIONS!
SMASH

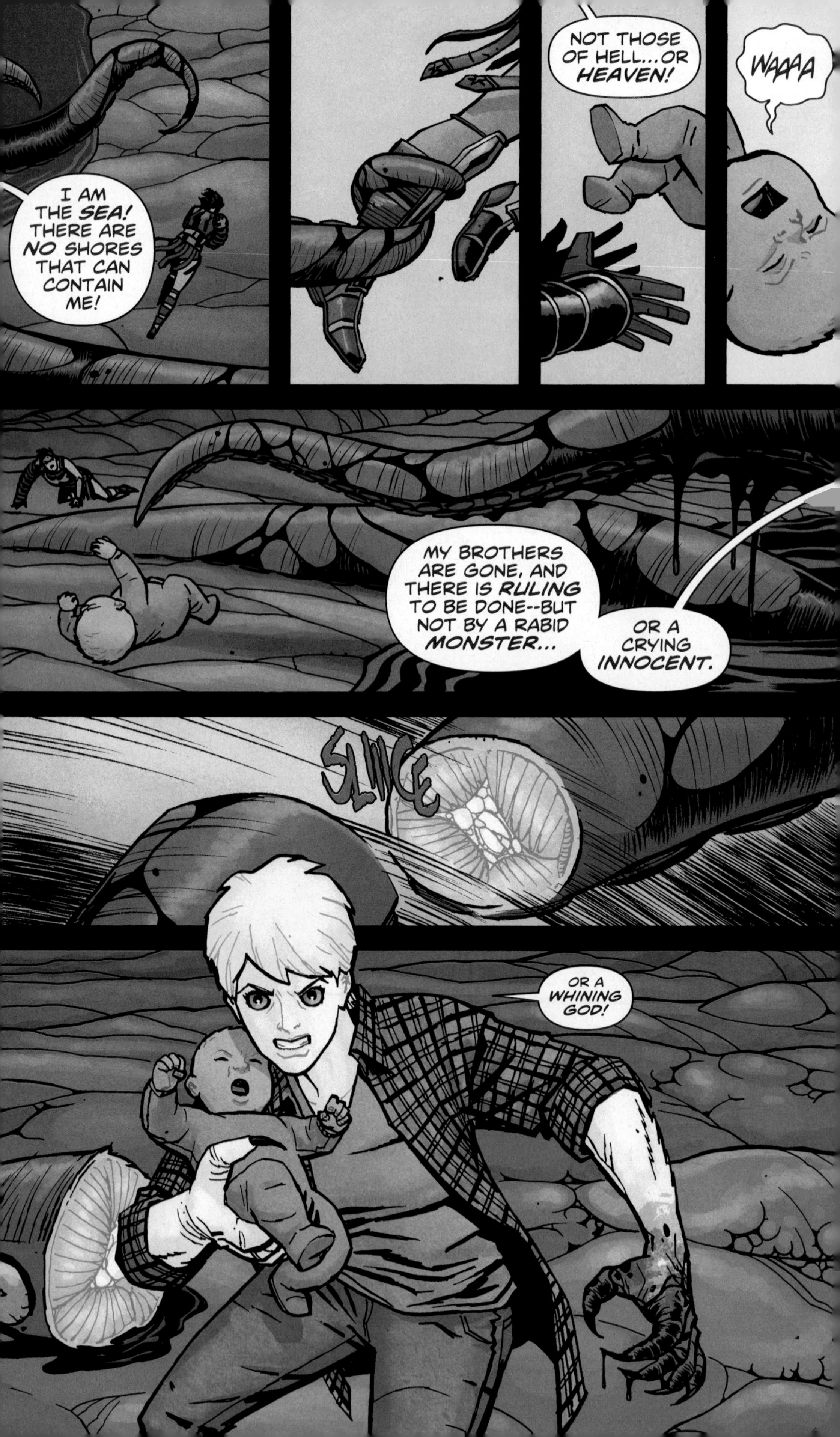
I AM THE SEA! THERE ARE NO SHORES THAT CAN CONTAIN ME!
NOT THOSE OF HELL...OR HEAVEN!
WAAAA
MY BROTHERS ARE GONE, AND THERE IS RULING TO BE DONE--BUT NOT BY A RABID MONSTER...
OR A CRYING INNOCENT.
SLIIICE
OR A WHINING GOD!

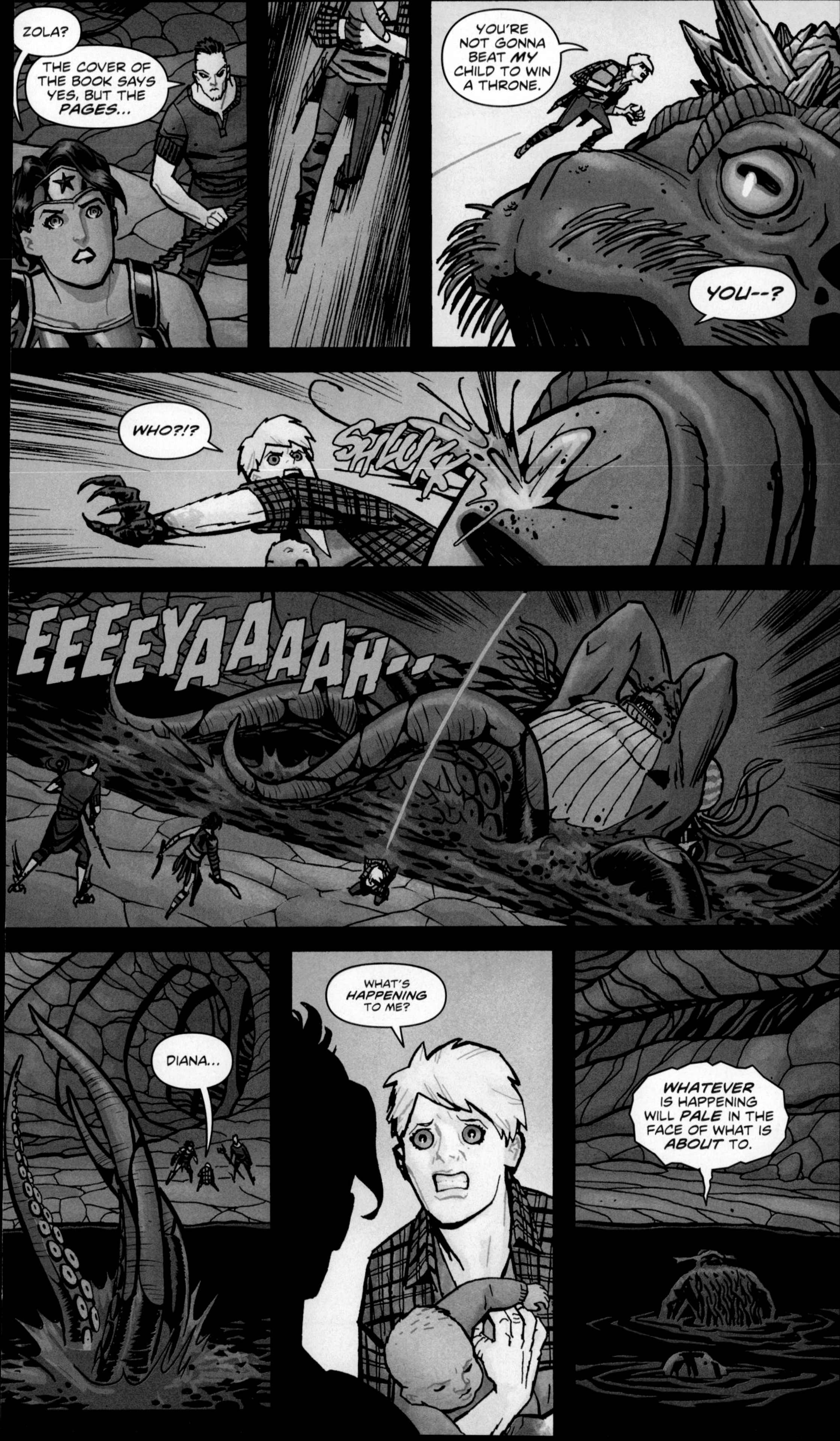

ZOLA?
THE COVER OF THE BOOK SAYS YES, BUT THE PAGES...
YOU'RE NOT GONNA BEAT MY CHILD TO WIN A THRONE.
YOU--?
WHO?!?
SHLOKK
EEEEYAAAAH--
DIANA...
WHAT'S HAPPENING TO ME?
WHATEVER IS HAPPENING WILL PALE IN THE FACE OF WHAT IS ABOUT TO.

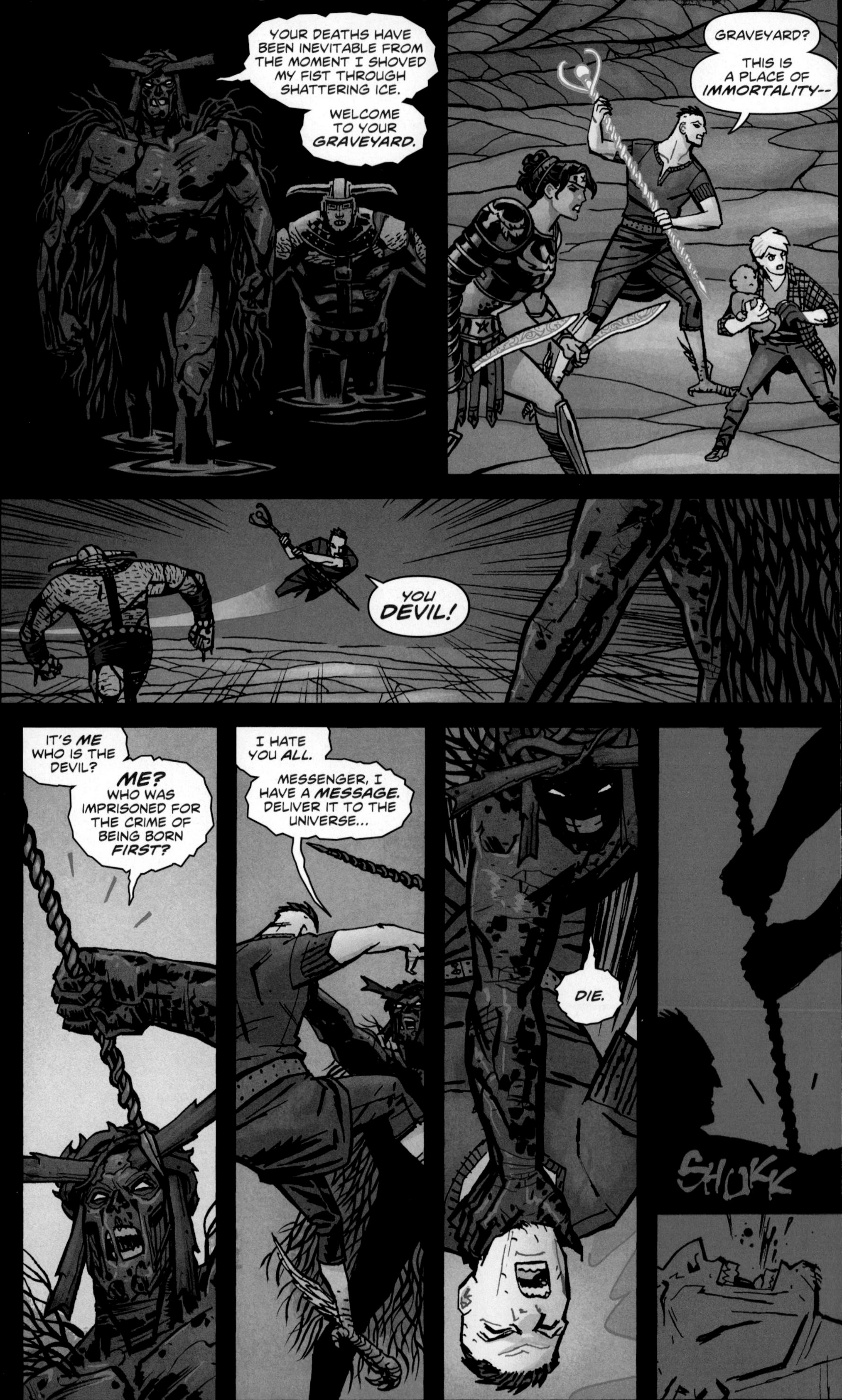
YOUR DEATHS HAVE BEEN INEVITABLE FROM THE MOMENT I SHOVED MY FIST THROUGH SHATTERING ICE.
WELCOME TO YOUR GRAVEYARD.
GRAVEYARD?
THIS IS A PLACE OF IMMORTALITY--
YOU DEVIL!
IT'S ME WHO IS THE DEVIL?
ME? WHO WAS IMPRISONED FOR THE CRIME OF BEING BORN FIRST?
I HATE YOU ALL.
MESSENGER, I HAVE A MESSAGE. DELIVER IT TO THE UNIVERSE...
DIE.
SHOKK

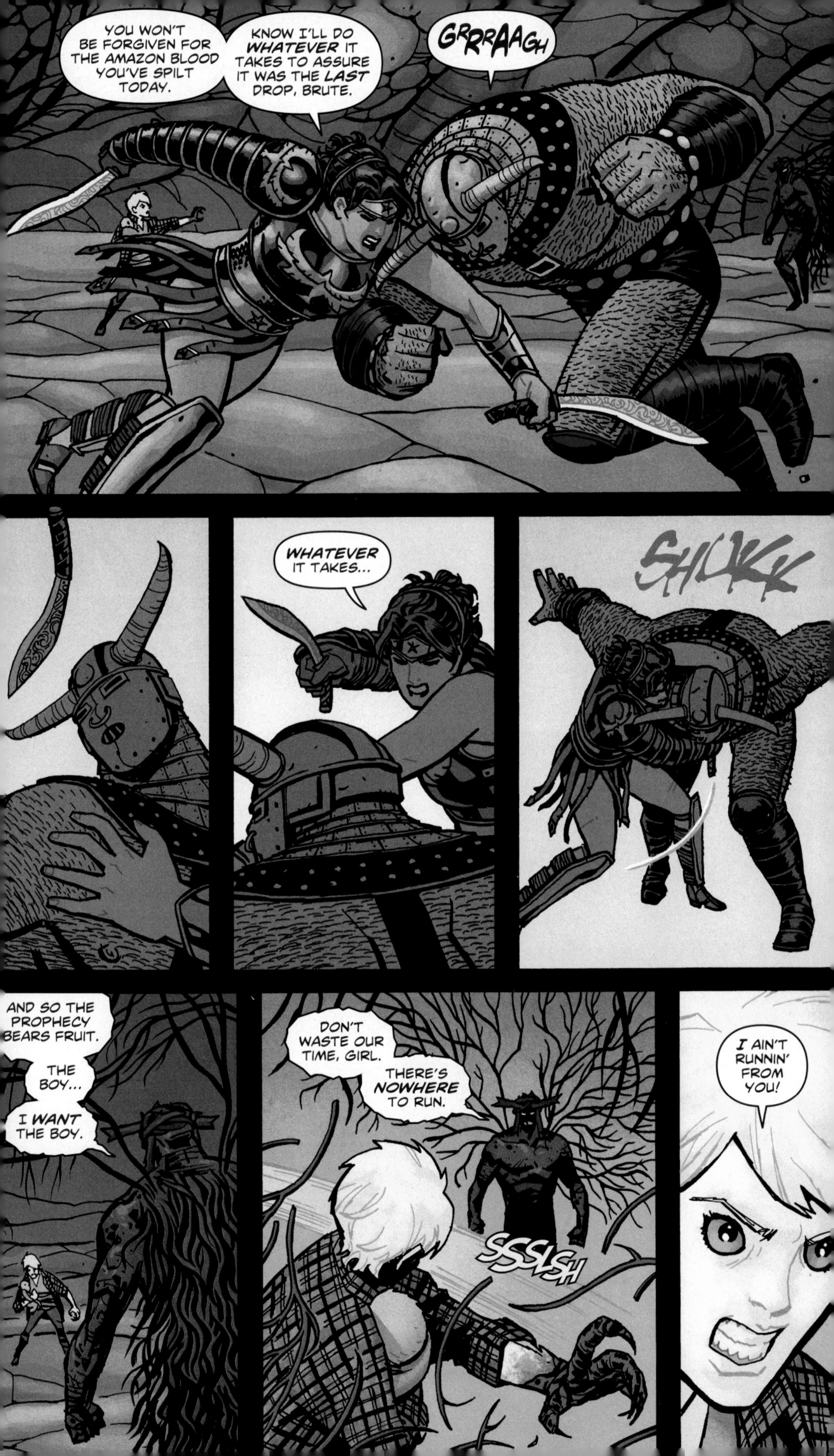
YOU WON'T BE FORGIVEN FOR THE AMAZON BLOOD YOU'VE SPILT TODAY.
KNOW I'LL DO WHATEVER IT TAKES TO ASSURE IT WAS THE LAST DROP, BRUTE.
GRRRAAGH
WHATEVER IT TAKES...
SHUKK
AND SO THE PROPHECY BEARS FRUIT.
THE BOY...
I WANT THE BOY.
DON'T WASTE OUR TIME, GIRL.
THERE'S NOWHERE TO RUN.
SSSLSH
I AIN'T RUNNIN' FROM YOU!

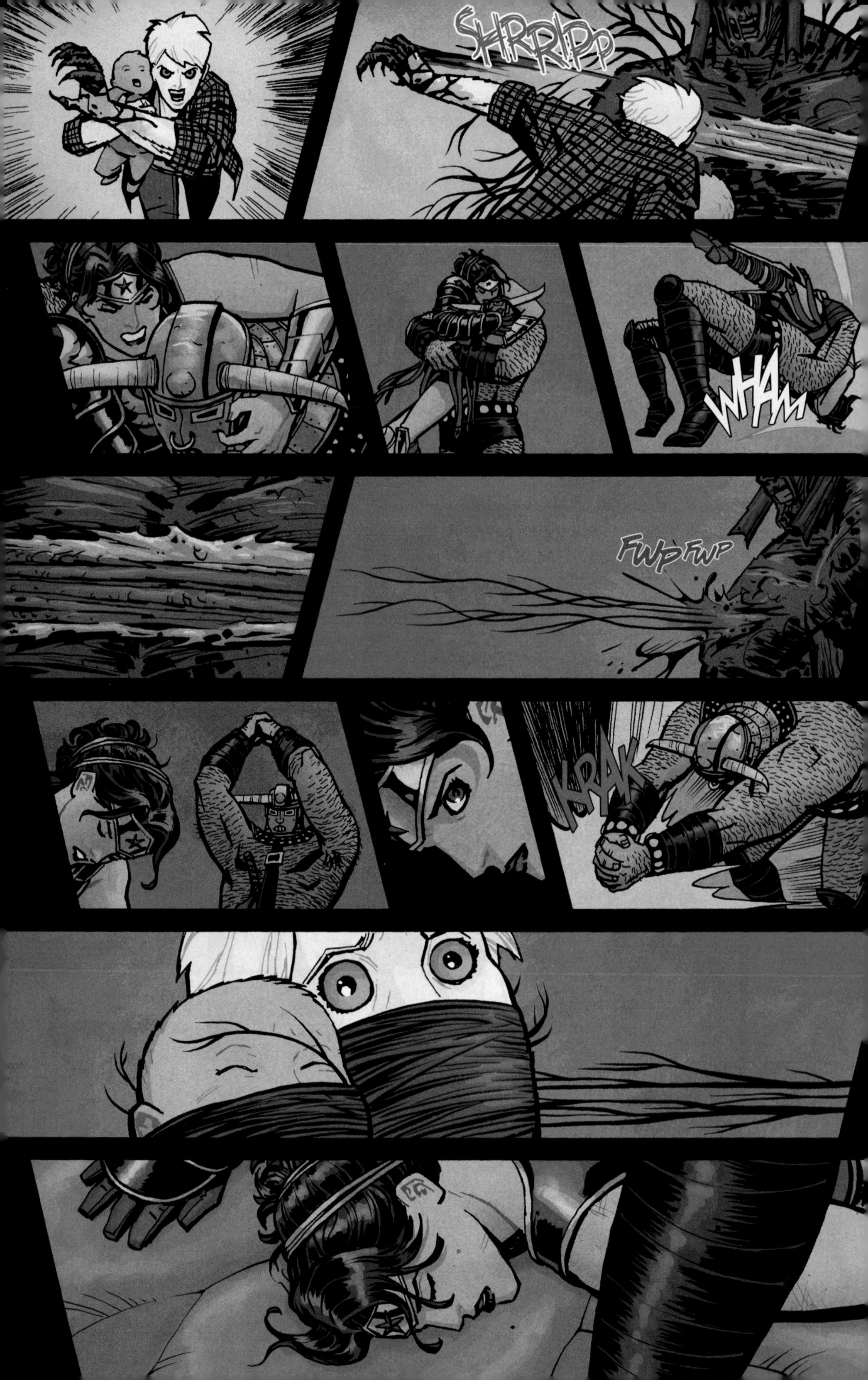
SHRRIPP
WHAM
FWP FWP
KRAK

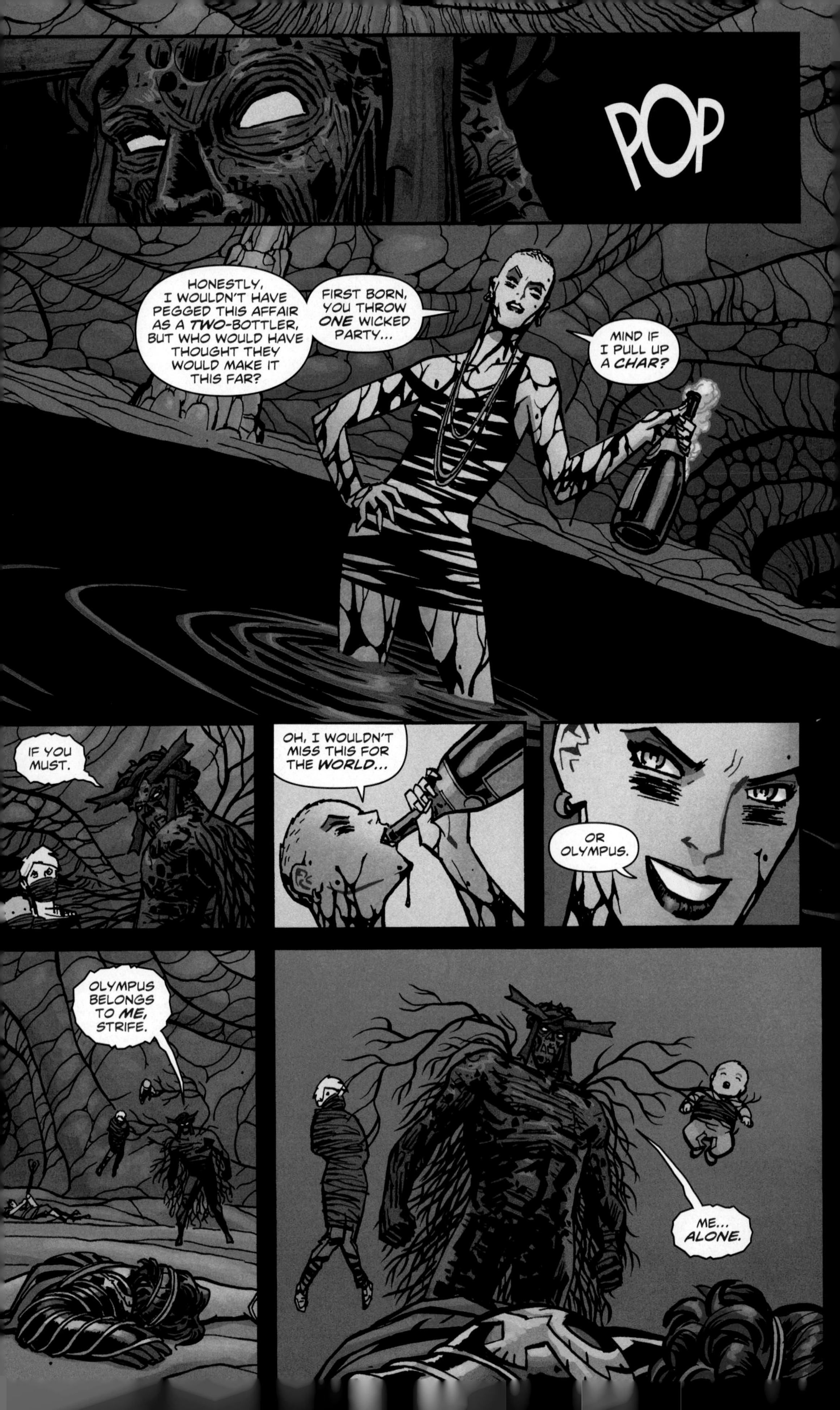
POP
HONESTLY, I WOULDN'T HAVE PEGGED THIS AFFAIR AS A TWO-BOTTLER, BUT WHO WOULD HAVE THOUGHT THEY WOULD MAKE IT THIS FAR?
FIRST BORN, YOU THROW ONE WICKED PARTY...
MIND IF I PULL UP A CHAR?
IF YOU MUST.
OH, I WOULDN'T MISS THIS FOR THE WORLD...
OR OLYMPUS.
OLYMPUS BELONGS TO ME, STRIFE.
ME... ALONE.

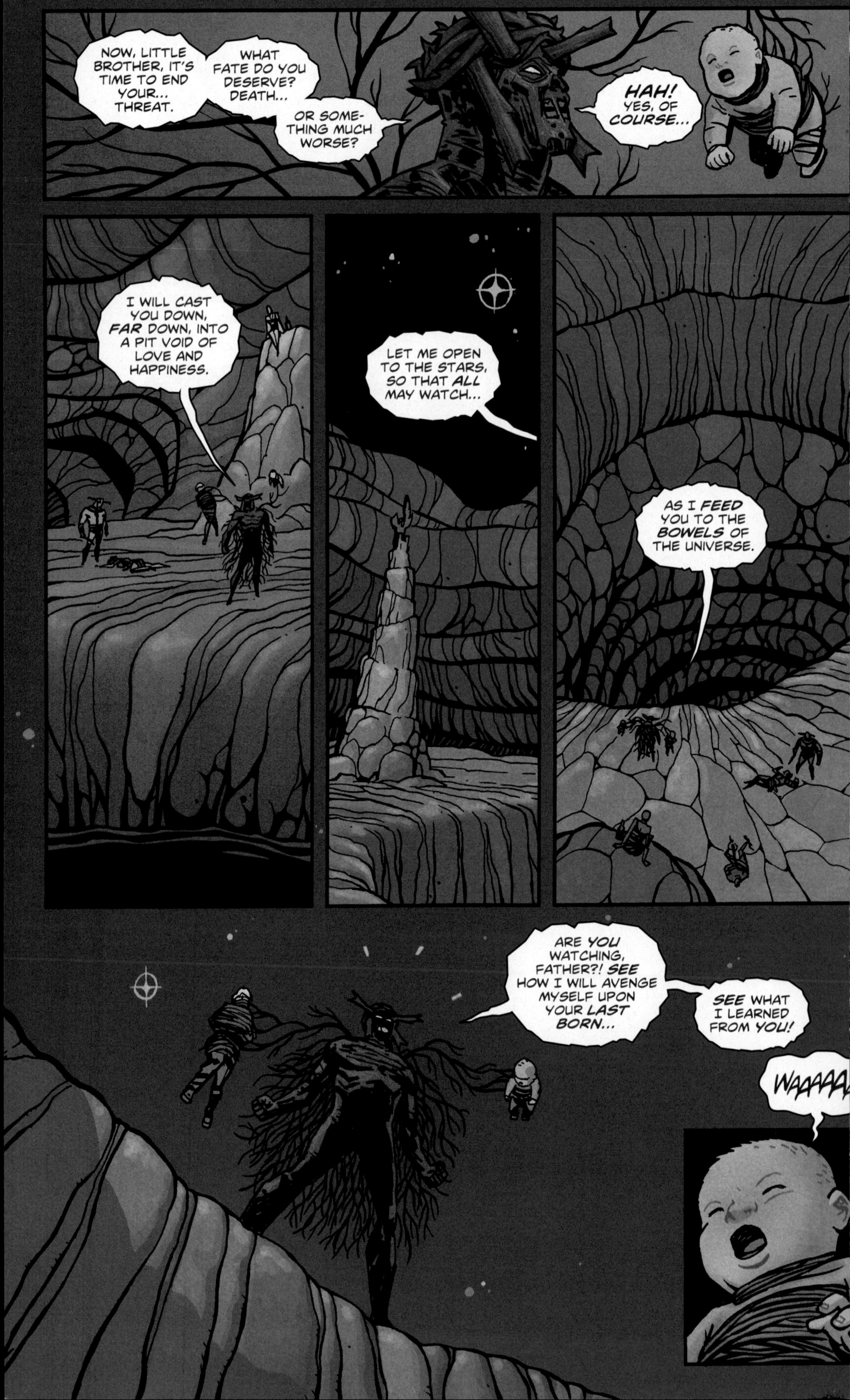
NOW, LITTLE BROTHER, IT'S TIME TO END YOUR... THREAT.
WHAT FATE DO YOU DESERVE? DEATH...
OR SOME-THING MUCH WORSE?
HAH! YES, OF COURSE...
I WILL CAST YOU DOWN, FAR DOWN, INTO A PIT VOID OF LOVE AND HAPPINESS.
LET ME OPEN TO THE STARS, SO THAT ALL MAY WATCH...
AS I FEED YOU TO THE BOWELS OF THE UNIVERSE.
ARE YOU WATCHING, FATHER?! SEE HOW I WILL AVENGE MYSELF UPON YOUR LAST BORN...
SEE WHAT I LEARNED FROM YOU!
WAAAAA

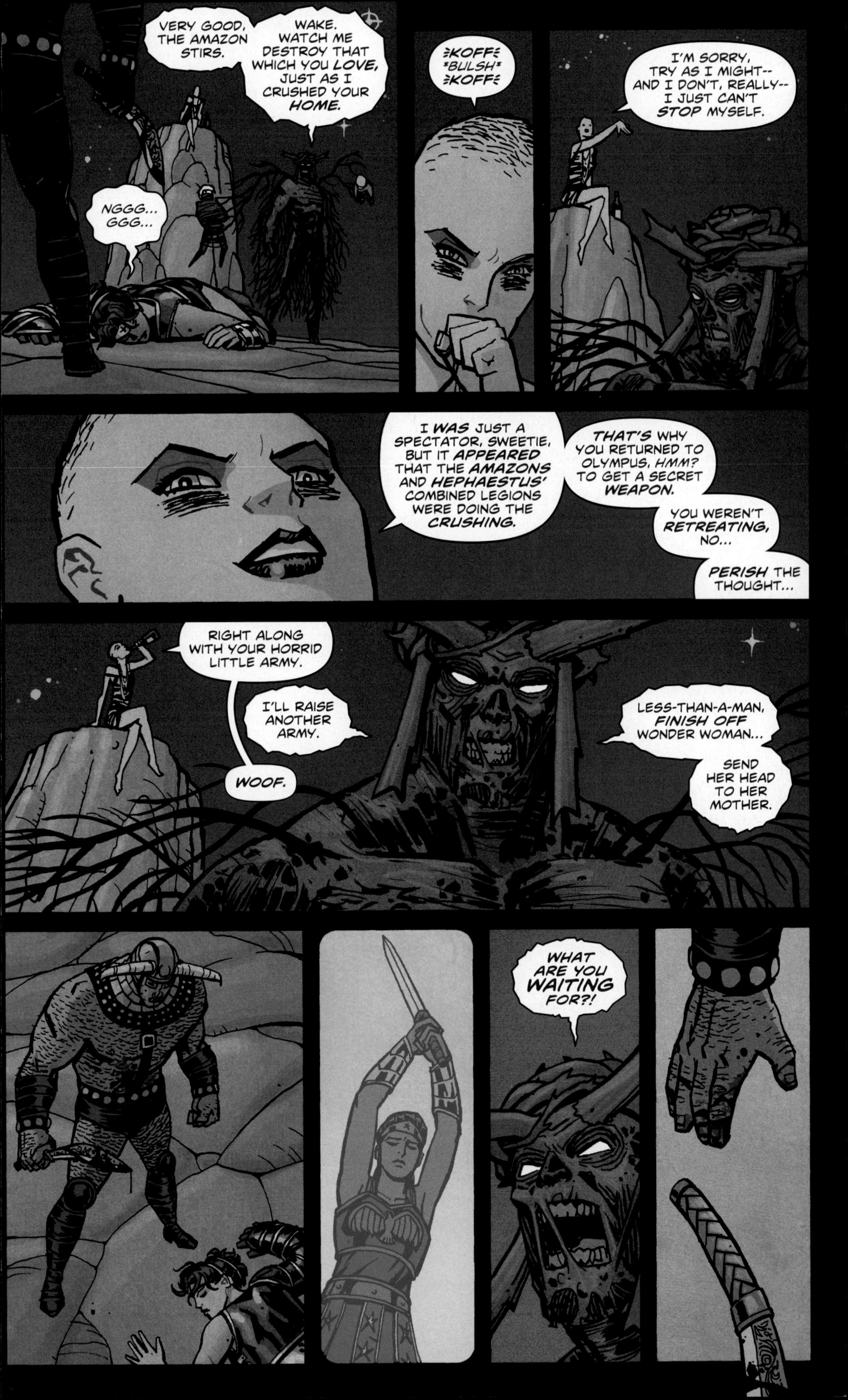
VERY GOOD, THE AMAZON STIRS.
WAKE. WATCH ME DESTROY THAT WHICH YOU LOVE, JUST AS I CRUSHED YOUR HOME.
NGGG... GGG...
KOFF *BULSH* *KOFF*
I'M SORRY, TRY AS I MIGHT-- AND I DON'T, REALLY-- I JUST CAN'T STOP MYSELF.
I WAS JUST A SPECTATOR, SWEETIE, BUT IT APPEARED THAT THE AMAZONS AND HEPHAESTUS' COMBINED LEGIONS WERE DOING THE CRUSHING.
THAT'S WHY YOU RETURNED TO OLYMPUS, HMM? TO GET A SECRET WEAPON.
YOU WEREN'T RETREATING, NO...
PERISH THE THOUGHT...
RIGHT ALONG WITH YOUR HORRID LITTLE ARMY.
I'LL RAISE ANOTHER ARMY.
WOOF.
LESS-THAN-A-MAN, FINISH OFF WONDER WOMAN...
SEND HER HEAD TO HER MOTHER.
WHAT ARE YOU WAITING FOR?!

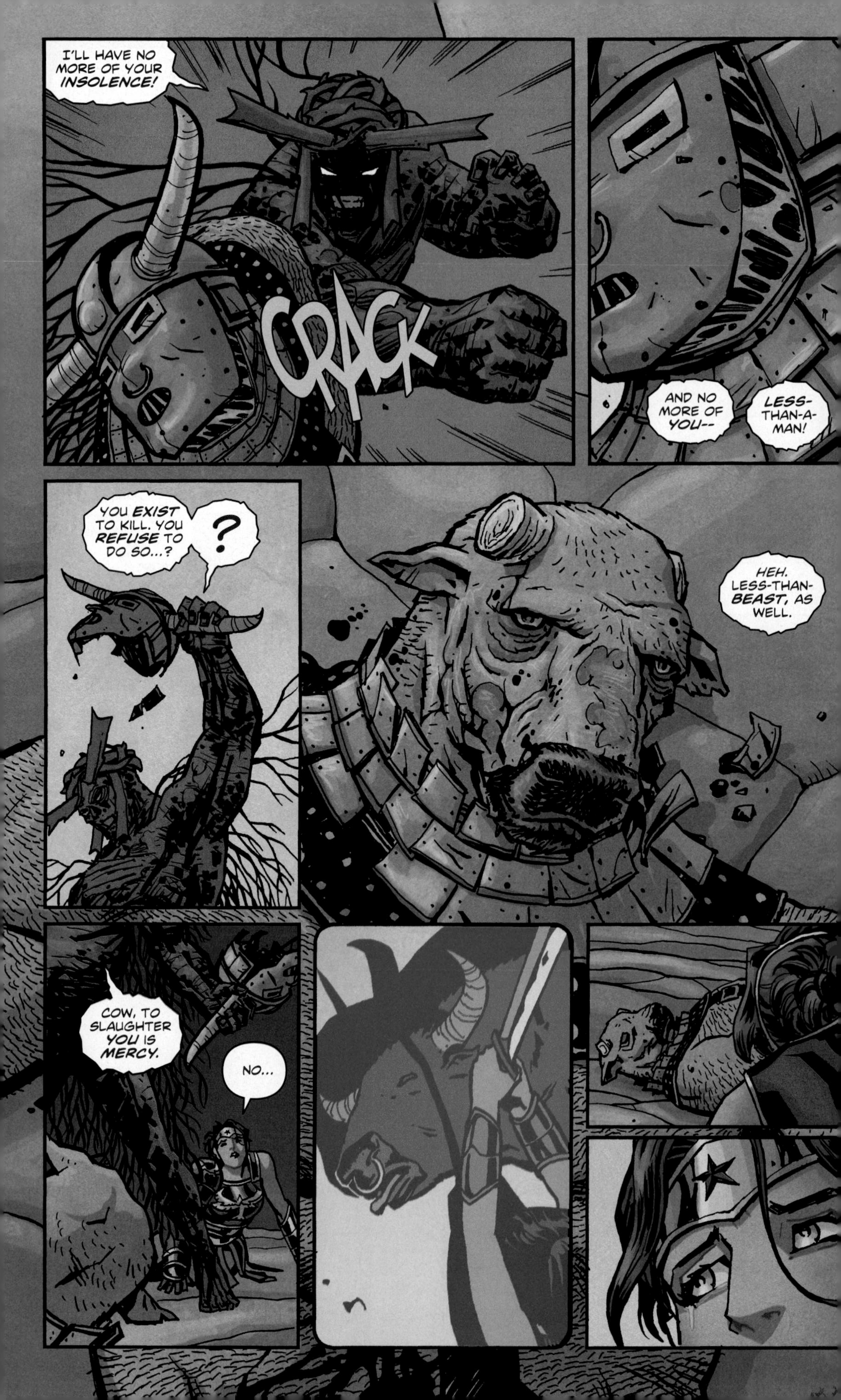

I'LL HAVE NO MORE OF YOUR INSOLENCE!
CRACK
AND NO MORE OF YOU--
LESS-THAN-A-MAN!
YOU EXIST TO KILL. YOU REFUSE TO DO SO...?
?
HEH. LESS-THAN-BEAST, AS WELL.
COW, TO SLAUGHTER YOU IS MERCY.
NO...

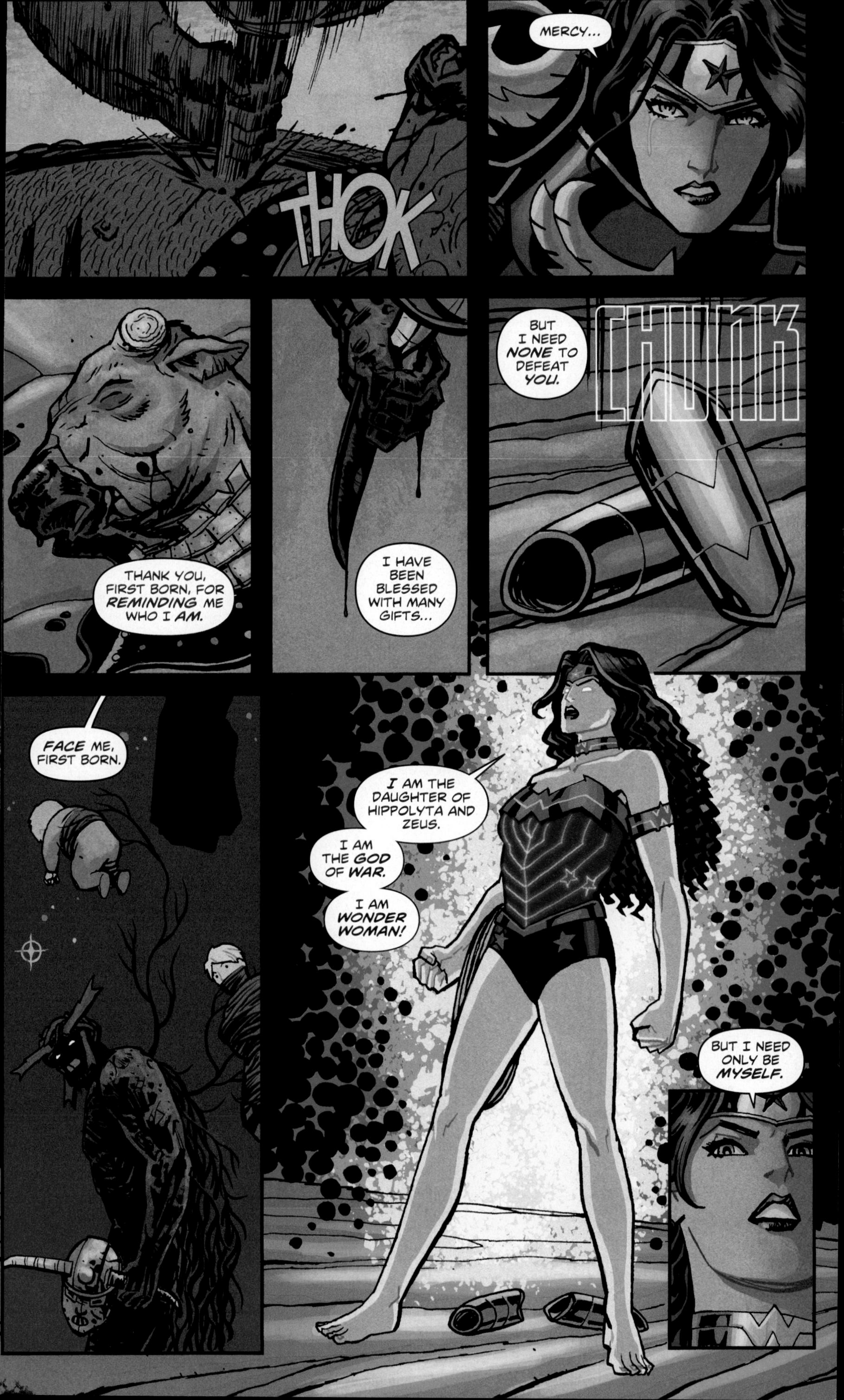
THOK
MERCY...
THANK YOU, FIRST BORN, FOR REMINDING ME WHO I AM.
I HAVE BEEN BLESSED WITH MANY GIFTS...
BUT I NEED NONE TO DEFEAT YOU.
CHUNK
FACE ME, FIRST BORN.
I AM THE DAUGHTER OF HIPPOLYTA AND ZEUS.
I AM THE GOD OF WAR.
I AM WONDER WOMAN!
BUT I NEED ONLY BE MYSELF.

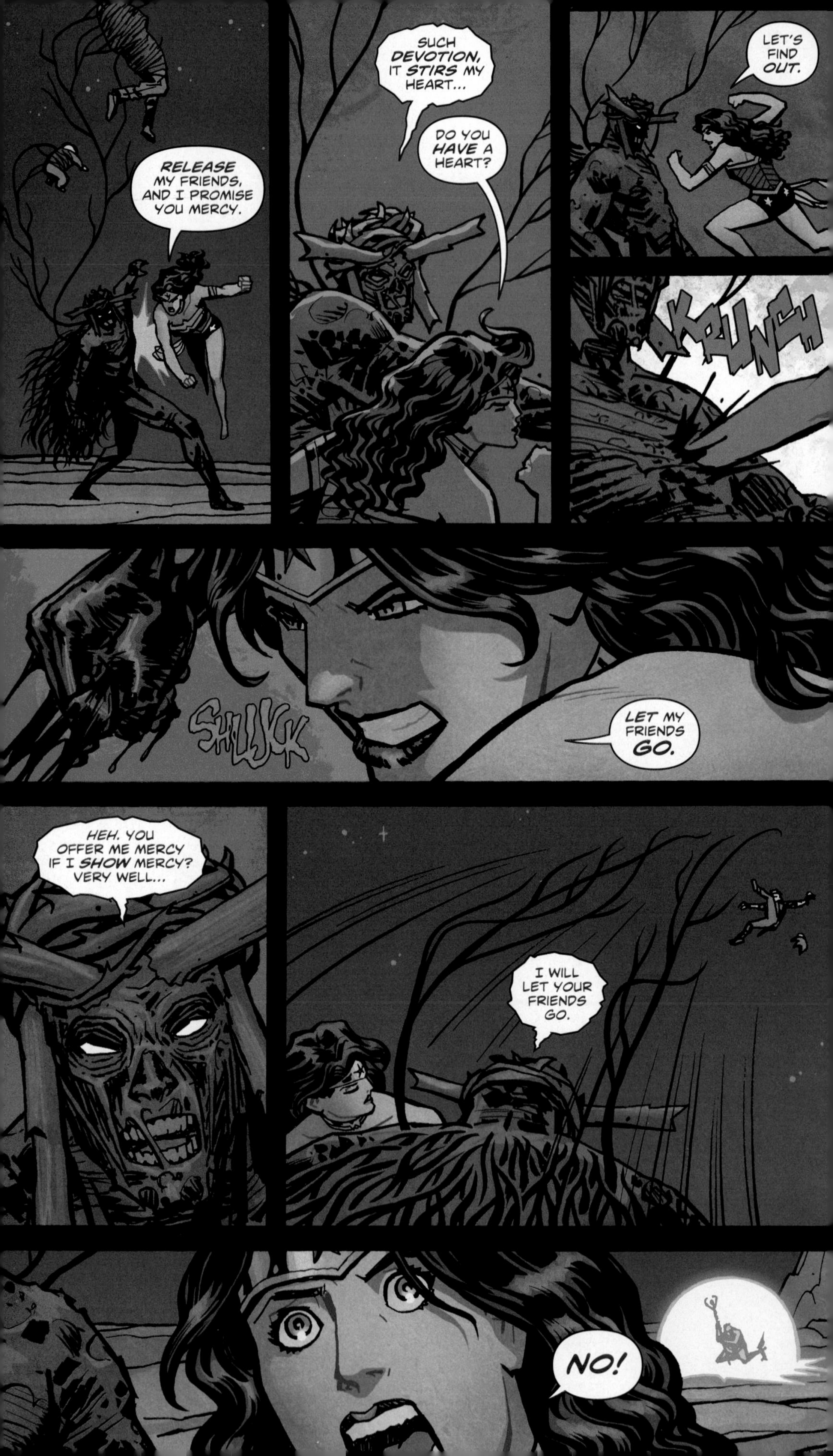
RELEASE MY FRIENDS, AND I PROMISE YOU MERCY.
SUCH DEVOTION, IT STIRS MY HEART...
DO YOU HAVE A HEART?
LET'S FIND OUT.
KRUNCH
SHLUKK
LET MY FRIENDS GO.
HEH. YOU OFFER ME MERCY IF I SHOW MERCY? VERY WELL...
I WILL LET YOUR FRIENDS GO.
NO!

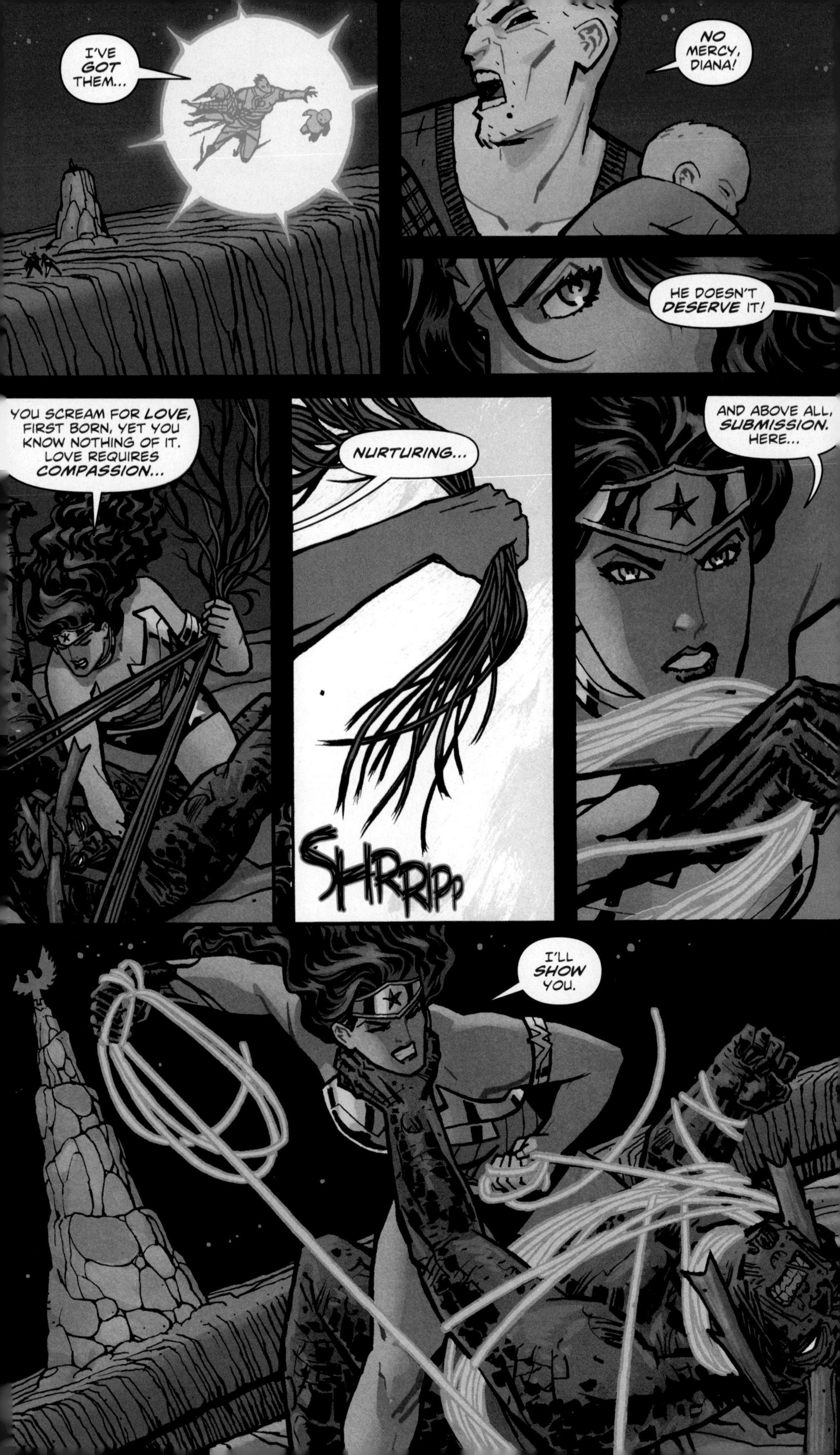
I'VE GOT THEM...
NO MERCY, DIANA!
HE DOESN'T DESERVE IT!
YOU SCREAM FOR LOVE, FIRST BORN, YET YOU KNOW NOTHING OF IT. LOVE REQUIRES COMPASSION...
NURTURING...
SHRRIPP
AND ABOVE ALL, SUBMISSION. HERE...
I'LL SHOW YOU.

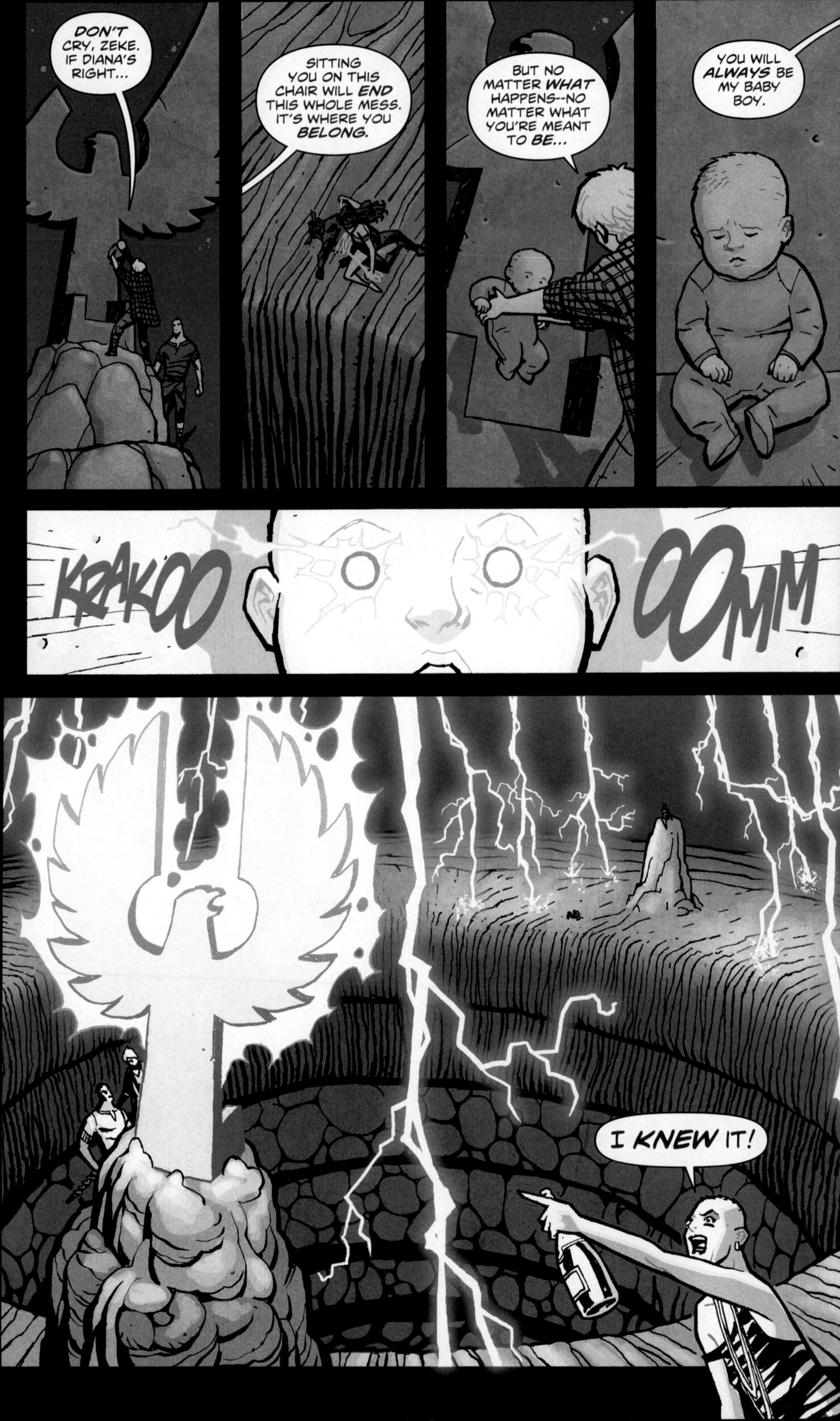
DON'T CRY, ZEKE. IF DIANA'S RIGHT...
SITTING YOU ON THIS CHAIR WILL END THIS WHOLE MESS. IT'S WHERE YOU BELONG.
BUT NO MATTER WHAT HAPPENS--NO MATTER WHAT YOU'RE MEANT TO BE...
YOU WILL ALWAYS BE MY BABY BOY.
KRAKOO
OOMM
I KNEW IT!

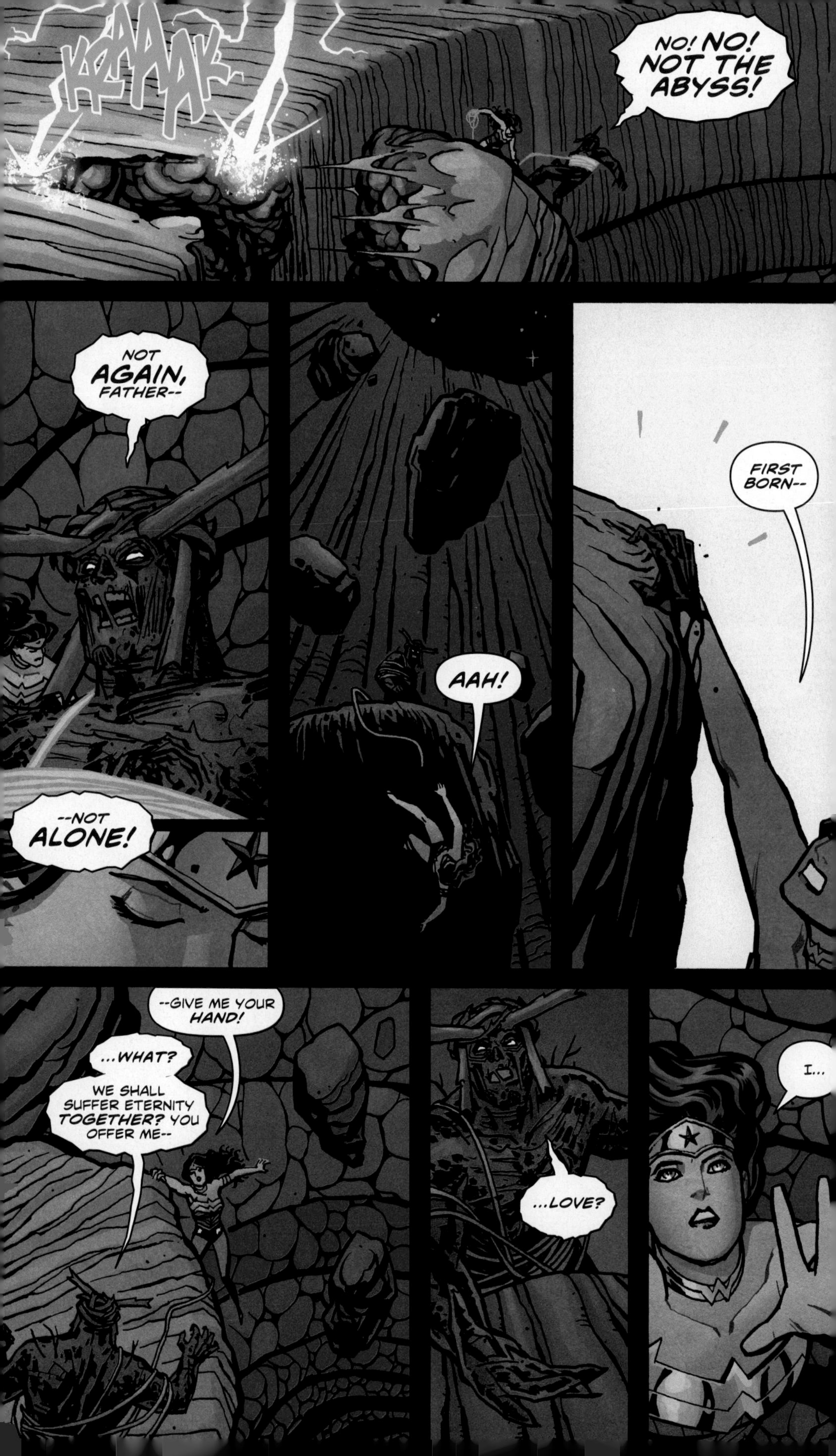
KRAAAK
NO! NO! NOT THE ABYSS!
NOT AGAIN, FATHER--
--NOT ALONE!
AAH!
FIRST BORN--
--GIVE ME YOUR HAND!
...WHAT?
WE SHALL SUFFER ETERNITY TOGETHER? YOU OFFER ME--
...LOVE?
I...

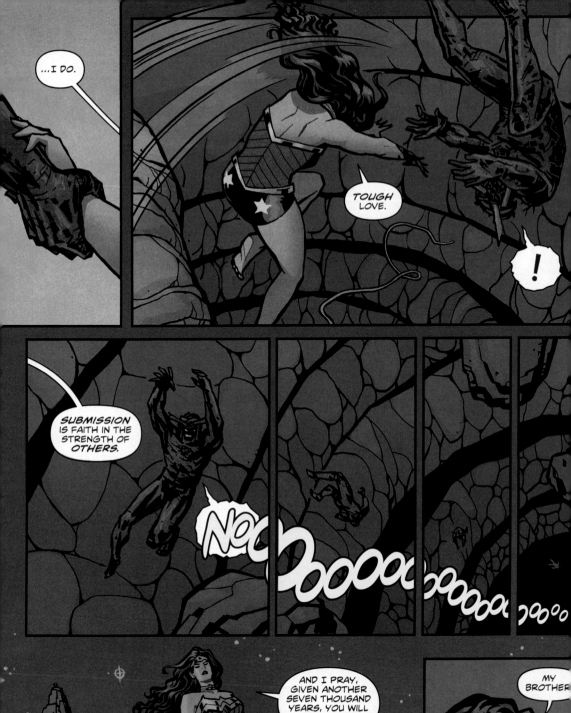

...I DO.

TOUGH LOVE.

!

SUBMISSION IS FAITH IN THE STRENGTH OF OTHERS.

NOOOoooooooooooooooo

AND I PRAY, GIVEN ANOTHER SEVEN THOUSAND YEARS, YOU WILL UNDERSTAND THAT...

MY BROTHER

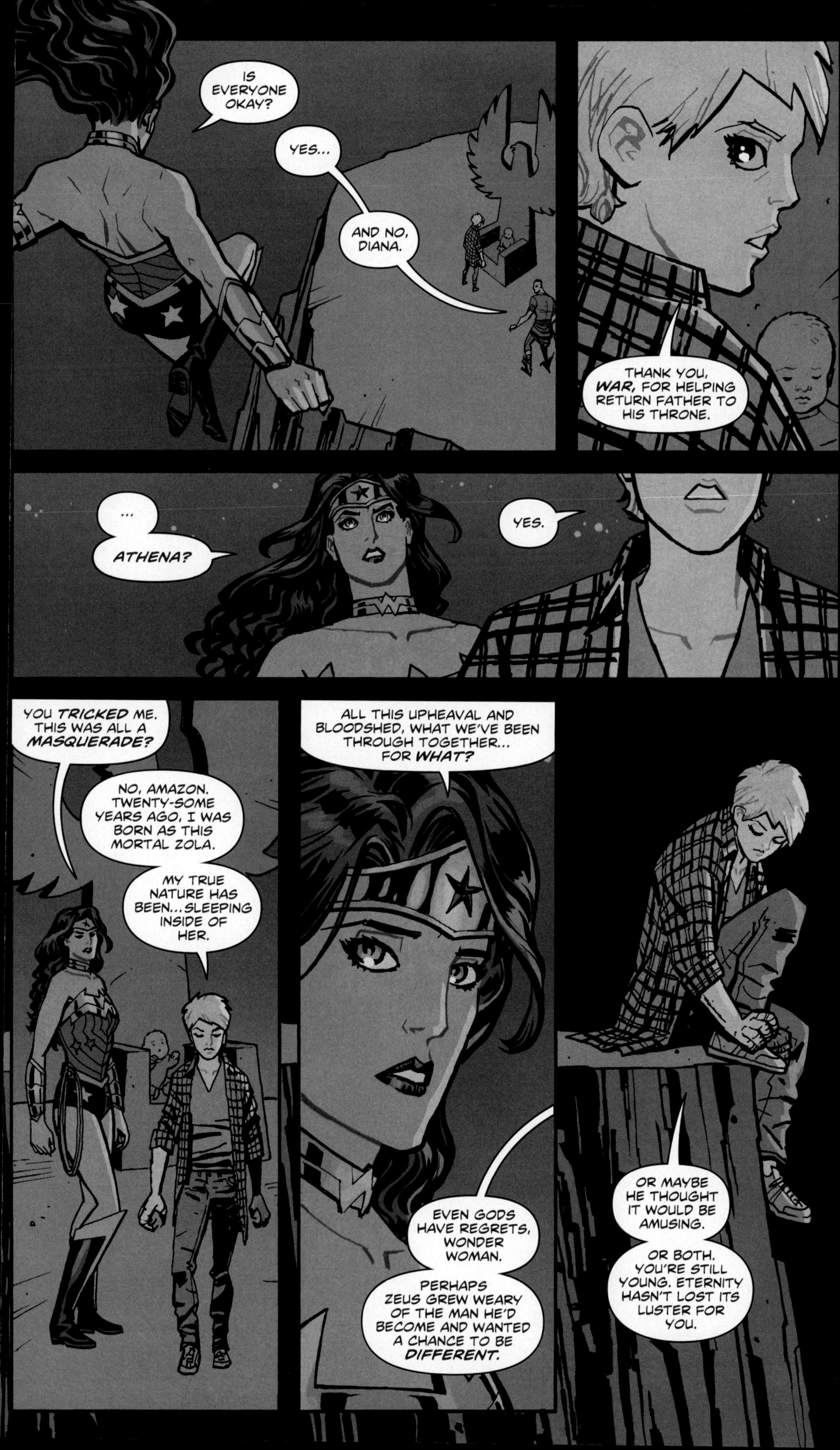
IS EVERYONE OKAY?
YES...
AND NO, DIANA.
THANK YOU, WAR, FOR HELPING RETURN FATHER TO HIS THRONE.
...
ATHENA?
YES.
YOU TRICKED ME. THIS WAS ALL A MASQUERADE?
NO, AMAZON. TWENTY-SOME YEARS AGO, I WAS BORN AS THIS MORTAL ZOLA.
MY TRUE NATURE HAS BEEN...SLEEPING INSIDE OF HER.
ALL THIS UPHEAVAL AND BLOODSHED, WHAT WE'VE BEEN THROUGH TOGETHER... FOR WHAT?
EVEN GODS HAVE REGRETS, WONDER WOMAN.
PERHAPS ZEUS GREW WEARY OF THE MAN HE'D BECOME AND WANTED A CHANCE TO BE DIFFERENT.
OR MAYBE HE THOUGHT IT WOULD BE AMUSING.
OR BOTH. YOU'RE STILL YOUNG. ETERNITY HASN'T LOST ITS LUSTER FOR YOU.

FATHER KNEW THAT WHEN HE DISAPPEARED, THE *FIRST BORN* WOULD RETURN.

AND THAT ARES WAS FALTERING.

AND THAT HE WANTED *MORE* FOR YOU.

STRIFE WAS TOLD THE SECRET OF YOUR BIRTH, KNOWING FULL WELL THAT HER NATURE WOULD START YOU ON THE PATH TO GODHOOD.

NONE SAVE I WAS PRIVY TO HIS FULL PLAN. IT WAS A RISKY GAMBIT, BUT YOU ALL PLAYED YOUR PARTS SPLENDIDLY.

AND I?

AS ZEUS ONCE GAVE BIRTH TO ME, I GAVE BIRTH TO HIM.

NOW ALL THAT IS LEFT IS TO DISCARD THE REMNANTS OF THIS *VESSEL'S* HUMANITY AND I SHALL BE MYSELF ONCE MORE.

ZO-- ATHENA!

WAIT!

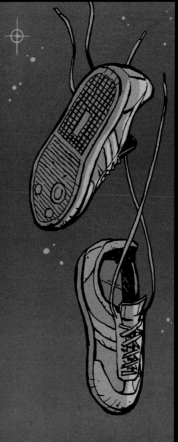

WAAAAAA

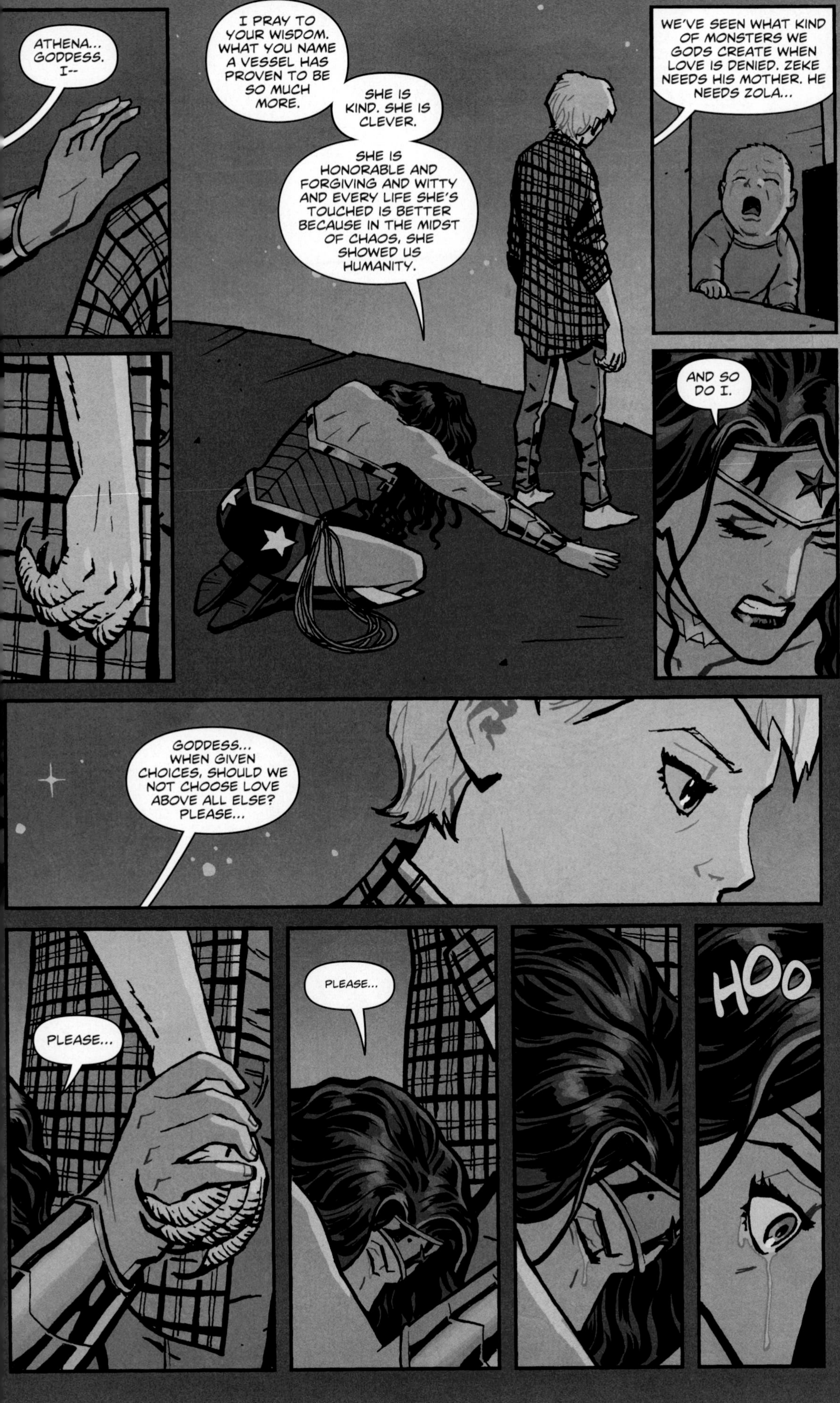
ATHENA... GODDESS. I--
I PRAY TO YOUR WISDOM. WHAT YOU NAME A VESSEL HAS PROVEN TO BE SO MUCH MORE.
SHE IS KIND. SHE IS CLEVER.
SHE IS HONORABLE AND FORGIVING AND WITTY AND EVERY LIFE SHE'S TOUCHED IS BETTER BECAUSE IN THE MIDST OF CHAOS, SHE SHOWED US HUMANITY.
WE'VE SEEN WHAT KIND OF MONSTERS WE GODS CREATE WHEN LOVE IS DENIED. ZEKE NEEDS HIS MOTHER. HE NEEDS ZOLA...
AND SO DO I.
GODDESS... WHEN GIVEN CHOICES, SHOULD WE NOT CHOOSE LOVE ABOVE ALL ELSE? PLEASE...
PLEASE...
PLEASE...
HOO

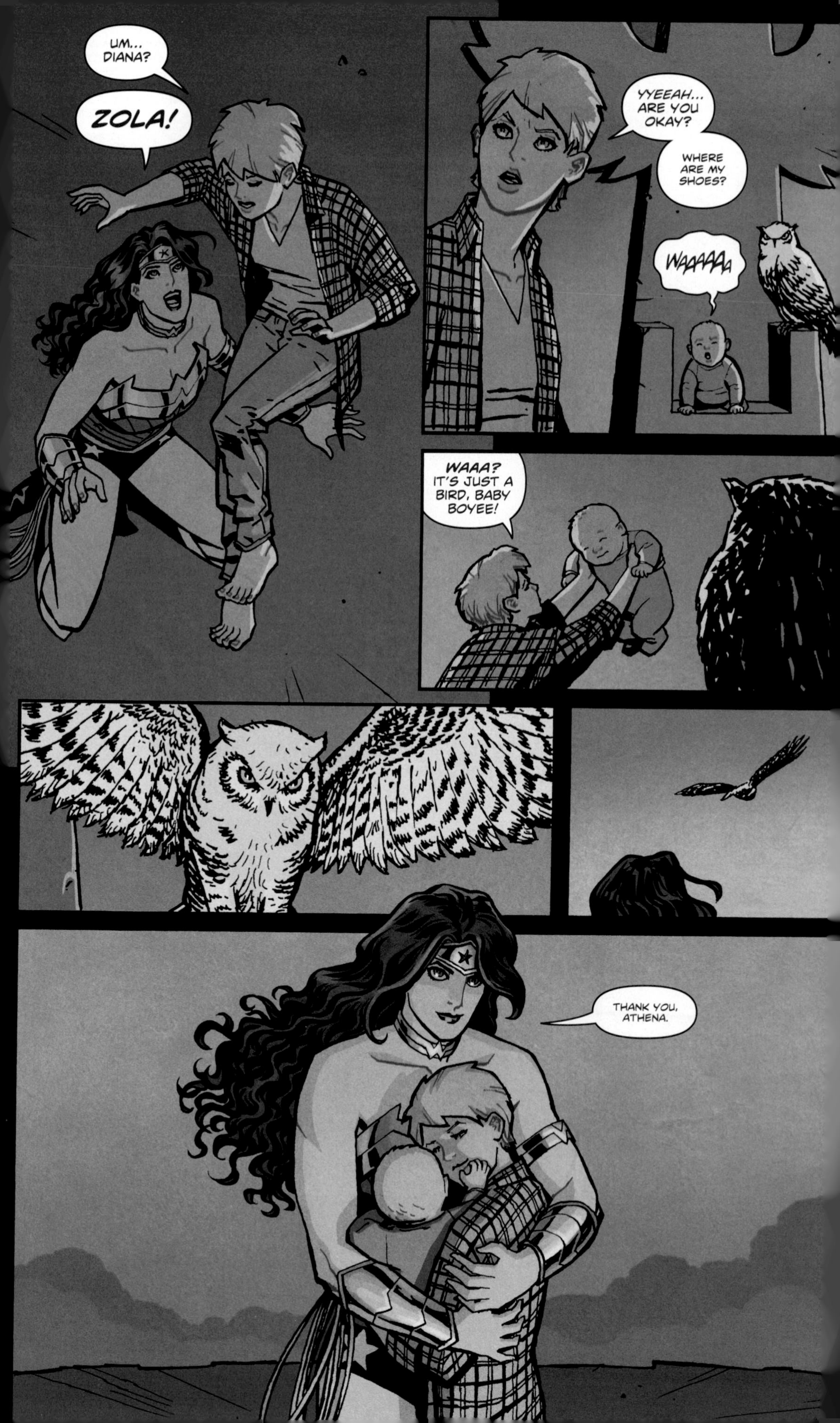
UM... DIANA?
ZOLA!
YYEEAH... ARE YOU OKAY?
WHERE ARE MY SHOES?
WAAAAAa
WAAA? IT'S JUST A BIRD, BABY BOYEE!
THANK YOU, ATHENA.

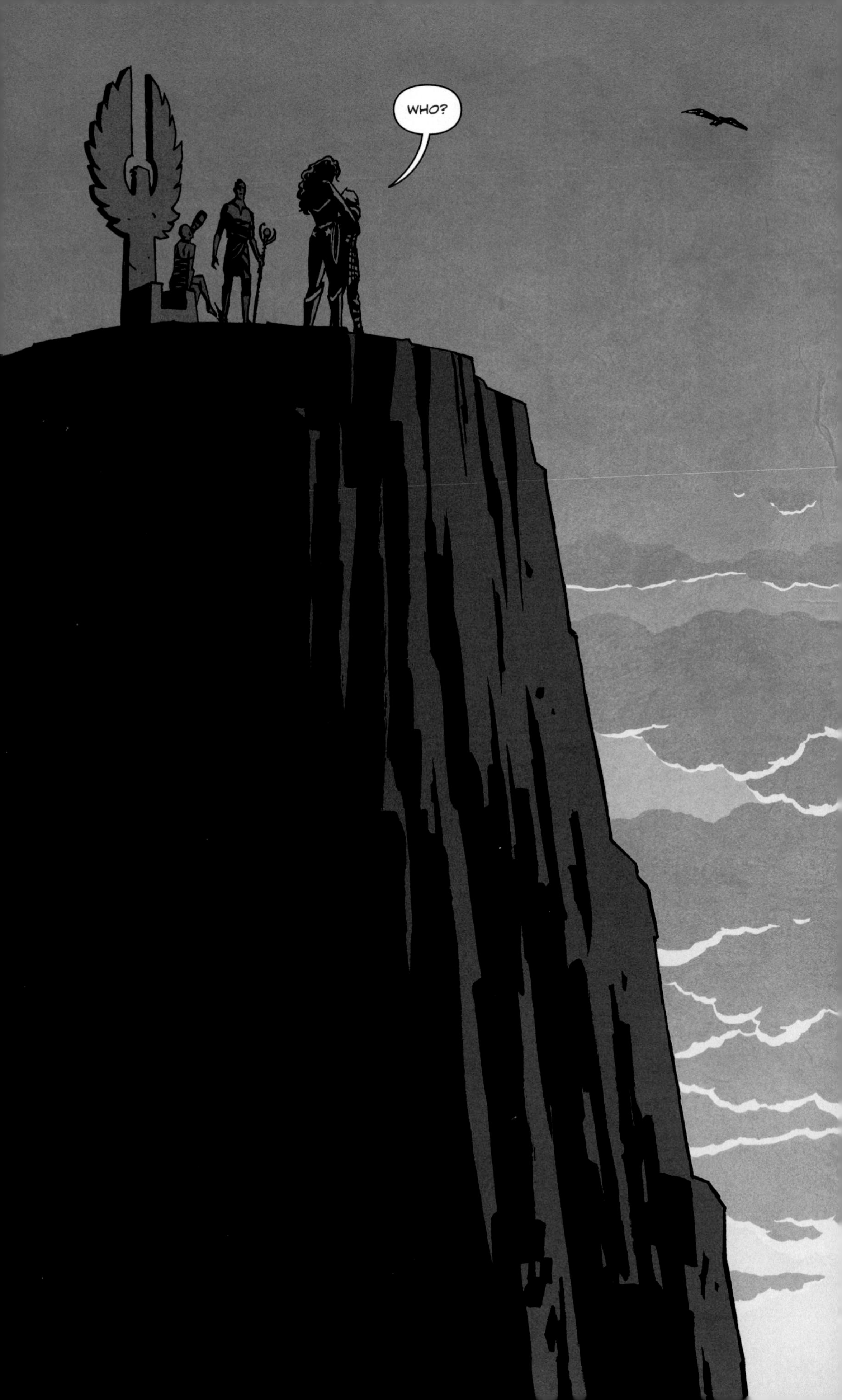
WHO?

SECRET ORIGINS #6 Cover by Lee Bermejo

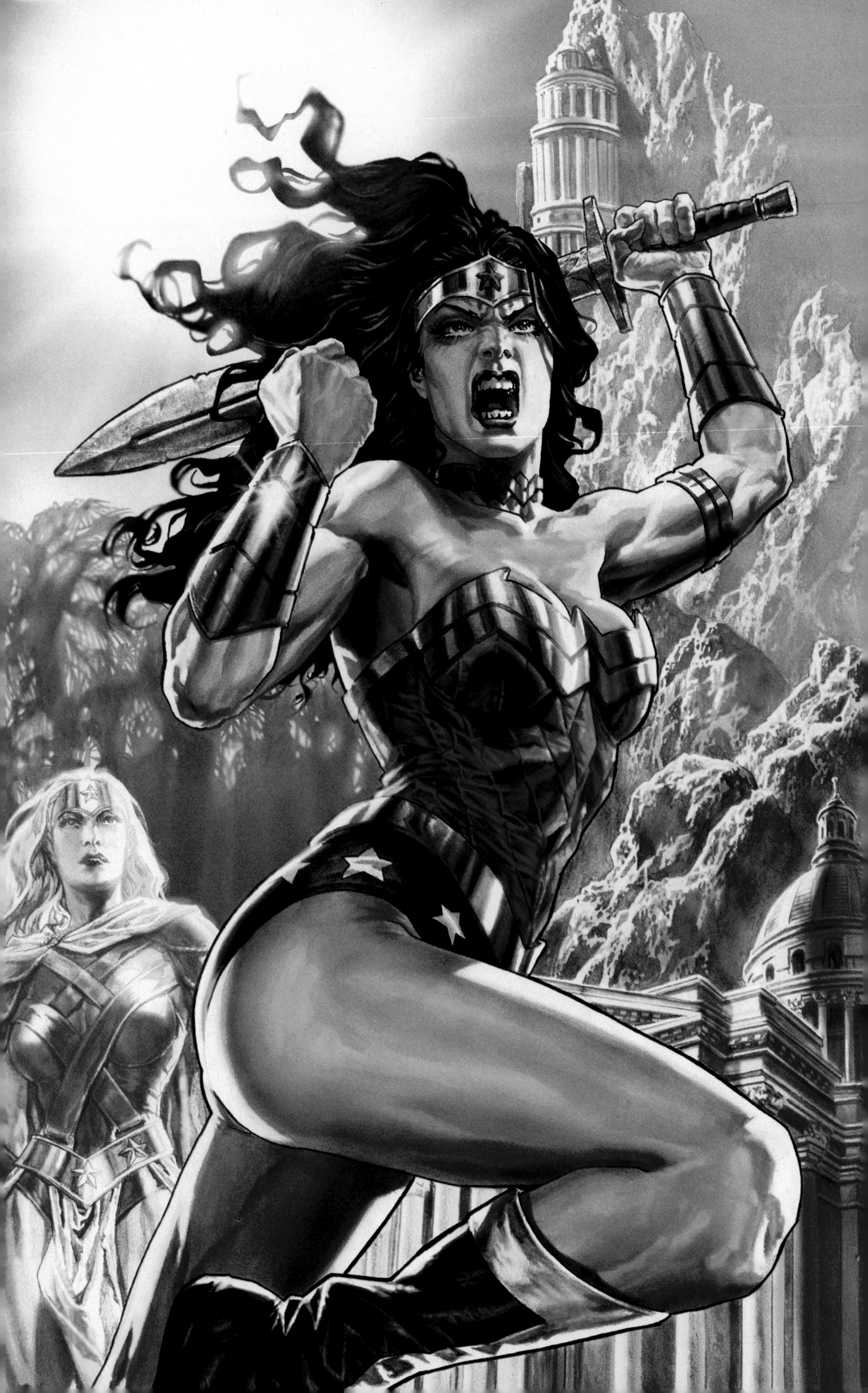

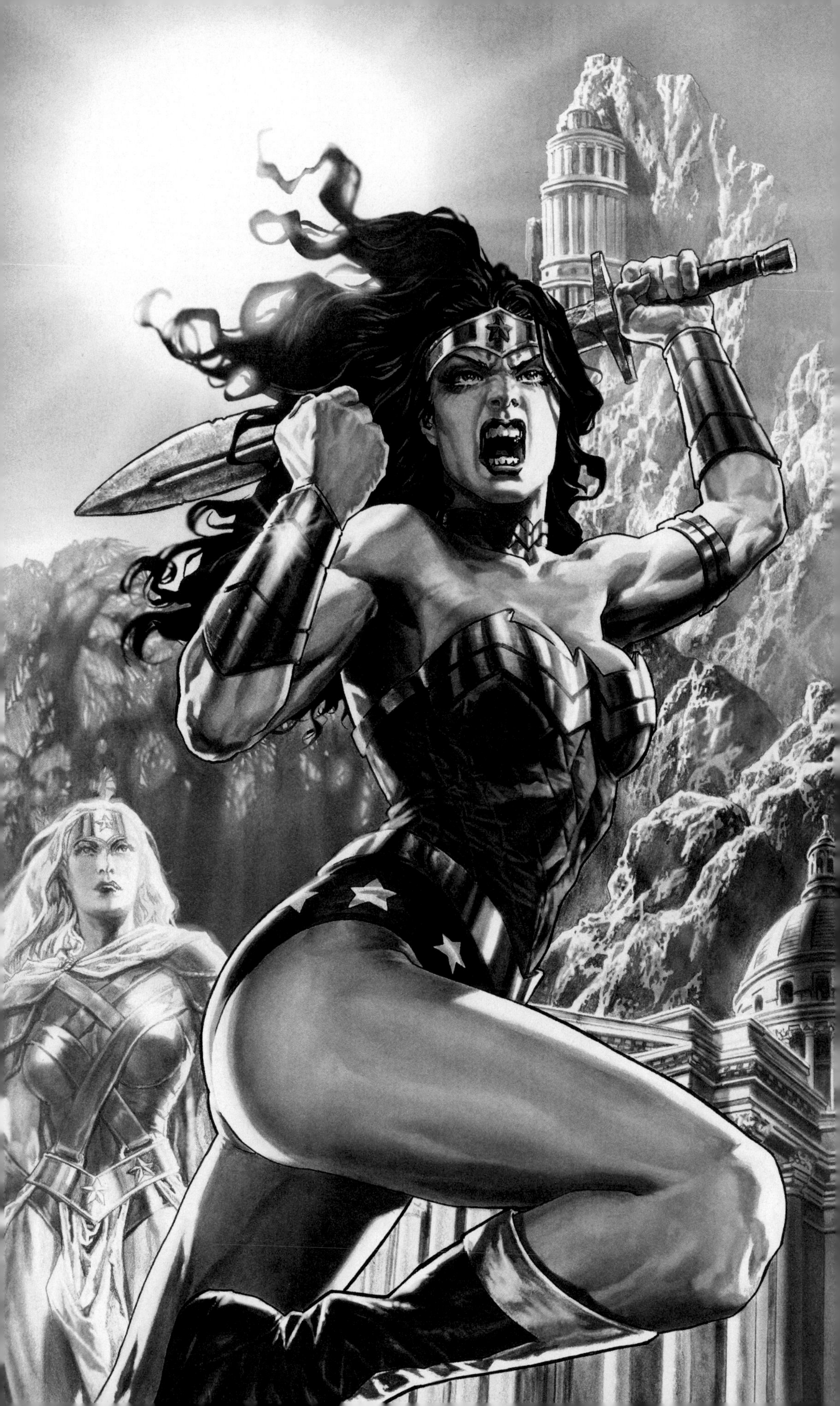

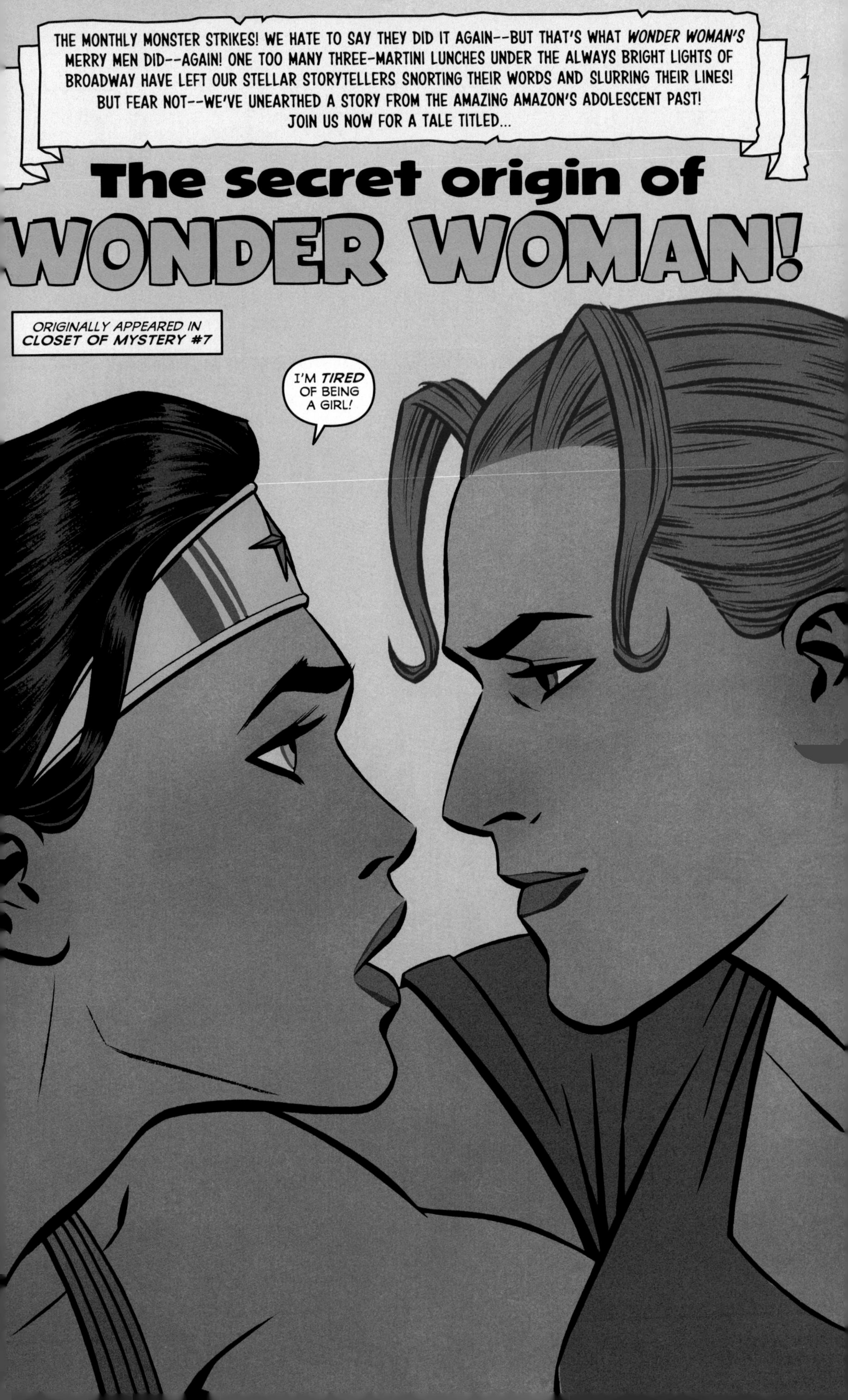

THE MONTHLY MONSTER STRIKES! WE HATE TO SAY THEY DID IT AGAIN--BUT THAT'S WHAT *WONDER WOMAN'S* MERRY MEN DID--AGAIN! ONE TOO MANY THREE-MARTINI LUNCHES UNDER THE ALWAYS BRIGHT LIGHTS OF BROADWAY HAVE LEFT OUR STELLAR STORYTELLERS SNORTING THEIR WORDS AND SLURRING THEIR LINES! BUT FEAR NOT--WE'VE UNEARTHED A STORY FROM THE AMAZING AMAZON'S ADOLESCENT PAST! JOIN US NOW FOR A TALE TITLED...
The secret origin of
WONDER WOMAN!
ORIGINALLY APPEARED IN CLOSET OF MYSTERY #7
I'M *TIRED* OF BEING A GIRL!

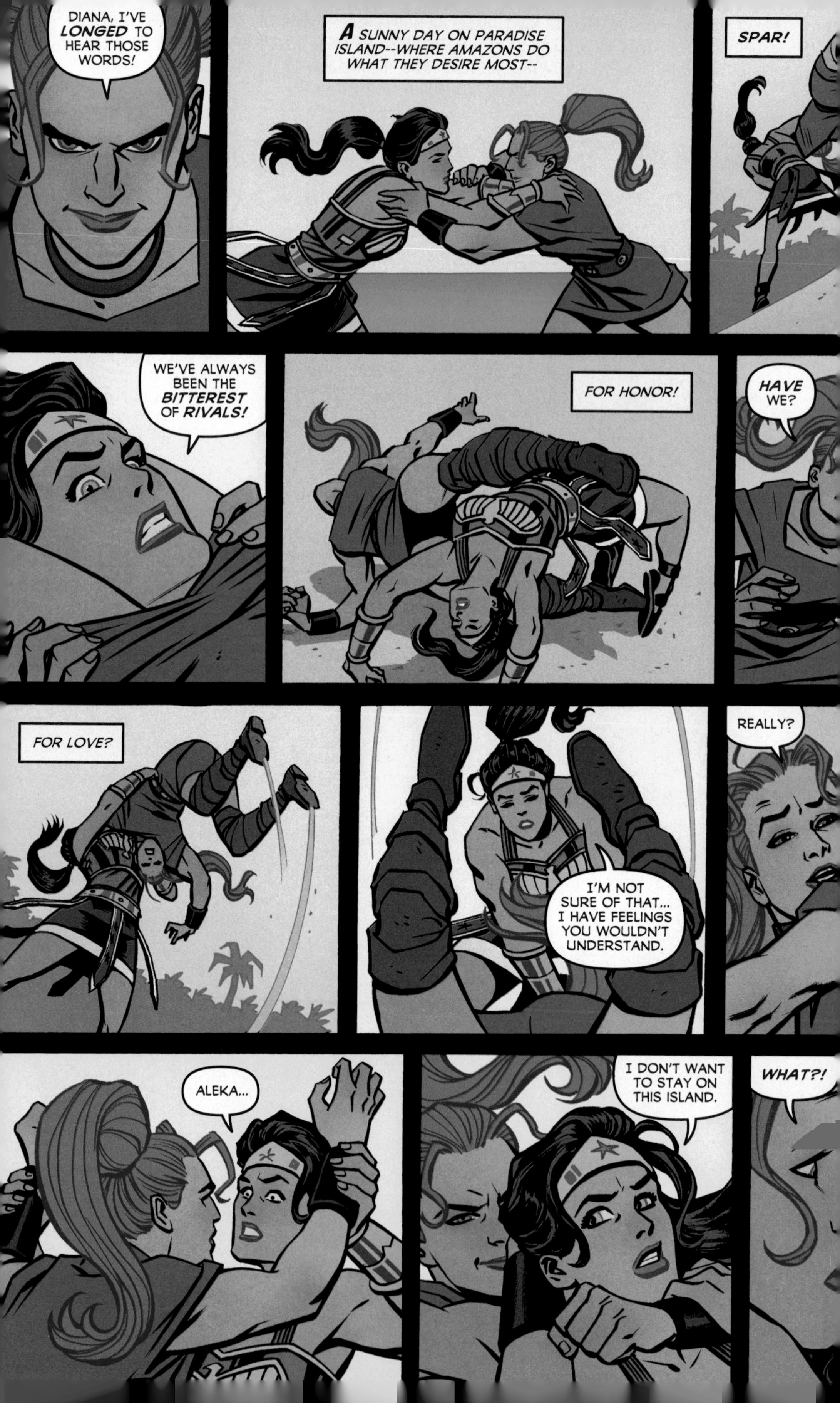
DIANA, I'VE LONGED TO HEAR THOSE WORDS!
A SUNNY DAY ON PARADISE ISLAND--WHERE AMAZONS DO WHAT THEY DESIRE MOST--
SPAR!
WE'VE ALWAYS BEEN THE BITTEREST OF RIVALS!
FOR HONOR!
HAVE WE?
FOR LOVE?
I'M NOT SURE OF THAT... I HAVE FEELINGS YOU WOULDN'T UNDERSTAND.
REALLY?
ALEKA...
I DON'T WANT TO STAY ON THIS ISLAND.
WHAT?!

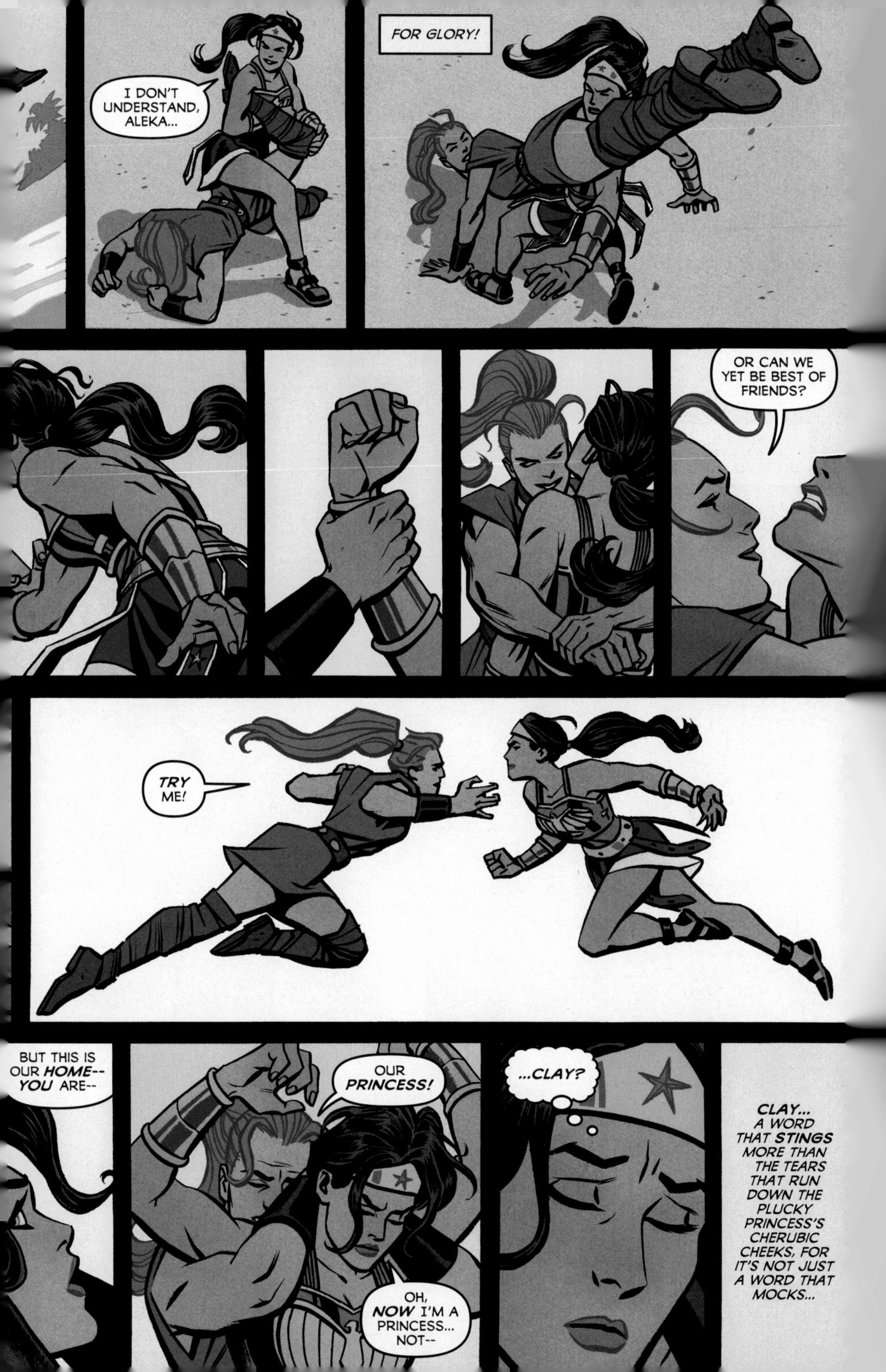
I DON'T UNDERSTAND, ALEKA...
FOR GLORY!
OR CAN WE YET BE BEST OF FRIENDS?
TRY ME!
BUT THIS IS OUR HOME-- YOU ARE--
OUR PRINCESS!
OH, NOW I'M A PRINCESS... NOT--
...CLAY?
CLAY... A WORD THAT STINGS MORE THAN THE TEARS THAT RUN DOWN THE PLUCKY PRINCESS'S CHERUBIC CHEEKS, FOR IT'S NOT JUST A WORD THAT MOCKS...

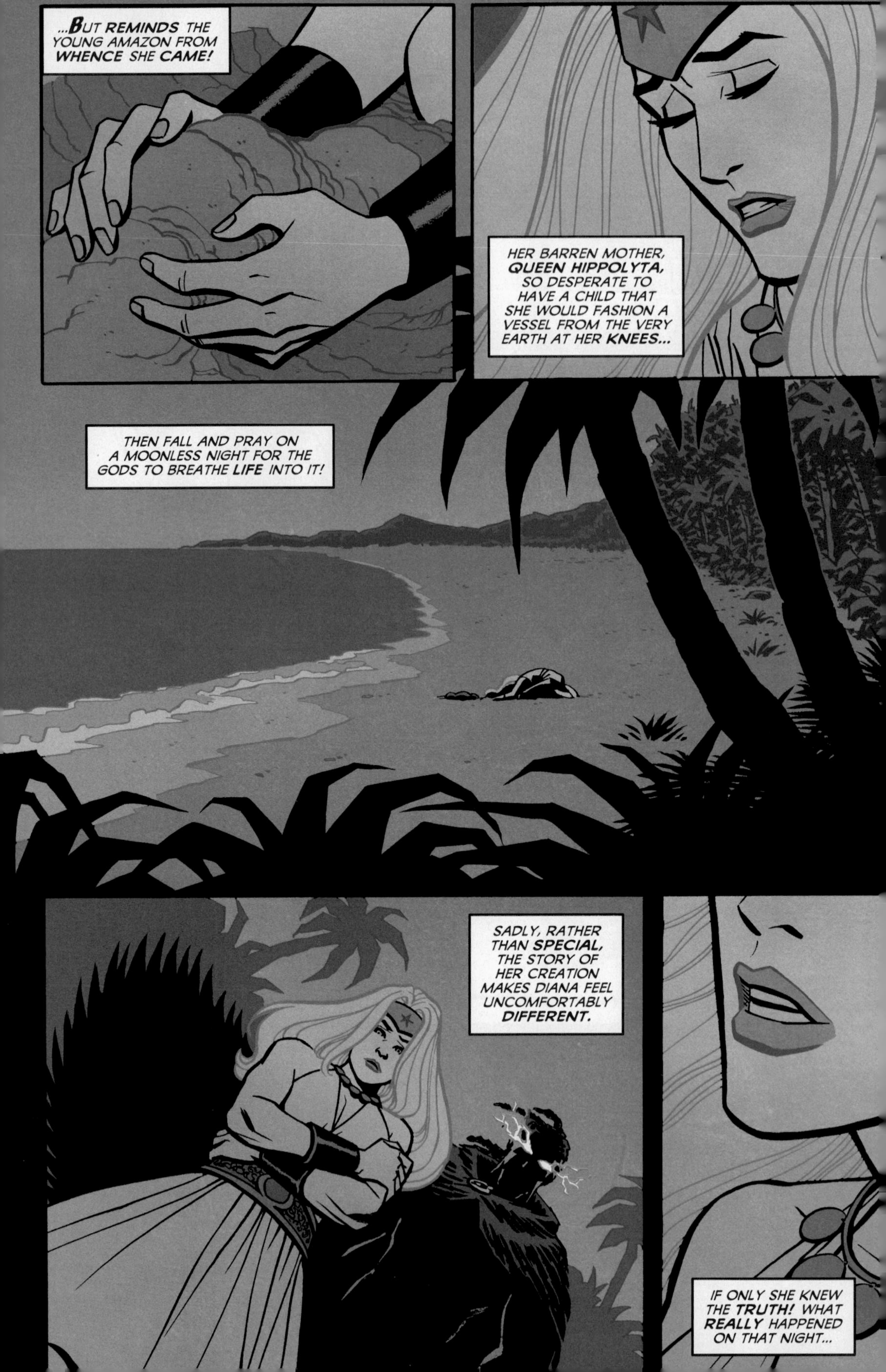
...BUT REMINDS THE YOUNG AMAZON FROM WHENCE SHE CAME!
HER BARREN MOTHER, QUEEN HIPPOLYTA, SO DESPERATE TO HAVE A CHILD THAT SHE WOULD FASHION A VESSEL FROM THE VERY EARTH AT HER KNEES...
THEN FALL AND PRAY ON A MOONLESS NIGHT FOR THE GODS TO BREATHE LIFE INTO IT!
SADLY, RATHER THAN SPECIAL, THE STORY OF HER CREATION MAKES DIANA FEEL UNCOMFORTABLY DIFFERENT.
IF ONLY SHE KNEW THE TRUTH! WHAT REALLY HAPPENED ON THAT NIGHT...

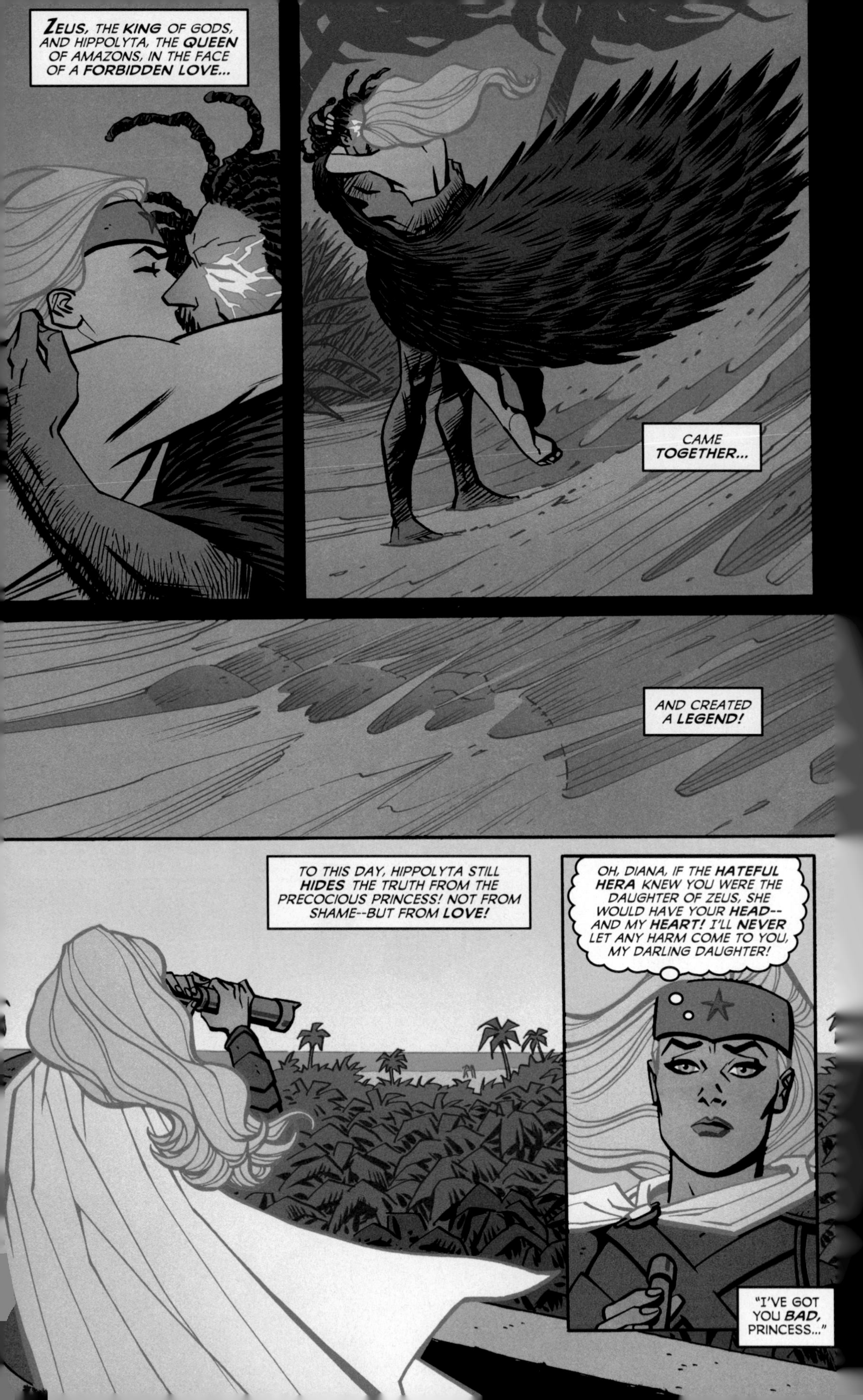
ZEUS, THE KING OF GODS, AND HIPPOLYTA, THE QUEEN OF AMAZONS, IN THE FACE OF A FORBIDDEN LOVE...
CAME TOGETHER...
AND CREATED A LEGEND!
TO THIS DAY, HIPPOLYTA STILL HIDES THE TRUTH FROM THE PRECOCIOUS PRINCESS! NOT FROM SHAME--BUT FROM LOVE!
OH, DIANA, IF THE HATEFUL HERA KNEW YOU WERE THE DAUGHTER OF ZEUS, SHE WOULD HAVE YOUR HEAD--AND MY HEART! I'LL NEVER LET ANY HARM COME TO YOU, MY DARLING DAUGHTER!
"I'VE GOT YOU BAD, PRINCESS..."

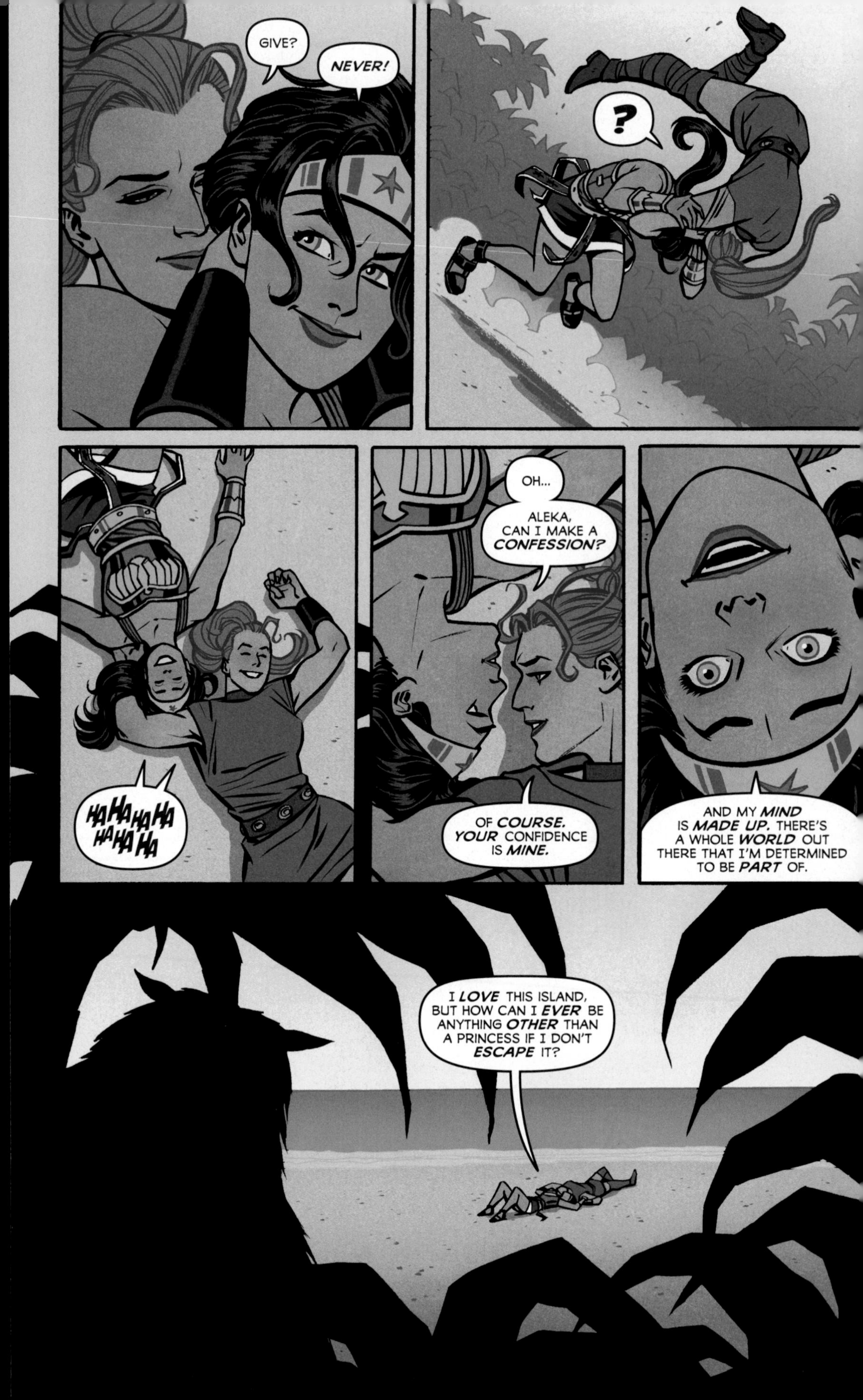
GIVE?
NEVER!
?
HAHAHAHA HAHAHA
OH...
ALEKA, CAN I MAKE A CONFESSION?
OF COURSE. YOUR CONFIDENCE IS MINE.
AND MY MIND IS MADE UP. THERE'S A WHOLE WORLD OUT THERE THAT I'M DETERMINED TO BE PART OF.
I LOVE THIS ISLAND, BUT HOW CAN I EVER BE ANYTHING OTHER THAN A PRINCESS IF I DON'T ESCAPE IT?

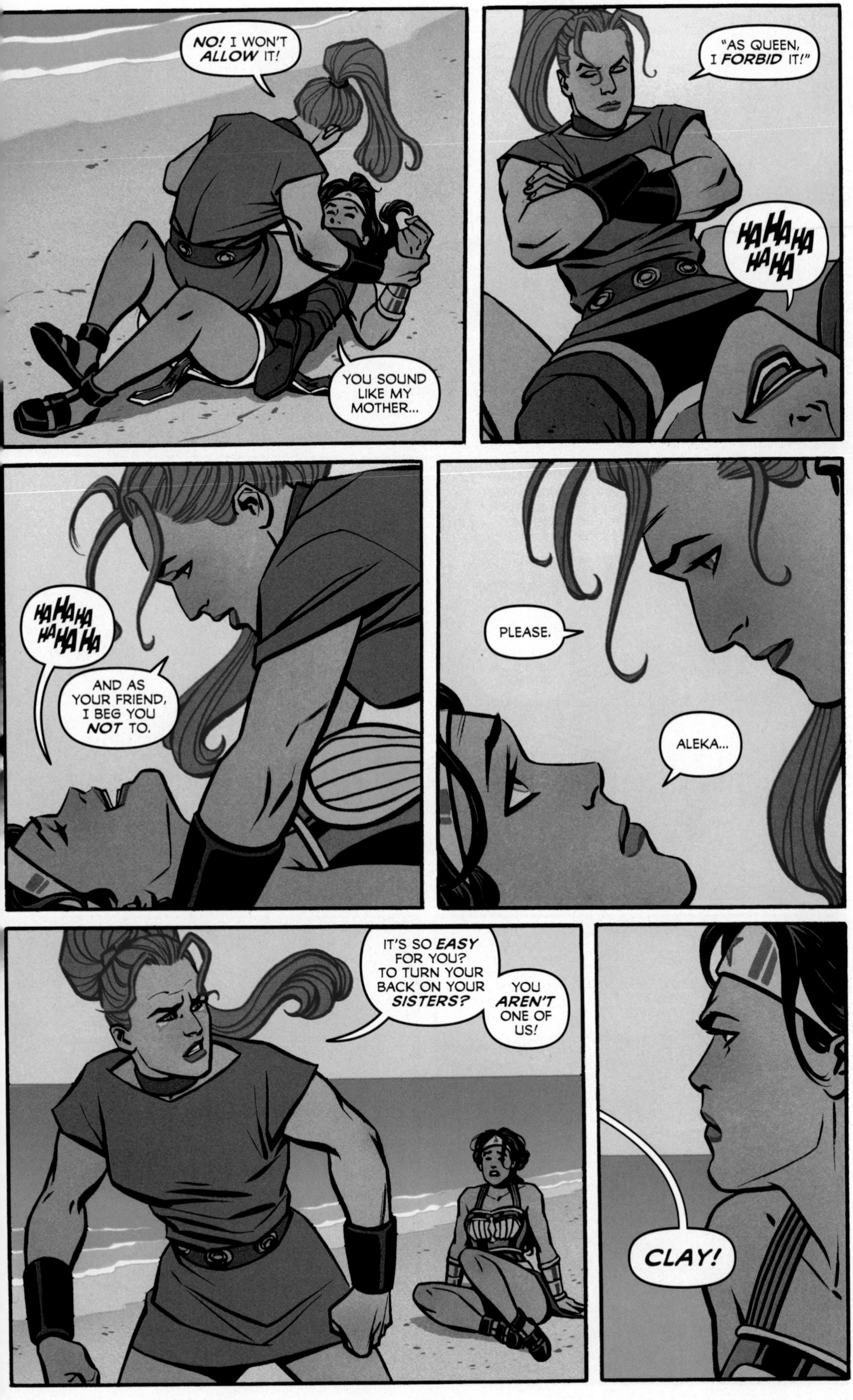
NO! I WON'T ALLOW IT!
YOU SOUND LIKE MY MOTHER...
"AS QUEEN, I FORBID IT!"
HAHAHA HAHA
HAHAHA HAHAHA
AND AS YOUR FRIEND, I BEG YOU NOT TO.
PLEASE.
ALEKA...
IT'S SO EASY FOR YOU? TO TURN YOUR BACK ON YOUR SISTERS?
YOU AREN'T ONE OF US!
CLAY!

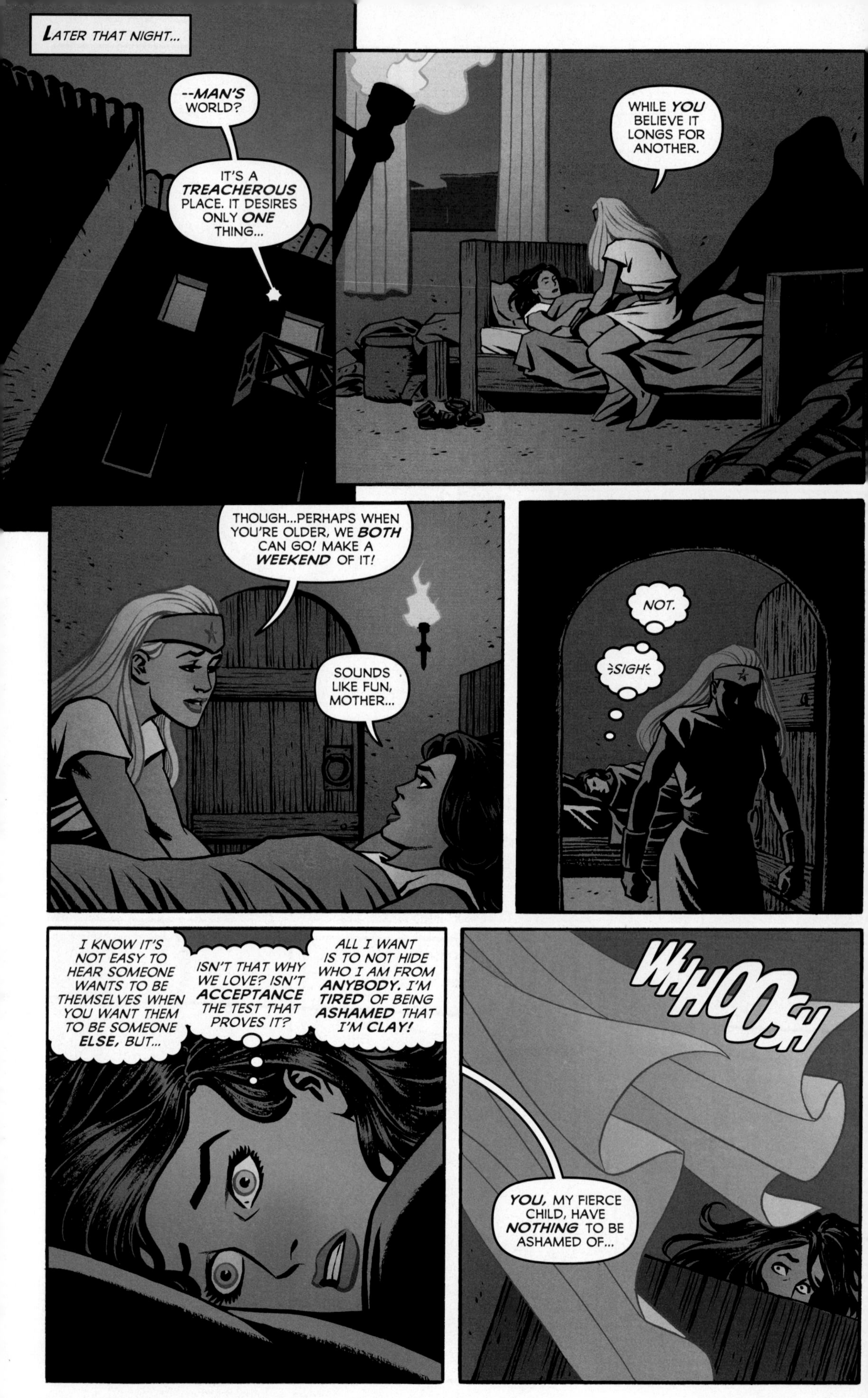
LATER THAT NIGHT...
--MAN'S WORLD?
IT'S A TREACHEROUS PLACE. IT DESIRES ONLY ONE THING...
WHILE YOU BELIEVE IT LONGS FOR ANOTHER.
THOUGH...PERHAPS WHEN YOU'RE OLDER, WE BOTH CAN GO! MAKE A WEEKEND OF IT!
SOUNDS LIKE FUN, MOTHER...
NOT.
SIGH
I KNOW IT'S NOT EASY TO HEAR SOMEONE WANTS TO BE THEMSELVES WHEN YOU WANT THEM TO BE SOMEONE ELSE, BUT...
ISN'T THAT WHY WE LOVE? ISN'T ACCEPTANCE THE TEST THAT PROVES IT?
ALL I WANT IS TO NOT HIDE WHO I AM FROM ANYBODY. I'M TIRED OF BEING ASHAMED THAT I'M CLAY!
WHHOOSH
YOU, MY FIERCE CHILD, HAVE NOTHING TO BE ASHAMED OF...

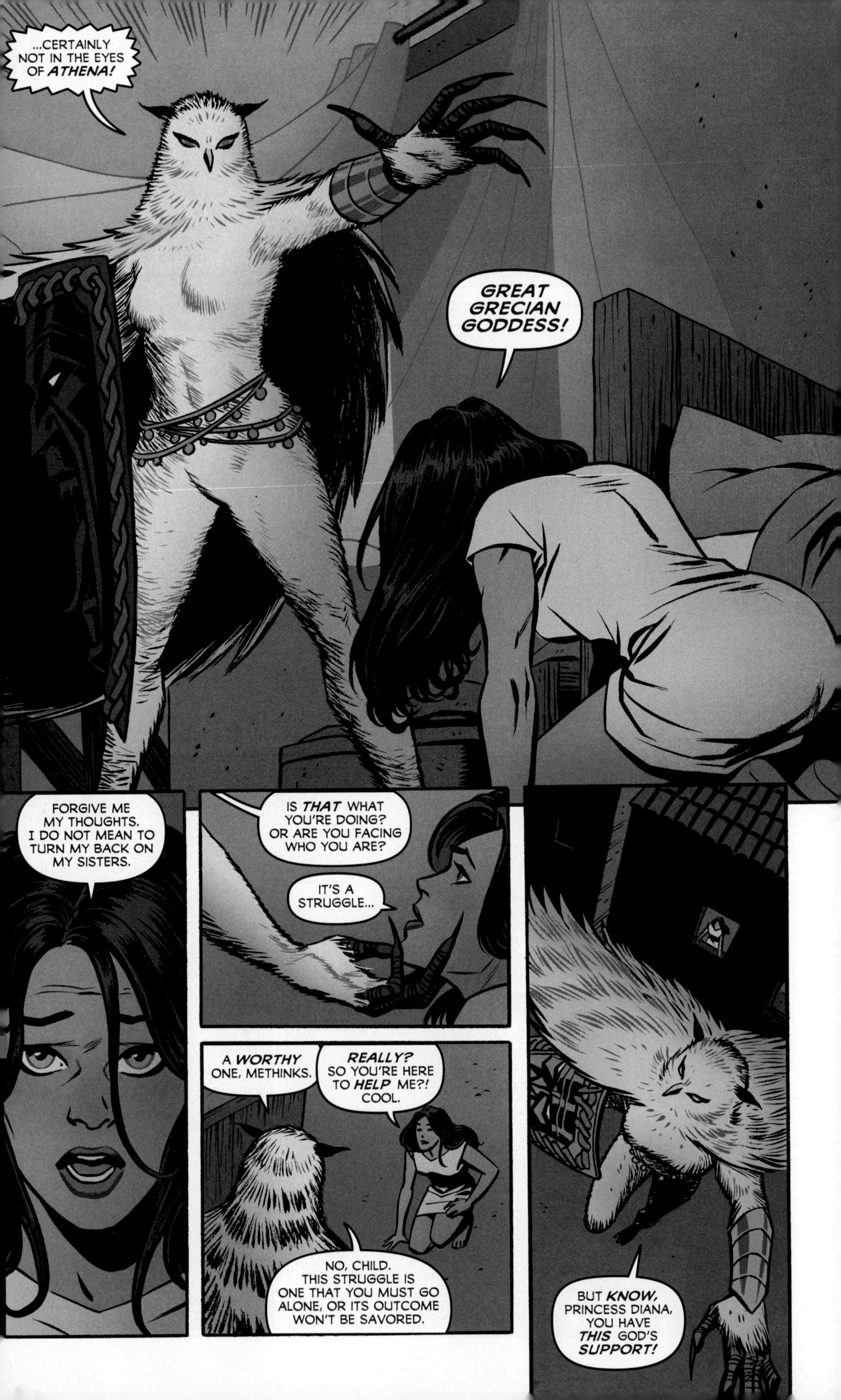

...CERTAINLY NOT IN THE EYES OF *ATHENA!*
GREAT GRECIAN GODDESS!
FORGIVE ME MY THOUGHTS. I DO NOT MEAN TO TURN MY BACK ON MY SISTERS.
IS *THAT* WHAT YOU'RE DOING? OR ARE YOU FACING WHO YOU ARE?
IT'S A STRUGGLE...
A *WORTHY* ONE, METHINKS.
REALLY? SO YOU'RE HERE TO *HELP* ME?! COOL.
NO, CHILD. THIS STRUGGLE IS ONE THAT YOU MUST GO ALONE, OR ITS OUTCOME WON'T BE SAVORED.
BUT *KNOW,* PRINCESS DIANA, YOU HAVE *THIS* GOD'S *SUPPORT!*

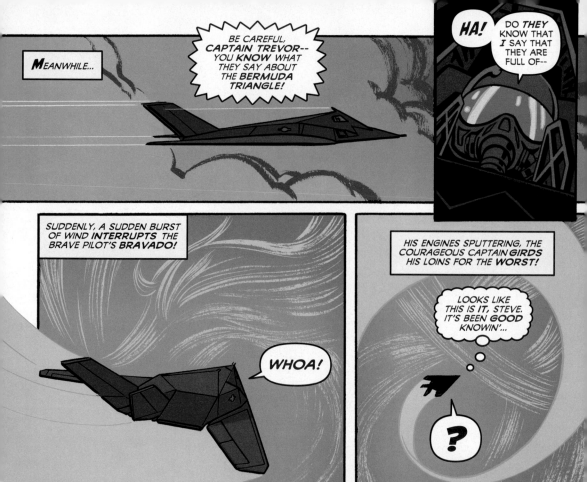

MEANWHILE...

BE CAREFUL, CAPTAIN TREVOR-- YOU KNOW WHAT THEY SAY ABOUT THE BERMUDA TRIANGLE!

HA! DO THEY KNOW THAT I SAY THAT THEY ARE FULL OF--

SUDDENLY, A SUDDEN BURST OF WIND INTERRUPTS THE BRAVE PILOT'S BRAVADO!

WHOA!

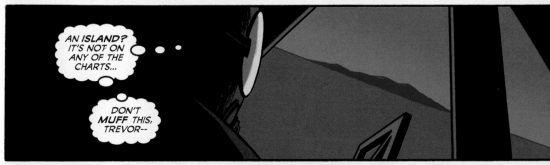

HIS ENGINES SPUTTERING, THE COURAGEOUS CAPTAIN GIRDS HIS LOINS FOR THE WORST!

LOOKS LIKE THIS IS IT, STEVE. IT'S BEEN GOOD KNOWIN'...

?

AN ISLAND? IT'S NOT ON ANY OF THE CHARTS...

DON'T MUFF THIS, TREVOR--

JUST GO DOWN!

BrRR.RrRr

CRASH

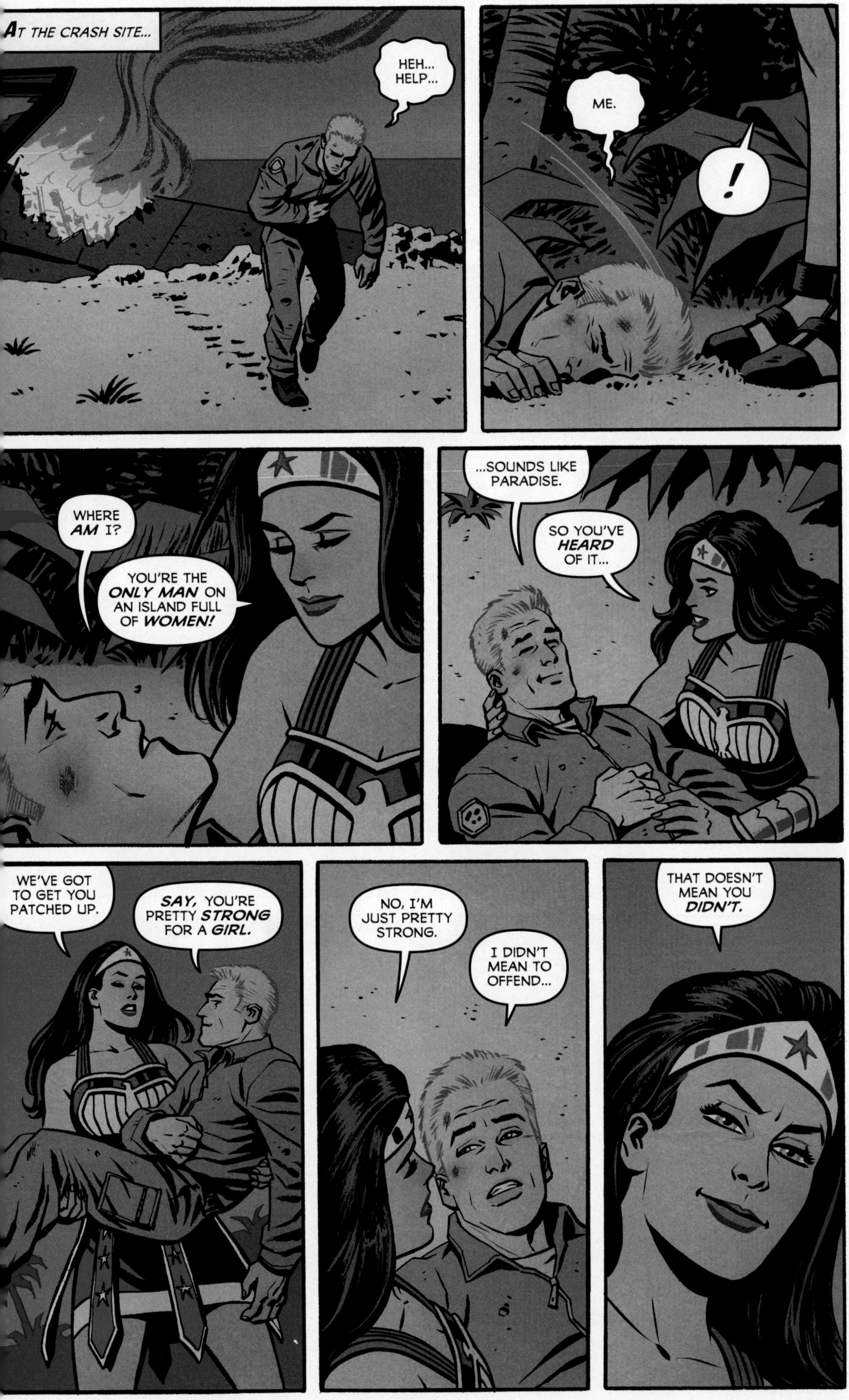
AT THE CRASH SITE...
HEH... HELP...
ME.
!
WHERE AM I?
YOU'RE THE ONLY MAN ON AN ISLAND FULL OF WOMEN!
...SOUNDS LIKE PARADISE.
SO YOU'VE HEARD OF IT...
WE'VE GOT TO GET YOU PATCHED UP.
SAY, YOU'RE PRETTY STRONG FOR A GIRL.
NO, I'M JUST PRETTY STRONG.
I DIDN'T MEAN TO OFFEND...
THAT DOESN'T MEAN YOU DIDN'T.

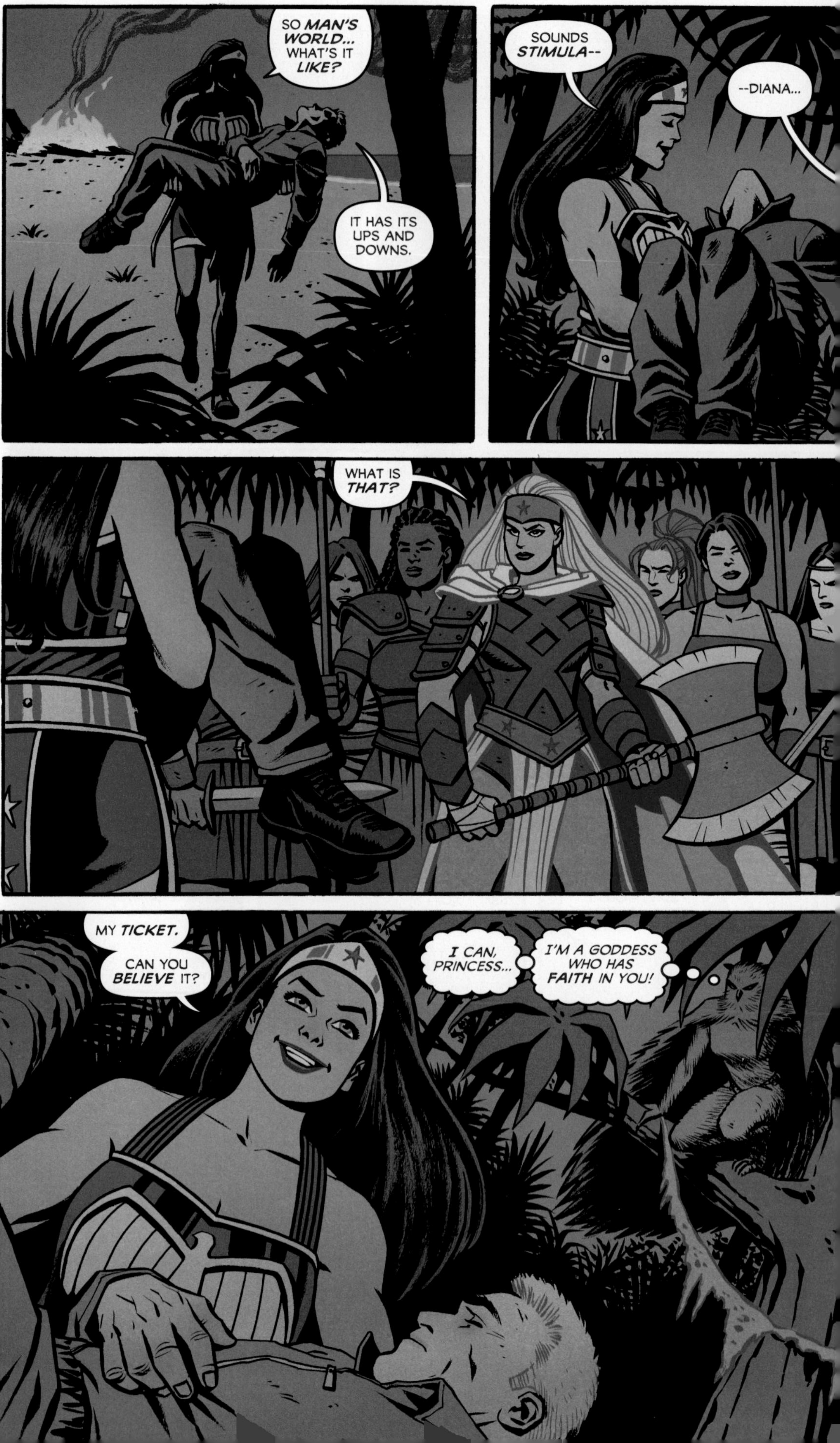
SO MAN'S WORLD... WHAT'S IT LIKE?
IT HAS ITS UPS AND DOWNS.
SOUNDS STIMULA--
--DIANA...
WHAT IS THAT?
MY TICKET.
CAN YOU BELIEVE IT?
I CAN, PRINCESS...
I'M A GODDESS WHO HAS FAITH IN YOU!

WONDER WOMAN
SKETCHES BY CLIFF CHIANG

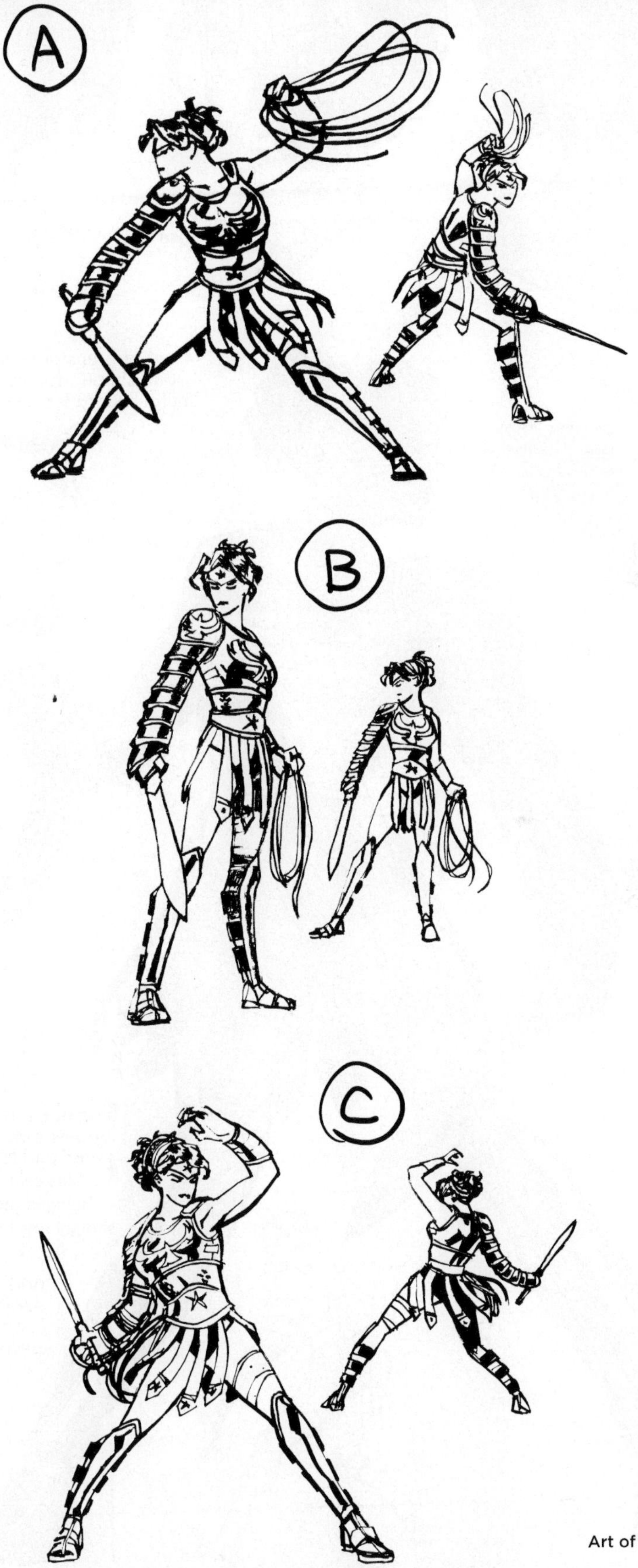
A
B
C

Art of War Statue

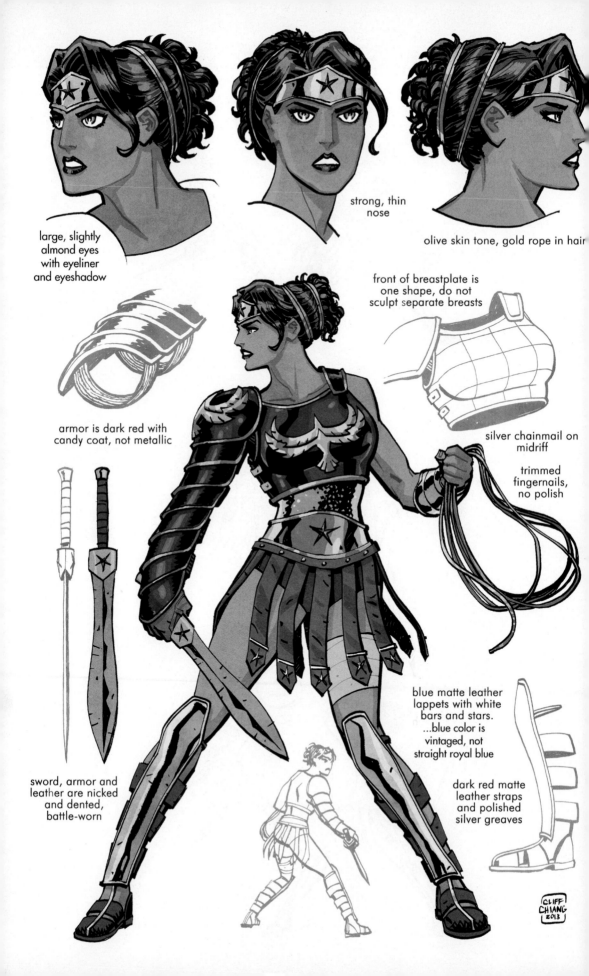

large, slightly
almond eyes
with eyeliner
and eyeshadow

strong, thin
nose

olive skin tone, gold rope in hair

front of breastplate is
one shape, do not
sculpt separate breasts

armor is dark red with
candy coat, not metallic

silver chainmail on
midriff

trimmed
fingernails,
no polish

sword, armor and
leather are nicked
and dented,
battle-worn

blue matte leather
lappets with white
bars and stars.
...blue color is
vintaged, not
straight royal blue

dark red matte
leather straps
and polished
silver greaves

CLIFF
CHIANG
2013

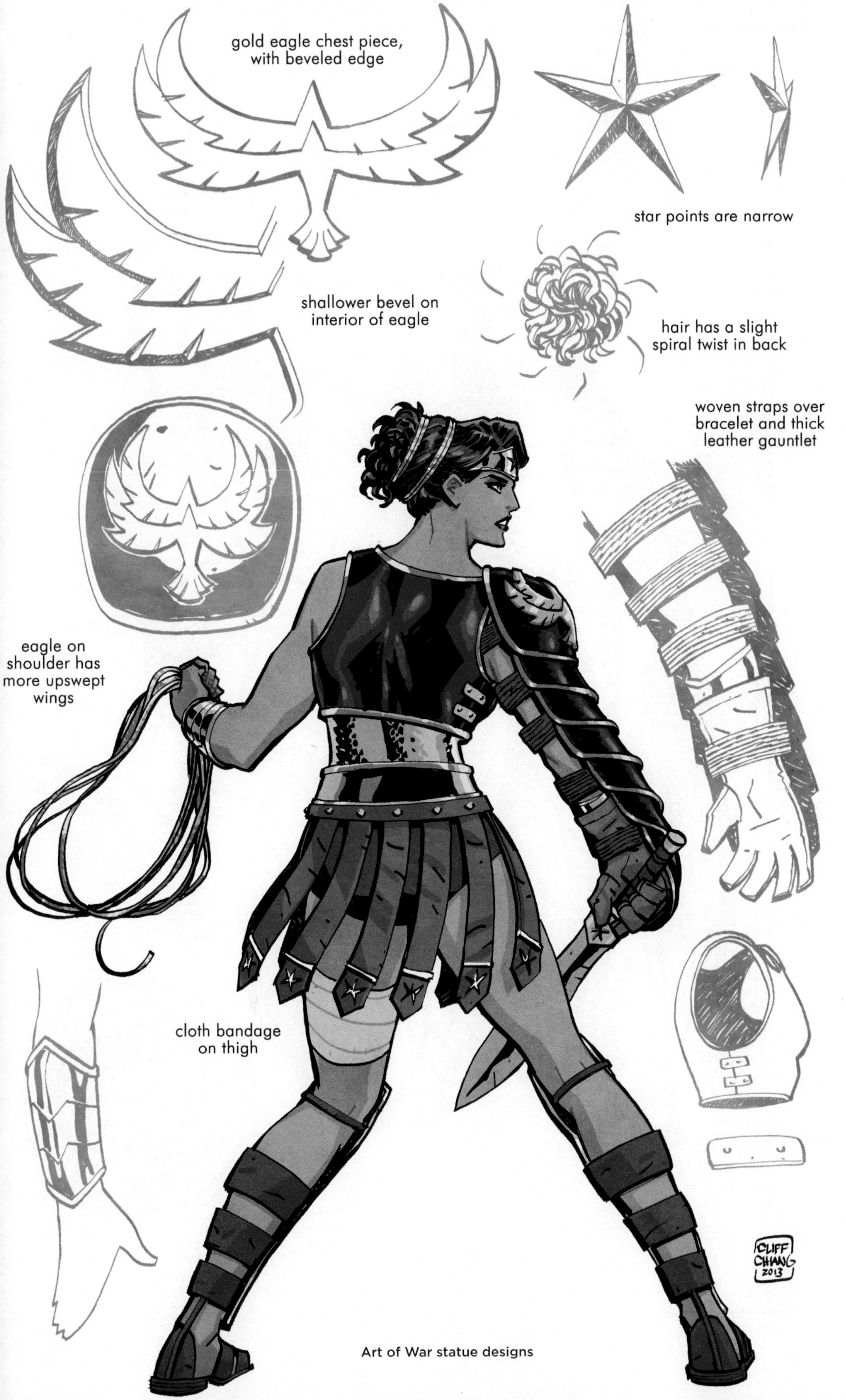
gold eagle chest piece, with beveled edge
star points are narrow
shallower bevel on interior of eagle
hair has a slight spiral twist in back
woven straps over bracelet and thick leather gauntlet
eagle on shoulder has more upswept wings
cloth bandage on thigh
CLIFF CHIANG 2013

Art of War statue designs

Athena sketches

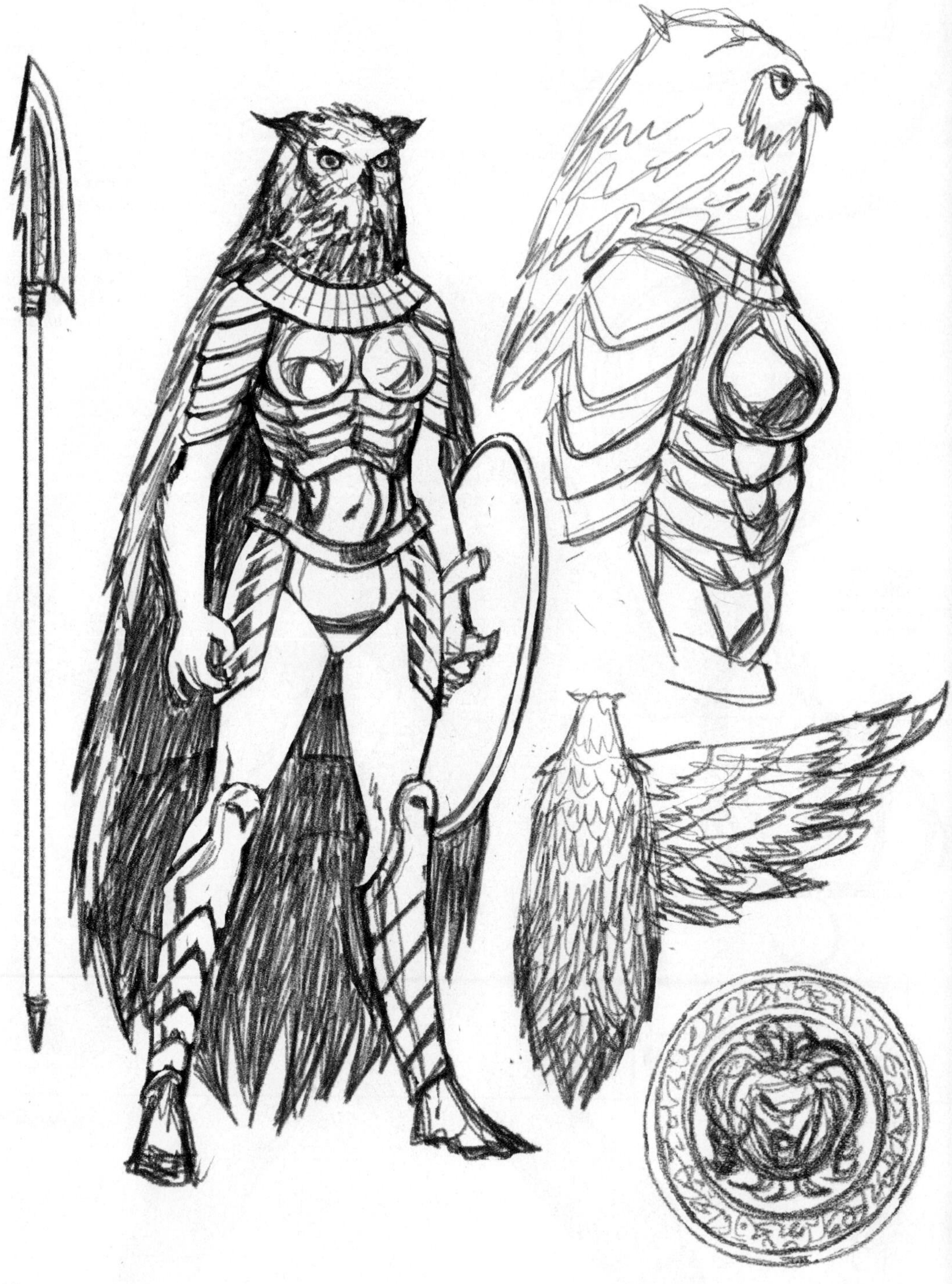

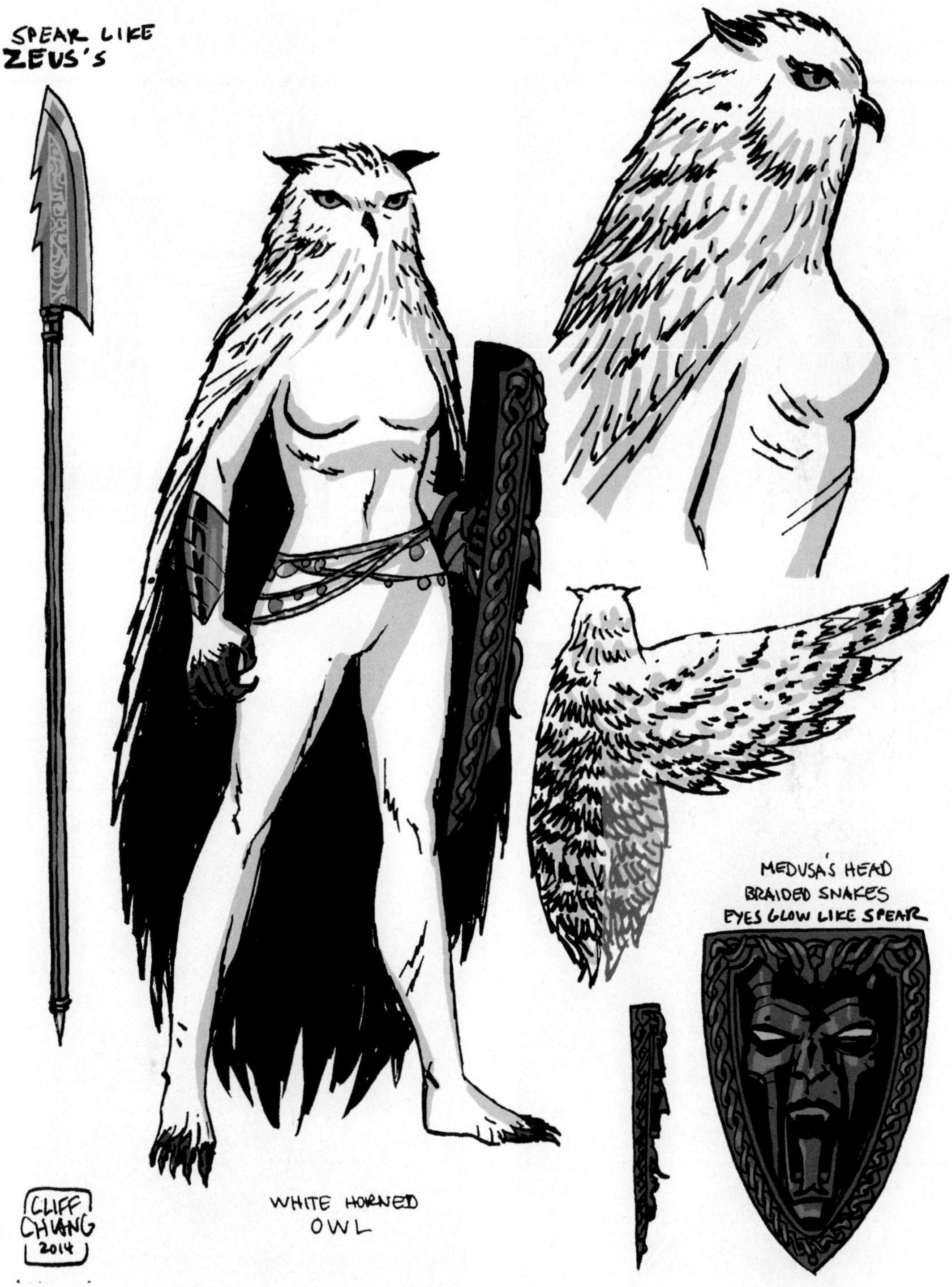
SPEAR LIKE
ZEUS'S
MEDUSA'S HEAD
BRAIDED SNAKES
EYES GLOW LIKE SPEAR
WHITE HORNED
OWL
CLIFF
CHIANG
2014

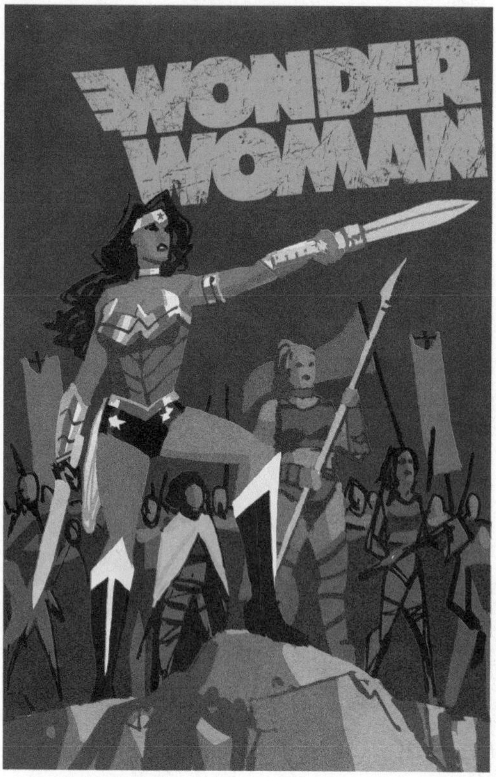
WONDER
WOMAN
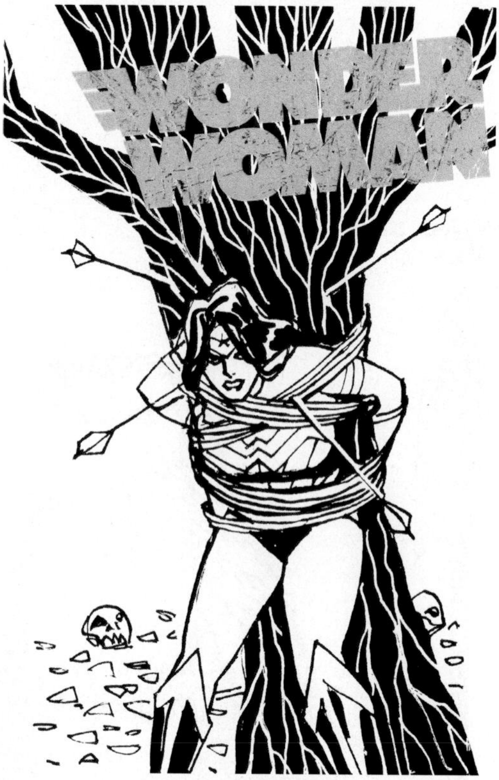
WONDER
WOMAN
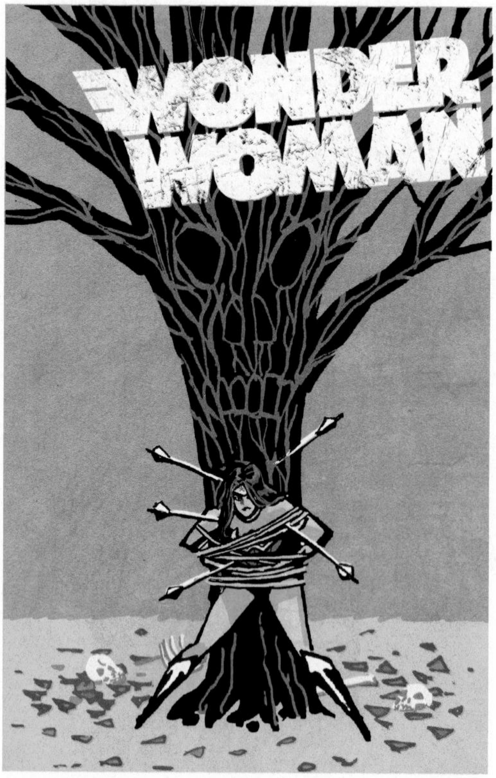
WONDER
WOMAN
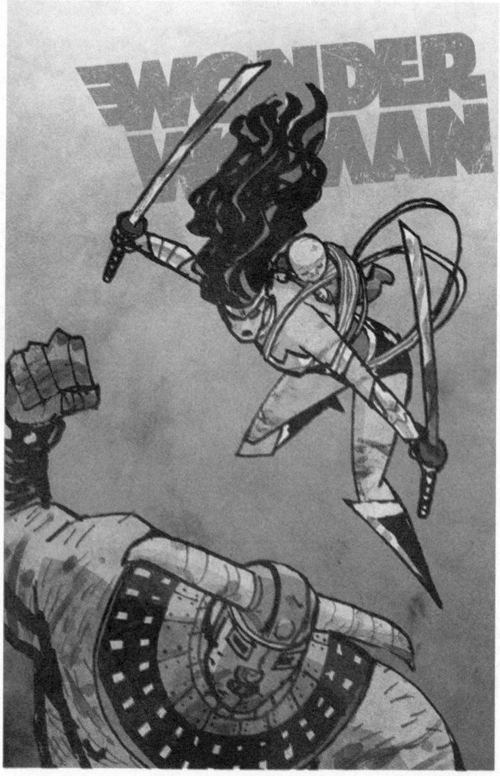
WONDER
WOMAN

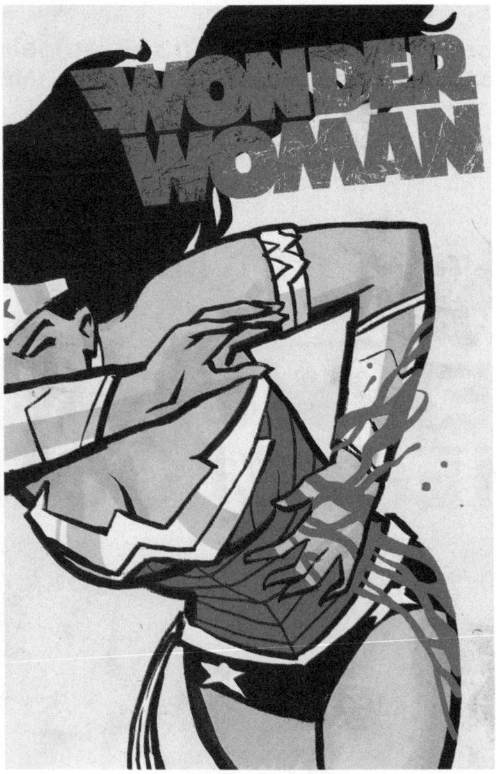
WONDER WOMAN

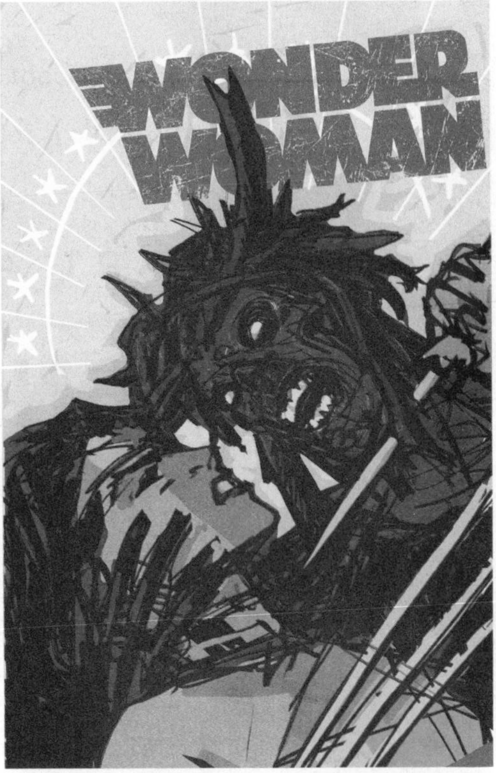
WONDER WOMAN

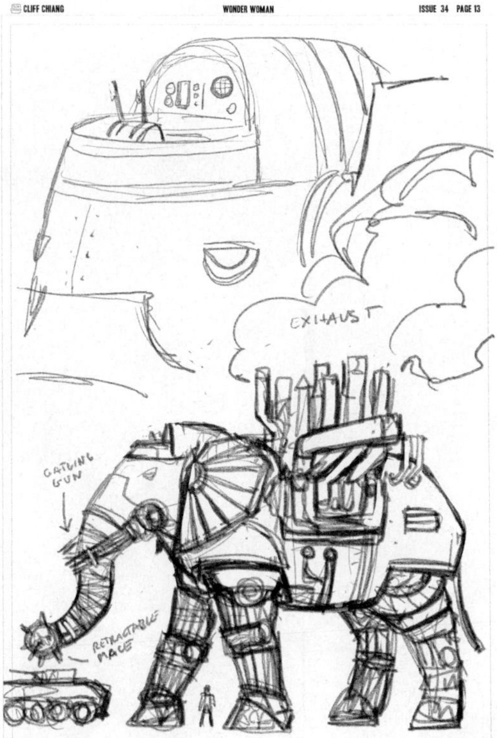
CLIFF CHIANG
WONDER WOMAN
ISSUE 34 PAGE 13
EXHAUST
GATLING GUN
RETRACTABLE MACE

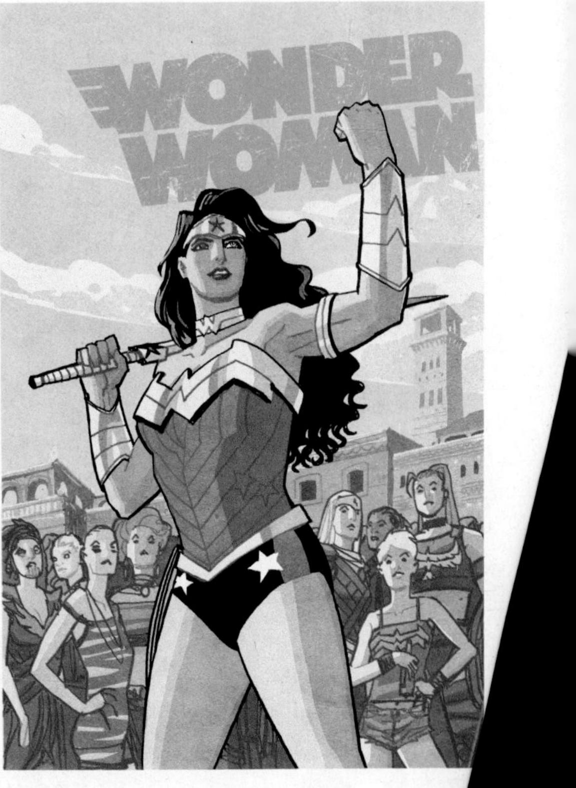
WONDER WOMAN